Engaging Theories in
Interpersonal
Communication

Engaging Theories in Interpersonal Communication

Multiple Perspectives

Leslie A. Baxter
University of Iowa

Dawn O. Braithwaite
University of Nebraska - Lincoln

editors

Los Angeles • London • New Delhi • Singapore

For information:

Sage Publications, Inc.
2455 Teller Road
Thousand Oaks, California 91320
E-mail: order@sagepub.com

Sage Publications India Pvt. Ltd.
B 1/I 1 Mohan Cooperative
    Industrial Area
Mathura Road, New Delhi 110 044
India

Sage Publications Ltd.
1 Oliver's Yard
55 City Road
London EC1Y 1SP
United Kingdom

Sage Publications Asia-Pacific Pte. Ltd.
33 Pekin Street #02-01
Far East Square
Singapore 048763

Printed in the United States of America

Library of Congress Cataloging-in-Publication Data

Engaging theories in interpersonal communication: multiple perspectives / Leslie A. Baxter, Dawn O. Braithwaite, editors.
    p. cm.
Includes bibliographical references and index.
ISBN 978-1-4129-3851-8 (cloth)
ISBN 978-1-4129-3852-5 (pbk.)
    1. Interpersonal communication—Philosophy.   I. Baxter, Leslie A. II. Braithwaite, Dawn O.

P94.7.E54 2008
153.6—dc22   2007036556

This book is printed on acid-free paper.

08   09   10   11   12   10   9   8   7   6   5   4   3   2

Acquisitions Editor:	Todd R. Armstrong
Editorial Assistant:	Katie Grim
Production Editor:	Astrid Virding
Copy Editor:	Alison Hope
Typesetter:	C&M Digitals (P) Ltd.
Proofreader:	Ellen Brink
Indexer:	Ellen Slavitz
Cover Designer:	Candice Harman
Marketing Manager:	Carmel Withers

Contents

Preface

This project began as we reflected on the current state and scope of interpersonal communication theory and scholarship. We observed that there are some fine books available about interpersonal communication, and that most are committed to examining communication at the different stages of relationships or are focused on the different interpersonal communication processes in play. In most books, theories play a supporting role and most often receive brief coverage. We wanted to produce a book where interpersonal communication theories take center stage.

A second motivation for this book came from a sense that the time was right to reflect on the maturity of the study of interpersonal communication theories. Tracing its roots in the college classroom back to about 1970, we saw this anniversary of approximately 35 years as a good time to take stock and to contribute to new generations of students and scholars. We have often heard communication scholars complain that we borrow theories from other disciplines more than create our own, and thus we wanted to examine the state of interpersonal communication theory, those that are *homegrown* (that is, constructed by scholars whose primary professional affiliation is Communication Studies) as well as those from other disciplines. While many disciplines say that they study communication, our goal was to focus on the unique contributions of Communication Studies scholars and theorists to understand what is foundational in our close relationships.

Third, both of us have felt frustrated at times when we read research that lacks a theoretical foundation or contribution. We are fans of theory-based research whenever it is feasible. We believe that we can best understand the breadth and strength of the study of interpersonal communication by focusing on the group of theories used most by researchers in recent years.

Last, our impetus for the present book sprang from our own sense and experience that, taken as a whole, interpersonal communication scholarship was not as inclusive or broad as it could or should be. We found it disheartening over the years to see that some scholars who began their careers in interpersonal communication had found homes elsewhere in our national associations, and that they have not perceived interpersonal communication to be open to different ways of studying and understanding. While we shared this perception ourselves, we had not done the work to track what theories were being used most in interpersonal communication and what meta-theoretical discourses or paradigmatic perspectives were perhaps over- or under-represented. As a result, we embarked on a study to examine the state of interpersonal communication research today in order to prepare for this book project.

Chapter 1 presents our interpretation of the landscape of interpersonal communication. We are grateful to Dr. Jill Tyler at the University of South Dakota who completed the study of interpersonal communication scholarship while she was a doctoral student at the University of Iowa. We entrusted to her the important task of compiling all of the empirical studies in interpersonal communication from 1990–2005. This was both a challenge and an education. Her careful, thoughtful work helped lay the groundwork for us to understand the state of interpersonal communication theory, and to choose what theories should be represented in this book. You will find theories that you would expect to see in the book because they have been used widely by interpersonal communication scholars, you will find some of the newer up-and-coming theories, and you will find some theories that you may have not seen explicitly connected to interpersonal communication in the past.

In our first chapter we trace the development of interpersonal communication theory from its beginnings, and we organize theory and research within the larger discussion of meta-theory, or paradigms. We asked the different authors to talk about the roots and paradigmatic homes of their individual theories in each of their chapters. While this task appears simple at first glance, it actually turned out to be quite knotty at times, because there were times when authors had different perspectives on meta-theory, even concerning what to call the different categories. To complicate matters, as we expected, some of the theories do not fit neatly into one category.

Following our first chapter are 28 theory chapters written by outstanding scholars. To help the reader make sense of the big picture, we begin each of the three main parts of the book with a description of what binds the theories in that section together and the meta-theoretical discourses represented by the theories in the particular section. Each chapter then presents the purpose and meta-theoretical or paradigmatic assumptions, main features of the theory, conceptualization of communication in the theory, uses of the theory, strengths and limitations of the theory, and directions for future research and applications.

This book would not exist without the expertise and dedication of this group of authors, many of whom created the theories about which they wrote. All of them have been active as theorists and researchers, challenging and refining the theories as they use them to enlighten us about interpersonal communication.

The authors have been more than cooperative and responsive during this project, benefiting all of us with their excellent work. We also appreciate the important contributions of Todd Armstrong, Senior Acquisitions Editor of Communication, Media, and Cultural Studies at Sage Publications, along with Katie Grim, his Editorial Assistant at Sage. We thank, as well, the several reviewers of this book in its draft stage: their detailed comments were very helpful to the contributing authors and to us during the revision stage of the project: Katherine L. Adams (California State University, Fresno), Karla Mason Bergen (College of Saint Mary), Marianne Dainton (La Salle University), René Dailey (University of Texas, Austin), Kathleen M. Galvin (Northwestern University), Daena J. Goldsmith (Lewis & Clark College), Maureen P. Keeley (Texas State University, San Marcos), Clark D. Olson (Arizona State University), Sally Planalp (University of Utah), Paul Schrodt (Texas Christian University), April R. Trees (Saint Louis University), Anita L. Vangelisti (University of Texas, Austin), and Stephen Yoshimura (University of Montana).

Finally, this book project also reflects our own interpersonal communication at every level. Our work as research partners, coeditors, and close friends has resulted in a project we are both proud of. Leslie thanks Dawn for her friendship—both personal and professional—over the years. She dedicates this book to her daughter, Emma, who, once again, heard from her mom the refrain, "Not right now. Give me just a little longer while I finish this task on the book." Dawn is grateful to Leslie for many years of friendship, good work, and family celebrations. She dedicates this book to Betsy, Leslie, Sandra, Steve, Clark, and Laura for being friends, to Chris for being Mom, and to Chuck for being the love of her life.

Leslie A. Baxter & Dawn O. Braithwaite

1

Introduction

Meta-theory and Theory
in Interpersonal Communication Research

Dawn O. Braithwaite and Leslie A. Baxter

O ur goal for this book is to provide a resource for students and researchers who are interested in studying interpersonal communication. Some of us will be studying the topic as students or instructors who want to better understand interpersonal communication theory. Others may be undertaking studies of interpersonal communication as researchers and may be looking for theories to guide their research projects. Some people will be studying interpersonal communication to better understand their own relationships—for example, their friendships, dating, or close workplace relationships. In most textbooks or handbooks of interpersonal communication (e.g., Knapp & Daly, 2002; Wood, 2000), a reader would expect to find summaries of research programs on different topics (e.g., deception, relational maintenance). Our goal in this book, rather, is to provide a collection and overview of important theories that are, or have the potential to be, useful for studying interpersonal communication. For the student and the scholar alike, this collection is a toolbox to help you approach and understand interpersonal communication from a variety of angles.

In this chapter we present first a brief background on the study of interpersonal communication, explain our approach to interpersonal communication, and discuss meta-theoretical perspectives for research on interpersonal communication. Second, we present findings from our own analysis of the 958 data-based studies of interpersonal communication conducted since 1990 by scholars affiliated with communication studies. Third, we discuss some of our own thoughts about the state of interpersonal communication theory today and where we wish to see the field move in the future. Finally, we overview the chapters in this book as top experts in interpersonal communication present more than 30 different theories to guide our thinking and studying about interpersonal communication.

Roots of Interpersonal Communication

Today's students likely think that interpersonal communication has been around forever. Well, yes, people have been communicating interpersonally since the beginning of human existence. However, the academic study of inter-personal communication is relatively recent and, in fact, most of the senior authors writing our chapters were students at its early stages. To help you understand how interpersonal communication theories have developed and why, we provide a brief history of the study of interpersonal communication in the larger context of the discipline of communication studies.

Those of us from the discipline of communication studies know that our roots trace back to ancient Greece and Rome, and most believe earlier than that, to Africa and China. The study of communication has always been a prac-tical one. The earliest studies were of rhetoric and persuasion where commu-nication was studied as a speechmaking activity in the public domain (Ehninger, 1968). Early theories of rhetoric and communication focused on speakers and the best way to get their ideas across to audiences.

Moving forward to the twentieth century, there were no communication departments in universities yet, but courses in public speaking, performance of literature, debate, and persuasion were taught most often in English or theatre departments under the title of "speech." In the early part of the twentieth cen-tury, two main approaches to the study of speech emerged. The Cornell School included those who approached the study of speech from a humanistic per-spective, and the Midwestern School included those who thought it best to study speech from a scientific basis (Pearce & Foss, 1990). These schools formed the two main approaches of rhetoric and speech (later, communica-tion) and these scholars later formed speech departments, breaking off from English and theatre departments. As many of you recognize from your own campuses, communication studies departments often include mass communi-cation and other specialties.

After World War II, speech teachers also began teaching courses in small group discussion. Social scientists, especially in psychology, began studying persuasion and obedience to authority, trying to understand the process of interpersonal influence to help explain some of the atrocities that happened during that war. While they were interested in the psychology of persuasion, many also realized that we needed to study how persuasion was enacted. After

World War II, scholars of communication who took a social scientific approach were focusing on persuasion and social influence in mass communication and models of information transmission, and on systems thinking about relationships (Berger, 2005; Bormann, 1980; Delia, 1987),

As the 1960s began, cultural shifts like the civil rights and women's movements, as well as changes in families and relationships, were in full swing. The practical reasons for wanting to understand communication persisted and, as Gerald Miller (1976) explained, "students themselves began to demand answers about how to relate communicatively with their acquaintances and close friends, and romantic partners" (p. 10). Some scholars whose work had originated in social psychology and sociology were moving to speech departments and took with them a social scientific and post-positivist orientation to research (see below), focusing mostly on cognitive approaches to understanding communication behavior (Delia, 1987; Miller, 1983). These scholars were studying topics such as interpersonal persuasion, nonverbal message transmission, interpersonal attraction, self-disclosure, and deception, to name a few. They joined the rhetoricians in speech departments and, to this day, most departments in our discipline are made up of a blend of humanities and social science approaches to understanding human communication.

The research interests of these social science scholars in the 1960s had an effect: interpersonal communication courses began to appear in college curricula in the early 1970s, and spread rapidly throughout the United States in the next 10 years. There was much excitement and momentum among those studying interpersonal communication during this time and the Interpersonal and Small Group Interaction Division formed and quickly became one of the largest in the Speech Communication Association. On college campuses, departments of speech were starting to change their names to "speech communication" and later to "communication." Simultaneously, the national association changed its name from the Speech Communication Association to the National Communication Association. Interpersonal communication scholars were importing theories from other disciplines and beginning to develop their own theories.

Interpersonal communication was joined in the 1970s and 1980s by research and by new college classes in nonverbal communication, conflict, gender, workplace communication, and intercultural communication, followed in the late 1980s and into the 1990s by family communication and health communication classes, among others. Some of the scholars studying in these contexts used qualitative data and interpretive methods that are humanistic in nature. Interestingly, most of these new topics were initially thought of as part of interpersonal communication. Slowly, they have developed into their own specializations, leaving us to wonder at times, "What is the center of interpersonal communication?"

Over the years, colleagues stressing humanistic and social science approaches to communication have gotten along well at times and less well at other times, largely because they do not speak the same research language, nor do they share the same perspectives on how communication works and how we should study it. Since the 1990s and into the twenty-first century, communication departments are also home to scholars who take a critical perspective on communication, which we will discuss below. While these groups of scholars pursue different approaches to understanding interpersonal communication, we will contend that, ultimately, it will be in this diversity of perspectives that our field will find strength.

Defining Interpersonal Communication

Before we define interpersonal communication, we need to focus on our definition of communication, as our perspective on interpersonal communication grows out of that. Early definitions of communication focused on the exchange of messages, for example in one of the early interpersonal communication textbooks, Giffin and Patton (1971) defined communication as "a process involving the sending and receiving of messages" (p. 5). As the thinking about communication developed, scholars began to focus on communication as a symbolic process humans use to create meaning. For example, John Stewart (1999) stressed that humans build their own reality:

> Communication is the way humans build our reality. Human worlds are not made up of objects but of peoples' responses to objects, or their meanings. And these meanings are negotiated in communication. Try not to think of communication as simply a way to share ideas, because it's much more than that. It's the process humans use to define reality itself. (p. 25)

From this perspective, interpersonal communication is more than information transmission between two people. Instead, it becomes the way that humans negotiate meanings, identity, and relationships through person-to-person communication.

In terms of interpersonal communication, different approaches to understanding it and studying it abound. A complete discussion is impossible here; we recommend sources dedicated to giving a more detailed history and overview (e.g., Berger, 2005; Knapp, Daly, Albada, & Miller, 2002). Authors often divide interpersonal communication into processes (e.g., social support), developmental stages (e.g., initiating, disengaging), contexts (e.g., family, workplace), or types or channels (e.g., nonverbal, computer-mediated). For our purposes in this book we would like to talk about three broad approaches to interpersonal communication theories that form our organization of theories in this book: interpersonal communication as (a) individually centered, (b) discourse or interaction centered, and (c) relationship centered.

The first focus of interpersonal communication theory is what we are calling individually centered theories of interpersonal communication. This perspective is centered on understanding how individuals plan, produce, and process interpersonal communication messages. These theories envision communication as an individually centered cognitive activity. This work began with Gerald Miller and others who argued that interpersonal communication occurs when people make predictions about the other interactants based on perceiving the person as an individual rather than based on a social role—for example, a teacher or store clerk (see G. R. Miller, 1976; G. R. Miller & Steinberg, 1975). Those taking this perspective on interpersonal communication focus on mental representations that influence how people interpret information and how they behave (Berger, 2005; Knapp, Daly, Albada, & Miller, 2002; Vangelisti, 2002). These approaches have been prominent in interpersonal communication research and theory, as we will see.

A second focus of interpersonal communication theory is what we are calling discourse- or interaction-centered theories of interpersonal communication. The central focus of this perspective is on understanding interpersonal communication as a message or a joint action behaviorally enacted between persons. The focus in this perspective moves from a focus on the individual and his or her dispositions or cognitive states to a wide variety of theories that share a focus on the content, forms, and functions of messages, and the behavioral interactions between interacting parties. Scholars are interested in "the ways our understandings, meanings, norms, roles, and rules are worked out interactively in communication" (Littlejohn & Foss, 2005, p. 45). Work in this second tradition has many origins, including the classic volume by Watzlawick, Beavin, and Jackson (1967) on behavioral patterns of joint actions, and scholarship by language philosophers such as Wittgenstein (1953) and Austin (1962).

The third focus of interpersonal communication theory is what we are labeling relationship-centered theories of interpersonal communication. Scholars taking this perspective on interpersonal communication focus on understanding the role of communication in developing, sustaining, and terminating social and personal relationships, including friendships, dating relationships, romantic relationships, and cohabiting relationships. Important classics in this third approach were two 1973 volumes, one by Murray Davis and the second by Irwin Altman and Dalmas Taylor. Beginning in the 1980s, scholars interested in personal relationships across psychology, communication, sociology, and family studies started meeting and founding journals. In fact, the initial goal of the founders of these associations was to create a separate interdisciplinary field devoted to studying personal relationships. While there are diverse approaches to studying relational communication, scholars taking a relational perspective on interpersonal communication focus on messages within relationships that influence (Guerrero, Andersen, & Afifi, 2001) or constitute (Baxter, 2004) those relationships.

What we notice about these three broad approaches to studying interpersonal communication is that they each have distinct differences in how they help us understand what interpersonal communication is and how it functions in human life. In order to be able to define interpersonal communication, we will need to concentrate on what these approaches have in common. As we examined books and articles on interpersonal communication, we found that all authors seem to agree that there are many different definitions and that defining interpersonal communication will be problematic, as it will highlight some dimensions and leave others out. Most scholars agree that interpersonal communication is a process; it involves a dyad or normally a small number of people; it involves creating meanings; and it is enacted through verbal and nonverbal message behaviors. Because our purpose in this book is to represent the breadth of interpersonal communication, we are best served by viewing interpersonal communication in the most inclusive way we can. Thus, our definition of interpersonal communication is the production and processing of verbal and nonverbal messages between two or a few persons. This definition includes elements that speak to each of the three broad approaches to interpersonal communication that organize this book: (a) "the production and processing of . . . messages" emphasizes the first approach, (b) "verbal and nonverbal messages between . . . persons" emphasizes the second approach, and (c) "two or a few persons" emphasizes the relational orientation of the third approach.

Meta-theory and Theory in Interpersonal Communication

As we seek to explore the theories of interpersonal communication, it is important to know that scholars do differ, at times greatly, on how to study and develop interpersonal communication theory. It will help to understand that scholars use different meta-theoretical discourses, which are intellectual traditions or paradigms that scholars use to think about and talk about a phenomenon of interest (Deetz, 2001). These discourses are points of view that help us to understand and appreciate the different approaches to asking questions about interpersonal communication, to choose research methods to answer these questions, and to provide the criteria by which to evaluate research findings and conclusions (Baxter & Babbie, 2004). Our goal here is not to argue for one of the discourses as superior, but rather to value them equally. For our purposes here, we have adopted three general discourses of interpersonal communication that have been identified by many scholars (e.g., Baxter & Babbie; Bochner, 1985; Habermas, 1971; Miller, 2002): post-positivist; interpretive, and critical.

POST-POSITIVIST PERSPECTIVE

Researchers adopting a post-positivist discourse take a scientific approach to research. This approach is often also called the "logical-empirical tradition." These scholars believe in an objective reality that can be discovered through appropriate research methods. That is, they believe in a knowable reality apart from the researcher. The goal of post-positivist theory and research is to advance predictions and to offer generalized, law-like cause and effect explanations or functional explanations about how variables or structures are interdependent with one another. Causal explanations view the social world as webs of variables, some of which function as independent variables in causing outcomes or effects on other variables known as dependent variables. Functional explanations are organized around the presumption that the social world is a system of interdependent parts: the functioning of one part depends on its patterns of interdependence with other parts of the system. Researchers committed to the discourse of post-positivism favor an a priori process in which they initially identify a theory relevant to the phenomenon they wish to explain and predict. Theories should consist of law-like statements, which apply across situations, about how variables or structures relate, causally or functionally. Post-positivists are committed to value-neutral theorizing in which researcher subjectivity should be controlled or neutralized. According to the post-positivist perspective, a good theory is one that is accurate (i.e., in agreement with observations), testable (i.e., capable of being falsified or proven wrong), logically consistent, parsimonious or simple, broad in scope, and useful in generating predictions and explanations about interpersonal communication.

In its idealized form, the researcher's task is to deduce testable hypotheses from a theory. For example, a researcher adopting this perspective might be interested in explaining how talk about one's occupation functions in self-presentation and impression management. He or she would begin with a relevant theory in which variables have been logically linked causally or functionally. From this theory, the researcher would derive testable hypotheses. For instance, a researcher might adopt one of the theories discussed in Part III of this book, Social Penetration Theory, because it focuses on the process of self-disclosure of personal information as people become acquainted. Based on this theory, the researcher might argue that there are various kinds of information that a person can reveal about his or her occupation and that this information can vary in its superficiality or depth. Because Social Penetration Theory argues that we disclose relatively superficial information early in a forming relationship and more in-depth information later in a relationship's development, our researcher might hypothesize that superficial disclosures about one's occupation (e.g., "I'm a professor of communication studies," "A professor's job has three components—teaching, research, and service") are more likely with strangers than are more in-depth disclosures about one's occupation (e.g., "I earn about half of what a physician earns," or "The worst part of my job is grading papers"). Additionally, more in-depth disclosures about occupation would be more characteristic of communication among acquaintances than among strangers. In this example, depth of disclosure about one's occupation is the dependent variable because it is the consequence of the independent variable, the closeness of the relationship with the other person (stranger versus acquaintance). The assumption of the researcher is that both relationship closeness and depth of disclosure can be objectively measured.

INTERPRETIVE PERSPECTIVE

The meta-theoretical discourse of interpretivism rejects a single objective view of reality that can be discovered. From the interpretive perspective, the social world consists of multiple realities according to the subjective position of the person or group. Humans are agents who act on their world in light of their subjective positions. Although humans often act to reproduce existing patterns, they can choose also to change those patterns. Interpretive researchers are committed to a detailed understanding of how particular social realities are produced and maintained through the everyday practices of individuals, relational parties, families, and so on. Researchers committed to the discourse of interpretivism value the "native's point of view": the perspectives and language choices of the individuals being studied. In addition, they tend to value context or situation-specific research. Because the interpretive project is committed to local meanings and rule-governed meaning-making processes, the theories valued by interpretive researchers are those focused on meanings and meaning-making.

Interpretive theories might be used by researchers as sensitizing devices or guides to getting started in a research study and subsequently put into conversation with locally emergent meanings. The goal is not to test a theory in a specific situation, but rather to engage the theory in conversation with the emergent observations and interpretations that flow from the natives' experiences. Thus, from an interpretive perspective, a theory can be a heuristic device, useful in sensitizing a researcher; it is a conversational partner, if you will; it is open to transformation when put into play with the native's point of view and the interpretations of the researcher.

For example, an interpretive researcher might be interested in how members of a local community—let's say neighbors in a given neighborhood populated with middle-class Euro-Americans—construct their identities in interaction with one another and the role that one's occupation holds in such identity work. That is, the researcher is interested in how the natives—members of the neighborhood—make sense of one another as persons and how occupation figures into the meaning-making process. There might be a local theory available in existing scholarship that examines the code of communication among middle-class Euro-Americans more generally. However, it does not directly address the question of interest to our researcher—the role of occupation talk in identity constructions. Nonetheless, our researcher could use this theory as a sensitizing device, which is perhaps helpful in guiding preliminary interview questions or in making findings intelligible at the analysis stage of the study. For example, the communication code for middle-class Euro-Americans might emphasize concepts of "self," "achievement," and "independence." These concepts might be helpful in rendering intelligible the observation by our researcher that neighbors appear to value more positively occupations that appear to have a great deal of autonomy of action. Our researcher would not test hypotheses derived from the theory. In the end, the researcher would conclude that the theory was more or less useful in illuminating the natives' experiences in the particular neighborhood group under observation.

Alternatively, an interpretive researcher might prefer to operate entirely inductively, developing a theory from the "bottom up" from observations. This process is often referred to as "grounded-theory construction." Returning to our example, our researcher might discover that no scholarship exists on how middle-class, Euro-American neighbors interact more generally, or in the neighborhood of interest more specifically. Our interpretive researcher would of necessity adopt an inductive approach with the goal of developing a grounded theory of the role of occupation talk in constructing the identity of persons.

Whether the researcher uses a general interpretive theory or constructs a grounded theory, common criteria apply in evaluating an interpretive theory. The theory needs to be heuristic—that is, it must shed fruitful insights into the meanings and meaning-making process of the "native" group of individuals under study. A heuristic theory moves beyond mere description: it does more than summarize the "native's point of view." Specifically, it provides an interpretation of observations that renders them intelligible or understandable. This goal of understanding or intelligibility differs from the prediction and explanation of post-positivist theories. Furthermore, the emphasis is on the local, not the general, which is (again) unlike post-positivist theories. However, like post-positivist theory, interpretive theory should be logically consistent and parsimonious.

CRITICAL PERSPECTIVE

Third, in contrast to both post-positivist and interpretive researchers, a critical scholar would view identity work in general and occupation talk in particular as social constructions that serve some interests more than others. A critical researcher would rely on a theory of institutional or ideological power to provide the analytic guide that would uncover silenced voices, and to inform his or her explanation or understanding of the process by which other voices become dominant. Key to this analysis would probably be the role of various societal structures and ideologies—for example, the ideology of individualism or the ideology of patriarchy, in personal identity. Critical researchers often focus on the interests of predetermined, identifiable groups, such as women, people of color, or nonelite social groups, such as people with disabilities. The work of critical researchers is often characterized by a goal of emancipation or enlightenment and an agenda that is activist and that supports social change. As Katherine Miller (2002) noted, critical theorists come in a variety of stripes. Some critical scholars (for instance, those who adopt late Marxism as their preferred critical theory) share a belief in an objective reality of material conditions typical of post-positivism. Other critical scholars (for instance, those who adopt early Marxism as their preferred critical theory) adopt a more subjective perspective typical of the interpretive tradition. In communication, most critical scholars probably align more with the assumptions of the interpretive tradition than with the assumptions of post-positivism. Regardless of basic assumptions, a good critical theory is evaluated by its capacity to accomplish social change, thereby emancipating disempowered groups from oppressive social structures or ideologies.

Returning to our example one final time, a critical researcher might be interested in examining whose interests are served (and whose are not served) when, for example, the media marks a person's occupation as the central feature of his or her identity. Such marking clearly privileges persons who are employed outside of the home, for example. One critical consequence of such marking might be that people whose occupation is relatively invisible (for example, homemakers and parents who work without pay in the home) might have reduced status in the society because their occupation is not formally legitimated.

Researchers rarely articulate explicitly their meta-theoretical commitments (and perhaps they should do so more than they do). Rather, scholars' philosophical alignments often float at a latent level, between the lines of their prose. The sophisticated reader needs to know how to interpret a given researcher's choices in order to infer what his or her meta-theoretical commitments are in a given study. Once one knows what key signs to look for, it is possible to locate a given researcher's commitments. Why is this helpful and important? Because it tells the reader what the researcher values about theory and how theory should be used and evaluated in the given study. Thus, we have asked each of the authors in the book to locate their theory, or cluster of theories, within its appropriate meta-theoretical discourse. As you read each chapter, we encourage you to work through the intellectual exercise of identifying the specific ways in which a meta-theoretical discourse seeps through in the articulation of that chapter's theory(ies).

But let's bring down the level of abstraction a bit, and turn our attentions to interpersonal communication research. In doing so, we will note some interesting patterns and trends with respect to both theories and the meta-theoretical discourses in which they are embedded.

Interpersonal Communication Research, 1990–2005

Before choosing the theories we wanted to include in this book, we needed to map the current state of research and theory in interpersonal communication. We knew an empirical study of interpersonal communication research would be an ambitious undertaking, because we had done a similar study two years earlier for our family communication theories book (Braithwaite & Baxter, 2006). We knew there would be much more interpersonal literature to analyze—and we were right: there were 958 interpersonal communication citations in our current data set, compared to 289 family communication citations. While we were aware that interpersonal communication research began well before 1990, we decided to start at that date, because our goal was to understand the current state of interpersonal communication theory, rather than to track its entire history.

We included in our analysis all data-based research that was published by interpersonal communication researchers who professionally identify with the communication studies discipline. Our goal was to analyze all interpersonal communication studies published during this period.[1] Our approach to interpersonal communication was intentionally broad, encompassing all studies of person-to-person communication (face-to-face or mediated). We included studies of dyadic interpersonal communication (e.g., communication in dating, committed, cohabiting, friendship, or marital relationships), and we excluded studies situated in role-based relationships (e.g., manager-employee, doctor-patient—what G. R. Miller and Steinberg (1975) would have categorized as "sociological"). The only family-related relationship we included was marital communication, because partners relate to one another as intimates, and not only in their respective roles as "husband" and "wife." We chose to include interpersonal communication research that is located at the level of the individual (e.g., studies of message planning, production, and processing) and we included persuasion research when the focus was interpersonal (e.g., compliance-gaining or planning and processing of persuasive messages in a person-to-person context). We also included research on language and social interaction in interpersonal contexts and data-based critical studies of interpersonal communication. Finally, we included only data-based studies (rather than conceptual essays) in this analysis because our goal was to assess the role of meta-theory and theory in qualitatively oriented or quantitatively oriented research.

For this study of the literature we identified 19 journals that would be most likely to contain the published research of interpersonal communication scholars. We included in our search 14 communication journals sponsored by the International Communication Association (ICA), the National Communication Association (NCA), or the four NCA-affiliated regional communication associations: *Communication Monographs, Communication Quarterly, Communication Reports, Communication Research Reports, Communication Studies, Human Communication Research, Journal of Applied Communication Research, Journal of Communication, Qualitative Research Reports in Communication, Quarterly Journal of Speech, Southern Communication Journal, Text and Performance Quarterly, Western Journal of Communication,* and the Western States Communication Association affiliate organization's *Women's Studies in Communication.* In addition, we included five journals that regularly published articles authored by interpersonal communication scholars: *Communication Research, Journal of Language and Social Psychology, Research on Language and Social Interaction,* and the two interdisciplinary journals on social and personal relationships: *Journal of Social and Personal Relationships* and *Personal Relationships.*

We are, of course, aware that researchers in other disciplines undertake studies on interpersonal communication. Thus, some may criticize our choice not to include these articles in our analysis. We certainly value the work on communication by scholars from outside the communication discipline, and there are excellent volumes of work that takes an interdisciplinary approach. However, our goal in the present project was to focus on work by the community of scholars whose primary intellectual affiliation is communication studies.

In the end, a total of 958 research-based articles on interpersonal communication were included in our analysis. For each study analyzed, we determined the meta-theoretical commitment (paradigm) of the researchers, and the theory(ies), if any, engaged by the researcher.

META-THEORETICAL COMMITMENTS

We analyzed the research articles included in the analysis to determine the meta-theoretical approaches taken by interpersonal communication researchers. From our analysis, we determined that 83.2% of the interpersonal communication research articles from 1990–2005 were embedded in a post-positivist discourse, 13.9% were interpretive in nature, and a scant 2.9% displayed a critical perspective. At this point in time, it is clear that interpersonal communication research springs largely from the discourse of post-positivism. There are some interpersonal communication scholars doing research from within the interpretive paradigm. Critical studies are rarely found in interpersonal communication.

THEORETICAL COMMITMENTS

We also wanted to know how much of the published interpersonal communication research displays theoretical presence and which specific theory(ies) were engaged. Determining theoretical presence is not as easy as it sounds. What does one count as a theory? Must the theory be used a priori, or may it be imposed post hoc after the data are analyzed, or both? How prominent must the use of theory in a study be to be counted as theory-based research? In the end, our choice was to be very generous in our approach to theory-based research. Thus, we included articles in which the author mentioned at least one theory in the introductory warrant or argument for the study, used at least one theory as a framework to analyze data, developed a grounded theory, or discussed at least one theory in the conclusions of the research report as a way to make post hoc sense of findings or to address their implications. As one of us commented to the other, "If the author waved the hot dog over the fire of theory, we counted it." While our approach to identifying theoretical presence departs little from the idealized use of theory among interpretive or critical theorists, we took a more generous approach to post-positivist work. In our current study we acknowledged theoretical presence in many post-positivist studies that did not deduce testable hypotheses from an identified theory. In the end, using our criteria, 66.5% (n = 638) of the interpersonal communication studies had a theoretical presence of some sort, while 33.4% (n = 320) did not.

Many different theories were cited in the data-based studies. The top 10 most-frequently cited theories, in descending order of frequency, were

Politeness Theory (cited 77 times)

Social Exchange Theories (64)

Uncertainty Reduction Theory (55)

Dramatistic Symbolic Interaction Theory (Goffman) (51)

Relational Dialectics Theory (44)

Expectancy Violations Theory (33)

Social Penetration Theory (31)

Communication Accommodation Theory (30)

Constructivism Theory (29)

Attribution Theory (28)

Obviously, we made a decision to include all of these theories in the book, given their salience in the research. Of these 10 most-frequently cited theories, half are homegrown. However, many other theories were cited with some frequency, as well, and we tried to include as many of those in the book as was feasible. In the end, all but seven of the theories in the book are "homegrown." We take this as evidence of maturity of the field of interpersonal communication. As we noted above, in the early years of scholarship on interpersonal communication, researchers relied heavily on importing theories from allied disciplines of psychology and sociology.

IMPLICATIONS

As you might anticipate, as editors of a book devoted to theories of interpersonal communication, we advocate theoretically centered research as opposed to research that is not based on theory. It is important to note that not all scholars will agree with us on this point. Some believe it is enough to embed a study within the conversation of accumulated findings from others' studies. While we appreciate all good research, we favor and recommend theoretically centered research for two reasons. First, we believe that theory helps researchers bring both intelligibility and coherence to their research findings. We understand that several atheoretical studies can produce a common finding, but we would argue that what makes these findings intelligible and useful is theory. We are also well aware that what we see and what we learn will be different depending on the theory guiding our attention, just as putting a different lens on a camera changes how we record our world. Given that theories operate out of different meta-theoretical discourses, we can change theories to enable us to take a different view of communication phenomenon. Not only does changing the lens of theory alter our view, but when we pay attention to theory we also have a heightened awareness that we are indeed seeing the world through a particular lens, focusing on certain things and not engaging others.

Second, we favor theory-based research because theory helps us launch new research, either by providing the basis of testable hypotheses (post-positivist) or by providing us with a heuristic sensitizing device (interpretive and critical). In addition, we believe that in the best of circumstances each study should also question and advance our body of theoretical knowledge. Thus, while we are heartened to see the percentage of theory-based research in interpersonal communication at 65.5%, we do hope to see it rise even higher as the years go on. We believe this book will be a helpful resource to researchers who want to see this happen, too.

A second implication of our study of interpersonal communication theory is that there is a clear imbalance among the meta-theoretical discourses, with the vast majority of research on interpersonal communication representing the post-positivist tradition. This is not a critique of the excellent research coming out of that paradigm. These scholars are doing important and high-quality work. In the end, what we are calling for is a greater balance among the perspectives. We contend that our ability as a field to shed light on some of the most important issues in the lives of humans rests in our ability to embrace and apply multiple perspectives and methods to capture the complexity that is interpersonal communication. Thus, we argue that all three perspectives should have a comparable presence at the scholarly table.

Related to the lack of paradigmatic balance, our third implication is to reflect on what a diversity of meta-theoretical perspectives might bring to interpersonal communication. Looking at the status quo, we conclude that interpersonal communication research is not as diverse as it could, and we believe, should be. We have also observed too little diversity within the ranks of interpersonal scholars and, we would argue, not enough diversity in the contexts, populations, and topics studied. We appreciate scholarship such as Wood and Duck's (1995) call to focus on understudied relationships. We agree that scholars need continually to expand the parameters of our research and the populations studied.

We note that most of the research on person-to-person communication by scholars about underrepresented groups is not appearing in interpersonal communication, but rather in intercultural communication, language and social interaction, and family communication. The same is true for work by scholars using critical and interpretive paradigms. While the most important thing is that the research is done, we have to ask what the study of interpersonal communication is missing for having this work appear elsewhere. Our sense is that interpretive scholars—and especially critical scholars—perceive that interpersonal communication is not the right place for their work, given the lack of meta-theoretical balance. Thus, we offer a challenge to interpersonal communication to open our minds and make sure that all voices are heard around the table.

We want to see a continuation of excellent post-positivist research and, at the same time, we want to see interpretive and critical research on interpersonal communication grow. To facilitate this goal, in this book we have intentionally included selected theories that interpretive and critical scholars will find relevant to and facilitative of their work, in addition to those theories important to scholars with post-positivist meta-theoretical commitments.

The Organization of the Book

Analyzing such a large number of studies confirmed what we already knew: there are many interpersonal communication theories to choose from and it would be difficult to make choices about which we could include in the book. We applied three criteria when choosing the theories. First, as noted above, we chose theories that represent the most frequent presence in the interpersonal communication literature. Second, we chose theories that we believe hold the greatest promise for researchers and students to use. Third, we chose a group of theories that produce a presence for all three meta-theoretical perspectives. This meant that we had to make some difficult choices and were not able to include all theories in one book.

We invited an outstanding group of researchers and theorists as first authors to write chapters for the book. We received enthusiastic responses from them and were delighted they wanted to be part of the project. Some invited coauthors to work with them, in some cases, scholars of equal senior status and in other cases, promising new scholars. We are pleased to welcome all of these colleagues and appreciate their contributions to interpersonal communication theory.

After we chose the chapters we wanted to include in the book, we needed to think about how to organize them. We knew that we did not want to divide the theories into the three meta-theoretical discourses because we wanted, as much as possible, to focus on how these discourses integrate (Deetz, 2001). In the end, we chose to organize the book into three sections, modeled after the three broad approaches to interpersonal communication we discussed earlier in this chapter: interpersonal communication theories that are individually centered, those that are discourse or interaction centered, and those that are relationship centered. We organized the theories alphabetically in each of the three sections.

Section I of the book presents individually centered theories of interpersonal communication. As we described above, these theories are centered in how individuals plan, produce, and process interpersonal communication messages. Theories in this section of the book primarily envision communication as an individually centered cognitive activity. Of the three sections in the book, this first section has the most meta-theoretical similarity—the post-positivist paradigm.

Section II of the book includes theories with a focus on discourse or interaction. These theories share an understanding of interpersonal communication as a message, a discourse (i.e., a system of meaning), or a joint action behaviorally enacted between persons. Meta-theoretical commitments are more diverse in this second section of the book, drawing primarily from post-positivist or interpretive traditions.

Section III includes relationship-centered theories of interpersonal communication. This group of theories focuses on understanding the role of communication in developing, sustaining, and terminating social and personal relationships. All three meta-theoretical commitments are evident in the third section of the book.

Interestingly, once we arrived at this structure for organizing the theories, we found that they divided fairly evenly between the three sections. While we highlighted some of our concerns about the state of interpersonal communication theory above, we also see great strengths, as this collection of theories by a superior set of scholars demonstrates. As the twenty-first century is underway, we can imagine few undertakings more important than understanding and improving interpersonal communication. We trust that the readers of this book will find the work of these scholars engaging and accessible.

Note

1. The editors express great appreciation to Dr. Jill Tyler, former doctoral candidate at the University of Iowa and currently Assistant Professor of Communication Studies at the University of South Dakota, for her assistance in the substantial undertaking of compiling the data for this analysis. Any interpretations or errors are those of the editors.

References

Altman, I., & Taylor, D. (1973). *Social penetration: The development of interpersonal relationships.* New York: Holt, Rinehart & Winston.

Austin, J. L. (1962). *How to do things with words.* Oxford, UK: Clarendon.

Baxter, L. A. (2004). Distinguished scholar article: Relationships as dialogues. *Personal Relationships, 11,* 1–22.

Baxter, L. A., & Babbie, E. R. (2004). *The basics of communication research.* Belmont, CA: Wadsworth.

Berger, C. R. (2005). Interpersonal communication: Theoretical perspectives, future prospects. *Journal of Communication, 55,* 415–447.

Bochner, A. P. (1985). Perspectives on inquiry: Representation, conversation, and reflection. In M. L. Knapp & G. R. Miller (Eds.), *Handbook of interpersonal communication* (pp. 27–58). Beverly Hills, CA: Sage.

Bormann, E. G. (1980). *Communication theory.* Salem, WI: Sheffield.

Braithwaite, D. O., & Baxter, L. A. (Eds.). (2006). *Engaging theories in family communication: Multiple perspectives.* Thousand Oaks, CA: Sage.

Davis, M. (1973). *Intimate relations.* New York: Free Press.

Deetz, S. (2001). Conceptual foundations. In F. M. Jablin & L. L. Putnam (Eds.), *The new handbook of organizational communication: Advances in theory, research, and methods* (pp. 3–46). Thousand Oaks, CA: Sage.

Delia, J. K. (1987). Communication research: A history. In C. R. Berger & S. H. Chafee (Eds.), *Handbook of communication science* (pp. 20–98). Newbury Park, CA: Sage.

Ehninger, D. (1968). On systems of rhetoric. *Philosophy and Rhetoric, 1,* 131–144.

Giffin, K., & Patton, B. R. (1971). *Fundamentals of interpersonal communication.* New York: Harper & Row.

Guerrero, L. K., Andersen, P. A., & Afifi, W. A. (2001). *Close encounters: Communicating in relationships.* Mountain View, CA: Mayfield.

Habermas, J. (1971). *Knowledge and human interest.* Boston: Beacon.

Knapp, M. L., & Daly, J. A. (Eds.). (2002). *Handbook of interpersonal communication* (3rd ed.). Thousand Oaks, CA: Sage.

Knapp, M. L., Daly, J. A., Albada, K. F., & Miller, G. R. (2002). Background and current trends in the study of interpersonal communication. In M. L. Knapp, & J. A. Daly (Eds.), *Handbook of interpersonal communication* (3rd ed., pp. 3–20). Thousand Oaks, CA: Sage.

Littlejohn, S. W., & Foss, K. A. (2005). *Theories of human communication* (8th ed.). Belmont, CA: Wadsworth.

Miller, G. R. (1976). Foreword. In G. R. Miller (Ed.), *Explorations in interpersonal communication* (pp. 9–16). Beverly Hills, CA: Sage.

Miller, G. R., (1983). Taking stock of a discipline. *Journal of Communication, 33,* 31–41.

Miller, G. R., & Steinberg M. (1975). *Between people.* Chicago: Science Research Associates.

Miller, K. I. (2002). *Communication theories.* New York: McGraw-Hill.

Pearce, W. B., & Foss, K. A. (1990). The historical context of communication as a science. In G. L. Dahnke & G. W. Clatterbuck (Eds.), *Human communication: Theory and research* (pp. 1–19). Belmont, CA: Wadsworth.

Stewart, J. (1999). Introduction to interpersonal communication. In Stewart, J. (Ed.) *Bridges not walls* (7th ed., pp. 15–65). New York: Random House.

Vangelisti, A. L. (2002). Interpersonal processes in romantic relationships. In M. L. Knapp & J. A. Daly (Eds.), *Handbook of interpersonal communication* (pp. 643–679). Thousand Oaks, CA: Sage.

Watzlawick, P., Beavin, J. H., & Jackson, D. D. (1967). *Pragmatics of human communication: A study of interactional patterns, pathologies, and paradoxes.* New York: W. W. Norton.

Wittgenstein, L. (1953). *Philosophical investigations* (*Philosophische Untersuchungen;* G.E.M. Anscombe, Trans.). New York: Macmillan.

Wood, J. T. (2000). *Relational communication: Continuity and change in interpersonal relationships* (2nd ed.). Belmont, CA: Wadsworth.

Wood, J. T., & Duck. S. (Eds.). (1995). *Understudied relationships: Off the beaten path.* Thousand Oaks, CA: Sage.

PART I

Individually-Centered Theories
of Interpersonal Communication

The contributors to Part I of this book address theories that hold prominence in understanding how individuals plan, produce, and process interpersonal communication messages. Theories in this section of the book are based on the basic assumption that individual cognitive activity is the heart of the communication process—both in producing and in processing messages. All but one of the theories is homegrown—that is, developed by scholars who identify professionally with the communication studies discipline. The one exception is the family of attribution theories, developed in the discipline of psychology.

The majority of theories in this section are positioned in the post-positivistic meta-theoretical tradition. The contributors flag this tradition using many terms, including

- logical-empirical,
- scientific,
- realism,
- prediction,
- causal explanation, and
- generalization.

In general, the theories examined in this section are based on the assumption that there is an objective reality organized by patterned regularities that researchers seek to predict and to explain by identifying basic cause-effect relationships. Although the chapters in this section focus on individual cognitive activity, the theoretical assumption is that regularities exist across individuals in how and why this activity takes place that can be objectively studied through sound scientific observation. Most of this observational work is quantitatively based.

Two of the theories examined in this section have been variously placed as either post-positivistic or interpretive: the uncertainty management theories of Problematic Integration Theory and Uncertainty Management Theory. Basically, the assumptions of these theories include an appreciation of meaning as locally organized and ultimately indeterminate, while the theories hold to a belief that fundamental regularities can still be identified.

The chapters in this section are organized alphabetically. If we were to organize this section historically, however, we would have begun with the two oldest homegrown members of this theoretical family, both originating with work by communication scholars in the 1970s: Uncertainty Reduction Theory and Constructivism Theory. These two theories helped to shape two of the major intellectual problems addressed by scholars of interpersonal communication over the past three decades: uncertainty management and communicator effectiveness.

Uncertainty Reduction Theory was formulated with a goal of explaining communicative activity organized around the goal of reducing uncertainty in initial interactions between strangers. Uncertainty management has emerged as a core intellectual problem for theorists of interpersonal communication, and several of the chapters in this part of the book illustrate different approaches to the problem of uncertainty. The three uncertainty management theories examined by Afifi and Matsunaga—Problematic Integration Theory, Uncertainty Management Theory, and the Theory of Motivated Information Management—challenge Uncertainty Reduction Theory's commitment to uncertainty reduction, instead focusing more broadly on how uncertainty is managed. Uncertainty management can involve the reduction of uncertainty, but does not necessarily do so. Scholarship in uncertainty reduction and uncertainty management has branched out well beyond the context of initial interactions between strangers, as becomes clear in reading the chapter authored by Afifi and Matsunaga and the chapter authored by Knobloch.

One way that communicators cope with uncertainty as they produce messages is to engage in a variety of mental planning or rehearsal work. Several of the chapters in this section focus on planning-related activity: in particular, the chapters devoted to Planning Theory, Action Assembly Theory, and Goals-Plans-Action Theory. All three of these chapters are committed to explaining how communicators produce messages through cognitive planning work. Planning Theory concentrates on characteristics of cognitive plans in general, whereas Goals-Plans-Action Theory focuses more narrowly on plans related to the goal of social influence, with particular attention on the role that goals play in the process of producing social influence acts. Action Assembly Theory takes a process approach, examining the general process by which messages are produced—that is, assembled—by communicators.

The intellectual problem of uncertainty management is one faced when we produce communication messages. In addition, we face the challenge of uncertainty when we undertake the processing of others' messages. Two of the theories in this section of the book focus directly on the processing of messages. The family of attribution theories, older in fact than either Uncertainty Reduction Theory or Constructivism Theory, has its origins in psychology. Nonetheless, it has proven its value to communication scholars, shedding light on the question of how people make sense of what causes others' actions. For example, did that person give you a compliment because he or she is dispositionally nice (an internal attribution), or because the situation requires it (an external attribution)? The ultimate meaning we ascribe to others' communicative messages depends on how we answer basic attributional questions such as this one. In the context of our relationships, we also must determine what another's communication means with respect to the underlying nature of our relationship. Was that comment a criticism (implying dominance) or a teasing joke (implying a relationship based on intimacy or affiliation)? When we make judgments like this one, we are engaged in a framing activity, attempting to understand the message in light of the underlying relationship between the parties. Such framing work is the topic of Relational Framing Theory.

Along with Uncertainty Reduction Theory, Constructivism Theory is the second homegrown theory that has origins in the 1970s. This theory focuses on message production with an eye toward communicator effectiveness or competence, asking what distinguishes more from less skilled communicative messages. This theory highlighted the second major intellectual problem of message production for scholars of interpersonal communication—effectiveness or competence. Constructivism Theory approaches the competence problem as one of individual differences, identifying cognitive complexity as a key variable on which people vary systematically. In turn, how "cognitively complex" someone is affects that person's ability to produce more or less person-centered messages, a key to communication effectiveness. Imagined Interaction Theory also examines the question of communicator effectiveness by examining differences in how people imagine interactions, whether retrospectively or prospectively. In its most recent turn, this theory examines the ways in which effective conflict management is related to how we construct in our minds both past and anticipated conflictual interactions with others. In addition, the intellectual problem of communicator effectiveness is a problem addressed in all of the planning theories. Communicators develop more or less efficacious plans and implement them with different degrees of skill. The planning theories, taken collectively, tell us a great deal about the role of planning in communicator effectiveness.

In summary, the chapters in this section examine two core issues of interest to scholars of interpersonal communication: coping with uncertainty and communicating effectively. They focus on the individual as the centerpiece of study, especially the role of individual cognitive activity in the production and processing of messages.

2

Action Assembly Theory

Forces of Creation

John O. Greene

T his is a sentence I have never written before.

Now you try it. No, don't copy my sentence (or anyone else's, for that matter). Keep your eyes on your own page and write your own novel sentence.

How did you do? Okay, I'm betting it's not the quote you'd want to pass on to your descendents as the essence of the wisdom you've acquired over your lifetime (although it might make the next person who reads this book snicker), but you were able to do it, weren't you?

This chapter is about the creative character of human behavior—about how it is possible for us to hear, say, think, and do things that we've never heard, said, thought, or done before. When you and I wrote our sentences we did something that is remarkable in many ways. It is remarkable that we have this capacity to create—to write (and say, and think) new things. And it is also remarkable that it is often relatively easy for us to do so—so much so that we tend to take this marvelous capacity for granted. In fact, it turns out that the property of creativity is always present in our behavior, even if we don't recognize it. It is rather like breathing in that it comes so naturally to us.

But these characteristics are only part of what makes this topic so fascinating. Two other aspects of our behavior might at first appear to be distinct from, or even opposed to, processes of creation, but in fact, they turn out to be essential for understanding the forces of creation that shape thought and action. First, it is true that novelty is an inherent and ubiquitous property of our behavior, but it is also true that we all experience situations where our creative genius fails us—times when we stutter, and stammer, and just can't think of the right things to say to help a friend feel better, tell a convincing lie, make a good impression in a job interview, or to ask someone for a date. Second, just as behavior is always "new," it is also always "old." Go back and look at your novel sentence. Sure, you never wrote that particular sentence before, but you've written sentences that followed the same rules of grammar (e.g., "singular subjects require singular verbs"), and you've used each one of those words in other sentences. It's as if we have a set of established building blocks that we use to make new structures. And the same applies to all our behavior. You may not know this, but your friends do: you have facial expressions and gestures and ways of moving that they would recognize in a second as being you, and, just like the words you own, these are building blocks that you combine and morph to produce something unique.

There is one more set of ideas we need to touch on in setting the stage for what is to come. There is a commonsense conception of how people produce messages that goes something like this: We formulate an idea or understanding that is then encoded as verbal and nonverbal cues that carry that meaning or understanding. And this everyday notion of message production has some common corollaries. For example, we often assume that we know what we mean, and, by extension, that our verbal and nonverbal behaviors capture or express this understanding. There are, however, two key points to make about this commonsense view of how it is that we speak and move. First, such a conception of message production is inadequate. To think in terms of formulating an idea that is then encoded as overt behaviors tells us virtually nothing about either of those processes. When you wrote your novel sentence, you constructed an idea and actually wrote the sentence, of course, but how was it possible for you to construct something new in your mind, and how was it possible for you to produce the overt action of writing down that something new? The second point to make about our everyday conception of message production as a sequence of formulation followed by encoding (along with the various corollaries of this notion) is that these understandings are simply wrong.

Purpose and Meta-theoretical Assumptions

Theorists make pretty crummy deities. They do not survey the void and speak their creations into being out of nothingness. Rather, theorists always work from and in a complex landscape of assumptions and biases that plays a key role in shaping what they do. Consequently, it is easier to understand a theory and appreciate its nuances when we have some insight about the influences that helped to shape that theory.

Now the truth of the matter is that the factors that influence and are reflected in a theorist's formulations are always numerous, often contradictory, sometimes idiosyncratic, and in many cases unrecognized even by the theorist. Nevertheless, we can make some headway in charting these influences if we remind ourselves of the simple fact that theory building is just another sort of human activity—like walking a dog or reading a book—and, as a result, reflects an underlying what-why-how logical structure. In other words, even though the landscape is complex, even jumbled, we can get some sense of the lay of the land if we ask, "What was the theorist trying to do, why was he or she trying to do this, and how did he or she seek to go about it?" Thinking about the process of theory building in what-why-how terms provides a convenient way of addressing the issues that are the focus of this section. That is, we learn about the theorist's purpose when we explore the "what" and "why" questions, and we gain insight about a theory's underlying meta-theoretical assumptions when we examine "how" the theorist went about the business of constructing the theory.

WHAT WAS THE THEORIST TRYING TO DO?

A good place to start in seeking to understand a theory is to determine what phenomena the theory seeks to address or illuminate. In other words, what was the theorist trying to explain? In the case of Action Assembly Theory (AAT), the focus is on two broad sets of phenomena. The first of these is people's overt behavior, and especially those aspects of behavior that are of interest to students of communication and social interaction. So AAT pertains to all the various activities that you engage in every day, including things like driving a car, hitting a baseball, and playing video games, but the theory is particularly concerned with why and how it is that you produce the verbal and nonverbal behaviors you exhibit when interacting with others—the things you say, the way you say them, your facial expressions, your gestures, and so on.

The second major focus of AAT follows directly from the first. The basic idea is that if you want to understand why and how people say and do what they do, you need to take into account how and what they think. Thus, the second set of phenomena addressed by AAT is the thought processes that make it possible for us to speak and move. In other words, the theory is concerned with what transpires in our minds when we formulate and produce our verbal and nonverbal messages: How are you able to tell your roommate about your vacation, explain to your little brother where the stars go during the day, or find the right words and actions to tell someone that you love her? And the thought processes of interest in AAT aren't limited to those involved in formulating and producing messages on the fly—they also include processes such as advance planning and rehearsing that may occur hours or even days before an interaction. Finally, it is worth noting that the thought processes that are the focus of AAT also include those related to what we do not say, processes such as "editing" (i.e., deciding not to say something we are thinking) and "encoding failures" (i.e., being unable to put our thoughts into words).

WHY WAS THE THEORIST TRYING TO DO THIS?

With an answer to the "what" question in hand, we can turn to the question of "why" one might want to understand the processes involved in formulating and producing messages. There are many reasons that might be given in response to this question, but I'll mention just two here. We all recognize that communication can be done well or poorly. There are times when our message behavior seems right on target—when we are able to express ourselves clearly (and cleverly!), when our messages have precisely the impact that we hoped they would. Nevertheless, every one of us is also all too familiar with the other side of the coin—the times when things just don't come out right, when what we say only seems to make matters worse. One of the great advantages of understanding the processes involved in formulating and producing messages is that we gain insights about how to enhance the quality of our message behavior. The situation is much like the advantage that comes from knowing how your car engine works. If you don't understand much about the way that engine works, then you're probably not going to be able to do much to improve things when it's not running well.

A second response to the "why" question is, to my way of thinking, even more compelling than the first. Simply put, the processes of formulating and producing messages are inherently fascinating. Think about just a few of the many manifestations of these processes that you experience on a daily basis: You have a conception of the person you are, your true self, that plays a role in guiding how you treat other people; you can carry on a conversation with another person while thinking about something else; you can carefully manage your facial expression to make it appear that you didn't just draw an inside straight; your consciousness flows effortlessly from one thought to another. And the list goes on and on, all of them examples of the workings of the system that produces thought and action.

HOW DID THE THEORIST SEEK TO GO ABOUT IT?

As I noted above, addressing the "what" and "why" questions informs us about the purpose of a theory; pursuing the "how" question involves an examination of the theorist's approach (or the "meta-theoretical assumptions" underlying a theory). Of the three general meta-theoretical perspectives described in Chapter 1, the meta-theoretical foundations of AAT are most similar to Braithwaite and Baxter's characterization of "post-positivist view." For our purposes, we can think about the approach reflected in AAT as a hierarchy consisting of three levels. At the most basic level of the hierarchy, AAT reflects a commitment to science as a way of knowing. Numerous lists of the characteristics of science are available. We need not delve into those characteristics here, but they include the notions that science rests on data rather than appeals to authority (i.e., something isn't true simply because someone, no matter how authoritative that persom might appear, says it is), that science attempts to minimize the error and bias inherent in human sense-making, and that science is public in the sense that researchers should be able to confirm or disconfirm one another's results and conclusions.

Moving up to the second level of our hierarchy, the particular brand of science reflected in AAT is that of "realism."[1] Scientists who are also realists (and almost all of them are) believe that there is a "real world" of causal mechanisms that exists independent of people's understanding of those mechanisms. For example, regardless of whether scientists understand them, there are processes that cause children to be autistic. The goal of theory building, then, is to describe the causal mechanisms at work in producing the phenomena of interest. The terms of the theory are taken to refer to real world entities and events, but of course the theorist recognizes that these descriptions will correspond only to some degree to the nature of the actual mechanisms at work in the world. The task of science is to continually refine our understanding of those mechanisms.

At the third and highest level of our hierarchy, AAT reflects the stance of "generative realism" (Greene, 1994). If, as realism suggests, the task of theory building is to describe the processes that give rise to some phenomenon, then generative realism is concerned with the kinds of theoretical terms that are likely to be required in those descriptions. In essence, generative realism says that people are simultaneously three things: (a) social beings, (b) psychological beings, and (c) physical beings. Theories of human behavior should incorporate all three of these elements. Theories that try to treat people as if they are only social beings (or only psychological beings, or only physiological beings) and that ignore either or both of the other two components can only provide an incomplete description of the causal processes responsible for the things people say and do.

Main Features of the Theory

THE CONCEPT OF ACTION FEATURES

I certainly would not do it, and I would not advise you to do it either, but you could express the basic idea of AAT by getting a small tattoo that reads "action is assembled." By that I mean that our thoughts and overt behaviors are built up out of smaller parts, just as a child builds a tower out of Tinkertoys, or as a composer "builds" a melody out of individual notes. Instead of Tinkertoy pieces or musical notes, though, in the case of human behavior the individual parts are "action features"—tiny snippets of thought and action that each of us has acquired over the course of our lives. When you finish reading this paragraph, put your book down and go to a mirror. Try to maintain a blank expression and examine your face for a few moments. You will be looking at dozens and dozens of action features corresponding to the positioning of your brows, eyelids, lips, and so on. Behind your eyes, countless other action features will make up each thought that runs through your mind as you stare into that mirror.

According to AAT, you have an enormous number of action features stored in your memory. The theory tells us a lot about the memory system where action features are held, but the only point that we really need to be concerned with here is the idea that action features are represented in multiple formats. For example, some action features are represented in memory in low-level codes that correspond to motor behaviors (e.g., the features involved in well-practiced skills such as hitting a tennis ball); others correspond to the routines you've acquired for pronouncing various word sounds; others reflect rules of grammar for combining words to make sentences; and still others reflect lessons from your parents, teachers, and friends about how to get along in life (e.g., "be kind to others" and "never give a sucker an even break").

THE ACTIVATION AND ASSEMBLY PROCESSES

AAT says that people have thousands and thousands of action features stored in memory. This is an important concept to grasp, but by itself it doesn't take us far toward understanding how it is that we are able to think and move (or how you were able to write your original sentence at the beginning of this chapter). The theory goes on, then, to specify two processes involved in utilizing action features to produce behavior.

The first of these processes, activation, is basically a selection process. It accounts for how, from the huge storehouse of action features one has acquired, only certain ones are involved in shaping our behavior at any given time. For example, it's probably a pretty safe bet that your action features for swimming weren't activated until you read this sentence. They are there in memory (assuming, of course, that you know at least a little about how to swim!), but they weren't activated. Stripped to the bare essentials, AAT says that action features are activated when they are relevant to our ongoing activities. For example, when you pick up a Sudoku puzzle, all of the action features related to strategies and shortcuts you've learned for solving Sudokus will become activated (although, according to the theory, some will be more highly activated than others).

Once a feature is activated, things really get interesting. On the one hand, an activated feature is in a race against time—activation decays quickly. You could think about activating a feature as being similar to striking a match—it will blaze for a short time and gradually burn out—but the truth is that for most features, the burn time of their activation level is closer to that of a camera flash than that of a match.

But it is also the case that once an action feature is activated, a second process, assembly, kicks in, and that changes the entire dynamic. Assembly occurs when two or more complementary action features are fit together, something like a key fitting in a lock or puzzle pieces fitting together. For example, when you lift a cold beer to your lips, the action features for moving your shoulder, elbow, and wrist mesh to produce a smooth, coordinated movement. The action features for what to say when introducing yourself (e.g., "Hi, my name is _____") complement the features for actually pronouncing your name. When attempting to express your perception that *American Idol*'s Simon Cowell is needlessly acerbic, the words "he," "is," "a," and "jackass" might lock in with that idea, with features representing the rules governing word order that you learned as a child, and with each other. As just one more example, when you are sitting through a boring lecture, an abstract action feature such as "try to look interested" may fit with lower-level features coding facial expression and direction of eye gaze to create a convincing package of an alert listener.

COALITIONS, OVERT BEHAVIOR, AND CONSCIOUSNESS

The entity that results from fitting together action features is termed a "coalition." Coalitions have several important properties. Remember that activation doesn't last long. However, when two features are fit together, they reinforce each other, and that coalition will remain activated longer than either feature alone (just as simultaneously striking middle C and upper C on a piano will cause the notes to reverberate longer than if you hit just one of those keys). This same idea applies as more and more features are added to a coalition; you get something of a snowball effect where coalitions that are able to recruit new features last longer, and, because they last longer, they are able to recruit more new features.[2]

The view of human behavior portrayed in AAT, then, is of an ever-evolving constellation of coalitions, some big, others small, emerging into existence and decaying. Nevertheless, most of these coalitions never show up in our overt behavior or enter our conscious awareness of what we're thinking and doing. So how is it that of all these coalitions some actually do become manifested in conscious thought, or overt action, or both?

There is more to what AAT has to say about these phenomena than can be unpacked here (see Greene, 2006), but the basic ideas are pretty simple. Regarding the question of how it is that some coalitions become manifested in overt behavior, recall that action features are represented in a number of different code systems that vary in level of abstraction. As a general principle, abstract action features will be manifested in overt behavior when they coalesce with lower level, motor-code features. If a person isn't able to translate some higher-level conception of what he or she wants to do into motor codes via the assembly process, that higher-order conception isn't going to show up in his or her overt behavior. The situation is analogous to those times when you've got some understanding in mind, but you just can't come up with words to express that emotion or understanding.

Then there is the question of why only a small subset of coalitions ever enters conscious awareness. Think for a moment about what consciousness is like—it flits over the landscape of your mind, lingering here and there, hovering as a succession of thoughts unfold, and sometimes abruptly shifting to something seemingly unrelated to what came before. In AAT, though, consciousness isn't simply a passive observer. To be sure, it is a slower player in the slam-bang world of activation and assembly, but it serves some important functions.

According to AAT (Greene, 1997) we become conscious of coalitions that are highly activated for longer periods of time (say, for seconds rather than for fractions of a second). As a result, we tend to be aware of abstract action specifications, which change slowly, rather than being aware of coalitions of low-level features, which tend to change rapidly. Moreover, when we run into assembly problems (as, for example, when we don't know how to say something without hurting someone's feelings), becoming conscious of the incompatible action specifications helps us to hold them in mind while we search for ways to solve the assembly problem.

FORCES OF CREATION

Because it is static and linear, Figure 2.1 is somewhat misleading, but it does give a rudimentary depiction of the features of AAT presented in this section. As we have seen, action features stored in memory are brought to bear in behavioral production via the activation process. The assembly process then serves to combine complementary action features to form coalitions. Some of these coalitions will be manifested in overt behavior because they are able to recruit low-level motor programs. Finally, some coalitions, because they are highly activated for extended periods of time, will enter conscious awareness.

With this basic model in place we're in a position to take a fresh look at the issues introduced at the beginning of this chapter. Recall that the overarching focus here is the creative character of behavior (i.e., how it is possible for

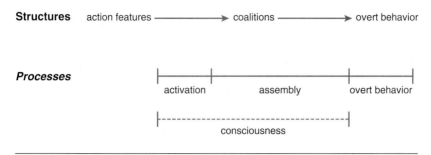

Figure 2.1   The Features of AAT

people to hear, think, say, or do things that they've never heard, thought, said, or done before). As I noted earlier, one important key in addressing the creative nature of behavior is recognizing that, although it is true that unfolding behavior is always new and unique, it is also always old in the sense that it reflects established elements and ways of doing things.

AAT addresses the simultaneous old and new character of behavior in a relatively straightforward way. The established elements of your behavior are those that are represented in memory as action features—all your characteristic ways of saying and doing things. The creative nature of your behavior comes from combining these action features in new sequences and configurations. An analogy I often invoke, although with some trepidation since it is grossly oversimplified, is a tune played on a piano (see Greene, 2007). The piano has just 88 keys (reflecting a single level of abstraction, and none are likely to be added); from those limited keys, an infinite number of unique compositions can be constructed by combining these 88 features in new ways. Imagine, then, what you can do with tens of thousands of action features (reflecting many levels of abstraction, and you can acquire new action features every day).

The simultaneous old-and-new character of behavior is only one of the paradoxes introduced earlier. There we also saw that while creativity comes effortlessly and naturally, there are also situations when our creative capacity fails us—situations where we stutter and stammer; where we just can't come up with the right thing to say; where we fail to think, say, and move as we want. A key precept of the intellectual tradition that fostered AAT is the notion that instances where a system fails to function optimally are just as important for understanding that system as the occasions where it runs smoothly. Breakdowns are not viewed as something to be ignored or passed off as insignificant; instead, they are prized as opportunities for deeper understanding.

In keeping with this perspective, AAT encourages scrutiny of our lapses and awkwardness, and explains them in terms of the properties of the activation and assembly processes (see below).

One other point raised in the introduction merits mention here as well. Models of message production typically are top down, in the sense that they assume that people formulate an abstract idea or understanding that then passes through a series of successively more concrete levels, terminating with verbal and nonverbal cues. AAT, however, tells a slightly different story about the creation of messages (see Greene, 2006). AAT holds that message behavior, especially verbal behavior, *tends* to be top down, but is not necessarily so. The nature of the coalition-building process is such that lower-level codes can actually drive the formation of higher-level thoughts. Thus, in AAT, the forces of creation include both top-down and bottom-up processes.

Conceptualization of Communication in the Theory

There are a number of properties of communication highlighted by AAT, some of which we've already touched on in this chapter. From the perspective of AAT, communication involves the interaction of two or more individuals, each of whom is, fundamentally, a physical, psychological, and social being. The presence of one's interlocutors and their behavior in such social contexts both poses assembly problems for the individual, and also affords solutions to assembly problems, such that interactions are inevitably characterized by mutual influence—and mutually driven creation, both intra- and interindividually. Each individual, in turn, via overt verbal and nonverbal behavior, expresses less than the individual means (i.e., the constellation of coalitions) and more than the individual knows (i.e., that they are consciously aware of)—and all of this unfolds at speeds faster than the individual is able to apprehend.

Uses of the Theory

Because it is a general theory of behavioral production, AAT is relevant to virtually any behavioral phenomenon one might wish to investigate (although, obviously, what the theory has to say about some sorts of phenomena is more interesting than the relatively superficial insights it might yield about others). As a result of its broad applicability, the theory has provided a foundation for addressing such diverse topics as the behaviors that distinguish liars from truth-tellers, processes underlying the experience of social anxiety, the nature of the self-concept, and the consistency (or lack of consistency!) of people's behavior from one situation to another (see Greene, 1995a).

Beyond these applications, others merit a little more discussion. One of these other applications is the topic of social skill and why we sometimes fail to communicate with others as we would like. We typically think of performance failures as stemming from a lack of either ability or motivation (or both). But Greene and Geddes (1993) noted that sometimes we have the necessary ability, and the motivation, but still are not able to produce a socially skilled response. For example, did you ever think of a great comeback to something someone said—but only after that person had left? Greene and Geddes attempted to show how we can understand these sorts of situations in terms of the properties of the activation and assembly processes.

Another realm in which AAT has found application is examination of the temporal (i.e., time) properties of message behavior. When we think about message behavior we typically focus on the content of what people say, but all of us have an intuitive understanding that the temporal properties of a message are important, as well (for example, we notice when a person pauses a long time before responding to a question). From the perspective of AAT, temporal features of a message, such as pauses and speech rate, are particularly fascinating because, on the one hand, they have social significance, and, on the other, they provide a window to the activation and assembly processes. This fact has led to applications of AAT in exploring such topics as the effects of advance planning on speech fluency, the impact of trying to accomplish multiple goals in a single message (see Greene, 1995b), and the ways that practice affects the acquisition of communication skills (see Greene, 2003).

Strengths and Limitations of the Theory

In a previous section of this chapter, I noted that there are various lists of the characteristics of science. In a similar vein, there are standard lists of criteria for evaluating scientific theories (e.g., range, scope, heurism, falsifiability, and so on), and you are encouraged to apply these criteria in evaluating AAT. But for present purposes, let us consider just one limitation and one strength of the theory. One of the former is that it may sometimes be difficult to take it all in—that is, to keep in mind all the details and at the same time to see the big picture of how they function together, and on top of this to apprehend the implications of the speed with which these processes unfold. The flip side of this same coin is one of the strengths of the theory. Science gives considerable weight to the "aesthetic value" of theories—that is, their elegance and the pleasure they afford. AAT is filled with puzzles and surprises that, like an undiscovered code, have always been embedded in the theory, and that emerge unexpectedly as you turn it over in your mind.

Directions for Future Research and Applications

As I noted earlier, the fact that AAT is a general model of behavioral production means that it can be applied to virtually anything that happens when people come together. If you've got some issue or phenomenon you've been pondering, try casting it in AAT terms to see what implications the theory has for understanding that process in a new way. One of the issues that my colleagues and I have focused on lately is why some people seem better than others at creating messages on the fly. You probably know people who are quick witted, who can think on their feet. We call this phenomenon "creative facility," and we're trying to understand why some people have more of it than others. As for you, you've already proven that you can create a novel sentence; now where are you going to apply your creative genius?

Notes

1. Realism, as a philosophical perspective, stands as an alternative to logical empiricism and perspectivism. A useful introduction to realism as a philosophical foundation for communication science is found in Pavitt (2001).

2. The snowball analogy is useful, but it does not convey a completely accurate picture because even as a coalition is adding new features it is also decaying and fragmenting, such that older features are being lost.

References

Greene, J. O. (1994). What sort of terms ought theories of human action incorporate? *Communication Studies, 45,* 187–211.

Greene, J. O. (1995a). An action-assembly perspective on verbal and nonverbal message production: A dancer's message unveiled. In D. E. Hewes (Ed.), *The cognitive bases of interpersonal communication* (pp. 51–85). Hillsdale, NJ: Erlbaum.

Greene, J. O. (1995b). Production of messages in pursuit of multiple social goals: Action assembly theory contributions to the study of cognitive encoding processes. In B. R. Burleson (Ed.), *Communication yearbook 18* (pp. 26–53). Thousand Oaks, CA: Sage.

Greene, J. O. (1997). A second generation action assembly theory. In J. O. Greene (Ed.), *Message production: Advances in communication theory* (pp. 151–170). Mahwah, NJ: Erlbaum.

Greene, J. O. (2003). Models of adult communication skill acquisition: Practice and the course of performance improvement. In J. O. Greene & B. R. Burleson (Eds.), *Handbook of communication and social interaction skills* (pp. 51–91). Mahwah, NJ: Erlbaum.

Greene, J. O. (2006). Have I got something to tell you: Ideational dynamics and message production. *Journal of Language and Social Psychology, 25,* 64–75.

Greene, J. O. (2007). Formulating and producing verbal and nonverbal messages: An action assembly theory. In B. B. Whaley & W. Samter (Eds.), *Explaining communication: Contemporary theories and exemplars* (pp. 165–180). Mahwah, NJ: Erlbaum.

Greene, J. O., & Geddes, D. (1993). An action assembly perspective on social skill. *Communication Theory, 3,* 26–49.

Pavitt, C. (2001). *The philosophy of science and communication theory.* Huntington, NY: Nova Science Publishers.

3

Attribution Theory

Finding Good Cause in the Search for Theory

Valerie Manusov and Brian Spitzberg

Humans are an inquisitive species: We wonder why and how things occur, and we develop religions, philosophies, and sciences as ways of answering our questions. Such curiosity influences our cultural, societal, interpersonal, and personal lives in intricate ways. We can easily see many everyday examples of this in our own minds and in our conversations with friends: We ask ourselves why another person looks so lonely, we think about why we did not get a job, and we talk to others to try to figure out why the person we went out with on Saturday has not called us since then. After all, it's Tuesday!

So fundamental is the process of asking and answering "why" questions—trying to figure out what caused something else—that it has been characterized as a basic human activity (Heider, 1958), and a family of theories has developed to illumine how and why things happen as they do. This set of theories, collectively called Attribution Theory, attempts to describe and explain the mental and communicative processes involved in everyday explanations, most typically explanations of individual and social events. In this chapter, we describe select parts of these theories and their related scholarship, and we offer critiques of its usefulness for understanding interpersonal communication processes.

Purpose and Meta-theoretical Assumptions

Even though attributions are talked about in everyday life and studied by people in many academic disciplines, most attribution theories arose in—and are most commonly researched as part of—the field of psychology. Not surprisingly, then, the various attribution theories lean heavily toward a logical-empirical view of the world. Although there are important cultural and personal differences in attribution making (see, for example, Lawrence, Murray, Banerjee, Turner, Sangha, Byng, et al., 2006; Maddux & Yuki, 2006), attribution researchers believe that the underlying process of attempting to understand the world around us is universal, pervasive, and predictable.

There are a number of definitions for attributions, but a common way to define "attributions" is as the internal (thinking) and external (talking) process of interpreting and understanding what is behind our own and others' behaviors. Thus, although there are different types of Attribution Theory, they all are concerned with the "how" and the "what" by which people process information in attempting to understand events, judge those events, and act on those events. We can, for example, see attributional processes at work in the following conversation, where three friends are trying to explain one of their professor's facial expressions. In this discussion, each is describing the cause he or she attributes to the same action:

Sheryl: Hey, did you see how Professor Smythe looked at me when I asked him that question?

Theo: Yeah, he looked like he was really confused!

Sheryl: Really? I thought he looked like he thought I was the dumbest student ever.

Theo: No way. I'm sure he was just trying to figure out the answer.

Kyle: I thought he was coming down with the flu.

This example illustrates that any communication event or behavior can be viewed as an effect that has some cause, and the cause we attribute (e.g., confusion, opinion, flu) is likely to influence the meaning of the action and how we might respond to it.

The person most often attributed as the originator of attribution models is Fritz Heider. In his early work, Heider reflected the logical-empirical backbone of attribution theories by making relatively global claims about what people do. Specifically, he argued that people act like naïve scientists as they attempt to make sense—in a relatively systematic way—of their larger social worlds. For Heider (1958), people are active interpreters of the events that occur in their lives, and they use consistent and logical modes of sense-making in their interpretations. They do so, in large part, to both understand and control the world around them.

Heider was concerned particularly with an action's "causal locus," focusing his work largely on when a person is more likely to judge a behavior's cause as internal (e.g., a disposition or a characteristic of a person) or external (i.e., an environmental factor) to another person. Causal locus continues to be a mainstay of attribution studies and is readily understandable. For example, if a good friend is late for a lunch date, it is likely that you would try to figure out why she was late. Heider argued that we do our best to determine the most likely causes.

Main Features of the Theory

Heider's (1958) initial ideas have been expanded in a number of ways to account for the complex process of attribution. For example, researchers have argued that attributions vary from one another not only based on causal locus but also on other dimensions. These include "stability," or whether or not we see the cause of something as stable ("He's late because he doesn't care about other people") or unstable ("He's late because he wasn't feeling well and it took him a while to get ready"); and "control," or whether or not we think a person was able to alter the cause ("He's late because he forgot to set his alarm again") or unable to alter the cause ("He's late because there was a traffic accident that delayed traffic").

In addition to a broadening of what form attributions take, four theoretical currents have emerged since Heider introduced the concept of attributions. Most research relies on just one of these currents, but, collectively, they make up the primary features of attributional scholarship.

A FOCUS ON CORRESPONDENCE

One of the ways that any action can be explained is as a product of some set of characteristics (i.e., "a kind person would act that way"). When attributions are informative of a person's nature or personality, they are considered "correspondent." Jones and his colleagues (Jones & Davis, 1965; Jones & Harris, 1967) developed this line of theorizing, and it has since been studied in a wide variety of disciplines and contexts. For example, Stamp and Sabourin (1995) found that relationally abusive or aggressive men tend to attribute their violence to things that were external to them, such as a wife's behavior or jealousy. Most of these external factors are considered correspondent, because abusive men tend to attribute such causes to intentional and negative factors in their partners. Importantly, such attributions reflected the men's thinking, rather than what may actually have prompted the behavior.

A FOCUS ON COVARIATION

Attributions are not tied only to dispositions. In order to understand the underlying structure of attributing causes to effects, Kelley (1967, 1971) proposed a normative model that came to be known as the ANOVA (an acronym for "analysis of variance") cube. In general, events are attributed to causes with which they covary or co-occur. Causes are attributed to factors that are present when an event or effect is observed, and not present when the event or effect is absent. If you find that your relationships tend to get more complicated and are more likely to dissolve only after one of you says "I love you," you might attribute the utterance or state of love as the cause of relationship problems. For you, these events covary.

A FOCUS ON RESPONSIBILITY

Not all attributions are about the cause of an action, however. When we are making sense of things, we often focus instead on who or what was responsible for that behavior or outcome (Weiner, 1986). Importantly, research following this reasoning has looked at the potential consequences of responsibility attributions, and these consequences can be extensive. For example, according to research by Badahdah and Alkhder (2006), people are, for example, more likely to feel sympathetic to a person with AIDS if that person is viewed as not responsible for his or her own plight (e.g., if AIDS was contracted through blood transfusion) as opposed to intentional risky conduct (e.g., unprotected sex). Thus attributions of responsibility can have significant repercussions.

A FOCUS ON BIAS

Whereas people can make relatively logical assessments of cause and responsibility, as Heider (1958) predicted, researchers have found there are often systematic biases in how we make attributions (see Ross, 1977). Perhaps the most well known bias is the "fundamental attribution bias," which is our tendency to make more internal attributions than external attributions for others' behaviors. But there are other biases as well. For example, Canary and Spitzberg (1990) predicted a self-serving bias in conflict situations, and found that actors in conflicts tend to view their behavior as significantly more appropriate than the behavior of their partners. They further predicted and found that more salient conflict behaviors such as anger and criticism would be more correlated between self and partner perceptions than less salient behaviors such as topic shifting and integrative discussion. To the extent that we generally view ourselves as competent and not responsible for negative events, and that we view our partners as stable and personally responsible for negative events, conflicts are springloaded to escalate in unpleasant ways (see Sillars, 1980).

SUMMARY

Every comment a person makes and every action in which a person engages can be subject to attributional analysis, by self and by others. The outcome of this analysis has potentially significant implications for the nature of how one responds to another's actions. Whether it is an achievement failure, a stigmatizing condition, a need for help, or an aggressive act, if these are attributed to controllable and intentional causes, responses of anger and reprimand or neglect are more likely, whereas uncontrollable and unintentional attributions are more likely to lead to sympathy and offers of assistance (Weiner, 2004).

Conceptualization of Communication in the Theory

Whereas attribution processes were perceived initially as the domain of psychologists, the past 20 years have also seen particular attention to attributions by communication scholars. Two key chapters written in 1982 (Seibold & Spitzberg, 1982; Sillars, 1982) helped to encourage communication researchers to address the nature of attributions, and the term "attribution" now shows up as a key word in an array of studies. Most scholarship on attributions in our field, however, has been done in the context of interpersonal encounters. For these scholars, attributions are employed typically in one of three ways.

ATTRIBUTIONS AS EXPLANATIONS
UNDERLYING SOCIAL ACTIONS,
INCLUDING COMMUNICATION BEHAVIORS

Initial work conceptualized attributions as a psychological process used to determine the cause of or responsibility for a behavior. The event that needed explaining was often an individual one such as why a person achieved or failed a goal. But attributions are also made for communication behavior, such as a facial expression directed to one person from another. That is, much like other behaviors, communication behaviors can be seen as occurring for different reasons. Work by Amy Bippus (2003) typifies the conceptualization of attributions as "explanations for communicative behavior." In her study, she asked people why a person used humor in an actual conflict situation. She also asked how they interpreted the cause and repercussions. For example, Bippus found that more internal attributions for humor use were associated with more negative outcomes (e.g., conflict escalation, progress, and face loss). Humor thought to be bad and humor that was attributed to the speaker's personality was particularly damaging to the relationship.

ATTRIBUTIONS AS CATEGORIES OF MEANINGS
GIVEN TO COMMUNICATION BEHAVIOR

Attributions not only help us explain communication behavior—they may also help us understand the diversity of meanings that people give to any communicative act. That is, if we look at the content of attributions made for communication we will see the many dimensions of attributions we discussed earlier (e.g., causal locus, responsibility, stability, and control). For more discussion of these dimensions, and to see other dimensions, read Weiner (1986). Different combinations of these dimensions lead to different conclusions about what something means. In the discussion between Sheryl, Theo, and Kyle, for example, each attribution discussed can be compared to the others based on an array of attributional dimensions. Furthermore, how these dimensions combine with one another has consequences. For example, Erina MacGeorge (2001) investigated the ways in which people offer social support to one another in times of crisis and found that when the crisis was attributed as more stable, more the affected person's responsibility, and more a result of the person's effort, it induced greater anger and reduced sympathy for the affected person's plight.

ATTRIBUTIONS AS THE ACTUAL MEANINGS GIVEN TO A BEHAVIOR, OFTEN IN TALK

The third conceptualization of attribution also points us toward the content of attributions, but in a somewhat different way. Rather than helping locate the source of difference in interpretations for communication behavior, some interpersonal communication researchers have looked at dialogue—like the dialogue between Sheryl, Theo, and Kyle—to investigate how spoken attributions reflect the meaning that people give to a communication act. That is, we can also look at attributions to see what a behavior means—what message value it has—for someone. As Brant Burleson (1986) noted,

> people frequently *talk* [emphasis in original] to one another about why someone acted in some way; indeed exploring why someone behaved as he or she did is probably one of the most ubiquitous conversational topics" (p. 64). . . . [Moreover] the *outcome* [emphasis in original] of a collaborative, publicly conducted attribution process . . . is a product that was socially constructed, tested, and verified. (p. 79)

That is, attributions do not just occur for communication behaviors; they also comprise some of what we communicate about (e.g., see Rempel, Ross, & Holmes, 2001) and are about what we have conflict (Orvis, Kelley, & Butler, 1976).

Uses of the Theory

These three conceptualizations reflect a strong interconnectedness between attributions and communication. They arise from a large body of context-based scholarship conducted by researchers interested in the interpersonal nature of attributions. Two of these are contexts are (a) marriage, and (b) the ways in which attributions are involved in some of the darker sides of communication. To follow, we discuss these somewhat overlapping areas of research.

ATTRIBUTIONS IN MARRIAGE

The majority of empirical work using Attribution Theory in relationships concerns the processes and effects of attributions in married couples. Only some of this work centers on communication processes, but all of it is relevant to understanding the role of attributions in interpersonal interaction. Most notably, researchers have looked at the ways in which one spouse's feelings about the relationship—his or her degree of marital satisfaction—influences or is influenced by the kind of attributions the spouse makes for his or her own and his or her partner's behaviors.

Overall, researchers find that

> distressed spouses . . . make attributions for negative events that accentuate their impact (e.g., they locate the cause in their partner, see it as stable or unchanging, and see it as global or influencing many of the areas of their relationship), whereas nondistressed spouses . . . make attributions that minimize the impact of negative events (e.g., they do not locate the cause in the partner and see it as unstable and specific). (Fincham & Bradbury, 1992, p. 457)

The tendency for nondistressed or satisfied couples to make low-impact attributions for negative behaviors (and, conversely, to allow positive events more influence) has been termed relationship-enhancing; the type of attributions more common for distressed or dissatisfied couples is called distress-maintaining (Holtzworth-Munroe & Jacobson, 1988).

The occurrence and impact of distress-maintaining attributions appears augmented when couples are categorized as aggressive. A study by a team of communication and psychology scholars (Sillars, Leonard, Roberts, and Dun 2002) concluded that aggressive couples tend to have negative styles of communication, and that their communication tends to get even more negative when the husbands drink alcohol. Couples in aggressive relationships tend to reveal quite divergent attributions in their beliefs about why they acted as they did and what accounts for their partners' behavior. Thus, one spouse may state that he engaged in certain conflict behavior because, "I'm trying to get her to talk about it," yet assert that his spouse engaged in the same behavior for a very different reason: "She's always got to have her way" (see Sillars et al., 2002, p. 97). In particular, the authors found that aggressive spouses tended to attribute less constructive engagement and more avoidance to their partner than they attributed to themselves ("He always runs away from conflict, but I try to argue it out") and concluded, ominously, that, in aggressive relationships, attribution-making "presents a combustible situation" (Sillars et al., 2002, p. 101).

Although researchers investigated the relationship between attributions and couples' behaviors less than would be expected, some researchers focus on it. In one study, Manusov (2002) reported evidence that attributions made by one spouse for his or her spouse's nonverbal cues may also influence the behaviors the attributor expresses toward the other (e.g., when one spouse attributed greater control to his or her partner's emotional expressions, the attributor was more likely to be facially pleasant, gaze more, and use a more upright posture when talking to his or her spouse). Other researchers have found links between the ways in which people assign responsibility and their own anger displays (Fincham & Bradbury, 1992), their overall use of negative behaviors in reaction to an attribution (Bradbury & Fincham, 1992), and their reciprocity of partners' negative behavior (Bradbury & Fincham). The links between attributions and other affective and behavioral outcomes show the extent to which attribution-making may permeate intimate relationships in both positive and negative ways.

THE DARKER SIDE OF ATTRIBUTIONS

As the section above on marriage reflects, the role of attribution processes has been the subject of increasing attention in the explanation of, among other things, intimate aggression and violence. Consistent with the responsibility principle discussed earlier, Byrne and Arias (1997) found that there was a substantial negative correlation between marital satisfaction and marital aggression among wives who attributed their husbands as responsible for negative behavior in the relationship (although the same was not true of husbands' attributions of responsibility to their wives). To explain this, Olson and Lloyd (2005) engaged in detailed interviews with a small sample of women who had experienced aggressive behaviors in their relationships. They found that a "glaring pattern was how often the women explained that aggression was the only way to get their partners' attention or to get the men to listen or acknowledge the women" (p. 615).

In contrast, however, and more consistent with the self-serving bias, Cantos, Neidig, and O'Leary (1993) found that spouses were more likely to blame their partners rather than themselves for domestic violence. Biased attributions occur in other ways in these relationships. For example, Tonizzo, Howells, Day, Reidpath, and Froyland (2000) found that physically violent men tend to blame their wives' negative behaviors on the wives' so-called selfish motivations. It appears that abusive men not only demonstrate these attribution biases in their own relationships but in their perception of others, as well. When asked to interpret the thoughts of videotaped interactions, Schweinle and Ickes (2002) learned that abusive men reveal an overattribution bias in which husbands assume that their wives' thoughts are more critical and rejecting than wives interpret their husbands' thoughts.

Strengths and Limitations of the Theory

The examples just discussed reflect the salience and consequences of attributions in interpersonal contexts. Despite the expansive and diverse domains and questions to which Attribution Theory has been applied, the theory is not without its problems, and Attribution Theory has received its share of critical review (e.g., Newcombe & Rutter, 1982; Semin, 1980). There are many criteria by which theories can be evaluated. We focus here on (a) explanatory power, (b) scope and generality, (c) conditionship specification, and (d) verifiability or falsifiability to show some of the strengths and limitations of Attribution Theory qua theory (Spitzberg, 2001).

"Explanatory power" refers to the most essential requirement of any theory: how well does it explain, or make sense of, phenomena? It is a near paradox that a theory explaining how people explain is itself required to be a good explanation. Attribution theories have the advantage of making good intuitive sense, developed as they were to account for laypersons as naïve scientists (Heider, 1958). Most of the dimensions and principles of attribution theories are recognizable immediately in everyday interactions. In Sheryl, Theo, and Kyle's conversation, for example, we can see evidence of the process of negotiating attributions and the normalcy of working together in conversation to determine why something occurred and what it meant.

"Scope and generality" refer to the breadth of phenomena and contexts in which a theory applies. A theory that only applies to a particular time, place, or behavior is narrow in scope and not very generalizable. Attribution Theory was developed originally as a universal theory of human sense-making, but research has limited its scope. Most research investigates contexts in which conscious attributional efforts are most likely: contexts involving actual or potential negative consequences and violations of expectations. For example, researchers have centered on shyness, loneliness, conflict, relationship satisfaction, accounts, abuse, anger, shame, achievement motivation, moral responsibility, and relationship breakups. Attributions may or may not work the same way in other contexts where the importance of making attributions is less necessary. Furthermore, there is increasing evidence that attributional thought processes may be culturally moderated to some extent. For example, Eastern and Asian cultures may be more situational in their attribution biases, compared to the West's dispositional attribution bias (Choi, Nisbett, & Norenzayan, 1999). Both of these, context and culture, limit how broadly general claims about attributions can legitimately be made.

"Conditionship specification" refers to the extent to which a theory articulates clearly the nature of the relationship among its concepts. Even some of the original theorists claim some strict parameters for the theory. For example, Heider's (1958) original propositions were quite formulaic, along the lines of the following: Personal causation is attributed as a multiplicative function of power (can) and trying (effort) plus environmental facilitation (or minus environmental obstruction). Weiner (2004) claimed boldly that "there are three, and indeed only three, underlying causal properties that have cross-situational generality. . . . locus, stability, and controllability" (p. 17). Bradbury and Fincham (1990) summarized their extensive review as indicating that "the dimensions of locus, stability, control, and globality are necessary and sufficient for assessing causal attributions in marriage" (p. 17). Yet, their own coding of research results indicates that many studies find no or only partial support for these dimensions.

The fact is that, almost 50 years after its inception, it is still not entirely clear how much the results of Attribution Theory support these condition specifications. This raises a significant question of the verifiability and falsifiability of this theory. "Verifiability" is the extent to which evidence in support of a theory can be generated through observation and investigation. "Falsifiability" is the extent to which evidence that contradicts a theory can be generated through observation and investigation. Consider the following proposition: all conflicts are blamed on the partner more than on self. A verification strategy would take any evidence that conflicts tend to be blamed on the partner more than on the self as evidence in support of the proposition. In contrast, a falsification strategy would take any evidence that it sometimes does not happen as evidence that the proposition is incorrect and must be modified or replaced. To date, it is easy to find researchers claiming to have supported or verified Attribution Theory. Even though lack of support and partial support are often reported, however, it is rare to find any scholar of merit claiming that Attribution Theory is fundamentally flawed and that some of its premises need to be replaced. We believe that the validity of Attribution Theory should be examined closely on these criteria.

Directions of Future Research and Applications

Despite our concerns with Attribution Theory as a theory, we contend that attribution processes have great potential for additional study and application by scholars interested in interpersonal communication and relationships. In particular, the research focusing on some of the very real consequences of the attributions we make suggest places for important exploration. For example, a recent study (Stewart, Keel, & Schiavo, 2006) examined attributions people gave for others who had been diagnosed with an eating disorder. Compared to the attributions made about people without the eating disorder, attributions about people with anorexia nervosa are to blame the affected person for his or her condition. That is, people implicated those with anorexia in their own disorder;

such attributions could affect others' treatment of and communication with that person and may, therefore, worsen the person's condition.

Attributions may have strong legal implications, as well. For example, Nancy White (2005) looked at the legal effects of responsibility attributions for juvenile delinquents and their parents. According to White,

> Recently, two families in Western Australia have felt the full force of being found guilty of failing to act responsibly in relation to their respective 14- and 15-year-old sons' delinquent actions. . . . Fines totalling A$60,000 were exacted, with one family ordered to pay A$45,000 and the other family A$15,000 remuneration to the victims of their sons' damage. . . . What, one asks, did these parents do or fail to do that allowed the Court to order such high compensation to be paid to the victims of their sons' acts? (p. 402)

What they did or failed to have done may well rest in how they communicated with their children.

In closing, we believe that attributional processes are a vital—and consequential—set of practices for interpersonal communication scholars to investigate. Their ubiquity in our everyday sense-making means that attributions are ripe for study by people in their everyday lives. Our hope is that this chapter energizes that curiosity in readers.

References

Badahdah, A. M., & Alkhder, O. H. (2006). Helping a friend with AIDS: A test of Weiner's attributional theory in Kuwait. *Illness, Crisis, & Loss, 14,* 43–54.

Bippus, A. M. (2003). Humor motives, qualities, and reactions in recalled conflict episodes. *Western Journal of Communication, 67,* 13–27.

Bradbury, T. N., & Fincham, F. D. (1990). Attributions in marriage: Review and critique. *Psychological Bulletin, 107,* 3–33.

Bradbury, T. N., & Fincham, F. D. (1992). Attributions and behavior in marital interaction. *Journal of Personality and Social Psychology, 63,* 613–628.

Burleson, B. R. (1986). Attribution schemes and causal inference in natural conversations. In D. G. Ellis & W. A. Donohue (Eds.), *Contemporary issues in language and discourse processes* (pp. 63–85). Mahwah, NJ: Erlbaum.

Byrne, C. A., & Arias, I. (1997). Marital satisfaction and marital violence: Moderating effects of attributional processes. *Journal of Family Violence, 11,* 188–195.

Canary, D. J., & Spitzberg, B. H. (1990). Attribution biases and associations between conflict strategies and competence outcomes. *Communication Monographs, 57,* 139–151.

Cantos, A. L., Neidig, P. H., & O'Leary, K. D. (1993). Men and women's attributions of blame for domestic violence. *Journal of Family Violence, 8,* 289–302.

Choi, I., Nisbett, R. E., & Norenzayan, A. (1999). Causal attribution across cultures: Variation and universality. *Psychological Bulletin, 125,* 47–63.

Fincham, F. D., & Bradbury, T. N. (1992). Assessing attributions in marriage: The relationship attribution measure. *Journal of Personality and Social Psychology, 62,* 457–468.

Heider, F. (1958). *The psychology of interpersonal relations.* New York: Wiley.

Holtzworth-Munroe, A., & Jacobson, N. S. (1988). Toward a methodology for coding spontaneous causal attributions: Preliminary results with married couples. *Journal of Social and Clinical Psychology, 7,* 101–112.

Jones, E. E., & Davis, K. E. (1965). From acts to dispositions: The attribution process in person perception. In L. Berkowitz (Ed.), *Advances in experimental social psychology* (Vol. 2, pp. 219–266). New York: Academic Press.

Jones, E. E., & Harris, V. A. (1967). The attribution of attitudes. *Journal of Experimental Social Psychology, 3,* 1–24.

Kelley H. H. (1967). Attribution theory in social psychology. *Nebraska Symposium on Motivation, 14,* 192–241.

Kelley, H. H. (1971). *Attribution in social interaction.* Morristown, NJ: General Learning Press.

Lawrence, V., Murray, J., Banerjee, S., Turner, S., Sangha, K., Byng, R., et al. (2006). Concepts and causation of depression: A cross-cultural study of the beliefs of older adults. *The Gerontologist, 46,* 23–33.

MacGeorge, E. L. (2001). Support providers' interaction goals: The influence of attributions and emotions. *Communication Monographs, 68,* 28–48.

Maddux, W. W., & Yuki, M. (2006). The "ripple effect": Cultural differences in perceptions of the consequences of events. *Personality & Social Psychology Bulletin, 32,* 669–684.

Manusov, V. (2002). Thought and action: Connecting attributions to behaviors in married couples' interactions. In P. Noller & J. A. Feeney (Eds.), *Understanding marriage: Developments in the study of couple interaction* (pp. 14–31). Cambridge, UK: Cambridge University Press.

Newcombe, R. D., & Rutter, D. R. (1982). Ten reasons why ANOVA theory and research fail to explain attribution processes. *Current Psychological Reviews, 2,* 95–108.

Olson, L. N., & Lloyd, S. A. (2005). "It depends on what you mean by starting": An exploration of how women define initiation of aggression and their motives for behaving aggressively. *Sex Roles, 53,* 603–617.

Orvis, B. R., Kelley, H. H., & Butler, D. (1976). Attributional conflict in young couples. In J. H. Harvey, W. J. Ickes, & R. F. Kidd (Eds.), *New directions in attribution research* (Vol. 1, pp. 353–386). Hillsdale, NJ: Erlbaum.

Rempel, J. K., Ross, M., & Holmes, J. G. (2001). Trust and communicated attributions in close relationships. *Journal of Personality and Social Psychology, 81,* 57–64.

Ross, L. (1977). The intuitive psychologist and his shortcomings. Distortions in the attribution process. In L. Berkowitz (Ed.), *Advances in experimental social psychology* (Vol. 10, pp. 174–177). New York: Academic Press.

Schweinle, W. E., & Ickes, W. (2002). On empathic accuracy and husbands' abusiveness. In P. Noller & J. A. Feeney (Eds.), *Understanding marriage: Developments in the study of couple interaction* (pp. 228–250). Cambridge, UK: Cambridge University Press.

Seibold, D. R., & Spitzberg, B. H. (1982). Attribution theory and research: Review and implications for communication. In B. Dervin & M. J. Voight (Eds.), *Progress in communication sciences* (pp. 85–125). Norwood, NJ: Ablex.

Semin, G. R. (1980). A gloss on attribution theory. *British Journal of Social and Clinical Psychology, 19,* 291–300.

Sillars, A. L. (1980). Attributions and communication in roommate conflicts. *Communication Monographs, 47,* 180–200.

Sillars, A. L. (1982). Attribution and communication: Are people "naïve scientists" or just naïve? In M. E. Roloff & C. R. Berger (Eds.), *Social cognition and communication* (pp. 73–106). Beverly Hills, CA: Sage.

Sillars, A. L., Leonard, K. E., Roberts, L. J., & Dun, T. (2002). Cognition and communication during marital conflict: How alcohol affects subjective coding of interaction in aggressive and nonaggressive couples. In P. Noller & J. A. Feeney (Eds.), *Understanding marriage: Developments in the study of couple interaction* (pp. 85–112). Cambridge, UK: Cambridge University Press.

Spitzberg, B. H. (2001). The status of attribution theory *qua* theory in personal relationships. In V. Manusov & J. H. Harvey (Eds.), *Attribution, communication behavior, and close relationships* (pp. 353–371). Cambridge, UK: Cambridge University Press.

Stamp, G. H., & Sabourin, T. C. (1995). Accounting for violence: An analysis of male spousal abuse narratives. *Journal of Applied Communication Research, 23,* 284–308.

Stewart, M. C., Keel, P. K., & Schiavo, S. (2006). Stigmatization of anorexia nervosa. *International Journal of Eating Disorders, 39,* 320–325.

Tonizzo, S., Howells, K., Day, A., Reidpath, D., & Froyland, I. (2000). Attributions of negative partner behavior by men who physically abuse their partners. *Journal of Family Violence, 15,* 155–167.

Weiner, B. (1986). *An attributional theory of motivation and emotion.* New York: Springer-Verlag.

Weiner, B. (2004). Attribution theory revisited: Transforming cultural plurality into theoretical unity. In D. M. McInerney & S. V. Etten (Eds.), *Big theories revisited* (Vol. 4, Research on sociocultural influences on motivation and learning, pp. 13–29). Greenwich, CT: Information Age Publishing.

White, N. (2005). Attribution and mitigation of parent and child responsibility: A qualitative analysis. *Psychiatry, Psychology and Law, 12,* 401–411.

4

Constructivism Theory

Explaining Individual Differences in Communication Skill

Brant R. Burleson and Jessica J. Rack

I magine that it is near the end of the semester, you are a student, and you are behind on a required term paper. You do not think you'll be able to complete it on time, so you meet with the professor to request an extension. Following are two different messages that might be used in this situation.

Message 1:   Dr. Jones, about the paper due this week, well, I really wanted to finish it on time but I've been so busy! I went on vacation for Thanksgiving and I couldn't find the time to write it then. When I came back I had another paper due for an important class, and it took forever! Plus I have meets with the paintball team, and I haven't been able to find the time to sit down and write the paper. So could I please, please, *please* have until the end of exam week to turn in the paper? It would be really helpful to have the extra week to work on it.

Message 2:   Dr. Jones, about the paper due this week, well, I love the topic that you chose and I've been doing tons of research on it. I've found so many articles that I haven't been able to read all of them! You said you wanted this paper to be something that I'm proud of, and I want that too. I know you'll enjoy reading a thorough paper, rather than something thrown together at the last minute. To write the great paper we both want, I need a little extra time. I know this will make grading it tough because you won't have as much time, but I think it won't take long to grade because it will be good. Could I have until next week to finish it?

Most people would regard the second message as more skillful, but why? What makes it skillful? More generally, what enables some people to communicate skillfully in a variety of contexts? What background and experiences contribute to skillfulness in communication? And what are some of the advantages associated with being skillful in this way? These are some of the questions that receive focal attention in the communication theory known as Constructivism Theory.

Constructivism, developed by Jesse Delia and his associates at the University of Illinois (e.g., Delia, 1977), is one of the older, most thoroughly tested, and most developed theories in interpersonal communication. The theory originally focused on explaining the development of interpersonal competence, especially during childhood (Delia & O'Keefe, 1979), but, in the last 25 years, it has been applied to numerous issues in diverse contexts, including close relationships (Burleson, Metts, & Kirch, 2000), business (Zorn & Violanti, 1996), education (Applegate, 1980), parenting (Applegate, Burleson, & Delia, 1992), health care (Kline & Ceropski, 1984), politics (Swanson, 1981), and intercultural interaction (Applegate & Sypher, 1988). The theory is one of the communication discipline's most fruitful approaches, serving as a rich resource for theory, research, and application (for reviews, see Applegate, 1990; Burleson, 2007; Burleson & Caplan, 1998; Coopman, 1997; Delia, O'Keefe, & O'Keefe, 1982; Gastil, 1995). Here, we seek to acquaint you with the basic elements of Constructivism Theory, some of the questions posed by constructivism, and how this approach tries to answer them.

Purpose and Meta-theoretical Assumptions

The main purpose of constructivism is to analyze the nature of functional communication competence and to develop testable propositions about this competence that lead to understandings of its various forms, determinants, antecedents, and consequences. Functional communication competence refers to the ability to generate and process messages in ways that enable people to accomplish their goals efficiently and effectively. Constructivism seeks to explain individual differences in functional communication skills: what these differences are, why they exist, where they come from, and why they matter. To do this, constructivism provides models of various communication skills and their causes, origins, and outcomes.

Constructivism is a scientific theory because it seeks to identify regularities in functional communication skills and develop explanations regarding the general nature, determinants, antecedents, and consequences of these skills. Like other scientific theories, constructivism seeks to evaluate its explanations by deriving testable predictions (i.e., hypotheses) and then evaluating their accuracy through empirical research (see Delia et al., 1982). To the extent that its predictions about communication skills are supported by experimentation and observation, constructivism provides a basis for the control of these skills (through, for example, training designed to enhance skills). As you know, scientific approaches to the study of human behavior are often distinguished from other approaches by the aims to explain, predict, and control.

Constructivism is most readily understood as a scientific theory, but it also contains elements of interpretive and critical theories (as do, perhaps, all good social scientific theories; see Fay & Moon, 1977). Similar to all interpretive theories, constructivism assumes that humans actively interpret the world and construct meaningful understandings of it. It assumes there are important regularities in how people make sense of experience, as well as in how interpretations inform actions. Thus, it seeks to provide scientific accounts of these regularities. Like most critical theories, constructivism assumes that humans inhabit a historical, sociocultural world that structures, constrains, and channels interpretation and action. Some of these structures may act as unwarranted constraints on the interpretations and actions of certain individuals or groups. Constructivism aims to emancipate individuals and groups by providing them with knowledge regarding interpretation, action, and communication skills in ways that foster skill development and empower skill use. In sum, constructivism is a scientific theory of human interpretation and "communicative action" that seeks (among other things) to clarify the nature of functional communication skills and, in so doing, to contribute to their development and enlightened use.

Main Features of the Theory

Constructivism views humans as agents who interpret experiences and act on the basis of these interpretations. People are active sense-makers who construe the world through varied interpretive schemes. Some of these originate in genetically based structures, others come from individual experience, and many more are inherited from the social group through language and other shared symbol systems. Different theories characterize these cognitive schemes in different ways. In constructivism, the primary cognitive structures through which we interpret events are termed (following Kelly, 1955) "personal constructs."

Each of us has many different systems of personal constructs that we develop and use in interpreting events. For example, you might have a system of constructs that applies to hip-hop music, another to plants, another to cars, another to types of government, and so on. Each construct system develops more or less independently, largely as a function of your interaction with and interest in the objects in the domain. Following Werner (1957), more developed systems of constructs are more differentiated (numerically larger), more abstract (focusing on more central and less superficial qualities), and more integrated (more organized and interconnected). Thus, if you are an avid football fan and regularly watch games, you likely have a highly differentiated, abstract, and integrated set of football constructs. This construct system enables you to see the positions played by each of the 22 athletes on the field, to understand their movements (such as a play-action fake to the running back followed by a naked screen pass to the flanker), and to appreciate coaching strategies (such as blitzing on second-and-long). You may know the teams in various divisions, standings in those divisions, the playoff contenders, and so on. In short, you are cognitively complex with respect to football; you have a rich, sophisticated understanding of the game. However, if you are uninterested in football, you probably have few constructs for the game (e.g., when watching, you may only see people dressed in strange costumes chasing and knocking each other around).

One system of constructs we all develop to some degree pertains to people. This system of "interpersonal constructs" includes schemas regarding others' appearances (blue versus brown eyes), behaviors (smiles versus frowns), roles (student versus teacher), attitudes (liberal versus conservative), and traits or dispositions (warm versus cold). People with developed systems of interpersonal constructs are said to have high levels of "interpersonal cognitive complexity" or to be cognitively complex in the social domain (see Burleson & Caplan, 1998). These individuals are highly skilled when it comes to understanding people, relationships, and actions in the social world. They are better able to store, retrieve, organize, and generate information about people and social situations. This expertise often enables them to make better judgments and decisions in the social world.

The last point (about making judgments and decisions) is important because it underscores the pragmatic character of our interpretations. We generally do not make sense of the world as an end in itself, but rather do so in service of our projects. We pursue projects through goal-based activity directed at achieving certain ends. Our actions are shaped by the interpretations generated through our cognitive schemes, which is why constructivism holds that it is important to understand how people interpret the world if we are to understand their actions.

People's actions are strategic because they are planned and executed with the intention of achieving a goal (or goals). Many of the goals that guide our actions may be implicit. We may have little awareness of our pursuit of them (Kellermann, 1992; Motley, 1990). For example, imagine that you and a friend are discussing where to dine. You want pasta and are trying to persuade your friend to dine at an Italian restaurant. If asked about your goals in this episode, you might respond, "Persuading my friend to go to an Italian restaurant"; this is your explicit goal. You probably have other goals in this interaction too, although you may be only minimally aware of them (i.e., they are tacit or implicit). You likely want to maintain a good relationship with your friend and not offend him or her (relationship management goals), and you probably want your friend to see you as likeable and reasonable (self-presentation goals). These goals are implicit, but they influence your actions: If you were unconcerned with maintaining the relationship, you might say "I don't care if you come, I'm going with or without you"; if you were unconcerned with appearing likeable, you might say "We are going to the Italian place because that is what I want and that's what matters to me." Generally, we do not say such things because our actions are shaped by both explicit and implicit goals. As we will see later, people differ in the extent to which, and how skillfully, they pursue multiple goals in their messages.

Communicative action is the principal means through which we seek to realize our social projects and goals, those that involve other people in some way. Thus, we next examine how constructivism conceptualizes human communication.

Conceptualization of Communication in the Theory

In constructivism, communication is seen as an intentional, strategic activity in which people convey internal states to others in the effort to accomplish goals (see Burleson, 1992; Delia et al., 1982). Specifically, communication is a process in which a person (the source) seeks to convey or make public some internal state to another (the recipient) through the use of signals and symbols (the message) in the effort to accomplish some pragmatic end (the goal). To the extent that the recipient recognizes the source's intention to convey an internal state, the source and receiver enter into a communicative relationship. To the extent that the recipient comprehends the content of the source's message, communication occurs. Finally, to the extent that the recipient responds to the message in the manner intended by the source (i.e., the source achieves the intended goal), the message is successful or effective. This conceptualization suggests that communication proceeds through four related processes: message production, message processing (or message reception), interaction coordination, and social perception. Each of these represents a particular form of pragmatic activity in which persons pursue distinct goals.

"Message production" is the process of generating verbal and nonverbal behaviors intended to obtain a desired response from others. When successful, this process enables individuals to efficiently and effectively accomplish their goals. Some of the primary goals people routinely pursue include persuading, informing, supporting, entertaining, and regulating (for a discussion of primary and secondary goals in social interaction, see Dillard, 2004; Chapter 5, this volume). We also produce messages directed at managing our relationships with others (e.g., initiating or terminating a relationship, resolving conflicts) and managing our interactions with others (e.g., beginning or ending a conversation, changing the topic). Message production is a complicated process that is composed of many constituents (see Berger, 2003; Chapter 7, this volume).

"Message processing" (sometimes called "message reception") involves interpreting the communicative behavior of others in the effort to understand the meaning and implications of that behavior. Skillful message processing involves grasping the meaning of another's messages and, when appropriate, going beyond these messages to understand the other's motivations. Message processing is a complex phenomenon (see Wyer & Adaval, 2003) made up of several components, including interpreting the meaning of another's words (what was said), the intention of those words (what the other was trying to do in saying these words), and the motive underlying the other's intention (why the other was trying to accomplish that intention).

"Interaction coordination" is the process of synchronizing message production and message-processing activities (along with other behaviors) in a social episode to achieve smooth and coherent interchanges. This requires learning and developing facility with the social rules governing particular interchanges (e.g., the rules for turn and topic management in conversations, the rules for classroom discussions, the rules for instant messenger exchanges). When mastered, these rules enable us to produce comprehensible, informationally adequate, and pragmatically relevant messages that fit appropriately into the sequential structure of the particular interaction in which we are engaged (see H. H. Clark & Bly, 1995).

"Social perception" is the process through which we make sense of the social world, including ourselves, others, and social relationships. For example, we try to "read" other people. We attend to their cues, movements, dress, and expressions in order to make inferences about who they are (particularly their role in the current episode), what they are doing (especially if we seem implicated in their conduct), and what they are thinking and feeling. To do this, we engage in a variety of processes, including identifying affect states, making attributions for actions, forming impressions, integrating information, and taking the other's perspective (see Moskowitz, 2005). Social perception is not a communicative process per se because it does not necessarily involve the production, processing, or coordination of messages. Rather, it is an aspect of social cognition. However, the cognitive processes involved in making sense about others are critical to effective communication. Constructivism maintains that social perception plays a crucial role in virtually all communicative conduct and thus should be examined when analyzing communication.

Consistent with its focus on individual differences, constructivism sees people as differentially skilled with respect to producing messages, processing messages, coordinating interaction, and perceiving social roles. By late childhood, most people exhibit basic competence in these processes, especially in everyday situations. However, some people routinely perform very well with regard to these processes while others perform less well. Moreover, in demanding situations (e.g., comforting a grieving parent, explaining a nonintuitive process to novices), some excel while others behave ineptly or even dysfunctionally. Constructivism makes its most incisive theoretical and pragmatic contributions in explaining these individual differences.

Uses of the Theory

Constructivism helps us understand interpersonal communication in several ways. In particular, constructivism provides theoretical and methodological tools for exploring the nature, determinants, antecedents, and consequences of individual differences in communication skills.

CONSTRUCTIVIST MODELS OF COMMUNICATION SKILLS

First, constructivism provides conceptual models of what count as more- and less-skilled message production, message processing, interaction coordination, and social perception. Its models of skill in message processing and interaction coordination are still rather underdeveloped, and so are not discussed here (but see Burleson, 2007; Burleson & Caplan, 1998). We focus here on its models of skill in social perception and message production.

The constructivist model of social perception skill builds from its analysis of interpersonal cognitive complexity. As noted previously, we perceive social things through interpersonal constructs. Furthermore, people vary in the complexity of their constructs. Because interpersonal constructs underlie all social perception processes (e.g., making attributions, forming impressions), people with more-complex constructs are more skilled in these processes: for example, they have been found better able to form and remember rich impressions of others, integrate inconsistent information about others, learn complex social information quickly, and take the other's perspective (see review by Burleson & Caplan, 1998). Assessments of cognitive complexity, typically obtained through an instrument called the Role Category Questionnaire (Burleson & Waltman, 1988), thus provide an overall index of social perception skill.

The constructivist model of skill in message production focuses on person-centered communication. Person-centered messages account for and adapt to the subjective, emotional, and relational aspects of communicative contexts. These messages are more responsive, more tailored to recipients, and more attentive to implicit goals (see Applegate, 1990; Coopman, 1997). Review the two messages that appear at the beginning of this chapter: Message 1 exhibits low person centeredness, whereas Message 2 exhibits high person centeredness. In both messages, a student has the primary goal of persuading a professor to grant an extension. But Message 2 is more sensitive and adapted to the goals of the recipient. Rather than simply emphasizing the student's need for an extension (as in Message 1), Message 2 details how granting the extension will benefit the professor (the student will produce a quality paper that will be easy to grade). Message 2 is also sensitive to self-presentation concerns. The student in Message 2 presents himself or herself as motivated, interested in the subject, and hardworking, whereas the student in Message 1 suggests that his or her vacation, other classes, and paintball team are all more important than the paper. Furthermore, the student in Message 2 attends to relationship issues, stating how much he or she likes the assignment and shares the professor's goal of writing an excellent paper, whereas the student in Message 1 gives no indication that his or her relationship with the professor matters. In sum, the highly person-centered Message 2 is a more skillful persuasive effort than Message 1 because it reflects an awareness and adaptation to goals of the recipient, as well as pursues other goals (self-presentation, relationship management).

Highly person-centered messages are unnecessary (and may be inappropriate) for many routine communicative tasks (e.g., saying "hi" to a friend, asking a question about the weather, making a request for the salt at dinner). But when dealing with more complicated situations (e.g., disciplining a child who hurt a peer's feelings, comforting someone upset about a loss, managing a disagreement with one's partner) highly person-centered messages represent more skilled ways of communicating. Constructivist researchers have developed models of person-centered communication for several functional contexts, including persuading others, regulating or disciplining others, informing and explaining, comforting or providing support, and managing conflicts, as well as models for more general communicative goals such as supporting face concerns, self-presentation, and relationship enhancement (see Burleson & Caplan, 1998).

A CONSTRUCTIVIST ANALYSIS OF DETERMINANTS OF INDIVIDUAL DIFFERENCES IN COMMUNICATION SKILLS

Why are some people able to generate highly person-centered messages, while other people generate less-skillful messages? Constructivism identifies several factors that underlie skillful message production, message processing, and interaction coordination. First, constructivism emphasizes the contribution of social perception skills (and hence, interpersonal cognitive complexity) to the production of person-centered messages. Speakers must perceive the characteristics of message recipients and social situations to adapt to them.

This is accomplished through complex interpersonal constructs. Cognitively complex individuals also view social situations in sophisticated ways, which leads them to pursue multiple social goals in their messages (e.g., managing their own and the recipient's identity, attending to relationship concerns). Extensive research has indeed found that interpersonal cognitive complexity is associated with both the generation of multiple goals for social situations and the use of person-centered messages in those situations (for reviews, see Burleson & Caplan, 1998; Coopman, 1997).

A second factor contributing to the use of highly person-centered messages is the availability of message plans (see Berger, Chapter 7, this volume) in the procedural memory store (see Greene, Chapter 2, this volume). People who have a lot of ideas about how to achieve a communicative goal (i.e., who have a large procedural memory or many canned plans) are more likely to use highly person-centered messages when pursuing this goal (see Burleson, 2007).

Having well-developed social perception skills and an extensive procedural memory of message plans underlies the ability to generate person-centered messages. However, producing person-centered messages requires effort, so their use is also dependent on several types of motivation. In particular, people are more likely to produce person-centered messages when they really want to achieve a certain outcome (goal motivation), feel capable of achieving this outcome (effectance motivation), and believe it is appropriate for them to use person-centered messages in the situation (normative motivation) (Burleson, Holmstrom, & Gilstrap, 2005).

A CONSTRUCTIVIST ANALYSIS OF ANTECEDENTS OF INDIVIDUAL DIFFERENCES IN COMMUNICATION SKILL

How do people come to acquire the interpersonal constructs, procedural memories, and motivational orientations that lead to skillful communication? Several aspects of the social environment influence these determinants of communication skill. Two caregiver practices contribute to a child's development of interpersonal constructs and use of skillful messages: (a) using language that explicitly mentions internal states (feelings, intentions), and (b) using person-centered messages when nurturing and disciplining the child (Applegate et al., 1992). These practices also contribute to the child's development of prosocial values that motivate the use of skilled messages (Hart, Newell, & Olsen, 2003). Later in life, frequent interaction with peers, especially those with good communication skills, may contribute to developing the constructs, procedural memories, and motivations underlying skillful communication (Buhrmester, 1996). Finally, research indicates that some educational programs and training efforts can facilitate the development of social perception and communication skills (e.g., R. A. Clark, Willihnganz, & O'Dell, 1985; Medvene, Grosch, & Swink, 2006).

A CONSTRUCTIVIST ANALYSIS OF CONSEQUENCES OF INDIVIDUAL DIFFERENCES IN COMMUNICATION SKILLS

Why do sophisticated social perception and communication skills matter? First, person-centered messages are often more effective forms of communication than are less person-centered messages: they do a better job of achieving the communicator's primary and secondary goals than do less person-centered messages (e.g., Jones, 2004). Second, people's skillfulness in communication is associated with broader indicants of personal and occupational success, such as satisfying close relationships at home (Burleson et al., 2000) and professional advancement at work (Zorn & Violanti, 1996). Third, those with well-developed communication skills tend to be better liked and more accepted by other people, perhaps because these skilled individuals are more oriented to helping others achieve their goals (Jones, 2004). If these are not enough reasons for using skilled messages, there is also evidence that these messages can promote the health of others and contribute to their development of communication skills (see Burleson, 2007).

Strengths and Limitations of the Theory

Constructivism is general, flexible, and broad. Constructivism Theory can be (and has been) applied to different skills exhibited by different types of people in different situations. Constructivism is testable; numerous researchers have developed innovative methods for measuring social perception and communication skills, and this has led to extensive empirical tests of the theory's predictions. Many of these predictions have been corroborated, which suggests the accuracy of the theory. Constructivism is heuristic; it has generated novel analyses of numerous communicative phenomena and has been fruitfully synthesized with other theories.

Constructivism has great potential for application, particularly with regard to developing communication skills. This potential, thus far, largely has gone unfulfilled, and this is an important limitation. Constructivism has also been criticized for focusing narrowly on the contribution of certain structures (i.e., interpersonal constructs) to the use of person-centered messages. It has given less attention to the processes through which messages are generated and the role that interpersonal constructs serve in these processes (see Burleson & Caplan, 1998). Others argue that several key concepts in the theory are ambiguous and need clarification (Gastil, 1995). Such concepts include, for example, (a) the model of social memory that is most consistent with constructivist analyses of person perception and social inference, (b) whether measures of cognitive complexity tap the availability or accessibility of interpersonal constructs, and (c) the precise way that cognitive complexity contributes to communicative functioning.

Directions for Future Research and Applications

One limitation currently receiving attention is the need for better models of message processing and interaction coordination. For example, Bodie and Burleson (in press) recently developed a dual-process model for the reception of comforting messages. This model may provide a general framework for explaining individual differences in message processing. Other scholars (e.g., Waldron & Applegate, 1994) have suggested integrating the constructivist analysis of message production with that provided by planning theory and other cognitive approaches. These efforts merit further research attention. Research exploring the pedagogical and training implications of constructivism is a particular need. Previous constructivist research clearly indicates that many people would benefit from programs that enhance communication skills. We need to know how to effectively and efficiently foster skill development. Research addressing this concern should contribute significantly to both theory and application.

References

Applegate, J. L. (1980). Adaptive communication in educational contexts: A study of teachers' communicative strategies. *Communication Education, 29,* 158–170.

Applegate, J. L. (1990). Constructs and communication: A pragmatic integration. In G. Neimeyer & R. Neimeyer (Eds.), *Advances in personal construct psychology* (Vol. 1, pp. 203–230). Greenwich, CT: JAI Press.

Applegate, J. L., Burleson, B. R., & Delia, J. G. (1992). Reflection-enhancing parenting as antecedent to children's social-cognitive and communicative development. In I. E. Sigel, A. V. McGillicuddy-Delisi, & J. J. Goodnow (Eds.), *Parental belief systems: The psychological consequences for children* (2nd ed., pp. 3–39). Hillsdale, NJ: Erlbaum.

Applegate, J. L., & Sypher, H. E. (1988). Constructivist theory and intercultural communication research. In Y. Kim & W. Gudykunst (Eds.), *Theoretical perspectives in intercultural communication* (pp. 41–65). Beverly Hills, CA: Sage.

Berger, C. R. (2003). Message production skill in social interaction. In J. O. Greene & B. R. Burleson (Eds.), *Handbook of communication and social interaction skills* (pp. 257–289). Mahwah, NJ: Erlbaum.

Bodie, G. D., & Burleson, B. R. (in press). Explaining moderators of the effects of supportive messages: Can a dual-process model account for extant findings? In C. Beck (Ed.), *Communication yearbook 32.* Mahwah, NJ: Erlbaum.

Buhrmester, D. (1996). Need fulfillment, interpersonal competence, and the developmental contexts of early adolescent friendship. In W. M. Bukowski, A. F. Newcomb, & W. W. Hartup (Eds.), *The company they keep: Friendship in childhood and adolescence* (pp. 158–185). New York: Cambridge University Press.

Burleson, B. R. (1992). Taking communication seriously. *Communication Monographs, 59,* 79–86.

Burleson, B. R. (2007). Constructivism: A general theory of communication skill. In B. B. Whaley & W. Samter (Eds.), *Explaining communication: Contemporary theories and exemplars* (pp. 105–128). Mahwah, NJ: Erlbaum.

Burleson, B. R., & Caplan, S. E. (1998). Cognitive complexity. In J. C. McCroskey, J. A. Daly, M. M. Martin, & M. J. Beatty (Eds.), *Communication and personality: Trait perspectives* (pp. 230–286). Cresskill, NJ: Hampton Press.

Burleson, B. R., Holmstrom, A. J., & Gilstrap, C. M. (2005). "Guys can't say *that* to guys": Four experiments assessing the normative motivation account for deficiencies in the emotional support provided by men. *Communication Monographs, 72,* 468–501.

Burleson, B. R., Metts, S., & Kirch, M. W. (2000). Communication in close relationships. In C. Hendrick & S. S. Hendrick (Eds.), *Close relationships: A sourcebook* (pp. 244–258). Thousand Oaks, CA: Sage.

Burleson, B. R., & Waltman, M. S. (1988). Cognitive complexity: Using the Role Category Questionnaire measure. In C. H. Tardy (Ed.), *A handbook for the study of human communication: Methods and instruments for observing, measuring, and assessing communication processes* (pp. 1–35). Norwood, NJ: Ablex.

Clark, H. H., & Bly, B. (1995). Pragmatics and discourse. In J. L. Miller & P. D. Eimas (Eds.), *Speech, language, and communication* (pp. 371–410). San Diego, CA: Academic Press.

Clark, R. A., Willihnganz, S., & O'Dell, L. L. (1985). Training fourth graders in compromising and persuasive strategies. *Communication Education, 34,* 331–342.

Coopman, S. Z. (1997). Personal constructs and communication in interpersonal and organizational contexts. In G. Neimeyer & R. Neimeyer (Eds.), *Advances in personal construct psychology* (Vol. 4, pp. 101–147). Greenwich, CT: JAI Press.

Delia, J. G. (1977). Constructivism and the study of human communication. *Quarterly Journal of Speech, 63,* 66–83.

Delia, J. G., & O'Keefe, B. J. (1979). Constructivism: The development of communication in children. In E. Wartella (Ed.), *Children communicating: Media and the development of thought, speech, understanding* (pp. 157–186). Beverly Hills, CA: Sage.

Delia, J. G., O'Keefe, B. J., & O'Keefe, D. J. (1982). The constructivist approach to communication. In F. E. X. Dance (Ed.), *Human communication theory: Comparative essays* (pp. 147–191). New York: Harper & Row.

Dillard, J. P. (2004). The goals-plan-action model of interpersonal influence. In J. S. Seiter & R. H. Gass (Eds.), *Perspectives on persuasion, social influence, and compliance gaining* (pp. 185–206). Boston: Allyn & Bacon.

Fay, B., & Moon, J. D. (1977). What would an adequate philosophy of social science look like? *Philosophy of Social Science, 7,* 209–227.

Gastil, J. (1995). An appraisal and revision of the constructivist research program. In B. R. Burleson (Ed.), *Communication yearbook 18* (pp. 83–104). Thousand Oaks, CA: Sage.

Hart, C. H., Newell, L. D., & Olsen, S. F. (2003). Parenting skills and social-communicative competence in childhood. In J. O. Greene & B. R. Burleson (Eds.), *Handbook of communication and social interaction skills* (pp. 753–799). Mahwah, NJ: Erlbaum.

Jones, S. M. (2004). Putting the person into person-centered and immediate emotional support: Emotional change and perceived helper competence as outcomes of comforting in helping situations. *Communication Research, 31,* 338–360.

Kellermann, K. (1992). Communication: Inherently strategic and primarily automatic. *Communication Monographs, 59,* 288–300.

Kelly, G. A. (1955). *The psychology of personal constructs.* New York: W. W. Norton.

Kline, S. L., & Ceropski, J. M. (1984). Person-centered communication in medical practice. In J. T. Wood & G. M. Phillips (Eds.), *Human decision-making* (pp. 120–141). Carbondale, IL: Southern Illinois University Press.

Medvene, L., Grosch, K., & Swink, N. (2006). Interpersonal complexity: A cognitive component of person-centered care. *The Geronotologist, 46,* 220–226.

Moskowitz, G. B. (2005). *Social cognition: Understanding self and others.* New York: Guilford.

Motley, M. T. (1990). On whether one can(not) not communicate: An examination via traditional communication postulates. *Western Journal of Speech Communication, 54,* 1–20.

Swanson, D. L. (1981). A constructivist approach to political communication. In D. Nimmo & K. R. Sanders (Eds.), *Handbook of political communication* (pp. 69–191). Beverly Hills, CA: Sage.

Waldron, V. R., & Applegate, J. L. (1994). Interpersonal construct differentiation and conversational planning: An examination of two cognitive accounts for the production of competent verbal disagreement tactics. *Human Communication Research, 21,* 3–35.

Werner, H. (1957). The concept of development from a comparative and organismic point of view. In D. B. Harris (Ed.), *The concept of development* (pp. 125–146). Minneapolis, MN: University of Minnesota Press.

Wyer, R. S., Jr., & Adaval, R. (2003). Message reception skills in social communication. In J. O. Greene & B. R. Burleson (Eds.), *Handbook of communication and social interaction skills* (pp. 291–355). Mahwah, NJ: Erlbaum.

Zorn, T. E., & Violanti, M. T. (1996). Communication abilities and individual achievement in organizations. *Management Communication Quarterly, 10,* 139–167.

5

Goals-Plans-Action Theory of Message Production

Making Influence Messages

James Price Dillard

I t is a fact of life that people often use communication in efforts to change the attitudes and behavior of others in ways that the former deem desirable. Consider the following:

"Could I borrow your notes from the last class?"

"He's not good for you. You should dump him."

"You need to do more on the group assignment. You're not pulling your weight."

"Would you mind if I handed in the assignment one day late?"

All of these messages illustrate one of the fundamental problems of social interaction: Influence. Goals-Plans-Action (GPA) Theory was developed to explain the process by which people produce messages like these—messages that are intended to change or maintain the attitudes or behavior of others (Dillard, 1990).

Purpose and Meta-theoretical Assumptions

GPA is a theory in the scientific tradition. As with scientific realism, it embraces the assumption that much of the world is patterned, knowable, and objective. Certain features of social interaction and the cognitive processes that undergird interaction are objectively real. For instance, memory for influence strategies is thought to reside in long-term memory, which is a physical record of behavior. But GPA Theory also assumes that many aspects of interaction are socially constructed. For example, a request to borrow class notes can be seen by both speaker and hearer as an act that has implications for the two participants' relationship. It might be viewed as an imposition or as an opportunity to help a friend. The interactants have the ability to jointly negotiate the preferred meaning.

GPA is a theory of purposeful behavior. It assumes that individuals make choices about the ways in which they try to influence others and that they do so with some degree of awareness. This does not mean that individuals are knowledgeable about all available options, nor does it mean that they are aware of every part of the message production process. It does mean that the theory embraces the idea that people usually know what they are doing. This may seem obvious, but it has important implications for theory and research strategy. For example, if people are acting purposefully, then their intentions should constitute valid explanations of their actions. Because they are aware of their intentions, truthful answers to the question "Why did you say that?" are invaluable data. Accordingly, much of the research that has been stimulated by GPA Theory has sought to understand influence behavior from the point of view of the message producer

Main Features of the Theory

The GPA Theory views message production as a three-step sequence. "Goals" are the first step. They are future states of affairs that an individual is committed to achieving or maintaining (Dillard, 1997). Goals motivate plans, the second component in the model. "Plans" are cognitive representations of the behaviors that are intended to enable goal attainment (Berger, 1997). "Actions" are the behaviors enacted in an effort to realize a goal. Whereas goals and plans are internal, actions are external. One aim of research on the GPA model has been to flesh out the nature of goals, plans, and actions, as well as their relationship to one another.

INFLUENCE GOALS

It might seem that people try to persuade others for an unlimited variety of reasons. However, research reveals a relatively small and recurring set of influence goals (Dillard, Anderson, & Knobloch, 2002). The most frequently identified reasons for influencing others are listed in Table 5.1, along with a description and an example of each.

Table 5.1   Most Frequently Identified Reasons for Influencing Others

Influence Goals		
Type	*Description*	*Example*
Gain assistance	Obtain material or nonmaterial resources	Can I borrow your car?
Give advice	Provide counsel (typically about health & relationships)	I think that you should quit using so many Prozac.
Share activity	Promote joint endeavors between source & target	Let's do something tonight. How about going to see that new band?
Change orientation	Alter target's stance toward a sociopolitical issue	There is another, more realistic, way to look at the abortion laws.
Change relationship	Alter the nature of the source-target relationship	I think that we ought to have a monogamous relationship.
Obtain permission	Secure the endorsement of the (more powerful) target	Would it be OK if I handed in the assignment one day late?
Enforce rights & obligations	Compel target to fulfill commitment or role requirement	You promised that you would keep the music down. So, how about it?

In the parlance of the GPA model, the goals listed in Table 5.1 are primary goals. They are so named because the theory attributes several unique properties to them. For one, primary goals lie at the beginning of the goals-plans-action sequence. They are primary in the sense that they initiate the series of constructs that model message production. Because primary goals energize cognition and behavior it can be said that they serve a "motivational" function.

Primary goals also allow individuals to bracket the interaction—that is, to identify its beginning and ending points. Such segmentation is surely valuable for making sense of what might otherwise be viewed as an undifferentiated outpouring of behavior. Bracketing is possible because the primary goal imbues the interaction with meaning. Knowledge of the primary goal allows the interactants to say what the exchange is about. Hence, primary goals are culturally viable explanations of the discourse produced by two or more speakers. This is the "social meaning function" of primary goals.

Finally, primary goals direct a number of mental operations. By providing an understanding of the intended purpose of an interaction, goals determine which aspects of a situation are perceived (Maruff, Danckert, Camplin, & Currie, 1999) and which are not. For example, a person who is on the receiving end of a threat may pay close attention to the speaker's size and emotional state while devoting little, if any, thought to evaluating the aesthetic qualities of the threatener's wardrobe. Thus, primary goals serve a (psychological) "guidance function" that results in some perceptions, memories, and thoughts becoming more accessible and others becoming less accessible.

In the course of pursuing or planning to pursue a primary goal, other concerns may arise. For example, one college student who hopes to initiate a relationship with another (Goal 1) might recognize the risk of rejection and wish to avoid feeling hurt (Goal 2). Such concerns are called "secondary goals" because they follow from the adoption of a primary goal. In the example above, the speaker holds a secondary goal only because he or she is considering trying to influence someone else. Thus, it is the desire to achieve the primary goal that brings about consideration of one or more secondary goals.

Research on the GPA model supports the existence of five secondary goals (Dillard, Segrin, & Harden, 1989; Schrader & Dillard, 1998), though not every goal will be relevant to every situation. "Identity goals" focus on ethical, moral, and personal standards for behavior. They arise from individuals' principles and values and, at the broadest level, individuals' conceptions of self. For instance, a child who wants a piece of chocolate cake might think nothing of knocking down a sibling and taking the piece of cake away. Most adults would reject that strategy on ethical grounds. In this way, the secondary goal of behaving ethically would limit the array of possible influence strategies.

"Conversation management goals" involve concerns about impression management and face. Though there are certainly exceptions, individuals usually prefer that interactions proceed smoothly, rather than awkwardly, and that neither interactant threaten the identity of the other. Thus, while conversation management goals may have implications that extend beyond the conversation, they also have a relatively short time horizon (i.e., typically the duration of the conversation). In this vein, when one person asks, "What did you mean by that?" the other person will generally provide some explanation of his or her behavior rather than simply ignore the question. By playing by the rules that govern conversation, interactants typically create a mutual understanding of what is occurring. This is true even when they disagree about the issues under discussion (e.g., both parties would agree that they had a fight).

"Relational resource goals" focus on relationship management. They are manifestations of the value that individuals place on desired social and personal relationships. Hence, it is most often the case that people try to maintain or improve their relationships with others. Of course, relationship resource goals do not really come into play unless one has a preexisting relationship with the hearer, or hopes to establish one. Relational resource goals focus on the benefits that flow to the source because of the relationship itself. As a consequence, relational resource goals have a longer time horizon than conversation management goals.

"Personal resource goals" reflect the physical, temporal, and material concerns of the communicator. More specifically, they arise from the desires to maintain or enhance one's physical well-being, temporal resources, finances, and material possessions. The statement, "I cut the conversation short because I realized that I was wasting my time," illustrates concern for a personal resource. The desire to behave efficiently is viewed as a personal resource goal (cf., Berger, 1997), although the GPA model does not suppose that individuals always prefer a high level of efficiency. Like some of the other secondary goals, personal resource goals will not be relevant to every interaction, but when they are relevant they can be important to determining how messages are created and uttered.

By positing the existence of "affect management goals," the model assumes that individuals strive to maintain preferred affective states. Importantly, affect management goals are not as simple as the wish to enjoy positive feelings and avoid negative ones. Sometimes people try to increase their level of anxiety because it motivates them, for example, to perform well on an exam or speech. In other instances, they enhance their level of anger so that they are emotionally aligned with a plan that takes a hard interactional stance.

The concept of secondary goals has at least one broad implication for how we conceive of interpersonal influence: It suggests that many interactions involve multiple goals that individuals try to achieve more or less simultaneously. Thus, interpersonal influence is often a complicated task.

RELATIONSHIPS AMONG PRIMARY GOALS AND SECONDARY GOALS

The most basic decision about communication that one can make is whether or not to engage another person in interaction. The interplay of primary and secondary goals can help to shed light on this choice point in the message production process. To simplify, assume a primary goal and just one secondary goal, then evaluate the degree of compatibility between the two (cf., Samp & Solomon, 1999). There are just three possibilities: First, that the two goals are *incompatible*. Imagine someone who intends to end a long-term romantic relationship but not hurt the other's feelings. Second, that the secondary goals are *irrelevant* to the primary goal. For example, concern for one's physical well-being is not often an issue when asking a friend to see a film. Third, that the primary and secondary goals are *compatible*. Relational initiation offers one context in which this might occur. The norm of reciprocity demands that individuals repay favors provided to them by others. When one person asks another for help (e.g., a ride to the grocery store) that he or she cannot immediately repay, the message source is signaling a willingness to enter into a relationship in which reciprocity will occur over time. This willingness is a defining feature of friendships. Thus, the speaker may obtain a ride and, in so doing, may also enhance a budding relationship.

Although the third possibility is clearly the most desirable of the three alternatives, it is also the least common. Most interactions can be characterized as a blend of the first and second possibilities. Because there are multiple secondary goals, it is likely that some of them create opposition to the primary goal, while others will be irrelevant. Hence, in most instances the set of relevant secondary goals will constitute a counterdynamic to the primary goal.

PLANS AND PLANNING

Plans can be differentiated in terms of hierarchy, complexity, and completeness (Dillard, 1990). Hierarchy refers to the level of abstraction at which the plan is cast, whereas complexity captures the number of steps in a plan as well as the number of contingencies (cf., Berger, 1997). Plan completeness is a measure of the extent to which the plan is fleshed out. Because others' behavior is sometimes difficult to predict, it is assumed that even when speakers engage in preconversational planning the resulting plans are necessarily incomplete (Bratman, 1987). These three properties may be used to analyze plans of any sort, but it is the *content* of influence plans that sets them apart from plans more generally.

Influence plans contain guidelines for the production of verbal and nonverbal behaviors. Whereas "strategy level plans" are concerned with lines of action and sequences of behavior, "tactic plans" exist at a lower level of abstraction. They are instructions for producing smaller units of behavior such as individual utterances. For example, although one might approach an influence attempt with the intention of implementing a liking strategy, there are many different ways to do so at the tactical level. The first move might consist of utterances such as, "You look great!" or, "That was a really smart thing that you said in our discussion group. I was impressed."

Research on the perception of message tactics suggests that four dimensions are particularly important to understanding influence plans (Dillard, Wilson, Tusing, & Kinney, 1997). The first of these dimensions, "explicitness," is the degree to which the message source makes her or his intentions transparent in the message itself. Whereas explicit messages require little or no guesswork regarding the speaker's wants, implicit messages necessitate more interpretation. When one roommate says to another, "I would like for you to come to the gym with me," the speaker's desire is clear. But, if the same person were to say, "Hey, I'm going to the gym," the other roommate would have to read between the lines to interpret the speaker's intention.

"Dominance," the second dimension, references the relative power of the source compared to the target as that power is expressed in the message. Message dominance expresses the source's perception of or desire for a particular source-target power relationship. Consider the following requests: "You said that you wanted to work out, so let's do it," and, "I would really, really appreciate it if you worked out with me." The first message is a little aggressive. It appears from this message that the speaker has the right to tell the message target how to behave. The second message, which beseeches the target to exercise, is submissive.

"Argument," the third dimension, is defined as the extent to which a rationale for the sought-after action is present (versus absent) in the message. Consider this message: "I sleep a lot better when I work out. I'll bet that you would, too." It suggests implicitly what the source wants the target to do, and it provides a reason for the source's wants. In contrast, the message "We should go work out" lacks any justification. In other words, the source's argument is absent.

"Control over outcomes" is the final dimension that characterizes influence plans. This message feature refers to the extent to which the source has control over the reasons for compliance. This distinction makes clear the difference between a threat (e.g., I will hurt you if . . .) and a warning (e.g., You could be harmed if . . .).

When the desire to influence another person arises, individuals will initially search their memory for stock plans that are likely to achieve the primary goal (Berger, 1997; Dillard, 1990; Meyer, 1997; Wilson, 1995). This search will probably yield plans that vary in abstraction, complexity, and completeness. If the available plans are seen as likely to succeed, then the individual moves toward translating the ideas into action. Of course, this involves a great many lower-level processes that must work in unison if a plan is to be successfully instantiated as behavior; these processes could fail to work in unison, leading to failure. For example, a plan that depends on flattering the target might fail because the speaker cannot find a way to deliver a compliment that does not sound transparently insincere. In this instance, the plan works at the level of strategy, but not at the level of tactic.

To the extent that the preexisting plans are judged to be less than satisfactory and the primary goal is viewed as important, individuals will try to (a) make existing plans more complete or more complex, or (b) create new plans. This kind of planning is constrained by the fact that successful interaction depends on the other person. If the message producer sees the other person as unpredictable, he or she will be less likely to go to the effort of plan development.

Although there may be many different ways to achieve a primary goal if none of the secondary goals are activated, it is more challenging to devise a plan that will satisfy the many competing desires that are present in an episode that is high in goal structure complexity. Students working in group projects often find themselves in the position of needing to tell one of the group members that he or she is not making a equitable contribution in terms of workload. This situation is more complex when the so-called slacker is a roommate or good friend. Achieving two goals simultaneously (i.e., changing behavior and not damaging the relationship) is much harder that achieving either goal alone.

When multiple plans or plan variations are available, the message source must select among them. The GPA model assumes that selection is made by searching for a satisfactory configuration of primary and secondary goals. This may be a drawn-out, contemplative process, but, due to the fact that conversation moves so quickly, often it is not. Indeed, opportunities for influence that require plan deployment in the next conversational turn may open up during the course of interaction. Hence, the planning process may be lengthy, but frequently it must move at least at the speed of ongoing conversation.

Conceptualization of Communication in the Theory

There are two answers to the question of how the GPA Theory views communication. The content answer is that communication is conceptualized in terms of explicitness, dominance, argument, and control. We might rephrase the issue as this question: "What is communication for?" The answer that GPA Theory provides to this question is that "communication is for getting things done." It is one means by which goals are achieved. Some readers of the theory have mistakenly equated goal achievement with self-interest (e.g., Shepherd, 1998), but goals can be egoistic or altruistic, self-serving or philanthropic. As the existence of the "Give advice" goal implies (Table 5.1), influence goals might arise for the purpose of benefiting others (Dillard & Schrader, 1998). In addition, influence goals may aim to improve the public good, as when one individual attempts to persuade another about some social issue ("Change orientation goal," Table 5.1). Finally, even when an individual's actions are the result of self-interest, they are often mundane, such as when we ask someone to pass the salt ("Gain assistance goal," Table 5.1). In short, the GPA Theory views communication as instrumental, seemingly for good reason.

Uses of the Theory

The components of GPA Theory are illustrated in Figure 5.1. The model proposes two pathways to the production of influence messages. In the first, individuals assess their goals, decide to engage the target, then move to plan generation and selection. This sequence is most likely when the importance of the primary goal substantially outweighs the set of relevant, incompatible secondary goals. In the other pathway, individuals think first about the possible means of influence. If they believe that they have a potentially successful plan, they make the decision to engage the other person. This path is more likely when the approach and avoidance forces are fairly closely matched.

The arrow that connects plans to action represents the implementation ideas about behavior into behavior itself. This process must necessarily involve many rapid processes, most of which do not involve conscious awareness. For instance, most of the time message producers do not have to devote conscious thought to expelling air from their lungs or moving their tongues and lips to form words.

The link from tactic implementation to target response assumes a target who processes the source's utterance and returns a more or less appropriate response. On the basis of that response, the source may return to the goal awareness stage and move through the entire process again. In such a sequence, goals are reevaluated in light of the target's behavior. Alternatively, the source may store a number of tactic plans in a buffer and iterate only as far back as the tactic selection stage. Metaphorically, the buffer can be seen as a checklist of options that is developed prior to the interaction. If the first option fails, it gets checked off and the individual moves to the next item on the list.

When the source encounters noncompliant behavior from the target, the first tendency will be to change low-level elements in the existing plan (Berger, 1997). To the extent that the plan itself is seen as having failed, however, the source may discard it wholesale and move to other options. In the event that no plan is available that can satisfy the primary-secondary goal array, and that the perceived likelihood of devising one is low, individuals may exit the episode either by changing the topic or by physically leaving the interaction. The following snippet of interaction illustrates movement on the model:

Student:　Would you mind if I turn in the paper a day late?

Professor:　No, that's not a problem. But, as it says in the syllabus, you'll receive no more than half credit if it is late.

Student:　But if I don't get full credit I'm probably going to fail this class. That means that I won't graduate.

Professor:　It's your call. But, I have to stick to the syllabus.

Student:　This isn't fair.

Professor:　I'm sorry. The syllabus is our contract.

Student:　(Leaves without speaking.)

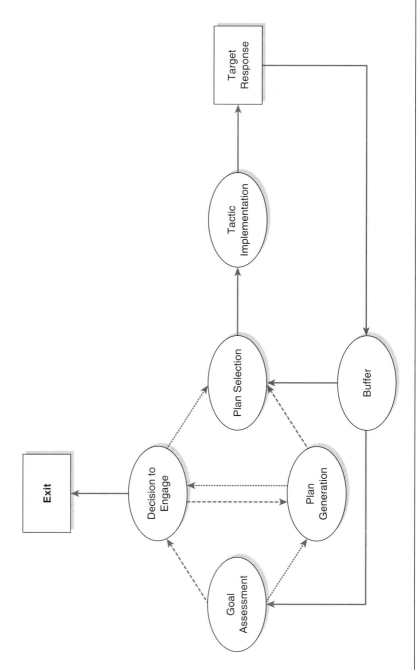

Figure 5.1   The Goals-Plans-Action Model of Message Production

Strengths and Limitations of the Theory

The GPA model is not without its critics. For example, Greene (2000) has argued that the GPA approach fails to give sufficient attention to the fleeting processes that underlie speech production. In his view, the theory is cast at the wrong level of abstraction because it is not psychological enough. Greene is certainly correct in saying that the theory could do more, but such criticism could be leveled at any theory. Perhaps a more realistic standard for evaluating the utility of theory is whether or not it has enhanced our understanding of message production processes. A quick review of the numerous investigations that utilize GPA logic suggests that the answer to this question is, "yes."

Shepherd (1998) complained that the GPA model is too psychological. He said that goals are essentially synonymous with self-interest and egoistic bias. This criticism seems to arise from a misreading of the theory. Whereas it is surely the case that individuals sometimes act out of self-interest, it would be a mistake to conclude from that observation that they always seek to satisfy only their own needs (cf., Shepherd, 1998). Goals can be egotistic or altruistic, self-serving or philanthropic. As the existence of the "Give advice" goal implies (Table 5.1), influence goals might arise for the purpose of benefiting others.

Directions for Future Research and Applications

Although there are many directions that research on GPA could take, there are two that are especially important: One involves elaborating the mechanisms that connect goals with plans and plans with action. Understanding of these processes is needed to provide insight into how message production fails as well as how it succeeds. Another important question concerns how primary and secondary goals are held in memory before, during, and after interaction. It has been suggested that primary goals recede in importance once one becomes committed to them, and that secondary goals subsequently occupy interactants' thinking (Schrader & Dillard, 1998). The answer to these and other questions awaits future inquiry.

References

Berger, C. R. (1997). *Planning strategic interaction: Attaining goals through communicative action.* Mahwah, NJ: Erlbaum.

Bratman, M. E. (1987). *Intentions, plans, and practical reason.* Cambridge, MA: Harvard University Press.

Dillard, J. P. (1990). A goal-driven model of interpersonal influence. In J. P. Dillard (Ed.), *Seeking compliance: The production of interpersonal influence messages* (pp. 41–56). Scottsdale, AZ: Gorsuch Scarisbrick.

Dillard, J. P. (1997). Explicating the goal construct: Tools for theorists. In J. O. Greene (Ed.), *Message production: Advances in communication theory* (pp. 47–69). Mahwah, NJ: Erlbaum.

Dillard, J. P., Anderson, J. W., & Knobloch, L. K. (2002). Interpersonal influence. In M. Knapp & J. Daly (Eds.), *The handbook of interpersonal communication* (pp. 423–474). Thousand Oaks, CA: Sage.

Dillard, J. P., & Schrader, D. C. (1998). On the utility of the goals-plans-action sequence: Commentary reply. *Communication Studies, 49,* 300–304.

Dillard, J. P., Segrin, C., & Harden, J. M. (1989). Primary and secondary goals in the interpersonal influence process. *Communication Monographs, 56,* 19–38.

Dillard, J. P., Wilson, S. R., Tusing, K. J., & Kinney, T. A. (1997). Politeness judgments in personal relationships. *Journal of Language and Social Psychology, 16,* 297–325.

Greene, J. O. (2000). Evanescent mentation: An ameliorative conceptual foundation for research and theory on message production. *Communication Theory, 10,* 139–155.

Maruff, P., Danckert, J., Camplin, G., & Currie, J. (1999). Behavioral goals constrain the selection of visual information. *Psychological Science, 10,* 522–525.

Meyer, J. A. (1997). Cognitive influences on the ability to address interaction goals. In J. O. Greene (Ed.), *Message production: Advances in communication theory* (pp. 71–90). Mahwah, NJ: Erlbaum.

Samp, J. A., & Solomon, D. H. (1999). Communicative responses to problematic events in close relationships II: The influence of five facets of goals on message features. *Communication Research, 26,* 193–239.

Schrader, D. C., & Dillard, J. P. (1998). Goal structures and interpersonal influence. *Communication Studies, 49,* 276–293.

Shepherd, G. J. (1998). The trouble with goals. *Communication Studies, 49,* 294–299.

Wilson, S. R. (1995). Elaborating the cognitive rules model of interaction goals: The problem of accounting for individual differences in goal formation. In B. R. Burleson (Ed.), *Communication yearbook 18* (pp. 3–26). Thousand Oaks, CA: Sage.

6

Imagined Interaction Theory

Mental Representations of Interpersonal Communication

James M. Honeycutt

I t is very common in everyday living to anticipate meetings with people that we know we are going to interact with. For example, you may imagine some of the questions that a job interviewer will ask you and how you might respond. Furthermore, after seeing people, we sometimes relive the encounter in our minds as we reflect on what was said or how we could have said things differently. These examples reflect imagined interactions (IIs), which are part of daydreaming and which reflect internal talk. They refer to a process of social cognition in which individuals imagine and therefore indirectly experience themselves in anticipated or past communicative encounters with others (Honeycutt, 2003, in press; Honeycutt, Zagacki, & Edwards, 1989). IIs focus and organize individuals' thoughts on communication, on the actors involved in specific acts of communication, and on the communicative context. IIs possess many of the same characteristics as real conversations in that they may be fragmentary, extended, rambling, repetitive, or coherent.

IIs serve multiple functions, including maintaining relationships and managing conflict. Individuals may feel anger as they relive old conflicts in their minds, or may feel happiness while imagining positive encounters. Our expectancies for interpersonal communication encounters emanate from IIs through replaying images from the electronic media as well as conversations with parents, siblings, peers, or novels. Furthermore, IIs can help form expectations or relational schemata for how individuals will perform in a variety of roles. They are a means of problem solving by allowing an individual to think through a problem. IIs have been used as a tool in therapy, allowing patients to visualize interaction with others who were not emotionally or physically available to them (Rosenblatt & Meyer, 1986). They can help people in planning messages and in enhancing communication effectiveness.

Purpose and Meta-theoretical Assumptions

The primary epistemology of IIs can be described as post-positivist. A variety of methods are triangulated in testing the theory out of the recognition that observations and measurements are inherently imperfect. IIs are measured through surveys, journals, and even through the use of a "talk-out-loud" procedure, in which individuals role play their imaginary dialogues with interaction partners prior to talking with them (see Honeycutt, 2003, in press). Numerous studies have tested hypotheses and theorems devoted to functions of IIs (see Honeycutt, 2003, for a review).

Imagined Interaction Theory is based in the work of symbolic interactionists and cognitive script theorists, including Mead (1934), Dewey (1922), Schutz (1962), and Abelson (1976). Mead discussed the internalized conversation of gestures in which individual actors are able consciously to monitor social action by reviewing alternative endings of any given act in which they are involved. Individuals use internal dialogues within their minds to test out the various possible scenarios of an event in advance of the act.

IIs also have their foundations in cognitive scripts (Zagacki, Edwards, & Honeycutt, 1992). For example, relational scripts are often partly formed through the process of mental imagery and daydreaming in which individuals think about conversations with significant others (Honeycutt & Cantrill, 2001). Cognitive researchers argue that much information is stored (sometimes unconsciously) in propositional form. The way in which information is processed is called "computational thinking" (Zagacki et al.). Yet propositional information located deep within cognitive structures may itself be transferred to or represented in phenomenal awareness in a variety of ways. One way is through IIs. Thus, when people experience IIs, they may be experiencing a representation of scripted or partially scripted knowledge, with the information being brought directly into explicit awareness for review. Hence, activating the script through an II may help to reconstitute the existing script. Our memories about relationships form later scripts or expectancies for appropriate behaviors in relationships (Honeycutt & Cantrill). Honeycutt and Cantrill discussed how scripts are a type of automatic pilot providing guidelines on how to act when one encounters new situations. Scripts are activated mindlessly and created through IIs as people envision contingency plans for actions.

Main Features of the Theory

It should be noted that the term "imagined interaction" is strategically used instead of "imaginary conversation" or "internal dialogue," because imagined interaction is a broader term that takes into account nonverbal and verbal imagery. Visual imagery reflects the scene of the interaction (e.g., office, den, and car). Verbal imagery reflects lines of dialogues imagined by the self and by others (e.g., I recall speaking to my sister on my cell phone when she told me that she had just been promoted in the state treasurer's office. I congratulated her with a pun saying, "They invested wisely in you.").

Early research spent considerable time examining the characteristics of IIs and their association with personality characteristics, gender differences, marriage types, and relational quality (for a review, see Honeycutt, 2003). The characteristics of IIs include

- frequency (how often persons experience IIs),
- emotional valence (how enjoyable or uncomfortable they are),
- discrepancy (the degree to which IIs are different from actual communication),
- dominance (the amount that the self or other dominates the talk),
- proactivity (whether IIs precede anticipated encounters),
- retroactivity (whether IIs follow encounters),
- specificity (the amount of detail in IIs), and
- variety (the number of different topics and partners experienced).

Research has examined the emotional valence of IIs and its association with other various characteristics of IIs. For example, negative emotions are associated with more discrepancy and more self-talk in the II, while mixed emotions are associated with replaying old arguments (Zagacki et al., 1992). More importantly, more IIs involve mixed emotions rather than purely being associated with positive affect. Once pleasant communicative experiences are acknowledged, they simply may be taken for granted and, as a result, are not recalled as much.

Conceptualization of Communication in the Theory

Because it concerns individual processing of information, a core feature of Imagined Interaction Theory is its reliance on intrapersonal communication as the foundation on which other types of communication rest. Intrapersonal communication involves all of the physiological and psychological processing of messages that happen within individuals as they attempt to understand themselves and their environment (Cunningham, 1989). Regardless if one speaks of dyadic, interpersonal, small group, organizational, societal, cultural, or mass communication, the individual processing of information is nested within all hierarchies of communication systems (Fisher, 1987).

Uses of the Theory

There are six basic functions that IIs serve: (a) maintaining relationships, (b) managing conflict (c) rehearsing messages, (d) aiding people in self-understanding through clarifying thoughts and feelings, (e) providing emotional catharsis by relieving tension, and (f) compensating for lack of real interaction (Honeycutt, 2003; Honeycutt & Ford, 2001). These functions are used in a variety of contexts.

Any combination of these functions can occur simultaneously. For example, the person may experience catharsis while thinking about how to manage conflict for an upcoming conversation. Simultaneously, the II may provide the opportunity to rehearse along with relational maintenance. An example is a female who, in a journal account, reported how she was rehearsing how to tell her boyfriend that she accepted a job offer in another city after telling him the week before that she was thinking about accepting a position in the city that he was living in. She felt tension release and the release of anxiety as she was rehearsing the anticipated encounter.

IIs help sustain relationships. People often imagine talking with others that are important in their lives. Research reveals that relational happiness is associated with having pleasant IIs (Honeycutt & Wiemann, 1999). IIs help maintain relationships as people think about their relational partners outside of their physical presence. Engaged couples who live apart use IIs to compensate for the absence of their partner compared to married couples. In addition, functions of talk that reflect enjoying serious discussion of topics, talking about events in the day, and equality of talk are associated with frequent, pleasant, and nondiscrepant IIs with partners.

An interesting area of research involves memorable messages in which people recall pleasant or negative messages in the form of maxims or clichés that impacted them. In recalling memorable messages, individuals are essentially experiencing retroactive IIs because they recall a statement made by someone from the past. Retroactive IIs allow us to relive prior messages. Memorable message research has revealed that these messages are remembered for long time periods, and they may be a major influence on the lives of people (Knapp, Stohl, & Reardon, 1981; Smith & Ellis, 2001). Memorable messages often reflect advice or attacks on competence. An example is a 63-year-old divorced woman who was a participant in one of our research projects. She told us a story about an event that had happened to her more than 25 years before. She recalled being in the kitchen with her ex-husband and he told her how to open a milk carton. While this is a simple task, he was indirectly communicating contempt for her in order to convey incompetence. She recalled the humiliation that she felt. Unfortunately, her memory maintained conflict with her ex-husband.

The conflict management function of IIs explains pervasive conflict in personal relationships and the difficulties in managing conflict in constructive ways. This function has resulted in the development of a secondary, axiomatic theory consisting of three axioms and nine theorems that explain the persistence and management of daily conflict (Honeycutt, 2004). The axioms are concerned with how relationships are conceptualized in terms of thinking about relational partners outside of their physical presence. Hence, IIs occur with important people in our lives including loved ones, work associates, and rivals. This secondary theory assumes that a major theme of relationships is concern with balancing cooperation and competition (Honeycutt & Cantrill, 2001). Indeed, a pioneer study on the dimensions of interpersonal relationships revealed that people view the relationships of others and ones they are involved with along four bipolar dimensions, one of which is competition-cooperation (Wish, Deutsch, & Kaplan, 1976).

The conflict management function of IIs highlights the role of rumination in which people have recurring thoughts about conflict and arguing that make it difficult to focus on other things. Research on rumination and depression reveals that it is difficult to either forgive or forget despite the cultural maxim to the contrary (McCullough, Bellah, Kilpatrick, & Johnson, 2001). Rumination about prior conflict is associated with depression, hopelessness, and lack of motivation (Honeycutt, 2003). Rumination is associated with vengefulness as people reflect on the injustices and harm they have suffered (McCullough et al.). Indeed, people believe that their rumination facilitates focusing on balancing the scales, retribution, or saving face, even though studies reveal that rumination is actually associated with poor problem solving (Nolen-Hoeksema, 1991). A comprehensive discussion of the various theorems and the research supporting them can be found in Honeycutt (2003, 2004, in press).

In terms of managing conflict, individuals often recall major arguments with other people. For example, Siegert and Stamp (1994) report how individuals may have vivid memories of their first, big fight. While recalling prior arguments, individuals also may use the rehearsal function in which they plan what they are going to say for anticipated encounters.

II research has spent considerable time examining planning and message rehearsal. For example, rehearsal has been analyzed in relation to attachment styles. Regression analysis revealed that a secure attachment is predicted by rehearsal as compared to other attachment types (Honeycutt, 1998–99). Perhaps strategic planning for various encounters may enhance security in romantic relationships. This use of IIs seems also to be linked to cognitive editing, which allows adjustments to messages after their potential effects on a given relationship have been assessed (Meyer, 1997). The implication here is that individuals rehearse messages, presumably through the use of IIs, and make changes as necessary for achieving desired outcomes.

Proactive IIs are a means by which to plan anticipated encounters. Plans are broader than IIs because rehearsal is just one function (see Berger, Chapter 7, this volume, for a discussion of plans). Plans may be nonverbal in the pursuit of actions or goals (e.g., realizing it's your anniversary and coming up with and buying a gift does not involve any communication). When used for rehearsal, IIs allow for a decrease in the number of silent pauses, shorter speech onset latencies during actual encounters, and an increase in message strategy variety (Allen & Honeycutt, 1997).

The self-understanding function of IIs emphasizes how IIs are used to understand ourselves better. IIs can help to uncover opposing or differing aspects of the self. Zagacki and his associates (1992) indicated that those IIs involving conflict increased understanding of the self. Self-understanding involved more verbal imagery with the self playing a greater role in the II, or being more dominant.

The catharsis function of IIs has to do with their ability to relieve tension and reduce uncertainty about another's actions (Honeycutt et al., 1989). Rosenblatt and Meyer (1986) proposed IIs as a means of emotional catharsis in counseling sessions, having found that IIs served as an outlet for their patients to release unresolved tension. Patients had noted feeling less relational tension after having experienced IIs. Allen and Berkos (in press) noted that individuals use IIs as a means of "getting things off their chest" when they know that certain behaviors or the expression of certain emotions would be inappropriate in actual interactions.

The use of IIs is also associated with a reduction in anxiety (Allen & Honeycutt, 1997). When planning for an interaction, making use of IIs also results in a lower occurrence of object adaptors. This seems to suggest that when one uses IIs, one experiences anxiety relief, perhaps experiencing a release of certain emotions in the form of catharsis. Honeycutt (2003) provided numerous accounts of individuals reporting how their IIs made them feel better and allowed them to release anxiety.

The final function of IIs is compensating for the lack of real communication. From their early development, IIs have been purported to serve in the place of real interaction when it is not possible to actually communicate with a given individual. In their discussion of IIs used for counseling, Rosenblatt and Meyer (1986) indicated that an individual may choose to use IIs in place of actually confronting a loved one because of fear that the loved one would be hurt by the message. Boldness has been identified as a possible function of IIs, but it appears to reflect compensation. McCann and Honeycutt (2006) discussed how individuals may feel emboldened in situations where there are sanctions for voicing opinion. They found that the Japanese, when compared to Thais and Americans, were more likely to use IIs to suppress communication and as a means of voicing disagreement because they felt empowered in their imaginary conflicts, which eliminated the possibility of repercussions. Indeed, scholars have described the highly elaborate rules of manners and conduct in Japan that include compliance to others, self-restraint (passivity), suppression of inner feelings, and observance of formal greetings, speech, and appropriate gestures (Rothbaum, Pott, Azuma, Miyake, & Weisz, 2000). McCann and Honeycutt concluded that IIs might have served as a safe, punitive-free outlet for self-expression for their Japanese participants. To the Thais and Americans, who perhaps operate under comparatively less rigid norms for individual expression (Embree, 1950; Triandis, 1995), this safe II outlet may not have been as necessary.

Strengths and Limitations of the Theory

At the foundation of all communication is intrapersonal communication in which individuals process information within their minds and think about communication encounters. Indeed, effective intrapersonal communication becomes the foundation on which interaction structures are built. An analogy to building construction is evident: Poorly laid foundations will not support a housing structure very well over time, particularly if the house is subjected to storms. An old maxim also reflects the power of II: Think before you speak.

Imagined Interaction Theory explains how conflicts are not isolated events, but rather are linked to the previous experiences of the communicators. For example, in the absence of actual conflict, retroactive IIs can be used to maintain conflict by reliving both the issues addressed and the emotions felt during prior encounters. Because conflict linkage takes into account prior conflict experiences, it incorporates relational patterns such as Caughlin and Vangelisti's (2000) demand-withdraw patterns, and contempt and defensiveness (Gottman, 1994). It also incorporates argumentative skills deficiency (Infante & Rancer, 1996) through lack of proactive IIs and rehearsal. Because the conflict-management function of IIs does not isolate the conflict encounter from other encounters within the relationship, it creates a deeper picture of conflict than is found in many theories of conflict (see Honeycutt, 2004, for a review).

Caughey (1984) contends that by rehearsing anticipated conversations, "we also bind ourselves tightly within a given culturally constructed framework. These inner conversations may be just as important as actual conversations" in managing our sense of social reality (p. 146). IIs provide a mechanism for managing and living on the edge of chaos and complexity. In some cases, IIs might prevent the sudden reorganizing of a complex system into a wholly new and possibly undesirable entity. Waldrop (1992) reminded us that, under the right conditions, small effects become magnified and precipitate self-organization. Furthermore, once a system has achieved its new pattern of organization, it does not spontaneously disorganize. The system may become inflexible or stagnant, as in numerous marketing cases where one product gains a permanent economic edge. Analogies with interpersonal communication abound. An example is the spouse whose spontaneous outburst precipitates a divorce, or who does not confine his or her interactions with alternative partners to the realm of the imaginary.

Any complete explanation of communication must ultimately be concerned with three components:

- input (preexisting attitudes, beliefs, experiences, or personality brought into an interaction),
- throughput (the process or actual unfolding of communication as evidenced in behaviors, messages, statements), and
- output (outcomes that emerge from the communication, including post-event attitudes, satisfaction, emotional ratings).

Many communication studies are simple input-output designs in which surveys and hypothetical scenarios are used in lieu of actual coding of verbal and nonverbal behaviors that are costly and time consuming. IIs are primarily focused on input and output. Indeed, a proactive II represents expectations about what may happen during a conversation. It resides within the individual, while ignoring group processes. However, it is possible to link IIs with process or throughput. For example, my colleagues and I code discrepancy in which individuals think about messages that they are going to discuss with their partner about some issue in their relationship (e.g., managing finances, social life, how they argue). After the discussion, the individuals watch themselves on DVD and discuss how discrepant the actual conversation was to what they had proactively imagined.

A criticism of Imagined Interaction Theory concerns the ability of cognitive researchers to identify or infer the existence of internal cognitive states from external behavior (Ericsson & Simon, 1980). Even though certain physiological measures allow researchers to document the occurrence of mental states, they tell us very little about these states beyond the physiological level. If one's interest is in the content of mental states or, in this case, the content of IIs, we must rely on individual self-reports. However, this criticism has been addressed by Ericsson and Simon and by Pelose (1989), who offer guidelines about the validity of retrospective reports. They indicate that providing contextual information and prompts to subjects can aid recall from long-term memory. The Survey of Imagined Interaction (SII) is designed to contextualize subjects through examples of IIs, and a new shorter version of the SII is available (Honeycutt, in press).

Directions for Future Research and Applications

Future research in Imagined Interaction Theory is limitless. Because IIs are a pervasive part of daily existence that occur across the lifespan, it is worthy to examine how they can be facilitated for maximizing outcomes. Indeed, sports imagists use mental imagery in which athletes are taught to imagine successful outcomes using the rehearsal function (e.g., imaging making a successful kick before kicking a field goal, making free throws, stopping a team from making a first-down on "4th and inches," hitting a baseball or a straight golf drive, and so on). Colleagues and I are currently testing physiological correlates of having IIs about pleasant topics (e.g., sharing news of success) and areas of disagreement in interpersonal relationships. For example, individuals imagine discussing a topic of concern about which they have had prior discussions or arguments with a relational partner. Blood pressure, heart-rate beats per minute, and heart-rate variability are measured while they are imagining the conflict as well as during a time period in which the partners actually discuss the topic. We often imagine what we are going to say to people before encounters (proactivity) and then relive what occurred (retroactivity). Relationships are maintained as well as dissolved through mental imagery. Indeed, my colleagues and I imagine great insights into the relationship between individual differences and productive communicative outcomes.

References

Abelson, R. P. (1976). Script processing in attitude formation and decision-making. In J. S. Carroll & J. W. Payne (Eds.), *Cognition and social behavior* (pp. 33–45). Hillsdale, NJ: Erlbaum.

Allen, T. H., & Berkos, K. M. (in press). Imagined interaction conflict-linkage theory: Examining accounts of recurring imagined interactions. In J. M. Honeycutt (Ed.), *Imagine that: Studies in imagined interaction.* Cresskill, NJ: Hampton.

Allen, T. H., & Honeycutt, J. M. (1997). Planning, imagined interaction, and the nonverbal display of anxiety. *Communication Research, 24,* 64–82.

Caughey, J. (1984). *Imaginary social worlds.* Lincoln, NE: University of Nebraska Press.

Caughlin, J. P., & Vangelisti, A. L. (2000). An individual differences explanation of why married couples engage in the demand/withdraw pattern of conflict. *Journal of Social and Personal Relationships, 17,* 523–551.

Cunningham, S. B. (1989). Defining intrapersonal communication. In C. V. Roberts & K. W. Watson (Eds.), *Intrapersonal communication processes* (pp. 82–94). Scottsdale, AZ: Gorsuch Scarisbrick.

Dewey, J. (1922) *Human nature and conduct: An introduction to social psychology.* New York: Henry Holt.

Embree, J. F. (1950). Thailand: A loosely structured social system. *American Anthropologist, 52,* 181–193.

Ericsson, K. A., & Simon, H. A. (1980). Verbal reports as data. *Psychological Review, 87,* 215–251.

Fisher, B. A. (1987). *Interpersonal communication: Pragmatics of human relationships.* New York: Random House.

Gottman, J. M. (1994). *What predicts divorce?* Hillsdale, NJ: Erlbaum.

Honeycutt, J. M. (1998–99). Differences in imagined interactions as a consequence of marital ideology and attachment. *Imagination, Cognition, and Personality, 18,* 269–283.

Honeycutt, J. M. (2003). *Imagined interactions.* Cresskill, NJ: Hampton.

Honeycutt, J. M. (2004). Imagined interaction conflict-linkage theory: Explaining the persistence and resolution of interpersonal conflict in everyday life. *Imagination, Cognition, and Personality, 23,* 3–25.

Honeycutt, J. M. (in press). Introduction. In J. M. Honeycutt (Ed.), *Imagine that: Studies in imagined interaction.* Cresskill, NJ: Hampton.

Honeycutt, J. M., & Cantrill, J. C. (2001). *Cognition, communication, and romantic relationships.* Mahwah, NJ: Erlbaum.

Honeycutt, J. M., & Ford, S. G. (2001). Mental imagery and intrapersonal communication: A review of research on imagined interactions (IIs) and current developments. In W. B. Gudykunst (Ed.), *Communication yearbook 25* (pp. 315–445). Mahwah, NJ: Erlbaum.

Honeycutt, J. M., & Wiemann, J. M. (1999). Analysis of functions of talk and reports of imagined interactions (IIs) during engagement and marriage. *Human Communication Research, 25,* 399–419.

Honeycutt, J. M., Zagacki, K. S., & Edwards, R. (1989). Intrapersonal communication, social cognition, and imagined interactions. In C. V. Roberts & K. W. Watson (Eds.), *Intrapersonal communication processes* (pp. 166–184). Scottsdale, AZ: Gorsuch Scarisbrick.

Infante, D., & Rancer, A. (1996). Argumentation and verbal aggressiveness: A review of recent theory and research. In B. Burleson (Ed.), *Communication yearbook 19* (pp. 319–351). Thousand Oaks, CA: Sage.

Knapp, M. L., Stohl, C., & Reardon, K. (1981). Memorables messages. *Journal of Communication, 31,* 27–42.

McCann, R. M., & Honeycutt, J. M. (2006). An intercultural analysis of imagined interaction. *Human Communication Research, 32,* 274–301.

McCullough, M. E., Bellah, C. G., Kilpatrick, S. D., & Johnson, J. L. (2001). Vengefulness: Relationships with forgiveness, rumination, well-being and the big five. *Personality and Social Psychology Bulletin, 27,* 601–610.

Mead, G. H. (1934). *Mind, self and society.* Chicago: University of Chicago Press.

Meyer, J. R. (1997). Cognitive influences on the ability to address interaction goals. In J. O. Greene (Ed.), *Message production: Advances in communication theory* (pp. 71–90). Mahwah, NJ: Erlbaum.

Nolen-Hoeksema, S. (1991). Responses to depression and their effects on the duration of depressive episodes. *Journal of Abnormal Psychology, 100,* 569–582.

Pelose, G. C. (1989). Metacognition as an intrapersonal communication process: The purposes of cognitive monitoring and methodology for its assessment. In C. V. Roberts & K. W. Watson (Eds.), *Intrapersonal communication processes* (pp. 135–165). Scottsdale, AZ: Gorsuch Scarisbrick.

Rosenblatt, P. C., & Meyer, C. (1986). Imagined interactions in the family. *Family Relations, 35,* 319–324.

Rothbaum, F., Pott, M., Azuma, H., Miyake, K., & Weisz, J. (2000). The development of close relationships in Japan and the United States: Paths of symbiotic harmony and generative tension. *Child Development, 71,* 1121–1142.

Schutz, A. (1962). Choosing among projects of action. In M. Natanson (Ed.), *Collected papers, Volume I: The problem of social reality* (pp. 67–96). The Hague, Netherlands: Martinus Nijhoff.

Siegert, J. R., & Stamp, G. H. (1994). "Our first big fight" as a milestone in the development of close relationships. *Communication Monographs, 61,* 345–360.

Smith, S. W., & Ellis, J. B. (2001) Memorable messages as guides to self-assessment of behavior: An initial investigation. *Communication Monographs, 68,* 154–168.

Triandis, H. C. (1995). *Individualism and collectivism.* Boulder, CO: Westview.

Waldrop, M. M. (1992) *Complexity: The emerging science at the edge of order and chaos.* New York: Simon and Schuster.

Wish, M., Deutsch, M., & Kaplan, S. J. (1976). Perceived dimensions of interpersonal relations. *Journal of Personality and Social Psychology, 33,* 404–420.

Zagacki, K. S., Edwards, R., & Honeycutt, J. M. (1992). The role of mental imagery and emotion in imagined interaction. *Communication Quarterly, 40,* 56–68.

7

Planning Theory of Communication

Goal Attainment Through Communicative Action

Charles R. Berger

M any communication theorists agree that communication is a tool for achieving goals: it is purposive. Even when people talk for the sake of talking, they are probably using communication to achieve a goal. In this case the goal might be to relieve boredom. People use both words and actions to accomplish such goals as persuading, entertaining, and informing others. The Planning Theory of communication seeks to explain how individuals arrive at an understanding of each other's goal-directed actions and discourse, and how individuals produce actions and discourse that enable them to attain their everyday goals.

Purpose and Meta-theoretical Assumptions

Planning Theory is a social-cognitive theory that identifies and describes the cognitive structures and processes that make possible both the understanding of others' actions and discourse, and the generation of purposive, goal-directed action, including verbal discourse. The theory's aim is to explain how mental plans influence communication. Although the theory has been developed and tested within face-to-face interaction situations, its scope goes far beyond this communication context. The theory also has relevance to explaining message production and message processing in print and electronic mass media, as well as communication through new technologies such as computer-mediated communication and mobile telephones. Whenever people communicate with each other, plans and planning processes come into play.

Planning Theory is post-positivist in orientation and represents the tradition of cognitive realism. It seeks to describe fundamental cognitive structures and processes that enable communication processes, as well as the mechanisms that prevent communication processes from taking place (Pavitt, 2001). It is well known that when persuasive messages are presented by sources who are perceived by audience members to be highly knowledgeable, audience members are more likely to be persuaded than when the same messages are presented by sources who others perceive to lack knowledge on the topic. However, being able to demonstrate that increases in perceived source credibility increase persuasive impact does not, by itself, constitute an explanation for this relationship. Explaining why sources perceived to be knowledgeable are more persuasive might involve the cognitive structures and processes individuals use to process information. Of course, not all people are necessarily persuaded by highly credible sources, so mechanisms that act to disable these links must be identified. Thus, answering the question "Why does persuasion occur?" by saying "Because of high source credibility" is not sufficient, even if the relationship between the two factors is well established. A detailed cognitive account of why the two factors are consistently related is necessary. Cognitive realism assumes that the cognitive structures and processes that enable these relationships are real.

Main Features of the Theory

This cognitive-realist, plan-based approach to interpersonal communication can be characterized by the following seven propositions:

Proposition 1. Organisms, including humans, seek to satisfy goals in order to survive. The satisfaction of goals is an ongoing activity in people's lives that gives rise to goal-directed, purposive actions on their part.

Proposition 2. The ability for humans to think has grown out of the need for us to satisfy goals (Bogdan, 1994, 1997, 2000). Cognitive abilities that enable people to anticipate and recognize opportunities to satisfy goals and to remember successful plans for achieving goals promote more effective and more efficient goal satisfaction.

Proposition 3. People use language to achieve goals, and not merely for the sake of using it. Language is used to accomplish such goals as persuading, informing, problem solving, and entertaining. Language is a tool or an instrument that people use to attain these goals (Clark, 1994; Wittgenstein, 1953).

Proposition 4. Goals are desired end states toward which people strive; plans are cognitive representations of action sequences that enable people to achieve their goals. Goals motivate action; plans guide action.

Proposition 5. Knowledge about goals is represented hierarchically in long-term memory with abstract goals at the tops of hierarchies and subgoals nested below them. Nested below the abstract goal "happiness" might be the subgoal "wealth" or "serving others," implying that the satisfaction of these subgoals will lead to the satisfaction of the more abstract goal. Achieving subgoals enables achievement of superordinate goals.

Proposition 6. Plans are hierarchically organized, and are cognitive representations of action sequences that enable people to reach goals. In the preceding example, individuals might develop or have available to them in long-term memory plans for becoming wealthy or for serving others. Plans can be consciously formulated and used to achieve goals, and previously used plans can be stored in long-term memory, and retrieved and used unconsciously to achieve current goals. The ability to store and reuse successful plans increases people's efficiency and effectiveness in satisfying many recurring goals in everyday life—obtaining food, exchanging money for goods and services, greeting others, and gathering information.

Proposition 7. Knowledge of goals and plans also plays a vital role in understanding the discourse and actions of other people. When people ask why other people have said or done what they have, their answers to these questions are couched in terms of the goals they infer others to be pursuing and the plans they believe others to be following to achieve those goals. Observers watching a person speak with great intensity in a two-person conversation might infer that the speaker's goal is to persuade the other person and that the message plan the speaker is following includes using intense verbal language and certain nonverbal behaviors. In order to understand others' discourse and actions in this example, observers must draw on their knowledge of what pursing a persuasion goal looks like and the typical plans people use to attain that goal. Persuasion plans might include what is said, as well as the vocal intensity with which it is said and the gestures that accompany the verbal message. Without goal-plan knowledge, it would be difficult for communicators to infer others' intentions that, in turn, would make it difficult for people to respond to others in a meaningful or effective way.

PLANS VS. PLANNING

Although the terms "plan" and "planning" are sometimes used interchangeably, they are not the same. "Plans" are hierarchical knowledge structures that represent goal-directed action sequences, but "planning" is a process that produces a plan or plans as its product. Planning includes assessing the situation, deciding what goal or goals to pursue, creating or retrieving plans, and then executing them (Berger, 1995, 1997). Most of the research motivated by Planning Theory has focused on characteristics of plans and how these characteristics influence communication effectiveness, rather than focusing on the processes involved in planning.

PLAN COMPLEXITY

A key aspect of plans is their degree of complexity (Berger, 1997; Waldron, 1997). Plans can be more or less complex depending on two factors: First, plans can vary with respect to their specificity. An abstract persuasion plan lacking specificity might simply include the action of offering a reward in exchange for compliance. By contrast, a detailed, more concrete plan might go on to specify the characteristics of the reward—material (money, goods) versus emotional (praise). Even more specifically, a plan might specify the words and actions that would be used to offer the reward to the other person—for example, "I want to give you this check for $10,000 . . ." said in a sincere voice while smiling at the other person, standing close to the person, and touching the person's arm. Note that the more abstract, less complex plan includes only one, highly abstract level (reward); conversely, the more detailed plan nests progressively more specific actions under the more abstract actions, as shown in Figure 7.1.

A second way that plans can be more complex is if they include action contingencies. Plans can be constructed to anticipate potential action failures by including alternative actions that might be pursued if failures occur. In the above example, what if the individual following the persuasion plan were to encounter resistance from the other person? That is, what if the planner (persuader) offered the $10,000 but the person who was the target of persuasion refused to take it? If the planner had no contingencies built into the persuasion plan, the next course of action would be problematic. By contrast, if the initial plan included the contingency that if the persuasion target refused the $10,000 offer the planner would offer $25,000, the planner would have a ready-made

Reward

Material (Money)

Verbal Content ("Here's $10,000 . . .") + Nonverbal Actions (Smile, Pleasant Voice)

Figure 7.1   A Message Plan Hierarchy

response to the failed action. Contingencies could be built into the plan at other levels of abstraction. In the example, a more abstract contingency might be that if a material reward such as money fails, the planner would try a non-material reward such as verbal praise. Alternatively, a plan might include the contingency that if the reward offer fails, threat would be used. As the contingencies represented in these conditional "if-then" statements are added to plans, plans exhibit a branching structure that reflects their increased complexity.

THE HIERARCHY PRINCIPLE

Planning Theory predicts and evidence supports the proposition that when individuals encounter failure, their first tendency is to alter plans at more concrete levels than at more abstract levels. This tendency is known as the "hierarchy principle" (Berger, 1997). The hierarchy principle is based on the idea that changing plans at more specific levels requires less cognitive effort than changing plans at more abstract levels. In the persuasion example, it is easier to change the amount of money offered for compliance in the event of failure than it is to switch from a reward to a threat strategy. When more abstract plan elements are altered, the communicator must figure out the specific actions that will be used to represent the new, abstract plan element. Minor adjustments to specific, concrete actions require much less thought.

Several studies have tested the hierarchy principle and have shown that when communicators are not understood by others, which thwarts the communicators' plans, communicators tend to repeat what they said previously but in a louder voice (a low-level plan alteration), even though the source of the communication failure may have nothing to do with others' failing to hear what was said (Berger, 1997). Research has also shown that when individuals are asked to alter message plans at higher levels—for example, trying another argument while persuading someone—they take longer to do so than when they are asked to make lower-level adjustments such as repeating what they said, but saying it more slowly the second time (Berger, 1997). High-level plan alterations are cognitively more demanding to accomplish; communicators usually try to avoid making such alterations, if possible. Of course, when the communicative stakes are high and goals must be attained—for example, if a salesperson is trying to close an important deal—communicators may be willing to expend greater cognitive effort to make high-level plan alterations.

Although plans that include contingencies have obvious advantages by providing communicators with the ability to respond quickly to action failures, increased plan complexity may come at a price, depending on the number of alternative actions or plans a message producer might have available. Communicators who pursue goals with no plan alternatives may not be able to respond rapidly if their sole plan or planned action fails. On the other side of the coin, however, message producers who have many alternative plans available or who have many action contingencies in a plan may have difficulty choosing among the alternatives when failure occurs, thus slowing down their response times. A communicator preparing to persuade a persuasion target might come up with 15 arguments to support his or her position. However, when one of these arguments fails to be persuasive, the communicator has the problem of choosing among the 14 remaining arguments. A communicator with fewer alternative arguments would face a less difficult decision-making task. Several experiments have shown that individuals with no alternative plans or actions, or as many as six alternative plans or actions responded equally less rapidly when their current plan or action failed, but individuals who had three alternative plans or actions responded to the same failure significantly more rapidly than both of these groups (Berger, 1997). Having alternative plans or actions available in the event of failure pays off in terms of circumventing failure, but too many alternatives may slow down communicators' ability to respond to failure. The inability to respond quickly in the event of plan failure could be costly in terms of others' perceptions of the slowly responding communicator. Because people who show longer pauses in their speech are judged to be less credible, how quickly individuals respond to plan failure may become an important determinant of how credible others perceive them to be (Berger).

PLANS AND COMMUNICATION EFFECTIVENESS

People can consciously devise plans before they become engaged in communication—for example, thinking up an excuse for being late to an important meeting—and plans can be retrieved, modified, or constructed as people communicate. Research spawned by Planning Theory has shown that planning while interacting with others helps to determine the degree to which communicators ultimately are effective in reaching their goals (Waldron, 1997). This research examined the plans individuals recalled using while pursuing such goals as obtaining sensitive information from conversational partners or trying to succeed in a job interview.

In general, this research has demonstrated that individuals whose plans look ahead in the conversation and anticipate their partners' future conversational moves, in much the same way as expert chess players anticipate their opponents' future moves, are more effective than those whose plans do not anticipate partners' future actions. Because plans that anticipate conversational partners' future actions are more complex than those that do not, increasingly more complex plans are increasingly more effective. This research also showed that individuals whose plans took into account their partners' goals were generally more effective than were those whose plans did not. The ability of individuals to integrate their partners' goals into their own plans implies that effective message producers have more flexible plans than do less effective communicators. Individuals who doggedly insist on pursuing their own goals without recognizing their partners' goals are less likely to achieve their own goals. Finally, this research revealed that plans that included concrete actions were more effective than were highly abstract or vague plans (Waldron, 1997). A plan for trying to persuade another person might include the abstract action of being pleasant, whereas, a more specific plan would detail the actions involved in being pleasant—for example, smiling and complimenting the other person. Those whose message plans are more concrete are generally more effective at achieving their interaction goals.

Conceptualization of Communication in the Theory

As the Planning Theory propositions suggest, verbal and nonverbal messages are instruments that individuals use to achieve goals in their everyday lives. Message exchanges between people enable them to achieve their goals. Over human history, people have developed progressively more sophisticated communication systems to make goal attainment more efficient and to make it possible to pursue multiple goals simultaneously. Individual human action and social interaction are hierarchically organized around goal pursuit, thus reflecting the role cognitive plans play in guiding human action and social interaction toward goals (Berger, 2002, 2003). Planning Theory suggests that social interaction and mediated-communication are instruments or tools that enable individuals to achieve their desired goals by enacting plans, and goal-plan knowledge helps provide meaning to others' discourse and actions.

Uses of the Theory

When individuals engage in unmediated social interaction or mediated communication, they do so because they are pursing goals. Even when individuals say they are talking with another person, watching television, or surfing the Internet "just to pass the time," implying that they do not have any particular goal for doing so, they are attempting to achieve goals. The goals they may be pursuing may not be accessible to their conscious awareness, but "passing the time" may be just another way of saying "relieving boredom" or "relieving feelings of loneliness and depression" or a similar goal.

Everyday observation suggests that individuals vary with respect to their ability to achieve their communication goals effectively and efficiently. Some individuals cannot succeed, even in the absence of direct resistance from others or unfortunate circumstances that interfere with the execution of the planned actions. Others can succeed in spite of substantial roadblocks that other people and situational factors put in their paths. Among those who succeed, some do so quickly and with apparent ease while others struggle for long periods of time to arrive at the same outcome. Planning Theory provides a partial explanation for these performance differences. Specifically, because of differences in prior experience and knowledge, some individuals have developed more effective plans for achieving the goal or goals in question than have others. Moreover, to the degree that these plans anticipate potential resistance or unfavorable circumstances and include contingencies for overcoming these sources of interference, these individuals will experience higher levels of success and do so more efficiently.

However, Planning Theory includes an important caution in this regard (Berger, 1997): no matter how effective plans may be, if communicators do not have the requisite performance skills to carry out the plan, effective plans may not be successful. This distinction between plan effectiveness and performance skills is reflected in the division of labor between those who plan messages—speech writers, script writers, and news writers—and the politicians, actors, and news anchors who ultimately perform or deliver the messages. This division of labor in these formal communication contexts suggests that the same individual may not necessarily possess both the ability to formulate effective message plans and the skills to effectively perform. An extremely effective planner may lack the necessary physical attributes and verbal and nonverbal skills to implement highly effective plans. The ineffective performer may have odd vocal characteristics or a limited range of nonverbal behaviors. Deep, resonant voices are preferred for radio and television announcers because voices with these characteristics are generally judged to be more persuasive than are high-pitched, nasal voices. No matter how effective a planner might be, one with a certain communication style might still be ineffective in achieving his or her goals. Conversely, an individual with excellent performance skills may lack the cognitive skills and knowledge necessary to devise effective message plans. Some successful actors and politicians with very strong performance skills are incapable of performing well unless they are provided with a script (plan) to follow.

Although this division of labor between plans and performance may be somewhat less obvious during informal, everyday social encounters, sometimes advice givers such as friends and relatives—acting in the role of planners—provide their peers and relatives (the performers) with information about actions they might take to achieve their goals that involve interactions with others. This division of labor possibility notwithstanding, the problem that many people must face when engaging in everyday social interaction is that they must at once have effective plans for achieving their goals and the performance skills necessary to carry out their plans effectively in discourse and action. Thus, when people fail to reach their social interaction goals, the problem may lie in faulty plans, inadequate performance skills, or both.

Planning Theory is also sensitive to the dynamic nature of social interaction and social relationships. This dynamism may render plans that have worked well in the past relatively ineffective at a later time (Berger, 1997). Spouses who use the same gift-giving plan (for example, a piece of jewelry) to determine what anniversary gift they will give their spouse, may, after several repetitions of the same plan, find it to be an ineffective one in reaching the goal of making the spouse happy. However, formerly effective plans may be rendered ineffective by more than their mindless, automatic repetition. A plan that was successful when first implemented, if used on a second occasion may prove to be ineffective because of changes that have occurred in the person or persons on whom the plan is being implemented or the environment in which the plan is being carried out, or both. Effective communicators must be sensitive to these changes and not lulled into the potentially false belief that a plan that has worked well in the past will necessarily work well again. Recognizing that an old and successful plan may not work in a current social situation is itself an important social skill.

Closely related to the problem of reusing plans is that of the "success bias" in planning. Research has found that when individuals devise plans to reach goals and they are then asked to estimate the likelihood that they will actually reach their goal, their estimated likelihood of success is significantly higher than that of individuals who have not devised a plan to reach the same goal (Berger, 1997). On logical grounds, the higher likelihood of success estimates of those who have generated plans are unwarranted. After all, these individuals have no idea whether or not their plans will be successful in attaining goals until they use them. By itself, the act of devising a plan should not induce planners to become more confident of success. In fact, effective planners anticipate the possibility of failure and develop contingencies to meet these potential failures.

Strengths and Limitations of the Theory

Planning Theory provides a way of explaining why some individuals are better than others at achieving their goals in social interaction situations and in mediated communication contexts. In addition to sensitizing those interested in improving communication skills to the difference between plan effectiveness and performance skills, Planning Theory explicitly identifies a knowledge structure (plan) and a set of cognitive processes that are amenable to improvement. That is, the theory identifies those aspects of plans and planning that are subject to improvement through instruction. The theory suggests that when groups are devising plans, it is important for the group to include individuals who may be skeptical of the potential effectiveness of the plans being developed rather than to include only like-minded "team players." Skeptics may spot potential problems with planned actions that would lead to failure if carried out. Raising these possibilities may prompt group members to think of contingencies that they may not have thought of in the absence of skeptics. Including skeptics in groups engaged in planning also helps counter the success bias (Berger, 1997).

By differentiating between plan and performance effectiveness, strategies for increasing communication effectiveness can be more accurately identified. As a result, strategies for improvement can be more finely tuned. Problems stemming from ineffective plans are not necessarily solved by focusing on improving presentational skills (gesturing effectively and increasing eye gaze toward conversational partners). In order to improve plan effectiveness, individuals may have to be encouraged to incorporate others' goals into their own plans, anticipate their partners' future conversational moves, plan at more detailed and concrete levels, consider the possibility of plan failure, and devise contingencies to meet anticipated failures. Similarly, presentation skill problems may not be solved by honing these planning skills. The important point is that these cognitive and presentational skill sets can be learned.

One limitation to Planning Theory is its bias toward the individual as the unit of analysis. Planning theorists have recognized that when individuals participate in social interaction, they engage in interactive planning (Waldron, 1997). That is, individuals must base their own plans on the goals and plans they infer others to be following in the interaction. This is most clearly the case in adversarial interactions in which parties attempt to anticipate each other's next attacks and devise plans to protect themselves against them. However, even when parties are engaged in cooperative interactions, they must coordinate their efforts through interactive planning. When participating in cooperative endeavors, individuals cannot fully articulate their goals and plans to each other: to do so would require large amounts of time and energy. Thus, there may be uncertainty and room left for partners to fill in these gaps by inferring each other's goals and the plans they are using to pursue their goals. Of course, even among individuals who know each other well, the inferences that fill these gaps may be erroneous, thus leading to communication failures and misunderstandings. Except for noting that interactive planning occurs continuously during everyday social interaction, Planning Theory does not provide the details of how individuals go about accomplishing interactive planning (Berger, 1997; Waldron, 1997).

Because the theory has focused intensely on the role that plans play in guiding message production, almost no attention has been paid to how people make inferences about each other's goals and plans. Those interested in understanding discourse and text comprehension have argued that inferences about goals and plans enable people to provide meaning to each other's words and actions (Berger, 1997). That is, people interpret each other's utterances and actions in terms of the goals they believe their co-interlocutors are trying to achieve, and the plans they think others are using to pursue their goals. The theory has not addressed such questions as how individuals are able to detect each other's goals and plans when they engage in social interaction, although the vital importance of goal detection in social interaction has been discussed (Berger, 2000). The theory has also ignored the issue of how inferences about others' goals and plans are integrated into ongoing message-production processes. Understanding how individuals use plan-based knowledge to make these inferences is crucial because message producers must rely on them when generating their own message plans and implementing them in action. Communicators base their own message plans and decisions about what to say, and how and when to say it, on the goals and plans they believe co-interlocutors are following.

Directions for Future Research and Applications

There are a number of potential avenues for further research on plans and planning; we discuss two of them here. First, because goal-plan inferences made during social interaction are frequently made quickly and outside of conscious awareness, and because individuals engage in dynamic, interactive planning while conversing with each other, effective methods for measuring these processes must be developed. This is an extremely difficult task because measurement methods that interrupt the flow of social interaction may artificially change its course, and methods that do not interrupt conversational flow and rely on people's memory for what they were thinking during a just-completed conversation may be inaccurate and distorted, even when people try their best to recall what they were thinking. It is difficult to measure automatic processes using methods that require individuals to make verbal reports. Perhaps advances in brain imagining techniques such as functional magnetic resonance imagining may enable researchers to gain insights into these automatic processes. At this time, however, using such techniques to study individuals during their interactions is difficult. There is widespread recognition that inferences about goals and plans enable individuals to understand each other's actions and discourse and to guide decisions about what to do and say in social encounters. Thus, the difficulties involved in measuring these complex, dynamic, fundamental processes are particularly frustrating.

Second, future research should address in more detail the relationships between plan effectiveness and performance skills. In many social interaction situations, the optimal condition might be for communicators to have highly effective plans implemented by equally high levels of performance skills. Unfortunately, however, individuals may not function at high levels simultaneously in both of these areas. In fact, it is doubtful that most individuals are capable of functioning at high levels in both areas in a given situation. When there is a discrepancy between the two dimensions, which there may often be, which discrepancy is more damaging to goal attainment? Can a highly effective plan overcome mediocre performance skills? Can highly skilled performance skills compensate for deficient plans? Another way to think about this question is to ask whether substance tends to trump style, or vice versa. The most probable answer to either question is, "It depends." Specifically what it depends on represents an opportunity for future research.

Approximately 60 years ago the psychologist Kurt Lewin, founder of the study of group dynamics, observed that nothing is more practical than a good theory. What Lewin meant is that because theories provide explanations for phenomena we observe every day, practical application based on good theory is more likely to succeed than application based on intuition and trial and error. Many individuals would like to be more effective in their everyday communication with other people. As I hope this chapter has made evident, Planning Theory provides one potential avenue for understanding and improving social interaction skills and the skills necessary for communicating effectively with mass audiences. At least, that was one of my goals in planning this chapter.

References

Berger, C. R. (1995). A plan-based approach to strategic communication. In D. E. Hewes (Ed.), *Cognitive bases of interpersonal communication* (pp. 141–179). Hillsdale, NJ: Erlbaum.

Berger, C. R. (1997). *Planning strategic interaction: Attaining goals through communicative action*. Mahwah, NJ: Erlbaum.

Berger, C. R. (2000). Goal detection and efficiency: Neglected aspects of message production. *Communication Theory, 10,* 156–166.

Berger, C. R. (2002). Goals and knowledge structures in social interaction. In M. L. Knapp & J. A. Daly (Eds.), *Handbook of interpersonal communication* (pp. 181–212). Thousand Oaks, CA: Sage.

Berger, C. R. (2003). Skillful message production. In J. O. Greene & B. R. Burleson (Eds.), *Handbook of communication and social interaction skills* (pp. 257–289). Mahwah, NJ: Erlbaum.

Bogdan, R. J. (1994). *Grounds for cognition: How goal-directed behavior shapes the mind.* Hillsdale, NJ: Erlbaum.

Bogdan, R. J. (1997). *Interpreting minds: The evolution of a practice.* Cambridge: MIT Press.

Bogdan, R. J. (2000). *Minding minds: Evolving a reflexive mind by interpreting others.* Cambridge: MIT Press.

Clark, H. H. (1994). Discourse in production. In M. A. Gernsbacher (Ed.), *Handbook of psycholinguistics* (pp. 985–1021). San Diego, CA: Academic Press.

Pavitt, C. (2001). *The philosophy of science and communication theory.* Huntington, NY: Nova Science.

Waldron, V. R. (1997). Toward a theory of interactive conversational planning. In J. O. Greene (Ed.), *Message production: Advances in theory and research* (pp. 195–220). Mahwah, NJ: Erlbaum.

Wittgenstein, L. (1953). *Philosophical investigations.* Oxford, UK: Basil Blackwell.

8

Relational Framing Theory

Drawing Inferences About Relationships From Interpersonal Interactions

Denise Haunani Solomon and Rachel M. McLaren

I magine yourself in a professional work environment, when your boss says, "I'm so glad you have been transferred to our office. You are always so friendly, and you're much better looking than our last analyst!" Or a friend comments, "I'd really like you to come with me to Matt's party. I don't want to go alone." Or imagine your parent says, "You remind me so much of your grandfather when you argue for your beliefs." Or an instructor returns your paper to you and tells you, "Although you did well on the paper, I know you have the potential to do much better." What do these messages mean? Are these comments friendly or unfriendly? Are you being coerced or admired? Situations such as these call for a response, but our reply depends on how we understand these messages. In this chapter, you'll learn about Relational Framing Theory, which seeks to explain how we make sense of ambiguous messages about our relationships with others.

Purpose and Meta-theoretical Assumptions

Relational Framing Theory (RFT) explains how people organize interpersonal messages to support inferences about the relationship that exists between communicators (Dillard, Solomon, & Samp, 1996). According to the theory, people make sense of relational messages by interpreting them as indicators of either dominance-submissiveness or affiliation-disaffiliation. Although these two dimensions are not new concepts, RFT positions these dimensions in a new way. In particular, the theory views dominance-submissiveness and affiliation-disaffiliation as functional frames that help people process social messages, resolve ambiguities, and draw relational inferences (Dillard & Solomon, 2005).

RFT emerges from a post-positivistic paradigm. This paradigm assumes that an objective reality does exist, and that it is the duty of science to discover reality through value-neutral research. RFT follows logical empiricism by offering a framework that is both logically deduced and informed by observable facts. RFT also theorizes about the causes of relational message processing at multiple levels. At the most precise level, RFT locates the immediate source of relational inferences in the contents of utterances, the goals of interactions, and features of the context. RFT also explains message processing in terms of the functions accomplished when people can efficiently resolve ambiguities. At yet another level, the theory recognizes that an ability to draw relational inferences is a human skill that is subject to both cognitive development and socialization. At the broadest level, RFT is rooted in assumptions about human evolution: in particular, our ancestors' abilities to decipher relational information would have influenced both survival and opportunities to reproduce. Thus, the theory links the dynamics of interaction to the evolution of the human species.

Main Features of the Theory

RFT is embodied in two sets of assumptions. The first set of claims addresses the nature of relational judgments. In other words, what evaluations are made when people draw inferences about their relationships? The second set of claims focus on the processes that guide relational inferences. This part of the theory describes how characteristics of the interaction context and cognitive processes jointly contribute to relational judgments.

THE NATURE OF RELATIONAL JUDGMENTS

In advancing RFT, Dillard and colleagues (1996) drew on the long history of research on relational communication (e.g., Bateson, 1935, 1958; Kemper, 1973; Leary, 1957; White, 1980). One important contribution to this body of literature was Burgoon and Hale's (1984) proposal that relational messages address as many as 12 facets of interpersonal associations. While recognizing the utility of the nuances revealed in Burgoon and Hale's perspective, Dillard and his colleagues (Dillard et al., 1996; Dillard, Solomon, & Palmer, 1999) argued that the domain of relational messages could be organized by three primary dimensions: dominance-submissiveness, affiliation-disaffiliation, and involvement.

Two of these dimensions encompass the substance of relational messages—or, in other words, the topic of the judgments people make about interpersonal associations. "Dominance-submissiveness" refers to the degree to which one person controls, influences, or has status over the other. For example, when a parent directs a child to clean his room, the parent is relying on status and authority to influence the child. "Affiliation-disaffiliation" captures the appreciation, esteem, or solidarity one person has for the other. As an example, consider how a love letter conveys affection and positive regard to the recipient. These two dimensions have been documented through a second-order factor analysis of responses to Burgoon and Hale's (1984) relational message scale (Dillard et al., 1999). Whereas dominance-submissiveness is defined by the corresponding factor of the relational message scale, affiliation is a more nuanced construct that subsumes six factors: similarity, affect, receptivity, equality, composure, and formality.

Beyond knowing the substance of interpersonal relationships, people make judgments about the intensity of their associations. The differences between positive regard and unmitigated devotion, authority, and subjugation, and between mild dislike and outright hatred are nontrivial distinctions within interpersonal relationships. RFT positions involvement as a third dimension of relational judgments that addresses the degree of coordination, engagement, and immediacy present in the interaction (see also Andersen & Andersen, 2005; Cegala, Savage, Brunner, & Conrad, 1982). Importantly, involvement is conceptualized as a unipolar construct that has no relational content. Rather, judgments of intensity can inform inferences about either dominance-submissiveness or affiliation-disaffiliation.

Consider interactions you might observe between two couples at a restaurant. As you glance at one pair, you see that they are maintaining direct eye contact, gesturing actively, and leaning forward. The other couple, in contrast, is talking quietly as they look at their plates. If you learned that both couples were celebrating a wedding anniversary, which pair would you conclude has the more loving relationship? If you learned that the dyads were involved in business meetings, which pair would you think was trying harder to exert influence or control? Odds are you would choose the same couple to answer both questions. In other words, partners that are more involved and active communicate both more liking for each other and more effort to influence or control each other. In this way, involvement is a modifier of the two substantive dimensions and does not have any experiential component on its own (Dillard et al., 1996). The theory implies that involvement can polarize judgments toward either extreme of the substantive dimensions (e.g., intense dislike, passionate love, obsequious submission, or total domination). Dillard and colleagues (1999) found that involvement correlates positively with affiliation and dominance within voluntary American peer relationships, however.

The concept of relational frames integrates the three dimensions of relational messages. "Relational frames" are mental structures that consist of organized knowledge about social relationships. They are similar to relationship schema or mental models of relationships (Baldwin, 1995; Planalp, 1985) in that they contain assumptions about interpersonal associations derived from prior experience. To understand how frames work, consider the classic image depicted in Figure 8.1. If you've seen this image before, you know that it is possible to perceive it as either a young woman with a feather in her hat or an older woman wearing a scarf. By instructing yourself to focus on one or the other you can detect the image you're looking for, but you cannot see both images at once. The way you frame the picture mentally determines what you perceive.

According to RFT, dominance-submissiveness and affiliation-disaffiliation constitute frames that guide the interpretation of interaction cues. As in our example, these mental structures direct what you pay attention to, how you organize information, and what you perceive. Because involvement can convey either dominance or affiliation, it is especially influenced by the relational frame through which it is viewed. Thus, relational frames both focus attention on particular cues and guide the meanings that people attach to more ambiguous indicators of message intensity.

Figure 8.1   The Old Woman and the Young Girl

THE PROCESS OF RELATIONAL JUDGMENTS

By taking a position with regard to the number and substance of relational judgments, RFT mirrors a number of previous efforts to clarify how people organize their social experiences (e.g., Burgoon & Hale, 1984; Kemper, 1973). RFT extends this tradition, however, by specifying the interface among cognitive structures, interaction cues, and relational judgments. Although other theoretical perspectives speak to the information processing patterns set in motion by violated expectations (Burgoon, 1983) or excessive or insufficient arousal (Cappella & Greene, 1982), RFT explains how relational inferences arise from both ordinary and extraordinary interactions.

The process of relational framing commences with the activation of dominance-submissiveness or affiliation-disaffiliation frames, which is influenced by a variety of factors (see Solomon, Dillard, & Anderson, 2002). Most specifically, the content of utterances themselves can clarify whether interactions are about social control ("If you don't follow my rules, I'll demote you") or social closeness ("I'm so glad that I have a friend like you at work"). At a higher level of abstraction, the function of the social episode can focus attention on issues of power (e.g., a performance review) or affiliation (e.g., a birthday greeting). If partners have a history of interactions that focus on dominance or affiliation, that pattern would direct attention within a particular exchange. Likewise, people might have a dispositional tendency to focus on dominance-submissiveness or affiliation-disaffiliation when they interact with others. At the most general level, norms dictated by the social or cultural context direct attention to the dominance-submissiveness or affiliation-disaffiliation features of an interaction.

The information provided by the interaction, present in the context, and brought to bear by the participants, combines to activate the dominance-submissiveness or affiliation-disaffiliation frames. An important assumption of RFT is that the activation levels afforded to each frame are often in competition (Dillard et al., 1996). In other words, the theory maintains that the frames tend to displace each other as lenses for making sense of interaction. To develop this point, Dillard and colleagues argued that the simultaneous operation of both frames would undermine efficient processing. This is not to say that it is impossible for both frames to be activated, but that doing so consumes cognitive capacity and is subjectively uncomfortable. Thus, the cognitive system tilts toward one frame or the other.

Consider the example of reading hastily scrawled text: When you encounter a word you cannot decipher, you can look to surrounding cues to guess what it is. Although you might be able to narrow down the options, you'll have trouble moving on in the text until you make a decision about what the word means. Moreover, maintaining alternative interpretations of the word will compromise your understanding of the text that follows. Because confusion about the meaning of ambiguous involvement cues undermines social functioning, human evolution may have promoted cognitive systems that facilitate sense-making. In other words, the activation of the dominance-submissiveness frame suppresses the affiliation-disaffiliation frame (and vice versa), to facilitate efficient and fluid processing of otherwise ambiguous involvement cues. This proposition is the differential-salience hypothesis.

The forces that influence frame activation, coupled with the tendency toward frame displacement, result in the primary activation of the dominance-submissiveness frame or the affiliation-disaffiliation frame. In turn, the salient relational frame directs attention to features of the interaction that inform relational judgments. When the content of interaction cues aligns with the activated relational frame, relational inferences are straightforward. In the case of more ambiguous involvement cues, the salient relational frame conveys meaning to the messages. Those involvement cues also inform the extremity of the relational judgment, such that involvement can lead to perceptions of either greater dominance or greater affiliation, depending on the salient relational frame. This proposition is the general-intensifier hypothesis.

In summary, relational frames are activated by a variety of contextual factors, ranging from the content of specific messages to the social and cultural norms for the interaction. The differential-salience hypothesis states that the two frames of dominance-submissiveness and affiliation-disaffiliation are in competition with one another; one necessarily displaces the other when individuals make sense of relational messages. In addition, the general-intensifier hypothesis positions involvement as a variable that polarizes salient relational judgments.

Conceptualization of Communication in the Theory

As the previous description of RFT reveals, the theory relies on two important assumptions about the nature of communication. First, RFT takes to heart the long-standing axiom that communication has both content and relational components (Watzlawick, Beavin, & Jackson, 1967). "Content messages" encompass the semantic or denotative meaning of the symbols exchanged; "relational messages" address assumptions about or preferences for the relationship that are implied by symbolic actions. For example, the ways in which your mom might ask for the salt ("Honey, could you please pass the salt," "Give me the salt," "I said I need salt now!") all convey the content of her goal, but the particular form of her request speaks volumes about how she sees your relationship. RFT centralizes the distinction between content and relational messages, and seeks to explain how people decipher the oftentimes ambiguous relationship component of messages.

Second, RFT highlights the polysemic nature of communication—in other words, the way in which communication supports multiple interpretations and multiple meanings. Of course, RFT is not the first perspective to recognize that meaning is subjective. Notably, however, RFT suggests that the same cues can support very different inferences, depending on whether they are viewed through a dominance-submissiveness frame or an affiliation-disaffiliation frame. Whether a loud voice is passionate or patronizing, whether mutual eye contact is intimate or intimidating, and whether a hand on a shoulder is comforting or controlling all depend on message interpretations. As these examples illustrate, the polysemic nature of communication allows people to reach a variety of conclusions from the same cues.

Uses of the Theory

RFT can help us to understand interpersonal communication on many levels, all of which reveal different nuances of the theory. The initial tests of the theory examined how people frame messages from friends based on the strategic goal of the episode. In the study reported in Dillard and colleagues (1996), participants were asked to imagine they were interacting with a same-sex friend who was pursuing either a compliance-gaining goal or an affinity-seeking goal. Results showed that the dominance-submissiveness frame was viewed as more relevant to compliance goals and that the affiliation-disaffiliation frame was judged as more relevant to affinity scenarios. This pattern was replicated in a study that included both same-sex and cross-sex dyads (Solomon et al., 2002).

Tests of the theory have also shown how personal characteristics can influence relational information processing. For example, Solomon and colleagues (2002) demonstrated that a dispositional tendency to be anxious about relationships was positively associated with the relevance of both dominance-submissiveness and affiliation-disaffiliation as people evaluated strategic messages from peers. Although speculative, Solomon and colleagues reasoned that paying attention to both relational dimensions at the same time could compromise a person's ability to draw relational inferences and might, in turn, perpetuate relational anxiety. Relatedly, Knobloch and Solomon (2005) found that relational uncertainty was positively associated with perceptions of the difficulty of an interaction, and that it corresponded with more conservative (i.e., less extreme) relational inferences. An RFT perspective on these findings suggests that relational uncertainty hinders a person's ability to frame an interaction and, in turn, to draw clear relational inferences.

RFT has also been applied to understanding normative and informational influence in groups (Henningsen, Henningsen, Cruz, & Morrill, 2003). Henningsen and colleagues manipulated whether decision-making group members prioritized group harmony or task performance and the level of involvement in the group. Results indicated that involvement intensified judgments of dominance in the task goal condition, and promoted evaluations of affiliation in both the task and group harmony goal conditions. Thus, Henningsen and colleagues' study demonstrates the applicability of RFT beyond interpersonal communication contexts.

In another application, RFT was used to understand the factors that shape people's perceptions of social-sexual messages in the workplace (Solomon, 2006). Social-sexual communication is often ambiguous, and it can lead to judgments of either liking or sexual harassment. Solomon and Williams (1997a, 1997b) have shown that perceptions of sexual harassment are affected by the formality of the context, the sex of the perceiver, the sex of the message initiator, and the explicitness of the message. By applying an RFT perspective, Solomon demonstrated that the effects of situational, personal, and message features are mediated by perceptions of dominance or affiliation.

Finally, Lannutti and Monahan (2002) examined how people interpret scenarios involving sexual escalation and coercion, and they manipulated alcohol consumption to evaluate how intoxication affected the salience of relational frames in these situations. As one might expect, the results indicated that people perceive affiliation-disaffiliation as the relational frame most relevant to consensual sexual episodes, and they tend to see dominance-submissiveness as more relevant to situations that involve both consensual and coercive activities. Moreover, perceptions of involvement were correlated with judgments of affiliation in the consensual scenarios. Involvement contributed to evaluations of both affiliation and dominance in the mixed cue interactions, however, especially when respondents in the study were intoxicated. Although these results are not wholly in line with RFT predictions, they shed light on relational information processing within sexual episodes.

This review of how RFT has been used to understand different aspects of interpersonal communication highlights two more central issues that the theory addresses. First, RFT provides a conceptual tool for representing interpersonal communication as a process. Although communication scholarship privileges the exchange of messages and the coconstruction of meaning as an important window on human behavior, few theoretical frameworks clarify how social norms, individual differences, and contextual features are woven together and intersect message processing. In the work reviewed in this section, the goal of the episode, personal traits, the interaction context, and temporary states have all been linked to the perceived relevance of the dominance-submissiveness and affiliation-disaffiliation frames and corresponding relational judgments. Thus, RFT provides a framework for embracing interpersonal communication as a dynamic and context-embedded social phenomenon.

In addition, the studies previously reviewed illustrate the particular applicability of RFT to ambiguous relational messages. When confronted with an explicit message—perhaps an expression of devotion or a threatening influence message—a person may be challenged to form a response to that message. But when the message itself is ambiguous, this challenge is two-fold. Not only must recipients form a response to the message, but they must first decipher its relational implications. In contexts such as ongoing relationships, problem-solving groups, the workplace, and first dates, misinterpreting cues and responding inappropriately can have serious consequences. Although the framing processes outlined in the theory are generally applicable to any interpersonal communication encounter, RFT is especially useful for understanding ambiguous and difficult communication experiences.

Strengths and Limitations of the Theory

As RFT has developed, both strengths and limitations of the theory and corresponding research have emerged. Perhaps the main strength of the theory is its heuristic value. RFT focuses on basic interpersonal communication processes that can shed light on a variety of interaction situations. Moreover, because the theory highlights the potential for confusing distinct relational judgments, it may be especially useful for understanding socially significant communication problems such as sexual harassment or unwanted sexual escalation. RFT also provides a framework that integrates cultural, personal, relational, and episodic forces that affect interpersonal communication. Thus, this perspective can be the source of many specific hypotheses about the effects of the interaction context on relational information processing within a variety of socially significant communication situations.

The primary limitation of RFT is the lack of clarity about the extent to which frame displacement occurs and under what conditions. Whereas the theory states that the dominance-submissiveness and affiliation-disaffiliation frames are differentially salient, empirical research suggests only a tendency toward frame displacement. These empirical patterns could reflect both theoretical and methodological ambiguities. At the conceptual level, the theory is unclear about how quickly a relevant frame can be activated and then replaced by the alternative frame. In fact, the factors that influence frame activation that are specified within the theory suggest that frames can fluctuate based on utterances, episodes, relationship contexts, interaction participants, or social contexts. Thus, the theory leaves ample room for ambiguity about the duration of an activated relational frame.

Conceptual ambiguity about the activation and deactivation of relational frames is compounded by the reliance on imprecise measures of frame activation in research on the theory to date. In particular, self-reports of frame relevance are, at best, indirect indicators of underlying cognitive processes. Moreover, because people can infer relational judgments from other evaluations they have made (Dillard, Palmer, & Kinney, 1995), they may perceive both frames as relevant to their perceptions of an interaction. At present, then, tests of RFT are limited by the methods used to assess frame activation.

The conceptual and methodological limitations noted thus far suggest the potential for a more far-reaching flaw in the theory. Namely, we wonder whether RFT is sufficiently falsifiable. As long as the details about frame activation and displacement are unspecified, any empirical data could be argued to fit the theory. Likewise, a lack of clarity about how the forces that affect frame activation work in concert invites alternative explanations for empirical observations that are all theoretically viable. Although these loopholes are not fatal flaws for a theory in its infancy, the falsifiability of RFT relies on the resolution of these ambiguities in the future.

As a final critique, we note that research on RFT is limited by the predominant use of hypothetical scenarios to operationalize interpersonal interaction (but see Dillard et al., 1999; Henningsen et al., 2003). On the one hand, constructing scenarios that describe specific and consistent interaction goals has allowed researchers to examine the role of involvement in situations that are clearly about issues of dominance or affiliation. At the same time, those scenarios fail to capture the dynamics and complexities people confront when they must make sense of real-time face-to-face interaction. Thus, support for the theory remains tentative until its claims can be evaluated in more ecologically valid research designs.

Directions for Future Research and Applications

RFT's strengths and limitations point to directions for improving and expanding the theory. First, RFT would benefit from empirical tests that use diverse research designs and tools. For example, response time measures that index cognitive processes could provide more precise tests of frame activation, frame duration, and frame displacement. Likewise, investigations of real-time interaction, either face-to-face or computer mediated, would enhance the external validity of research on RFT. Relatedly, research on RFT needs to expand beyond its current focus on verbal messages to consider how people process nonverbal cues. Because nonverbal indicators of involvement (e.g., eye contact, forward lean, animated gestures) often convey especially ambiguous relational information, the effects of relational frames on interpretations of nonverbal messages may be particularly pronounced.

Another avenue for future research is suggested by evidence that the degree of frame displacement can vary. What are the conditions that make it more or less easy for people to discern the relevance of dominance-submissiveness and affiliation-disaffiliation? Prior research implies that anxiety about relationships (Solomon et al., 2002), intoxication (Lannutti & Monohan, 2002), and relational uncertainty (Knobloch & Solomon, 2005) might make it difficult for people to privilege one frame over the other. And what are the consequences of paying attention to both relational frames simultaneously? RFT was founded on the assumption that frame displacement allows people to process ambiguous social information in a timely fashion, and Solomon and colleagues speculated that people who are unable to commit to one or the other relational frame will have difficulty drawing relational inferences. We see research dedicated to exploring these claims as a priority for future inquiry.

Additional directions for research stem from the applicability of RFT to diverse social contexts. For example, we wonder how relational framing might influence how parents and children make sense of interactions about sensitive topics such as sexual activity or drug and alcohol use. Whereas conversations that are viewed through a dominance-submissiveness frame might invite psychological reactance, the same conversations viewed through an affiliative parent-child interaction might have a dramatically different effect. Similarly, we see value in applying RFT to doctor-patient interaction. Collaborative approaches to doctor-patient interaction are beneficial (Kaplan, Greenfield, & Ware, 1989). Power dynamics can inhibit cooperation and the open exchange of information when doctors and patients discuss medical conditions and treatment options, however. Applying RFT to medical interactions would highlight the forces that privilege the dominance-submissiveness frame, as well as strategies for suppressing this view of communication between doctors and patients.

In this chapter, we have examined RFT's account of the processes by which people draw relational inferences from interpersonal interaction. Because the theory is relatively young and the empirical base limited, further research is needed to explore core assumptions and clarify conceptual ambiguities. At the same time, we are encouraged that the theory has heuristic value as a framework for making sense of communication—and miscommunication—within a variety of socially significant communication contexts.

References

Andersen, P. A., & Andersen, J. F. (2005). Measurements of perceived nonverbal immediacy. In V. Manusov (Ed.), *The sourcebook of nonverbal measures: Going beyond words* (pp. 113–126). Mahwah, NJ: Erlbaum.

Baldwin, M. W. (1995). Relational schemas and cognition in close relationships. *Journal of Social and Personal Relationships, 12,* 547–552.

Bateson, G. (1935). Culture and contact with schismogenesis. *Man, 35,* 178–183.

Bateson, G. (1958). *Naven* (2nd ed.). Stanford, CA: Stanford University Press.

Burgoon, J. K. (1983). Nonverbal violations of expectations. In J. M. Wiemann & R. P. Harrison (Eds.), *Nonverbal interaction* (pp. 77–111). Beverly Hills, CA: Sage.

Burgoon, J. K., & Hale, J. L. (1984). The fundamental topoi of relational communication. *Communication Monographs, 51,* 193–214.

Cappella, J. N., & Greene, J. O. (1982). A discrepancy-arousal explanation of mutual influence in expressive behavior for adult and infant-adult interaction. *Communication Monographs, 49,* 89–114.

Cegala, D. J., Savage, G. T., Brunner, C. C., & Conrad, A. B. (1982). An elaboration of the meaning of interaction involvement: Toward the development of a theoretical concept. *Communication Monographs, 49,* 229–248.

Dillard, J. P., Palmer, M. T., & Kinney, T. (1995). Relational judgments in an influence context. *Human Communication Research, 21,* 331–353.

Dillard, J. P., & Solomon, D. H. (2005). Measuring the relevance of relational frames: A relational framing theory perspective. In V. Manusov (Ed.), *The sourcebook of nonverbal measures: Going beyond words* (pp. 325–334). Mahwah, NJ: Erlbaum.

Dillard, J. P., Solomon, D. H., & Palmer, M. T. (1999). Structuring the concept of relational communication. *Communication Monographs, 66,* 49–65.

Dillard, J. P., Solomon, D. H., & Samp, J. A. (1996). Framing social reality: The relevance of relational judgments. *Communication Research, 23,* 703–723.

Henningsen, M.L.M., Henningsen, D. D., Cruz, M. G., & Morrill, J. (2003). Social influence in groups: A comparative application of relational framing theory and the elaboration likelihood model of persuasion. *Communication Monographs, 70,* 175–197.

Kaplan, S. H., Greenfield, S., & Ware, J. E., Jr. (1989). Assessing the effects of physician-patient interactions on the outcomes of chronic disease. *Medical Care, 27,* S110–27.

Kemper, T. D. (1973). The fundamental dimensions of social relationship: A theoretical statement. *Acta Sociologica, 16,* 41–58.

Knobloch, L. K., & Solomon, D. H. (2005). Relational uncertainty and relational information processing: Questions without answers? *Communication Research, 32,* 349–388.

Lannutti, P. J., & Monahan, J. L. (2002). When the frame paints the picture: Alcohol consumption, relational framing, and sexual communication. *Communication Research, 29,* 390–421.

Leary, T. (1957). *Interpersonal diagnosis of personality.* New York: Ronald Press.

Planalp, S. (1985). Relational schemata: A test of alternative forms of relational knowledge as guides to communication. *Human Communication Research, 1,* 222–239.

Solomon, D. H. (2006). A relational framing perspective on perceptions of social-sexual communication at work. In B. A. LePoire & R. M. Dailey (Eds.), *Applied research in interpersonal communication: Family communication, health communication, and communicating across social boundaries* (pp. 271–298). New York: Peter Lang.

Solomon, D. H., Dillard, J. P., & Anderson, J. W. (2002). Episode type, attachment orientation, and frame salience: Evidence for a theory of relational framing. *Human Communication Research, 28,* 136–152.

Solomon, D. H., & Williams, M. L. (1997a). Perceptions of social-sexual communication at work as sexually harassing. *Management Communication Quarterly, 11,* 147–184.

Solomon, D. H., & Williams, M. L. (1997b). Perceptions of social-sexual communication at work: The effects of message, situation, and observer characteristics on judgments of sexual harassment. *Journal of Applied Communication Research, 25,* 196–216.

Watzlawick, P., Beavin, J. H., & Jackson, D. D. (1967). *Pragmatics of human communication.* New York: W. W. Norton.

White, G. M. (1980). Conceptual universals in language. *American Anthropologist, 82,* 759–781.

9

Uncertainty Management Theories

Three Approaches to a Multifarious Process

Walid A. Afifi and Masaki Matsunaga

The history of research on uncertainty and uncertainty management is long. However, the past decade has seen an explosion in new efforts to understand uncertainty management within interpersonal settings. This chapter reviews three of the most recent efforts to explain this behavior. By limiting the summary to three theories we hope to capture at least the major contribution of each, but we recognize that we are also missing the contribution of other important scholars in this area. To help you see the three theories' similarities and differences, we will discuss how each theory would address the following scenario: "Bill, a 22-year-old college senior, had unprotected sexual intercourse with an acquaintance over spring break. For a week since that encounter, he has regretted the decision and has developed some uncertainty about whether he now has an STD. He hasn't seen any physical symptoms, but also knows that such symptoms sometimes do not appear for months after infection." On to the theories . . .

Problematic Integration Theory:
Purpose and Meta-theoretical Assumptions

Austin Babrow developed Problematic Integration Theory (PIT; Babrow, 1992, 2001) because of dissatisfaction with existing communication frameworks' understanding of how people deal with uncertain situations and what role communication plays in this process. PIT assumes that individuals form both cognitive and emotional thoughts as they experience uncertainty and that those thoughts are integrated in complex ways. It mostly uses existing social-scientific theories to form its explanations, but extends them by highlighting factors that help predict the complexities of uncertainty and explain how these perceptions emerge in a given situation. In this sense, PIT originally shared assumptions with post-positivistic approaches. Not long after its inception, though, Babrow recognized ways in which the interpretive paradigm contributed in important ways to the theory (see Babrow, 1995), and the theory has increasingly morphed into an interpretive framework (see Babrow, Kline, & Rawlins, 2005). Along this line, Babrow (2001, p. 559) stressed the need for the theory to consider "lay epistemology" and account for "what it means to know." The theory's meta-theoretical journey has even included forays into the critical perspective (for review, see Babrow, 2007). So, what meta-theoretical box holds PIT? Babrow himself (personal communication, June 16, 2006) perhaps best summarized the theory's evolution this way: "The theory is in motion, as are all living things."

Main Features of the Theory

PIT "has ties to 'warm' psychological models" (Babrow, 1995, p. 296) because it accounts for not only reason-based, cold cognitive mechanisms, but also emotion-based, hot dynamics of perceptions. PIT argues that individuals form two psychological orientations: probabilistic (the cold component) and evaluative (the hot component). "Probabilistic orientation" refers to one's belief or expectation about what the world is and will be, whereas "evaluative orientation" represents an idea about what the world should be and whether the world is good or bad (Babrow, 2001).

The "integration" part of the theory's name comes from the idea that those probabilities and values are often integrated or intertwined (Babrow, 1995). The "problematic" label reflects the idea that such integrations are sometimes difficult. If someone is uncertain, but is also certain that a search for information will bring about positive news, the management of uncertainty is relatively unproblematic. It is rarely the case, however, that such situations arise. Instead, there is often ambiguity about the outcome of an information search: there is an expected outcome that is unwanted, or there are other difficulties that make the decision about how to respond to uncertainty difficult. The two general factors that determine the difficulty of integration are the probability-value configuration and the centrality or importance of the issue. In other words, integration is difficult to the extent that (a) you do not really know how likely an outcome will be, (b) there are both positive and negative values attached to the outcome, (c) expectations about the outcome differ from what is desired—all aspects associated with the configuration of probabilities and values—and (d) the given issue is important.

Conceptualization of Communication in the Theory

PIT considers communication as a medium, source, and resource for uncertainty. First, communication is deemed as a medium of problematic integration (PI), meaning that individuals "create, shape, clarify, obscure, challenge, and transform probabilistic and evaluative orientations" through interactions with others (Babrow, 2001, p. 555). Second, communication serves as a source of PI. The mere act of communicating brings with it probabilistic and evaluative orientations related to that action. Babrow (2007), for example, noted that bearers of bad news struggle with a host of uncertainties related to the disclosure, from questioning what would serve as the best strategy for disclosure to assessing the various reactions that each might elicit. Finally, communication provides a resource in that it helps cope with uncertainty. When in uncertain situations, people often turn to others in hopes of managing the problem of managing the uncertainty. Similarly, when others are facing a problem, we engage in various communicative acts (e.g., advise, encourage, warn) in an attempt to provide assistance and alleviate the problem.

Uses of the Theory

PIT has been used in a wide variety of contexts. For example, Hines, Babrow, Badzek, and Moss (1997) applied PIT to the end-of-life (EOL) decision-making process. They found that the current practice often focuses on issues that are least likely to result in PI, indicating the potential of the theory to help enhance the EOL quality. For example, Hines and colleagues found that patients desire more encouragement and coping advice (to address emotional or evaluative concerns), whereas nurses emphasize the need for patients to be fully informed and alert to the consequences of treatment (to address probabilistic uncertainty). In another context, McPhee and Zaug (2001) presented an application of PIT to understand patterns of communication among employees of an organization. They argued that changes in organizational contexts likely beget intended or unintended chains of problematic integration among group members.

PIT would address the scenario presented at the top of the chapter this way: Bill's assessment of the possibility of having an STD (probabilistic orientation) would likely make Bill anxious (evaluative orientation). Seeing no symptoms, however, he might eventually feel less worried and more optimistic, which, in turn, would change the initially conceived likelihood of having an STD (probabilistic orientation), and so on. So, what should he do? Should he see a physician now, or should he wait until any symptom arises? Of course, the action under consideration (e.g., seeing a physician) itself is a target for uncertainty and both probabilistic and evaluative thoughts. For example, Bill might wonder if anybody will see him go to a hospital (probabilistic orientation—how likely is that to happen?) and fear the embarrassment likely to follow (evaluative orientation—how costly is that embarrassment factor?). As a result, he would again find it difficult to integrate thoughts and emotions and have trouble deciding what to do. So, there is multiple layering of uncertainty concerns, but back to the specific issue of the possibility of an STD. How to manage the uncertainty in this scenario? PIT argues that we often turn to others in hopes of managing our uncertainty. However, PIT also notes that communicative acts are often a source of additional uncertainties. So, Bill's decision to talk to others is, by no means, a guarantee of solving the uncertainty dilemma, but is only a context in which his problematic integrations play out. In the end, PIT offers a relatively detailed description of what Bill might do and why he might do it, but is unwilling to pin down the precise strategy in which he would engage and its likely consequence.

Strengths and Limitations of the Theory

The strength of PIT is its ability to capture the nuanced dynamics of uncertainty experience and communication. It not only allows researchers to see different aspects of cognitive and emotional experiences of uncertainty but also illuminates how those thoughts are integrated, under what circumstance the integration is likely to be problematic, and how individuals live perceived PIs through communication (Babrow, 2001; Hines, Babrow, Badzek, & Moss, 2001).

On the other hand, the capability of PIT to incorporate the subjective psychological experiences poses a limitation because, presumably, different individuals with different historical and cultural backgrounds have different probabilistic and evaluative orientations (see Babrow, 2001). As Babrow himself noted, some cultures are rife with "habitual uncertainty" (p. 566) while others are relatively stable and lack uncertainty. Thus, the predictive power of PIT is limited by what Babrow considered inherent limitations of social, situational, and cultural factors that shape our experience of uncertainty. Besides this general critique about predictive precision, Bradac (2001) asked whether the relationship between probabilistic and evaluative thoughts is "apparent in the everyday subjective experiences of persons who are not technical theorists?" (p. 463). So, one question is whether we are really that cognitive in our assessment of likely outcomes and their values. That critique, as you will see, is one that could be brought against the third theory discussed in this chapter, as well.

Directions for Future Research and Applications

PIT could be applied to help us understand several issues. First, its recognition of the social construction of uncertainty and its meanings lends itself very well to studying differences in the management of uncertainty across the globe. We need to know more about the ways in which cultures differ in their weighing and integrating of probabilistic and evaluative orientations—something of which we know relatively little. Not surprisingly, the little that we do know on this front comes from scholars who have applied PIT (e.g., Mookerjee & Babrow, 2002). Second, the theory's recognition of the multifaceted ways in which various uncertainties ebb and flow make it ideal to help scholars better understand the connection between uncertainty in one area (e.g., your health) and uncertainty in another (e.g., your relationship's future). Finally, PIT's periodic application to domains outside health communication (for review, see Babrow, 2007) offers promise for its future use in distinct areas of study. One such area is relational communication. Within that area of study, recent investigations into obsessive relational intrusions (e.g., stalking) suggest that PIT may provide a fruitful framework through which to understand that behavior (see Cupach & Spitzberg, 2004). Stalkers, for example, may have problems in integrating their probabilistic orientations (the perception that achieving an intimate relationship with the target is unlikely) and evaluative orientations (the anger caused by that perception). Understanding stalking from that perspective may lend insight into the decisions they make and how they might be changed.

Uncertainty Management Theory: Purpose and Meta-theoretical Assumptions

Dale Brashers followed on the heels of PIT with the development of Uncertainty Management Theory (UMT; Brashers, 2001a; Brashers, Neidig, Cardillo, Dobbs, Russell, & Haas, 1999). As a graduate student at the University of Arizona, Brashers first became disenchanted with the way that uncertainty was discussed in much of the research literature. Like Babrow, he saw the experience of uncertainty to be much more complex than previous models would lead us to believe. His interest in health communication led him to work in nursing by Merle Mishel (for a recent summary of Mishel's work, see Mishel &

Clayton, 2003) that brought the spotlight on uncertainty during illness and revealed cases where patients sometimes preferred uncertainty to certainty about their illness. Mishel's research with HIV patients added to his conviction that the current state of knowledge about our experience of uncertainty was incomplete (Brashers, Neidig, Haas, Dobbs, Cardillo, & Russell, 2000) and led to his development of UMT. The theory includes aspects that reflect the assumptions of interpretive paradigms, but, as a whole, most closely aligns with post-positivistic positions (Brashers, personal communication, June 16, 2006). The theory hopes to systematically predict individuals' experience of uncertainty and related communication decisions, but shares the intepretivists' understanding of meanings (in this case, the meaning of uncertainty) as a situationally constructed phenomenon (see Brashers, Goldsmith, & Hsieh, 2002).

Main Features of the Theory

UMT's primary contribution to the landscape of uncertainty theories is its emphasis on the different ways that people respond (both psychologically and communicatively) to uncertainty. Although the notions can be applied across contexts, the theory's clear emphasis is on health decisions. The theory emphasizes three features: (a) the meaning and experience of uncertainty, (b) the role of emotion in our response to uncertainty, and (c) the various communicative and psychological strategies for managing uncertainty.

UMT makes an important distinction between information and uncertainty. While most earlier theories of uncertainty married the two concepts (i.e., more information equals less uncertainty), Brashers noted that the two should be separated. As he writes, "I may have a great deal of information about a topic . . . yet I still may feel uncertain" (Brashers, 2001a, p. 478). Consistent with that separation, the theory defines uncertainty as existing "when people feel insecure in their own state of knowledge or the state of knowledge in general about a topic" (p. 478). Such an insecurity may occur regardless of the actual level of information that someone has on the topic. Yet, perhaps the most important statement of UMT is that we need to "abandon the assumption that uncertainty will produce anxiety" (p. 477). Central to Brashers's work is the effort to make us realize that uncertainty causes an array of emotions wider than simply anxiety.

Brashers's work has centered on the experience of illness for HIV patients. That research has been directly responsible for his understanding of the emotions that people feel related to uncertainty. Indeed, up to the mid-1990s or so, certainty that one had HIV was essentially certainty that one would die a gruesome death. In contrast, keeping some uncertainty about that HIV-positive prognosis meant continued hope. Given the role that positive psychology plays in maintaining our well-being, such hope undoubtedly improved immunity to the disease and served to prolong life, even if for a short period. In other words, UMT emphasizes that we must shift our understanding about uncertainty if we are going to understand how people deal with it. If we continued to think of uncertainty as always being an anxiety-producing experience, we would never have understood the responses to uncertainty that we see among HIV patients. Brashers (2001b) argued that negative emotional responses to uncertainty occur when uncertainty is seen as a dangerous state (i.e., not knowing could lead to harm), positive emotional reactions result from a sense that uncertainty is a preferred state (i.e., not knowing is better than knowing that harm is inevitable), and neutral emotional responses can occur when the uncertainty about the issue is not particularly relevant or important to the person (i.e., it does not matter whether or not I know more about this issue). He also argued that uncertainty can sometimes cause both positive and negative emotions simultaneously (e.g., when cliff diving). This emphasis on the range of emotional responses to uncertainty necessitates a shift from thinking about the ways in which we seek to reduce uncertainty (the predominant way of thinking until Babrow's and Brashers's models) to thinking about the ways we manage uncertainty.

Conceptualization of Communication in the Theory

While seeking information was previously considered to be the best way to reduce uncertainty, UMT's awareness of the different reactions to uncertainty also opens the door to look more closely at the ways we communicate to increase, decrease, or maintain uncertainty (Brashers et al., 2000). Patients who want to maintain hope about their illness may look for a doctor who challenges the earlier diagnosis and offers them uncertainty about whether they have that illness and, as a result, gives them hope. Another response in the face of uncertainty might be simple avoidance. Think about the times that parents "turn a blind eye" to the possibility that their child is doing drugs. These parents' reaction is partly due to preferring uncertainty over knowing that their child is in trouble. We also know that people often avoid getting tested for an illness, whether it is an STD, cancer, or something else, because they would prefer to not know than find out they have something they consider to be devastating. So both avoidance of information and the search for information serve uncertainty management purposes.

Besides direct information seeking or avoidance, though, Brashers (2001a) noted three other ways that people manage their uncertainty levels. First, those who experience a chronic illness or who otherwise live with consistently high uncertainty states often simply learn to adapt to chronic uncertainty. For example, Brashers and his colleagues (1999) found that people living with HIV often focused on short-term plans and goals, which offered more opportunity for certainty, than on the longer-range, more uncertainty-producing, goals. Second, people often rely on the social support of others to help manage their uncertainty. It is through the positive outlook of others that we might regain hope in times of despair, or through the actions of others that we find relief from high uncertainty. Finally, Brashers noted that we manage uncertainty management. That process works in two ways: First, we manage our uncertainty management by balancing our needs for certainty in one domain with the desire for uncertainty in another domain. Second, we do so by becoming skilled at knowing what information to trust and what information to ignore as we manage our level of uncertainty.

Uses of the Theory

Given Brashers's interest in interpersonal uncertainty management within health settings, it is not surprising that UMT has been exclusively tested within that context. In fact, more specifically, the theory has been primarily used to understand HIV patients' management of the uncertainty that comes with their diagnosis (for applications to a broader patient population, see Brashers, Hsieh, Neidig, & Reynolds, 2006; Barbour, Rintamaki, Ramsey, & Brasher, 2005).

The theory would address this chapter's scenario this way: Bill's wavering about whether to get tested may partly reflect a belief that the cost of reducing his uncertainty is greater than the benefit of doing so. In other words, given his lack of symptoms, Bill may prefer to manage his uncertainty by avoiding information (and maintaining his elevated uncertainty levels) than by seeking it. Of course that decision comes at potentially serious costs to well-being—untreated STDs can be much more serious than treated ones, and symptoms often never appear and are not easily visible for certain STDs. UMT would likely point to this case as a classic example where uncertainty is not met with efforts to reduce it. Instead, Bill may manage his uncertainty in other ways.

Strengths and Limitations of the Theory

UMT has improved our knowledge of individuals' reactions to uncertainty in important ways. Its greatest strength is that, on the heels of Babrow's work, it has further broadened our understanding of the ways in which people respond to health-related uncertainty. Its limitation is more about its infancy as a theory than any glaring weakness. If one approaches the theory from a primarily post-positivistic perspective, then a general limitation may be its relative lack of precision about the process. For example, it seems insufficiently specific about when or why uncertainty should be experienced as hope (and thereby considered comforting) and when or why it should be experienced as threat (and thereby considered something to be reduced). In other words, the theory seems unable to explain when and why we will sometimes experience uncertainty as a positive emotion. The earlier theories of uncertainty have noted that prolonged uncertainty is, by definition, threatening. For example, not knowing about a threat to one's life would be evolutionarily harmful because of one's inability to defend against that threat. When and why would more uncertainty be evolutionarily beneficial?

Another area of possible imprecision is in the factors that might predict individuals' decisions to avoid versus seek information. UMT makes us aware that people respond to uncertainty differently, but when might someone choose to avoid information as a strategy to maintain hope (i.e., maintain or increase uncertainty) and when might someone choose to seek information with that goal in mind? Currently the theory is unable to offer guidance on that question. We know that we have a choice of uncertainty management strategies, but we do not know much about when and why we choose one strategy over another.

Of course, these critiques about predictive imprecision assume a post-positivistic perspective. If a person adopts a more interpretive approach, then such predictive precision would be impossible and critiquing the theory for absence of such precision would be foolish. Given that Brashers has sometimes straddled the post-positivistic–interpretive fence, it may not be fair to him or the theory to critique it for maintaining some ambiguity in what he would likely see as a highly complex, flowing, and ambiguous process (uncertainty management).

Directions for Future Research and Applications

Given the theory's infancy, there are many ways it could continue to grow. First, applying the theory to illnesses beyond life-threatening ones such as HIV might illuminate assumptions that Brashers made and help clarify and extend the theory's framework. Second, expanding further on the uncertainty management strategies would help explain when and why individuals choose one uncertainty-management route over another (see Barbour et al., 2005, for efforts on this front). Third, Brashers consistently addressed the role of the information provider in development of the theory (e.g., referencing support from friends as an uncertainty management strategy; recognizing the role of the physician in patients' uncertainty management efforts). Nevertheless, the theory might benefit from more direct attention to the role of the information provider in the uncertainty management process. Finally, like PIT, it is well suited to help account for uncertainty management decisions outside of health contexts. For example, it seems perfectly capable of lending insight into the uncertainty management strategies that parents use when coping with uncertainties about their adolescents' risky behavior, or into the strategies that employees use to cope with uncertainty about their job security, or into myriad other situations in which uncertainty is sometimes preferable to complete information.

Theory of Motivated Information Management: Purpose and Meta-theoretical Assumptions

The latest effort to explain uncertainty management behavior in interpersonal settings is Walid Afifi's work on the Theory of Motivated Information Management (TMIM; Afifi & Weiner, 2004). An office mate of Brashers's during graduate school, Afifi borrowed extensively from both UMT and PIT's frameworks, but developed TMIM to increase precision in our understanding of uncertainty management decisions, to address the failure of past models to include efficacy perceptions, and to more closely examine the role of the information provider in the uncertainty management process. The theory is postpositivistic in orientation.

Afifi and Weiner (2004) expressly noted that the theory is limited to understanding uncertainty management within interpersonal encounters and only applies to situations in which individuals are motivated to manage their uncertainty. In other words, the theory relates only to important issues that motivate uncertainty management action. As such, the sort of instances that Brashers identified as emotionally neutral uncertainty experiences are not addressed in the theory, and cases in which information is accidentally discovered (without any effort to seek it) are also not accounted for in the theory's framework.

Main Features of the Theory

TMIM envisions the uncertainty management process as a three-phased process that consistently repeats itself. The first phase is called the interpretation phase. That phase starts with the person noticing a difference between the amount of uncertainty the person has and the amount that the person wants. That difference is labeled "uncertainty discrepancy" and is what starts the process of uncertainty management. Any difference between the uncertainty one has and the amount one wants (whether more or less) is said to initiate efforts to manage that discrepancy. In that way, TMIM shares

Babrow's and Brashers's ideas that people sometimes want more uncertainty than they have, but Afifi identified an equilibrium between haves and wants as the engine that starts the process. Someone might have very high uncertainty, but be comfortable with that level. In that case, the person has no discrepancy and TMIM would not apply. The next claim of the theory is that the discrepancy causes anxiety. It is important to note that the theory does not argue that uncertainty causes anxiety: both Babrow and Brashers showed that it sometimes does not. Instead, that difference between wants and needs is anxiety producing. That anxiety pushes people into the second phase of the process, the evaluation phase.

The evaluation phase is where people think about the possible outcomes of an information search (labeled "outcome expectancy") and whether they have the ability to gather the information and cope with it (labeled "efficacy"). Once the anxiety is felt, TMIM proposes that people think about what a search for information would produce. They consider the pluses and minuses of searching for information. For example, a benefit from visiting a doctor could be that the person receives a clean bill of health, but a cost could be a discovered illness. Other costs come from the mere act of searching for information. A cost of meeting with the boss about your performance may be that others around the office gossip about the meeting. TMIM argues that people consider all sorts of costs and rewards, both about the outcome of the search for information (what will be revealed) and about the process of information seeking itself. Once the costs and benefits are considered, TMIM argues that people then decide whether they have the ability to both gather the information and cope with it once they have it. This process is still part of the evaluation phase and is what scholars call efficacy assessment. TMIM discusses three types of efficacy: communication efficacy, target efficacy, and coping efficacy. Communication efficacy involves a determination by the person about whether or not the person has the skill to seek information about the issue at hand. For example, some people avoid seeking information from their boss about an issue because they know that they freeze in those situation (i.e., they do not have the skill to talk to their boss about the issue). Target efficacy is an assessment about whether the target of the information search (i.e., the person that the person is considering going to for the information) actually has the information and would be willing to share it. Parents might not ask their child about a grade in a course because they think that their child either does not have the information yet or would not be honest about it even if their child had the information. Finally, coping efficacy reflects a determination about whether a person could cope with the information she or he expects to get. People sometimes avoid asking their partner if they are cheating because they do not feel that they have the emotional resources or friendship support to psychologically cope with such a discovery. TMIM argues that all three of these assessments go into the strategy that individuals ultimately use to manage their uncertainty discrepancy. The theory predicts that people are increasingly less likely to seek information when they expect negative outcomes and even less likely when they feel that they do not have the ability to gather or cope with those expected outcomes.

Conceptualization of Communication in the Theory

The third and final phase, according to TMIM, is the decision phase—where the various uncertainty management strategies are housed. In other words, once people pass through the interpretation and evaluation phases, they arrive at a decision about what to do. That decision could involve direct information seeking (asking the person directly), indirect information seeking (beating around the bush with the person or asking a mutual friend), active avoidance (going out of one's way to avoid any information on the topic), or passive avoidance (not doing much either way; not seeking information but not actively avoiding it, either). This decision then goes back around to influence the amount of uncertainty discrepancy, at which point the process may start over.

As noted earlier, one of the key features of TMIM is explicit recognition of the information provider in the uncertainty management process. The theory argues that the provider goes through a similar process, though limited to the evaluation and decision phases. Specifically, once asked a question by the information seeker, the provider makes a judgment about whether she or he has the skills to respond to the information request (communication efficacy), has the ability to cope with the result that comes from providing the information sought (coping efficacy), and believes that the information seeker is able and willing to manage the information given (target efficacy).

Afifi and Weiner (2004) saw this process as extremely fluid, such that these assessments are changed during the interaction and immediately affect assessments. For example, a person may approach someone with the intent of seeing whether that person would be interested in going on a date. After the first couple of words, however, the initiator might get feedback that dramatically changes perceptions of the outcomes of that search. As a result, the person might immediately shift strategies and change the communication goal. That sort of example reflects the dance between information seeker and provider that TMIM believes is central to understanding the uncertainty management process.

Although TMIM is in large part a psychological framework, communication is the key ingredient that moves the engine. First, the decisions that are being made during this three-phase process are entirely communication decisions (i.e., to avoid information, to seek information, and the manner of doing each). Second, it is in the interaction itself where uncertainty management decisions are adjusted based on the feedback they receive.

Uses of the Theory

TMIM is in its infancy so there have been only a few tests of its framework. Nevertheless, the theory has met at least partial success in three different published applications—college students' searches for general information from their dating partners (Afifi, Dillow, & Morse, 2004), college students' searches for sexual health information from their sexual partners (Afifi & Weiner, 2006), and community members' searches for organ donation–related information from their family members (Afifi et al., 2006).

When applied to this chapter's scenario, TMIM would predict the following: There is still much to know about Bill before TMIM could offer a prediction. Has Bill's level of uncertainty reached a point where it is more (or less) than he desires? If so, he has an uncertainty discrepancy that will produce anxiety that needs to be reduced. The next question is, in part, similar to PIT's notion of evaluative orientation: TMIM would need to know what costs and benefits Bill sees in getting tested (i.e., he would need to assess his outcome expectancies). Once we know his outcome expectancies, TMIM would need to know his level of efficacy on the three types of interest: (a) Can he bring himself to talk competently and honestly to a physician about this (communication efficacy)? (b) Could he cope with finding out he has an STD (coping efficacy)? (c) Would the physician be able to tell him whether he has an STD at this point? TMIM would predict that the more confidence he has in his abilities to seek the information, the more likely he'll see a physician in this case (i.e., seek information directly).

Strengths and Limitations of the Theory

As with all young theories, there is much yet to be done before we can feel comfortable with all aspects of TMIM. Nevertheless, the theory does offer some advantages over other uncertainty management theories. First, its recognition of efficacy has been shown to be an important way in which it can improve on our understanding of why individuals choose certain uncertainty management strategies over others. Second, its explicit reference to the information provider's decision-making process offers considerable promise. Finally, the theory explicitly notes some scope conditions that limit its applicability (to interpersonal uncertainty management and to important issues). As such, it can focus on unique aspects of those conditions (i.e., interpersonal contexts and important issues) and perhaps more successfully account for behavior in those situations.

The limitations of TMIM are also important to consider. First, like PIT, the theory assumes that people are relatively cognitive. In other words, it suggests that we go through much processing (outcome expectancies and efficacy assessments) before deciding on a course of action. Some scholars have questioned the extent to which this captures how people truly make decisions. Second, the theory lacks adequate recognition of the role played by emotion in the process. While PIT and UMT devote considerable attention to understanding emotion and uncertainty, TMIM barely references it. While Afifi acknowledged that limitation elsewhere (see Afifi & Weiner, 2006), it nevertheless is a gaping hole in the theory that needs to be addressed before the theory can advance.

Directions for Future Research and Applications

Given the broad scope of TMIM and the mixed results from initial tests, there are many avenues for future applications of the theory. Three will be discussed here. First, results from the first three tests of the theory show that outcome expectancies influence the process in some situations more than others and that some efficacy components work better than others. More thinking needs to go into the situations that explain these differences and more effort into studies that explore them. Second, the theory references the role of the information provider but no studies have focused on the provider or predicted the decisions the provider might make. Clearly, more attention needs to be given to the provider's role if the theory is to live up to its promise. Third, currently planned projects hope to apply the framework to help account for parent-child interactions following community-wide trauma (e.g., terrorist events, natural disasters). Success in that realm would continue to extend the study of interpersonal uncertainty into socially meaningful and important domains. In sum, TMIM contributes to our understanding of the uncertainty management process and offers promise as a framework to guide studies in this area, but there is still much to be done before confidence in the theory can be had.

Summary

This chapter has summarized three theories that try to understand the reasons why people manage uncertainty. The central assumption across all three theories is that the experience of, and response to, uncertainty differs across people and situations. As such, these three theories differ from theories of uncertainty that consider uncertainty as an inherently negative state that individuals always (or almost always) seek to reduce. (For example, see Knobloch, Chapter 10, this volume). However, all three theories are also relatively new and all three are still in the process of development and change. There is still much to know about uncertainty and its impacts on us, but we hope that this chapter jogged the reader's mind about some of the issues that we need to consider when thinking about this topic.

References

Afifi, W. A., Dillow, M., & Morse, C. (2004). Seeking information in relational contexts: A test of the theory of motivated information management. *Personal Relationships, 11*, 429–450.

Afifi, W. A., Morgan, S. E., Stephenson, M., Morse, C., Harrison, T., Reichert, T., & Long, S. D. (2006). Examining the decision to talk with family about organ donation: Applying the theory of motivated information management. *Communication Monographs, 73*, 188–215.

Afifi, W. A. & Weiner, J. L. (2004). Toward a theory of motivated information management. *Communication Theory, 14*, 167–190.

Afifi, W. A., & Weiner, J. L. (2006). Seeking information about sexual health: Applying the theory of motivated information management. *Human Communication Research, 32*, 35–57.

Babrow, A. S. (1992). Communication and problematic integration: Understanding diverging probability and value, ambiguity, ambivalence, and impossibility. *Communication Theory, 2*, 95–130.

Babrow, A. S. (1995). Communication and problematic integration: Milan Kundera's "Lost Letters" in *The Book of Laughter and Forgetting. Communication Monographs, 62*, 283–300.

Babrow, A. S. (2001). Uncertainty, value, communication, and problematic integration. *Journal of Communication, 51*, 553–573.

Babrow, A. S. (2007). Problematic integration theory. In B. B. Whaley & W. Samter (Eds.), *Explaining communication: Contemporary theories and exemplars* (pp. 181–200). Mahwah, NJ: Erlbaum.

Babrow, A. S., Kline, K. N., & Rawlins, W. K. (2005). Narrating problems and problematizing narratives: Linking problematic integration and narrative theory in telling stories about our health. In L. M. Harter, P. M. Japp, & C. M. Beck (Eds.), *Constructing our health: The implications of narrative for enacting illness and wellness* (pp. 31–52). Hillsdale, NJ: Erlbaum.

Barbour, J. B., Rintamaki, L. S., Ramsey, J., & Brashers, D. E. (2005, May). *Health information avoidance as uncertainty management.* Paper presented at the annual meeting of the International Communication Association, New York.

Bradac, J. J. (2001). Theory comparison: Uncertainty reduction, problematic integration, uncertainty management, and other curious constructs. *Journal of Communication, 51*, 456–476.

Brashers, D. E. (2001a). Communication and uncertainty management. *Journal of Communication, 51,* 477–497.

Brashers, D. E. (2001b). HIV and uncertainty: Managing treatment decision making. *Focus: A Guide to AIDS Research, 16*(9), 5–6.

Brashers, D. E., Goldsmith, D. J., & Hsieh, E. (2002). Information seeking and avoiding in health contexts. *Human Communication Research, 28,* 258–271.

Brashers, D. E., Hsieh, E., Neidig, J. L., & Reynolds, N. R. (2006). Managing uncertainty about illness: Health care providers as credible authorities. In B. Le Poire & R. M. Dailey (Eds.), *Applied interpersonal communication matters: Family, health, and community relations* (pp. 219–240). New York: Peter Lang.

Brashers, D. E., Neidig, J. L., Cardillo, L. W., Dobbs, L. K., Russell, J. A., & Haas, S. M. (1999). "In an important way, I did die." Uncertainty and revival among persons living with HIV or AIDS. *AIDS Care, 11,* 201–219.

Brashers, D. E., Neidig, J. L., Haas, S. M., Dobbs, L. K., Cardillo, L. W., & Russell, J. A. (2000). Communication in the management of uncertainty: The case of persons living with HIV or AIDS. *Communication Monographs, 67,* 63–84.

Cupach, W. R., & Spitzberg, B. H. (2004). *The dark side of relationship pursuit: From attraction to obsession and stalking.* Mahwah, NJ: Erlbaum.

Hines, S. C., Babrow, A. S., Badzek, L., & Moss, A. H. (1997). Communication and problematic integration in end-of-life decisions: Dialysis decisions among the elderly. *Health Communication, 9,* 199–217.

Hines, S. C., Babrow, A. S., Badzek, L., & Moss, A. (2001). From coping with life to coping with death: Problematic integration for the seriously ill elderly. *Health Communication, 13,* 327–342.

McPhee, R. D., & Zaug, P. (2001). Organizational theory, organizational communication, organizational knowledge, and problematic integration. *Journal of Communication, 51,* 574–591.

Mishel, M. H., & Clayton, M. F. (2003). Uncertainty in illness theory. In M. J. Smith & P. R. Liehr (Eds.), *Middle range theory for nursing* (pp. 25–48). New York: Springer Publishing.

Mookerjee, D., & Babrow, A. S. (2002, November). *Information-seeking in family planning: what women say about their experiences in West Bengal, India.* Paper presented at the annual meeting of the National Communication Association, New Orleans, LA.

Spitzberg, B. H., & Cupach, W. R. (2001). Paradoxes of pursuit: Toward a relational model of stalking-related phenomena. In J. A. Davis (Ed.), *Stalking crimes and victim protection: Prevention, intervention, threat assessment, and case management* (pp. 97–136). Boca Raton, FL: CRC.

10

Uncertainty Reduction Theory

Communicating Under
Conditions of Ambiguity

Leanne K. Knobloch

E veryday life is infused with uncertainty. We experience uncertainty in the day-to-day experiences of chatting with the person next to us on the bus, keeping an appointment with our doctor, investing our money in the stock market, meeting a new coworker, and dining with friends at the restaurant that just opened downtown. We also grapple with uncertainty when we negotiate more significant events such as switching careers, getting married, moving to a new city, becoming a parent, coping with a serious illness, and retiring from the workforce. Because life is unpredictable, our daily interactions are rife with uncertainty.

Uncertainty Reduction Theory (URT) seeks to explain how we communicate when we are unsure about our surroundings (Berger & Bradac, 1982; Berger & Calabrese, 1975; Berger & Gudykunst, 1991). URT, developed by Charles Berger and his colleagues, sparked the systematic study of communication under conditions of uncertainty. URT was a pioneer in two ways: First, it was one of the first theories to originate in the field of interpersonal communication (rather than in other scholarly disciplines such as psychology or sociology). Second, it paved the way for subsequent generations of theorists to verify, refine, extend, challenge, and even refute its premises (see Afifi & Matsunaga, Chapter 9, this volume; Kramer, 2004; Sunnafrank, 1986). I devote this chapter to explicating URT and its contributions to the field of interpersonal communication.

Purpose and Meta-theoretical Assumptions

In its original form, URT focused on how strangers communicate; the theory was limited to behavior within an initial interaction (Berger & Calabrese, 1975). Almost immediately after the theory's conception, however, scholars began applying it to other contexts. URT has provided a foundation for understanding communication in romantic relationships (Knobloch, in press), intercultural interactions (Gudykunst, 1995), organizational settings (Kramer, 2004), and health domains (Albrecht & Adelman, 1984). More than three decades of theorizing and research have underscored the strong connection between uncertainty and communication.

URT adopts a post-positivistic orientation toward inquiry (Berger & Bradac, 1982; Berger & Calabrese, 1975). The theory highlights uncertainty as a causal force shaping communication behavior, and it advances quantifiable predictions about how people behave when they are uncertain. It works to identify principles of interpersonal communication that generalize across specific episodes.

Main Features of the Theory

URT begins with the premise that people are motivated to reduce uncertainty about their social environment; the theory argues that individuals seek to predict and explain their surroundings. URT draws on information theory (Shannon & Weaver, 1949) to define uncertainty as a function of the number and likelihood of alternatives that may occur (Berger & Bradac, 1982). Uncertainty is high when several outcomes are equally plausible; uncertainty is low when only one outcome is likely. URT identifies two types of uncertainty that arise in dyadic interaction: "Cognitive uncertainty" refers to the doubts people experience about their own beliefs and the beliefs of others. "Behavioral uncertainty" refers to the questions individuals have about their own actions and the actions of others. In sum, uncertainty arises when people lack information about themselves and others.

URT characterizes uncertainty as feeling unsure about interaction (Berger & Bradac, 1982). Whereas ambiguity is an objective state that occurs because messages are only partial or conflicting representations of meaning (Sillars & Vangelisti, 2006), uncertainty is a subjective experience that stems from people's awareness of ambiguity. For example, consider our response when a friend says, "I'll see you soon." The message contains ambiguity about when, where, and how we will spend time with our friend in the future, but we do not experience uncertainty unless we attend to the ambiguity. In other words, "a person who believes himself or herself to be uncertain is uncertain" (Brashers, 2001, p. 478), and a person who believes himself or herself to be certain is certain.

The theory delineates three situational parameters that enhance people's desire to reduce uncertainty (Berger, 1979). One such parameter is deviation: we are curious when an individual violates our expectations. Another is anticipation of future interaction: we are particularly motivated to reduce uncertainty when we expect to interact with someone again. A third situational parameter is control over resources: we feel especially compelled to alleviate uncertainty when an individual determines the rewards and costs we will receive.

URT adopts a post-positivistic structure by proposing axioms—or causal relationships assumed to be true. It then pairs each axiom with every other one to derive theorems—predictions of covariation between variables (Berger & Calabrese, 1975; Berger & Gudykunst, 1991). The axioms emphasize the correspondence between uncertainty and communication:

Axiom 1: Uncertainty is negatively associated with verbal communication.

Axiom 2: Uncertainty is negatively associated with nonverbal affiliative expressiveness.

Axiom 3: Uncertainty is positively associated with information-seeking behavior.

Axiom 4: Uncertainty is negatively associated with the intimacy of communication content.

Axiom 5: Uncertainty is positively associated with reciprocity rate.

Axiom 6: Uncertainty is negatively associated with the degree of similarity between partners.

Axiom 7: Uncertainty is negatively associated with liking.

An eighth axiom was added based on Parks and Adelman's (1983) research documenting a link between uncertainty and the overlap in people's social networks:

Axiom 8: Uncertainty is negatively associated with shared communication networks between partners.

An example may help to illustrate the axioms. Morgan and Chris are strangers when they cross paths at the grocery store. They chat about superficial topics such as the price of cereal (Axiom 4), reciprocate self-disclosures about their beverage preferences (Axiom 5), and ask questions about each other's occupation (Axiom 3). The more they talk, the less uncertainty they experience (Axiom 1), the more they like each other (Axiom 7), and the more they engage in eye contact, head nods, and arm gestures (Axiom 2). Their uncertainty is further reduced when they discover that they both enjoy the local music scene (Axiom 6) and that they have some friends in common (Axiom 8).

Conceptualization of Communication in the Theory

URT identifies two roles of communication within interpersonal situations (Berger & Calabrese, 1975). First, we seek to predict and explain communication. Communication functions in this capacity when we ask ourselves "What should I say next?" or "Why did she do that?" or "What's going on here?" Second, communication provides information to help us predict and explain. Communication operates in this way when we receive answers to questions ("Your explanation really helps clarify things for me"), glean insights from nonverbal cues ("He must not be angry because he's smiling"), and learn information from disclosures ("Wow! I didn't know that you enjoy skydiving"). Hence, URT proposes that communication can be both a cause and an effect of uncertainty.

Because some degree of ambiguity is always present within social interaction, individuals must find ways to produce messages under conditions of uncertainty. Berger and his colleagues (1989) have identified three strategies that people use to cope with uncertainty: (a) seeking information, (b) planning, and (c) hedging. I describe these methods in the subsections that follow.

SEEKING INFORMATION

Consistent with the theory's focus on communication as a vehicle for acquiring knowledge, URT delineates three categories of information-seeking behavior: passive strategies, active strategies, and interactive strategies (Berger & Bradac, 1982; Berger & Kellermann, 1994). Passive strategies involve observing the target person from a distance. One example of a passive strategy is a reactivity search, in which people watch how the target person reacts to others in social situations. A second example of a passive strategy is a disinhibition search, in which individuals observe the target person in an informal setting. An advantage of passive strategies is that they minimize face threats; a disadvantage is that they may not produce the information the observer is most interested in.

Active strategies occur when individuals take action to acquire information but do not actually interact with the target person. One example is asking others about the target person. Although communicating with a third party may generate answers to specific questions, it carries a number of risks. In particular, the third party may (a) notify the target person, (b) lack the desired information, or (c) distort the information provided. Research suggests that individuals recognize these risks and process third-party information with a healthy degree of skepticism (Hewes, Graham, Doelger, & Pavitt, 1985). Another active strategy is environmental structuring, in which people manipulate the situation to glean information about the target person. Active strategies offer more control over information acquisition than passive strategies, but they also require more effort and involve more risk.

Interactive strategies entail communicating with the target person. One interactive strategy is interrogating. Question-asking permits individuals to gain insights and discover similarities, but norms of politeness limit the number and explicitness of questions that are appropriate (Berger & Kellermann, 1983). A second interactive strategy is seeking reciprocated disclosures. To implement this strategy, an individual reveals information and hopes that the target person matches the disclosure. A third option is relaxing the target person: individuals who are at ease may be more likely to disclose information about themselves. Interactive strategies may be the most direct method of reducing uncertainty; on the other hand, they may produce anxiety, embarrassment, discomfort, and awkwardness.

PLANNING

Individuals also cope with uncertainty by planning before and during social interaction (Berger, 1997b). A "plan" is a cognitive representation of the actions a person can deploy to achieve a goal (see Berger, Chapter 7, this volume). To be effective, individuals must plan at an optimal level of complexity: Plans that are too simplistic lack breadth and depth (Berger & Bell, 1988), but plans that are overly complex prevent people from being flexible (Berger, Karol, & Jordan, 1989). When a plan fails to accomplish a goal, individuals tend to modify concrete, low-level aspects of the plan to conserve their cognitive resources (Berger & diBattista, 1993). Individuals are most successful in ambiguous environments when they are able to generate, enact, and modify plans to address the contingencies that may transpire (Berger, 1997a, 1997b).

HEDGING

A third strategy is to hedge against the negative outcomes that could occur when producing messages under conditions of uncertainty (Berger, 1997a, 1997b). Consider asking a boss for a raise. Individuals may frame messages in ways that minimize face threat: they may use humor to soften their request ("I'll bet you're getting ready to double my salary"), or they may redirect their message if they need to backtrack ("You misunderstood. I didn't mean that"). Another option is using ambiguous messages to mask true intent ("What does the budget look like for next year?"). People may use disclaimers to ward off negative reactions ("I don't mean to be pushy, but I'd like to request a raise"). In addition, they may deploy retroactive discounting to mitigate an assertion ("I think I've earned a raise this year. I don't know what you think, though"). Another alternative is to control the floor to gain information while the other person does the talking ("I'm interested in how you make decisions about salary increases. What are all the steps involved?"). These hedging strategies, although diverse, serve the common goal of circumventing embarrassment in ambiguous situations (Berger, 1997b).

Uses of the Theory

The legacy of URT is visible in the diverse literatures to which it has contributed. One body of work has evaluated the tenets of URT within initial interaction (e.g., Kellermann & Reynolds, 1990). A second body of work has used URT to explain initial interaction between people of different cultural groups (e.g., Gudykunst, 1995). A third line of research has jettisoned the initial interaction context in favor of examining uncertainty within established relationships (e.g., Knobloch, in press). The following subsections introduce these programs of research.

UNCERTAINTY IN INITIAL INTERACTION

Some work, following the original scope condition of URT, has investigated conversations between strangers. These findings demonstrate support for some axioms but not others. For example, Gudykunst (1985) found evidence linking uncertainty to verbal communication (Axiom 1), the intimacy of communication content (Axiom 4), and similarity between partners (Axiom 6). Other work has garnered support for Axiom 7, which predicts a negative association between uncertainty and liking (Clatterbuck, 1979; Douglas, 1994; Gudykunst, Yang, & Nishida, 1985). Conversely, some results contradict Axiom 3, which anticipates a positive association between uncertainty and information seeking (Gudykunst, 1985; Kellermann & Reynolds, 1990). These findings led Berger (1987) to concede that URT's original framework possessed "some propositions of dubious validity" (p. 40).

UNCERTAINTY IN CROSS-CULTURAL INTERACTION

A second program of research has evaluated uncertainty in intercultural contexts. In particular, URT was a catalyst for Gudykunst's Anxiety/Uncertainty Management (AUM) Theory (Gudykunst, 1995). AUM proposes that both anxiety (an emotion) and uncertainty (a cognition) arise when an individual interacts with a person from a different cultural group. AUM argues that anxiety and uncertainty, in turn, guide how people communicate. Like URT, AUM adopts a post-positivistic structure by proposing 94 axioms about how individuals communicate in cross-cultural interactions. (See Gudykunst, 1995, for an overview of AUM.)

UNCERTAINTY IN ESTABLISHED RELATIONSHIPS

URT also sparked interest in uncertainty in ongoing relationships. Early findings examined the link between uncertainty and social network involvement within courtship (Parks & Adelman, 1983), the nature of uncertainty-increasing events within friendships and dating relationships (Planalp & Honeycutt, 1985; Planalp, Rutherford, & Honeycutt, 1988), and the issues about which people experience uncertainty within marriage (Turner, 1990). Results provided tantalizing evidence of the salience of uncertainty within established relationships.

These first investigations closely followed URT's conception of uncertainty. Once a critical mass of findings emerged, however, it became clear that the new context required a reformulation of the uncertainty construct. To that end, Knobloch and Solomon (1999) built on Berger and Bradac's (1982) passing observation that "in order for a relationship to continue, it is important that the persons involved in the relationship consistently update their fund of knowledge about themselves, their relational partner and their relationship" (pp. 12–13). Knobloch and Solomon (1999, 2002a) defined "relational uncertainty" as the degree of confidence people have in their perceptions of involvement within interpersonal relationships.

Relational uncertainty stems from self, partner, and relationship sources (Knobloch & Solomon, 1999, 2002a). "Self-uncertainty" entails the questions people have about their own participation in a relationship (e.g., "How certain am I about my view of this relationship?"). "Partner uncertainty" involves the questions individuals experience about their partner's participation in the relationship (e.g., "How certain am I about my partner's view of this relationship?"). "Relationship uncertainty" includes the questions people have about the relationship itself, apart from either self or partner concerns (e.g., "How certain am I about where this relationship is going?"). Whereas self and partner uncertainty refer to questions about individuals, relationship uncertainty exists at a higher level of abstraction because it refers to questions about the dyad as a unit.

An extension of URT to intimate associations implies that relational uncertainty may make relationships more volatile. Research corroborates this assumption. People grappling with relational uncertainty judge irritating partner behavior more negatively (Solomon & Knobloch, 2004), feel more jealousy (Knobloch, Solomon, & Cruz, 2001), report less helpfulness from social network members (Knobloch & Donovan-Kicken, 2006), and appraise unexpected events to be more severe, more negatively valenced, and more emotionally upsetting (Knobloch & Solomon, 2002b). Taken together, these studies suggest that relational uncertainty increases the challenges of relating.

Relational uncertainty may also make communication, in particular, more difficult. Romantic partners experiencing relational uncertainty engage in more topic avoidance (Knobloch & Carpenter-Theune, 2004) and are less likely to confront each other about unexpected events (Knobloch & Solomon, 2002b). Individuals craft less fluent, less affiliative, and less effective date request messages under conditions of relational uncertainty (Knobloch, 2006). Moreover, people grappling with relational uncertainty have trouble gleaning relationship-focused information from conversation (Knobloch & Solomon, 2005). This evidence implies that relational uncertainty may present obstacles to both message production and message processing.

In sum, work on relational uncertainty is consistent with URT's intimation that uncertainty may be an impediment to relating. Some scholars, however, have cautioned against assuming that the effects of relational uncertainty are universally negative. Baxter and Montgomery (1996), working from a dialectical framework, argued that too much certainty or too much uncertainty can be detrimental to close relationships. Similarly, Knobloch and Solomon (2002a) proposed that the process of reducing uncertainty offers people occasions to confirm their loyalty to each other (see also Livingston, 1980). Additional work is needed to determine the conditions under which relational uncertainty is helpful and harmful to intimate associations.

Strengths and Limitations of the Theory

Three decades of work on URT have illuminated both its strengths and weaknesses. One such strength is the centrality of communication within the theory. When Berger and Calabrese (1975) first formulated URT, the fledgling field of interpersonal communication had few theories to call its own. URT was among the first frameworks to focus on dyadic interaction, to foreground communication variables, and to originate in the discipline. Even now, the field of interpersonal communication tends to borrow more ideas than it lends to other scholarly disciplines (Berger, 1991). Not only did URT break new ground by making communication its epicenter, but also ongoing extensions of the theory continue to redress the imbalance of inputs versus outputs within the field of interpersonal communication.

A second strength of URT is its graceful hypodeductive structure. A hallmark of post-positivistic theories is falsifiability: a theory should take a clear stand in its predictions to allow scholars to conduct definitive tests. URT performs well on this criterion because its axioms and theorems are precise, exact, and unequivocal. On the other hand, the falsifiability of URT can also be viewed as a liability. Empirical results that contradict just one theorem call into question the tightly woven web of axioms (Kellermann & Reynolds, 1990). Thus, URT's orderly structure permits rigorous evaluation, but it also opens the door to criticism if the tests do not produce results that are compatible with the theory.

A specific assumption that has generated criticism is URT's premise that uncertainty drives people's communication behavior. Predicted Outcome Value (POV) Theory, Sunnafrank's (1986, 1990) reformulation of URT, argues that communication is motivated by resource acquisition rather than by uncertainty reduction. POV proposes that people's desire to gain rewards—and not their drive to reduce uncertainty—is the causal mechanism shaping their communication behavior. POV posits that individuals engage in uncertainty reduction to forecast whether an acquaintance has the potential to generate rewards. For example, imagine that Joan and John meet for the first time: URT predicts that Joan will ask questions because she wants to dispel uncertainty; POV predicts that Joan will ask questions because she wants to gauge whether a friendship with John may be valuable. Berger (1986) defended URT against this critique by arguing that uncertainty reduction is a prerequisite for estimating predicted outcome values.

A second criticism stems from work demonstrating that people often prefer to maintain (or even cultivate) rather than to reduce uncertainty. Consider these situations: (a) You're hoping that a friendship will blossom into a romantic relationship, but you're reluctant to ask your partner where your relationship is headed. (b) You're uncertain about your new stepfather's role in your family, but you're uncomfortable raising the issue with your mother. (c) You're in line for a promotion at work, but you do not want to ask your boss about it because you do not want to jinx it. (d) You suspect you may have a serious illness, but you're afraid to be diagnosed by a doctor. Individuals experiencing uncertainty in situations like these may refrain from information seeking in romantic associations (Knobloch & Carpenter-Theune, 2004), family relationships (Afifi & Schrodt, 2003), work settings (Kramer, 1999; Teboul, 1995), and health contexts (Brashers, 2001). This work suggests that people's drive to reduce uncertainty may be supplanted by their desire to save face, protect others, evade bad news, and maintain optimism.

Directions for Future Research and Applications

Berger and Calabrese (1975) concluded their seminal piece by issuing a challenge: "Hopefully, subsequent research and reformulation will result in a more general theory of the developmental aspects of interpersonal communication" (p. 110). Scholars have work left to do to fulfill this charge. One task is to expand the understanding of how uncertainty operates in different interpersonal settings. URT offers a conceptualization of uncertainty that is tailored to initial interaction; uncertainty in other contexts may possess unique features. For example, URT emphasizes questions about a partner's personality characteristics as particularly relevant to acquaintance, but questions about the dyad are especially salient within intimate associations (Knobloch & Solomon, 2002a). In health contexts, questions about illness, prognosis, and stigma arise along with questions about social support (Brashers, 2001). In intercultural interactions, anxiety occurs alongside uncertainty (Gudykunst, 1995). As scholars continue to pursue Berger and Calabrese's (1975) aspirations for a comprehensive theory, they must carefully attend to the nuances of uncertainty across domains.

A second task is to more fully illuminate how uncertainty corresponds with message processing. URT is a theory of message production; it considers both communication strategies and features of messages. URT has generated a voluminous literature about how uncertainty coincides with message production, but evidence also suggests that uncertainty predicts message processing (Knobloch & Solomon, 2005). Accordingly, theorizing is needed to explain how uncertainty shapes message processing. A next generation of URT would be well poised to accomplish that task.

References

Afifi, T. D., & Schrodt, P. (2003). Uncertainty and the avoidance of the state of one's family in stepfamilies, post divorce single-parent families, and first-marriage families. *Human Communication Research, 29,* 516–532.

Albrecht, T. L., & Adelman, M. B. (1984). Social support and life stress: New directions for communication research. *Human Communication Research, 11,* 3–32.

Baxter, L. A., & Montgomery, B. M. (1996). *Relating: Dialogues and dialectics.* New York: Guilford.

Berger, C. R. (1979). Beyond initial interaction: Uncertainty, understanding, and the development of interpersonal relationships. In H. Giles & R. St. Clair (Eds.), *Language and social psychology* (pp. 122–144). Oxford, UK: Basil Blackwell.

Berger, C. R. (1986). Uncertain outcome values in predicted relationships: Uncertainty reduction theory then and now. *Human Communication Research, 13,* 34–38.

Berger, C. R. (1987). Communicating under uncertainty. In M. E. Roloff & G. R. Miller (Eds.), *Interpersonal processes* (pp. 39–62). Newbury Park, CA: Sage.

Berger, C. R. (1991). Chautauqua: Why are there so few communication theories? Communication theories and other curios. *Communication Monographs, 58,* 101–113.

Berger, C. R. (1997a). Message production under uncertainty. In G. Philipsen & T. L. Albrecht (Eds.), *Developing communication theories* (pp. 29–55). Albany, NY: SUNY Press.

Berger, C. R. (1997b). Producing messages under uncertainty. In J. O. Greene (Ed.), *Message production: Advances in communication theory* (pp. 221–244). Mahwah, NJ: Erlbaum.

Berger, C. R., & Bell, R. A. (1988). Plans and the initiation of social relationships. *Human Communication Research, 15,* 217–235.

Berger, C. R., & Bradac, J. J. (1982). *Language and social knowledge: Uncertainty in interpersonal relationships.* London: Edward Arnold.

Berger, C. R., & Calabrese, R. J. (1975). Some explorations in initial interaction and beyond: Toward a developmental theory of interpersonal communication. *Human Communication Research, 1,* 99–112.

Berger, C. R., & diBattista, P. (1993). Communication failure and plan adaptation: If at first you don't succeed, say it louder and slower. *Communication Monographs, 60,* 222–238.

Berger, C. R., & Gudykunst, W. B. (1991). Uncertainty and communication. In B. Dervin & M. J. Voight (Eds.), *Progress in communication sciences* (Vol. 10, pp. 21–66). Norwood, NJ: Ablex.

Berger, C. R., Karol, S. H., & Jordan, J. M. (1989). When a lot of knowledge is a dangerous thing: The debilitating effects of plan complexity on verbal fluency. *Human Communication Research, 16,* 91–119.

Berger, C. R., & Kellermann, K. A. (1983). To ask or not to ask: Is that a question? In R. Bostrom (Ed.), *Communication yearbook 7* (pp. 342–368). Newbury Park, CA: Sage.

Berger, C. R., & Kellermann, K. A. (1994). Acquiring social information. In J. A. Daly & J. M. Wiemann (Eds.), *Strategic interpersonal communication* (pp. 1–31). Hillsdale, NJ: Erlbaum.

Brashers, D. E. (2001). Communication and uncertainty management. *Journal of Communication, 51,* 477–497.

Clatterbuck, G. W. (1979). Attributional confidence and uncertainty in initial interaction. *Human Communication Research, 5,* 147–157.

Douglas, W. (1994). The acquaintanceship process: An examination of uncertainty, information seeking, and social attraction during initial conversation. *Communication Research, 21,* 154–176.

Gudykunst, W. B. (1985). The influence of cultural similarity, type of relationship, and self-monitoring on uncertainty reduction processes. *Communication Monographs, 52,* 203–217.

Gudykunst, W. B. (1995). Anxiety/uncertainty management (AUM) theory: Current status. In R. L. Wiseman (Ed.), *Intercultural communication theory* (pp. 8–58). Thousand Oaks, CA: Sage.

Gudykunst, W. B., Yang, S. M., & Nishida, T. (1985). A cross-cultural test of uncertainty reduction theory: Comparisons of acquaintances, friends, and dating relationships in Japan, Korea, and the United States. *Human Communication Research, 11,* 407–454.

Hewes, D. E., Graham, M. L., Doelger, J., & Pavitt, C. (1985). "Second-guessing": Message interpretation in social networks. *Human Communication Research, 11,* 299–334.

Kellermann, K. A., & Reynolds, R. (1990). When ignorance is bliss: The role of motivation to reduce uncertainty in uncertainty reduction theory. *Human Communication Research, 17,* 5–75.

Knobloch, L. K. (2006). Relational uncertainty and message production within courtship: Features and appraisals of date request messages. *Human Communication Research, 32,* 244–273.

Knobloch, L. K. (in press). The dark side of relational uncertainty: Obstacle or opportunity? In B. Spitzberg & W. Cupach (Eds.), *The dark side of interpersonal communication* (2nd ed.). Mahwah, NJ: Erlbaum.

Knobloch, L. K., & Carpenter-Theune, K. E. (2004). Topic avoidance in developing romantic relationships: Associations with intimacy and relational uncertainty. *Communication Research, 31,* 173–205.

Knobloch, L. K., & Donovan-Kicken, E. (2006). Perceived involvement of network members in courtships: A test of the relational turbulence model. *Personal Relationships, 13,* 281–302.

Knobloch, L. K., & Solomon, D. H. (1999). Measuring the sources and content of relational uncertainty. *Communication Studies, 50,* 261–278.

Knobloch, L. K., & Solomon, D. H. (2002a). Information seeking beyond initial interaction: Negotiating relational uncertainty within close relationships. *Human Communication Research, 28,* 243–257.

Knobloch, L. K., & Solomon, D. H. (2002b). Intimacy and the magnitude and experience of episodic relational uncertainty within romantic relationships. *Personal Relationships, 9,* 457–478.

Knobloch, L. K., & Solomon, D. H. (2005). Relational uncertainty and relational information processing: Questions without answers? *Communication Research, 32,* 349–388.

Knobloch, L. K., Solomon, D. H., & Cruz, M. G. (2001). The role of relationship development and attachment in the experience of romantic jealousy. *Personal Relationships, 8,* 205–224.

Kramer, M. W. (1999). Motivation to reduce uncertainty: A reconceptualization of uncertainty reduction theory. *Management Communication Quarterly, 13,* 305–316.

Kramer, M. W. (2004). *Managing uncertainty in organizational communication.* Mahwah, NJ: Erlbaum.

Livingston, K. R. (1980). Love as a process of reducing uncertainty: Cognitive theory. In K. S. Pope (Ed.), *On love and loving* (pp. 133–151). San Francisco: Jossey-Bass.

Parks, M. R., & Adelman, M. B. (1983). Communication networks and the development of romantic relationships: An expansion of uncertainty reduction theory. *Human Communication Research, 10,* 55–79.

Planalp, S., & Honeycutt, J. M. (1985). Events that increase uncertainty in personal relationships. *Human Communication Research, 11,* 593–604.

Planalp, S., Rutherford, D. K., & Honeycutt, J. M. (1988). Events that increase uncertainty in personal relationships II: Replication and extension. *Human Communication Research, 14,* 516–547.

Shannon, C. E., & Weaver, W. (1949). *The mathematical theory of communication.* Champaign, IL: University of Illinois.

Sillars, A. L., & Vangelisti, A. L. (2006). Communication: Basic properties and their relevance to relationship research. In A. L. Vangelisti & D. Perlman (Eds.), *The Cambridge handbook of personal relationships* (pp. 331–352). New York: Cambridge University Press.

Solomon, D. H., & Knobloch, L. K. (2004). A model of relational turbulence: The role of intimacy, relational uncertainty, and interference from partners in appraisals of irritations. *Journal of Social and Personal Relationships, 21,* 795–816.

Sunnafrank, M. (1986). Predicted outcome value during initial interactions: A reformulation of uncertainty reduction theory. *Human Communication Research, 13,* 3–33.

Sunnafrank, M. (1990). Predicted outcome value and uncertainty reduction theories: A test of competing perspectives. *Human Communication Research, 17,* 76–103.

Teboul, J. B. (1995). Determinants of new hire information-seeking during organizational encounter. *Western Journal of Communication, 59,* 305–325.

Turner, L. H. (1990). The relationship between communication and marital uncertainty: Is "her" marriage different from "his" marriage? *Women's Studies in Communication, 13,* 57–83.

PART II

Discourse/Interaction-Centered
Theories of Interpersonal
Communication

T he contributors to this part of the book address theories that hold prominence in understanding interpersonal communication as an interaction
process that unfolds between interlocutors. Theories in Part II are focused on
the content, forms, and functions of messages and the behavioral interaction
patterns between persons. In contrast to the theories in Part I that emphasize
what transpires in individual minds to produce or interpret messages, the
theories in this part take a decidedly more social turn to study communication
as it is enacted between persons. Seven of the chapters reflect homegrown
theories—that is, theories that were developed within the discipline of communication. However, sociology is the discipline of origin for Goffman's Face
Theory and for Conversation Analysis Theory. Sociolinguistics is the originary
discipline for Politeness Theory. In addition, as Koenig Kellas makes evident,
many narrative theories have been developed, only some of which originate
with communication studies scholars.

In contrast to the post-positivistic orientation that prevails in Part I, the
theories in Part II are more eclectic with respect to meta-theoretical inclina-
tions. Three of the chapters—representing Communication Accommodation
Theory, Expectancy Violations Theory and Interaction Adaptation Theory, and
Interpersonal Deception Theory—are straightforward exemplars of the post-
positivistic project. These theories were developed with a goal of predicting
and explaining patterned regularities among key communication variables.

Theorists who developed these theories presume an objective reality whose underlying cause-and-effect patterns can be discovered through scientific observation. A fourth theory is also post-positivistic in nature, although it is quite different from the theories just mentioned: Conversation Analysis Theory. Conversation Analysis Theory is an inductively derived theory designed to describe the features of conversation that enable interactants to construct their own social realities. The theory is radically empirical in nature in its search for universal-like characteristics of enacted talk. The theory focuses on functional explanation, in contrast to the cause-and-effect explanations that characterize the first three theories.

Two of the chapters discuss theories that are best categorized as interpretive: Action-Implicative Discourse Analysis Theory and Speech Codes Theory. These theories privilege understanding from the so-called native's point of view, and appreciate that meaning-making is a highly contextualized affair.

Four of the chapters present theories that are more complicated to categorize. Information Manipulation Theory is post-positivistic in nature, yet it is based on Grice's work on conversation maxims, which many interpretive scholars claim as important to their own work. Goffman's Face Theory has roots in the interpretive tradition, yet it has been used productively by both interpretive and post-positivistic researchers, as Metts and Cupach make evident. Similarly, most narrative theories have roots in interpretive or critical traditions, yet Koenig Kellas usefully calls attention to the value of post-positivistic narrative research. Last, as Goldsmith discusses, Politeness Theory has appealed to both post-positivistic and interpretive traditions.

The theories in this part of the book can be productively mapped in ways other than meta-theoretical orientation. Many of the theories share a common focus on the role of communication in giving us our sense of reality. Several theories adopt a constitutive view, presuming that social reality is constructed through communicative action: they are Action-Implicative Discourse Analysis Theory, Conversation Analysis Theory, Face Theory, several of the narrative theories, and Speech Codes Theory. Politeness Theory presumes that "face" is a socially enacted phenomenon, and the performance of facework holds implications for the meaning of the relationship between parties. The two deception theories—Information Manipulation Theory and Interpersonal Deception Theory—presume that a reality (a truth) exists in an objective sense, but that people's perception of what is true can be manipulated through deceptive communicative practices.

Several of the theories represented in Part II recognize that interpersonal communication is a complicated business, fraught with problems and challenges of one kind or another. Action-Implicative Discourse Analysis focuses most explicitly on the dilemmatic nature of a variety of communication practices. Conversation Analysis Theory focuses more generally on the fundamental problem of how it is that interactants pull off seamless interaction that allows us to take much of our everyday social world for granted. Expectancy Violations Theory examines what happens when a person's expectations are violated, and Interaction Adaptation Theory examines the complexities of how a person responds to such violations in light of other factors. Politeness Theory captures the face-threat implications of speaking directly and efficiently, and why speakers might opt instead for less direct forms of expression. The two deception theories focus on the problem of manipulating information in order to convince someone that a deception is a truth. Both Communication Accommodation Theory and Interaction Adaptation Theory concentrate on the problem of coordination between speakers—whether they respond with similar or different behavioral responses. Narrative theories address the challenge of how narrative coherence is rendered from the less coherent, and more chaotic, experiences of living.

Identity, including face, is the focus of several of the theories in Part II. Communication Accommodation Theory, Face Theory, several narrative theories, Politeness Theory, and Speech Codes Theory address, in different ways, the matter of who we are when we communicate interpersonally. Communication Accommodation Theory emphasizes identity as social group identity—for example, whether we are socially positioned as a member of the older or the younger generation. Speech Codes Theory emphasizes identity as cultural membership—for example, whether we are American or Norwegian. Several narrative theories emphasize how our identities are storied phenomena. Whereas Goffman's Face Theory focuses at a general level on face as a dramatistic performance in which we are always on stage playing a role, Brown and Levinson's Politeness Theory affords a more micro-oriented examination of how interlocutors enact facework on the other's behalf. Although not directly addressing issues of face, Expectancy Violations Theory holds relevance to face threat as a specific form of expectancy violation. Of course, both Action-Implicative Discourse Analysis Theory and Conversation Analysis Theory also implicate issues of identity and face in their commitment to communication as a constitutive enterprise. Identity and face, and their complications, come to be through people's communication actions and choices. Additionally, both of the deception theories implicate indirectly the issue of identity; both address the question of how it is that speakers come across as "truthtellers" rather than "liars." Information Manipulation Theory addresses the message features by which "truth" and "deception" are constructed (usually through hybrid forms that are both truthful and deceptive at once). Interpersonal Deception Theory, by contrast, focuses less on the micro-level details of manipulating basic features of conversation cooperation and more on the interactive factors that affect the implementation and success of a deceptive act.

Three of the theories in Part II remind us that culture is important in interpersonal communication. Communication Accommodation Theory has been examined in diverse cultural contexts and has proven especially useful in addressing intergroup communication encounters. Politeness Theory explicitly notes that not all cultures are alike in the details of facework, despite sharing more abstract principles of facework. Speech Codes Theory is explicitly a theory oriented toward an understanding of how cultures differ in their codes of communication.

Taken as a whole, the contrast between the theories in Parts I and II is somewhat stark. Whereas the theories in Part I are more psychologically and individualistically centered, the theories in Part II have moved beyond the individual to examine interpersonal communication as messages between speakers.

11

Action-Implicative Discourse Analysis Theory

Theorizing Communicative Practices

Karen Tracy

- How does the small talk preceding a company's weekly staff meeting display the group to be both a mainstream American business and an especially health-and-fitness conscious community (Mirivel & Tracy, 2005)?

- What dilemmas do graduate students face as they talk to departmental faculty and other graduate students about their research (Tracy, 1997a)?

- How did the situated beliefs of FBI negotiators at Waco about "good negotiation" differ from what was espoused in negotiation training manuals (Agne, 2003)?

- What meeting strategies did participants (elected officials, citizens) use to manage conflicts related to developing their school district's policy about sexual orientation (Tracy & Ashcraft, 2001)?

- How does cosmetic surgeons' talk manage tensions between selling elective surgeries (such as breast augmentation) and being good, patient-focused physicians? (Mirivel, in press).

The above are examples of questions that action-implicative discourse analysis (AIDA) has addressed. AIDA is an approach to communication study that is a theory-method package. AIDA focuses on a small set of questions related to describing and cultivating interaction in existing communicative practices, whereas a "communicative practice" is one in which talking is central to what people are doing. Communicative practices that AIDA has studied have included physician-patient consultations, school board meetings, law enforcement crisis negotiations, academic brown bag discussions, and routine business meetings. AIDA is also a methodology. It pursues the study of a focal communicative practice by audiotaping or videotaping segments of the inter-action (or accessing existing tapes), making a transcript that captures specifics of how participants talked, and then, in light of other kinds of data about the practice (e.g., observations and field notes, interviews, policy and training manuals), analyzing the discourse to answer one or another of a small set of questions that AIDA investigates. AIDA's name draws attention to its method-ological side. When the theoretical side is highlighted the focus shifts to "grounded practical theory."

Purpose and Meta-theoretical Assumptions

As is true of any category system, the trifold distinction among post-positivistic, interpretive, and critical meta-theoretical orientations oversimplifies the diver-sity among existing theoretical approaches; many theories do not fit neatly into a single category. AIDA, for instance, is a combination of interpretive and crit-ical approaches. To use Flyvbjerg's (2001) invented label, grounded practical theory is a "phronetic" approach to inquiry, melding the goal of constructing a rich understanding of how a practice operates (interpretive) with the goal of aiding a practice's participants in reflecting about how they might act more wisely (critical). In contrast to most critical approaches, however, the principle motivating critique is not that of exposing inequities in power arrangements. Instead, "AIDA draws on the Aristotelian idea of phronesis—good judgment, pru-dence, practical wisdom, sound and thoughtful deliberation, reasonableness— as its key concept" (Tracy, 2005, p. 314).

Grounded practical theory seeks to reconstruct communicative practices at three levels. The first, and the most important, level is that of a practice's prob-lems. From studying the discourse of a practice, grounded practical theory aims to describe the web of problems that participants face in their different roles. The second level of reconstruction—the technical level—specifies the conversational moves that reflect problems and the interactional strategies that participants use to manage them. At the most abstract level—the philosophi-cal level—a practice "can be reconstructed in the form of elaborated normative ideals and overarching principles that provide a rationale for the resolution of problems" (Craig & Tracy, 1995, p. 253). To develop normative ideals, the com-ments of praise and blame that a practice's participants make about specific interactional moments, their "situated ideals," are the building blocks.

A basic assumption of AIDA is that most communicative practices are shaped by interactional dilemmas. In academic discussions, for instance, grad-uate students and faculty members want to appear intelligent but do not want to be seen as self-aggrandized and out to show off (Tracy & Baratz, 1993).

In school boards, the meeting chair wants to move the meeting along so that decisions can be made, but wants to do so in a way that ensures citizens feel they have had a fair chance to be heard (Potter & Hepburn, in press). As a result of the dilemmas that are part of virtually all practices, a normative proposal about how participants ought to act needs to weigh the multiple goods to which a practice is committed. Usefulness for thought and action, rather than accuracy of predicting theorized relationships or showing how power is naturalized in a situation, is the criterion for evaluating grounded practical theory.

Main Features of the Theory

To illustrate how the key theoretical concepts of AIDA—(a) problems/dilemmas, (b) discourse strategies/moves, and (c) situated ideals—are worked out in the study of actual communicative practices, I focus on two rather different practices: police/9-1-1 telephone calls and academic colloquia. For the police calls, I describe the data that provided the practice's grounding, characterize several problems within the practice, and identify a few discourse strategies that were used to manage one of the problems. For academic colloquia, I describe the ideal for good discussion that was developed using participants' situated ideals as the starting point.

POLICE/9-1-1 TELEPHONE CALLS

The focal discourse data for studying citizen calls to 9-1-1 and the police were 650 calls in a major city's police department. Audiotaped copies of calls were downloaded from police archives, a log was made describing features of each call, and then a transcript was made of calls selected for detailed analysis. In addition to the discourse data, the researchers spent 10 months observing in the emergency center, sitting with calltakers and listening to conversations with citizens, attending training workshops, going on police ride-alongs, and studying the center's policy and training manuals. This immersion in a communicative practice, with particular attention given to the transcribing and analysis of discourse, is the first step of an AIDA study. In creating a transcript, discourse analysts seek to capture what was said, including the uhs, ums, and restarts. Depending on a project's purposes, the sound and pacing of talk may also be represented (see Ochs, 1979, for a discussion about transcription decisions). Then the researcher begins analysis, working to identify the interactional problems that faced participants and the discourse strategies they used.

In studying citizen-police exchanges, dilemmas were identified that confronted police calltakers answering calls and the citizens making them. Calltakers, for instance, need to deal with the fact that citizens usually brought a customer-service frame to their requests for help, assuming that all they needed to do was name what they desired and help would be forthcoming (Tracy, 1997b). In reality, police departments have limited resources, necessitating careful screening of requests. Police departments also have concerns about officer safety that lead calltakers to seek information that citizens might believe delays the arrival of desired services. In addition, although the goal of the calltakers is to be as helpful as possible, their ability to accomplish this goal is constrained by institutional requirements not to give legal advice and to manage calls quickly so that they can be available for a next call (Tracy & Agne, 2002).

In initiating calls to the police, citizens, too, face problems. Consider one problem that callers sometimes faced (Tracy & Anderson, 1999):

> When citizens call the police to report a problem with (or caused by) another, they need not only to characterize the problematic action/event, but they must position themselves in relation to the complained-about person. This conversational work of positioning self, and describing the other's actions, is delicate business when the complained-about person is connected to the caller. Different constructions of the other and the problem affect whether callers get the help they are seeking. At the same time, alternate constructions offer different pictures of the other's blameworthiness and self's contribution to the problem. Furthermore, these verbal pictures become actions that others—calltakers, police officers, the complained-about person, and additional people in the caller's web of connections—may interrogate for plausibility and evaluate as signs of a caller's character and moral fairness. (p. 202)

In a nutshell, a person calling the police to report a difficulty caused by someone with whom that person has a relationship is a "problem." On the one hand the caller wants the trouble that the other person has caused resolved; on the other hand, it is generally regarded as inappropriate, unless the trouble is highly serious (e.g., violence), to cause a connected other to be in trouble with the police. How then, did citizens manage this dilemma?

To minimize their closeness to an other without explicitly lying, one strategy that citizens used was to describe the person causing the difficulty using generic terms such as "the man," "someone," and "the gentleman." Of note, while these terms are literally true—all males can be referred to as men, some-ones, or gentlemen—the terms are misleading. When a referred-to person is more closely linked to a speaker, these terms imply the absence of a closer relationship, such as being a friend, ex-boyfriend, or neighbor. Often, as the police call continued and the calltaker pursued particular pieces of information, the fact that "the man" was a family friend became apparent by virtue of the caller having information about the other that did not fit the frame of a stranger or a barely acquainted relationship.

A second strategy citizens used to mask the degree of closeness they had to another was to refer to the troublecauser as "a friend." Call number 167, below, offers an extended example of how a caller used the word "friend" as a relational distancing strategy. Through a variety of discourse specifics, identified in Tracy and Anderson (1999), the caller's term initially implied that the complained-about other was "just a friend" rather than a "boyfriend." As a second calltaker came on the phone to explore whether the police could help the caller retrieve her car, the ambiguity that the caller's use of the term "friend" was trading on became apparent.

(Call 167, 3:30 PM, female calltaker, female caller)

[transcript notations: (a) underline = vocal stress; caps = loud speech; (b) (.) = brief pause of 0.2 sec, and ((pause)) is a longer, untimed pause; (c) brackets = overlapping talk; (d) .hhh = inhalation; number of h's indicates length; (e) colons = prolonged sound]

CT1   Citywest Police?

C   Um, yeah, I need to file a complaint about my car being taken?

CT1   (.) It was stolen?

C   Well .hhhhh a friend borrowed it and h-he never brought it back.

    . . .

C   Well, I didn't loan it, he took it.

CT1   ((pause)) I mean wh- are you saying that, you know did you say to him at a:11, and be ho:nest with me, did you say, yeah go ahead borrow it but bring it right back?

C   Um no, I was in the hospital ((clear throat)) and (.) he was here staying with me, and he (.) took it while I was in the hospital, and then when I got out I couldn't reach him.

CT1   ((pause)) And have you talked to him at all since [he took] the car?

C   [No, no]

CT1   ((pause)) Does he have a history of drinking or drugs?

C   YES.

CT1   Okay hold on a second okay?

C   °Thank you°

    . . .

CT2   Good afternoon auto theft, this is Ellen.

C   Um yeah I don't know what to do ((clearing throat)) A friend of mine uhmm was using my car wh-ile I was in the hospital? And he's been gone now for (.) well it's been, gosh about 36 hours. And I haven't been able to get in touch with hi:m or (.) he doesn't have a local phone number, and I don't know what to do.

CT2   Okay a friend of yours, meaning an acquaintance friend? or a friend [a boyfriend?

C   [He was staying with me

CT2   Pardon?

CT2   A boyfriend?

C   Ye:ah.

CT2   Okay. So it's a boyfriend and he stayed with you for how long?

C   Pardon?

CT2   How long has he stayed with you?

C   About a month.

CT2   Okay, so you're (.) together as a boyfriend then.

C   Yeah.

CT2   Okay well he has access to the ca:r, doesn't he?

C   Well, h-he never did before, because I, uhm always drove, or he drove but this ih-is the first time I wasn't there with him, using the car

CT2   But still you gave him permission to drive the ca:r.

C   Umm, not really. I mean I was in the ho:spital and he used my car and (.) uhmm

CT2   Well do you know why, it comes from you. Y-you let him drive the ca:r when you're together, he drives it sometimes, he drives it sometimes but yet he has t- the permission to be able to drive the car.

        . . . [call continues]

Citizens and calltakers face dilemmas that are affected by their positions in the practice of police/9-1-1 calls. As they confront problems, each party's talk reflects one or more problems, as well as attempts to manage the problems. AIDA is interested in identifying the interactional problems and discourse strategies of existing communicative practices.

ACADEMIC COLLOQUIA

A second practice that AIDA has investigated is that of academic colloquia. Faculty and graduate students face a variety of problems in participating in research paper discussions. These problems include how to present oneself during the oral description of the research project so that the right level of expertise is established. If presenters hedge their experience and expertise too much, they set in motion implications that they are intellectually limited (i.e., not that smart). If, on the other hand, their talk suggests they possess a high level of expertise, they license especially difficult questions and the potential embarrassment of not having good answers (Tracy & Baratz, 1993).

Graduate students and faculty also face dilemmas as they pose questions to presenters (Tracy & Naughton, 1994), because questions imply how knowledgeable, interesting, and sophisticated a questioner sees a presenter to be, as well as how knowledgeable, interesting, and sophisticated the questioner is. Interviews with graduate students and faculty at two universities were used to identify the situated ideal for good intellectual discussion. Rather than a single ideal, two different ideals were identified. The first was constructive criticism and the second was dialectic.

Constructive critics focused on avoiding hostility and creating positive effect. Within the constructive criticism ideal, high-status participants (i.e., faculty) were responsible for dealing with low-status participants (graduate students) in careful, supportive ways. The dialectic ideal, in contrast, emphasized faculty responsibility to create equality and minimize differences of status. For faculty to treat students in markedly different ways was to reify status and hinder the transformation of graduate students from novices into full-fledged colleagues. Interestingly, while faculty and graduate students generally favored one or the other ideal, traces of the other ideal could be found in just about everyone's talk. The upshot of this, I argue, is the need for a dilemmatic ideal for intellectual discussion. Intellectual discussion is a communicative practice in which both discussion and ideas matter, and in which people and their feelings need to be considered. When faculty and graduate students discuss ideas that are personally important to them, their competence and character are implicated. "Unrestrained pursuit of the dialectical ideal may injure people and relationships and may rend the social fabric without which intellectual discussion becomes impossible," but talk that is geared centrally to being supportive can produce a discussion that "will degenerate into therapy and will render unlikely the intellectual growth that constructive criticism can foster" (Tracy, 1997a, p. 144). To do academic colloquia well, participants need a dilemmatic ideal that keeps dialectic and constructive criticism in an ongoing tension with each other.

Conceptualization of Communication in the Theory

There are many ways to frame communication. A recent reader (Shepherd, St. John, & Striphas, 2006) identified 27 different theoretical conceptualizations. Communication, for instance, can be understood as a process of social influence (Boster, 2006), as centrally about rituals (Rothenbuhler, 2006), or, as is key with AIDA, it can be constructed as a practice. To conceive of communication as a practice is to recognize it as a connected, meaningful set of activities for people in particular cultural communities. A practice may be described at different levels of generality (e.g., emergency calltaking versus questioning upset callers). Of note, practices are surrounded by larger discourses that include talk about desirable and problematic ways to participate in specific practices. It is this talk about practices that occurs among people as they go about their ordinary life activities that makes communicative practices socially significant: What should be standards of good conduct? What is or is not ethical? Does using a particular conversational technique have this positive or that negative effect? This everyday meta-discourse surrounding practices is a large part of how conduct in any particular practice is actually regulated.

In drawing on "practice" as the central concept, theorizing communication is taken to be a normative enterprise rather than an explanatory scientific one. As Craig (2006) puts it, "A theory of a practice provides a particular way of *interpreting* [emphasis in original] practical knowledge, a way of focusing attention on important details of a situation and weaving them into a web of concepts that can give experience a new layer of meaning, reveal previously unnoticed connections, and suggest new lines of action" (p. 43). To conceptualize communication as a practice is to work to develop communication theories that are useful for action. "Useful," however, is not a synonym for expedient and effective action. Rather, it is the morally serious judgments about action and consequences that pragmatist philosopher John Dewey (1910) advocated.

Uses of the Theory

One way of defining interpersonal communication is to see it as people interacting, whether they are in institutional settings or in intimate relationships. When interpersonal communication is defined broadly, AIDA is very much an interpersonal communication theory. With its interest in the problems, conversational strategies, and situated ideals of talk-focused, face-to-face or telephone exchanges, it is all about understanding interaction between people.

As a method as well as a theory, AIDA provides a framework for future studies of interpersonal interaction. With its questions about communicative problems, conversational strategies, and normative ideals of conduct, AIDA is a useful guide for observation, enabling study of interpersonal practices that have been overlooked and ignored.

A second way of conceptualizing interpersonal communication is to see it as a community of scholars who identify themselves as interpersonal communication folks. When interpersonal communication is thought about this way, AIDA's differences with other theoretical approaches (particularly its hybrid critical-interpretive epistemology and its language and interaction grounding) make apparent the diversity of theoretical approaches—not always recognized—that exists in interpersonal communication studies.

Strengths and Limitations of the Theory

AIDA's focus on institutional practices is a strength of the theory, and it is a limitation. Consider why this is so. As a theoretical-methodological hybrid, AIDA maps how to study a variety of socially consequential practices. In making its central focus the problems of a practice, it presupposes that a practice is meaningful at the sociocultural level, that it can be described in terms of multiple aims and purposes, and that the practice will be shaped by espoused organizational values and practical constraints related to time, money, and energy. It is this assumptive frame that grounds an AIDA study and enables an analyst to identify problems or dilemmas, as well as novel discourse strategies. For institutional practices, such as the ones I have mentioned throughout this chapter, it makes sense to ask what are better and worse ways for participants to conduct themselves as they juggle the multiple aims of the practice. The relative uniformity of goals and ideals that can be assumed for police departments dealing with citizens, however, does not work as well with intimate relationships. For communicative practices that are central to close relationships, there is much less agreement about what constitutes right action. Strong cultural differences, as well as within-culture, social class, and value differences shape how people negotiate marrying or living together, parenting in blended families, and having (or not having) cross-cultural friendships. Although not everything goes, there is huge cultural variation. In American society, at least, there is a much stronger assumption that ideas as to what should count as better (and worse) ways to run a meeting, make a presentation, negotiate a contract, or give feedback to an employee are socially shared. In contrast, although close relationships are also clearly cultural products (Fitch, 1998), there is a stronger expectation that there is not a single "best" way to do close relationships. The ability of people to craft good, albeit idiosyncratic, relationships is one of the delights of intimate life. For this reason, posing normative questions about the best ways to participate in and structure communicative practices makes more sense in institutional than it does in intimate practices.

A second strength (and limitation) of AIDA is that it "bridges" interpersonal and organizational communication theorizing. As a limitation, this strength would be described as "not fitting" into the major research interests in either interpersonal or organizational communication. With its focus on institutional practices, AIDA finds itself reflecting about communicative practices in many of the same places as organizational scholars do. With its focus on interaction and its preference for practices in nonbusiness settings, it is different from most organizational communication. In the field of communication, a fairly sharp line is drawn between interpersonal communication and organizational communication theories. This line drawing does not work well for AIDA, because it reflects features of both research communities, and it also differs from each of them. The choice of sites and practices, as I have noted, are the clearest features that distinguish AIDA from other interpersonal work.

Two additional limitations of AIDA deserve mention. First is that AIDA works best for communicative practices that are site-based and nameable (e.g., divorce mediation [Tracy & Spradlin, 1994]) versus practices that are dispersed across many different sites such as is the case with negotiation, questioning, or story-telling. This is not to rule out dispersed practices as a focus for AIDA, but it is important to recognize that AIDA's theoretical frame rather strongly presupposes communicative practices that are attached to particular institutions. Second, AIDA tends to assume that an institutional practice deserves cultivation. There are practices—extraction of information through torture mixed with talk—in which an AIDA frame would be nonsensical and unethical. In practices that are socially controversial, such as cosmetic surgery, AIDA can be useful for understanding the problems and conversational techniques of the practice (e.g., Mirivel, 2005), but it does not deal particularly well with the normative questions. AIDA does not offer much guidance, at least in its current form, as to how cultivating and improving a practice could and should be applied to practices that are socially contested.

Directions for Future Research and Applications

There are two possible directions for AIDA research. A first would be to reexamine communicative practices that have already been extensively studied, such as classroom teaching, divorce mediation, therapy, or labor-management negotiation, bringing an AIDA theoretical agenda to the study. To the degree that it is useful to have a firm grasp of the problems and dilemmas of a practice, its routine conversational strategies, and its situated ideals, AIDA could bring fresh insights to reflection about conduct in communicative practices that society already assumes are important.

A second direction would be to focus on socially consequential practices that have not yet been studied. Almost any activity that regularly occurs in some spot in institutional or public life deserves a careful look. What AIDA could be applied to is virtually unlimited. There is an issue, though. Thus far I have referred to "communicative practice" as if it were straightforward, an event we would all see and name the same way. This is not the case. The name for a practice frequently privileges the viewpoint of one category of participant over others, thereby making the analyst's task of naming a crucial one. In addition, practices may be embedded in each other and conceptualized at different levels of abstraction.

Consider how this issue applies to what I have referred to as the practice of school board meetings (Tracy, unpublished). Other labels for this practice could be local governance, public meetings, or places of ordinary democracy. Alternatively, one could focus on smaller activities that are embedded in or related to one of these larger practices: One could study citizen participation, agenda-setting meetings, candidate debates, board discussions, community discussions of controversial issues, advisory committee meetings, persuading taxpayers to vote for a school bond, or communication between those whose power base is expertise (e.g., teachers, superintendents) and those who derive power from being democratically elected. All of these are reasonable and valuable ways to frame school governance, but each directs observation and analysis into different channels and makes likely the construction of different problems, discourse strategies, and ideals of conduct. What a practice (or problem) is named matters.

AIDA offers a different view of theory—including what theory should and could be—from what usually comes to mind when one hears the word "theory." AIDA is about understanding complexities of existing practices and helping a practice's participants reflect, plan, and act more wisely. In communicative practices in which people spend time and invest emotional energy, AIDA seeks to be implicative for reflection, the first and most important action of all.

References

Agne, R. (2003). *Crisis negotiations: The FBI and Branch Davidians at Waco.* Unpublished doctoral dissertation, University of Colorado, Boulder, CO.

Boster, F. (2006). Communication as social influence. In G. J. Shepherd, G. St. John, & T. Striphas (Eds.), *Communication as . . . perspectives on theory* (pp. 180–187). Thousand Oaks, CA: Sage.

Craig, R. T. (2006). Communication as a practice. In G. J. Shepherd, G. St. John & T. Striphas (Eds.), *Communication as . . . perspectives on theory* (pp. 38–47). Thousand Oaks, CA: Sage.

Craig, R. T., & Tracy, K. (1995). Grounded practical theory: The case of intellectual discussion. *Communication Theory, 5,* 248–272.

Dewey, J. (1910). *How we think.* Boston: D. C. Heath and Company.

Fitch, K. L. (1998). *Speaking relationally: Culture, communication and interpersonal connection.* New York: Guilford.

Flyvbjerg, B. (2001). *Making social science matter.* Cambridge, MA: Cambridge University Press.

Mirivel, J. (2005). *Getting "nipped and tucked" through talk: A communication take on cosmetic surgery.* Unpublished doctoral dissertation, University of Colorado, Boulder, CO.

Mirivel, J. (in press). The physical examination in cosmetic surgery: Communication strategies to promote the desirability of surgery. *Health Communication.*

Mirivel, J., & Tracy, K. (2005). Premeeting talk: An organizationally crucial form of talk. *Research on Language and Social Interaction, 38,* 1–34.

Ochs, E. (1979). Transcription as theory. In E. Ochs & B. B. Schieffelin (Eds.), *Developmental pragmatics* (pp. 43–72). New York: Academic Press.

Potter, J., & Hepburn, A. (in press). Chairing democracy: Psychology, time, and negotiating the institution. In K. Tracy, J. P. McDaniel, & B. E. Gronbeck (Eds.), *The prettier doll: Rhetoric, discourse, and ordinary democracy.* Tuscaloosa, AL: University of Alabama Press.

Rothenbuhler, E. (2006). Communication as ritual. In G. J. Shepherd, G. St. John & T. Striphas (Eds.), *Communication as . . . perspectives on theory* (pp. 13–31). Thousand Oaks, CA: Sage.

Shepherd, G. J., St. John, G., & Striphas, T. (Eds.). (2006). *Communication as . . . perspectives on theory.* Thousand Oaks, CA: Sage.

Tracy, K. (1997a). *Colloquium: Dilemmas of academic discourse.* Norwood, NJ: Ablex.

Tracy, K. (1997b). Interactional trouble in emergency service requests: A problem of frames. *Research on Language and Social Interaction, 30,* 315–343.

Tracy, K. (2005). Reconstructing communicative practices: Action-implicative discourse analysis. In K. Fitch & R. Sanders (Eds.), *Handbook of language and social interaction* (pp. 301–319). Mahwah, NJ: Erlbaum.

Tracy, K. (in press). *Ordinary democracy: Argument and emotion in school board meetings.* Albany, NY: SUNY Press.

Tracy, K., & Agne, R. R. (2002). "I just need to ask somebody some questions": Sensitivities in domestic dispute calls. In J. Cottrell (Ed.), *Language in the legal process* (pp. 75–89). Brunel, UK: Palgrave.

Tracy, K., & Anderson, D. L. (1999). Relational positioning strategies in calls to the police: A dilemma. *Discourse Studies, 1,* 201–226.

Tracy, K., & Ashcraft, C. (2001). Crafting policies about controversial values: How wording disputes manage a group dilemma. *Journal of Applied Communication Research, 29,* 297–316.

Tracy, K., & Baratz, S. (1993). Intellectual discussion in the academy as situated discourse. *Communication Monographs, 60,* 300–320.

Tracy, K., & Naughton, J. (1994). The identity work of questioning in intellectual discussion. *Communication Monographs, 61,* 281–302.

Tracy, K., & Spradlin, A. (1994). "Talking like a mediator": Conversational moves of experienced divorce mediators. In J. Folger & T. Jones (Eds.), *New directions in mediation* (pp. 110–132). Thousand Oaks, CA: Sage.

12

Communication Accommodation Theory

"When in Rome . . ." or not!

Howard Giles[1]

People can vary their communicative styles and strategies in ways that reflect their differing personalities and temperaments, roles and relationships, and social identities. The verbal and nonverbal outcomes selected have significant social meanings: some, such as British Standard English, are lauded, and others, such as so-called "gayspeak," are often stigmatized. Indeed, the same communicative act will be appreciated by some, yet abhorred by others—as with the case of a baseball cap worn backwards. Such differences in interpersonal communicative styles are abundant, varying by ethnicity, occupational status, gender, age, and so on.

Purpose and Paradigmatic Assumptions

As an arguably paradigm case of such interpersonal tensions in language choice, recent attention has been afforded the growth of new language forms among young people, and this especially so regarding new media technologies (e.g., text messaging). Not only can these language forms invoke the wrath of older adults (Thurlow, 2007), they are often viewed as inappropriate and ridiculed when adopted by the latter. In that regard, note this Web site commentary:

> This ever-changing teen terminology not only defines each new generation, it also keeps the older generation guessing: "This was so whack, dawg. He was

completely up in my kool-aid. He may think he's all that, but he's such a poser flashin all that cheddah. Yo dude, gotta bounce, the lights are on. . . ." So, how is anyone supposed to keep up with the rapidly changing teen terminology? Well, the point is, as adults, we aren't. . . . [You can use] a quick cheat sheet to help you translate what your kids might be saying. Don't get too comfortable: By the time you learn these terms they'll probably be bunk, fo shizzle!" (Talking Tips, 2005)

How then do we communicatively manage such evolving interpersonal diversity that is committed to understanding such processes? While commentators have caricatured Communication Accommodation Theory (CAT) as "one of the best-developed theories relating to interpersonal adjustment" (Littlejohn, 1999, p. 107), it emerged originally as a sociopsychological account of how our dialects and words change depending on to whom we are speaking (Giles & Powesland, 1975). Empirical work in this vein persists today and continues to garner attention in the popular media. For instance, Kuznia (2006) cited a mother talking about her daughter's communicative style as saying, "at home . . . she could always tell whether the friend her daughter was talking to on the phone was white or Latina. When she talked like an adult, it was a white student. When she peppered her diction with the words 'like' and 'you know,' it was a Latina" (p. A19).

The theory quickly embraced interpersonal adjustments in other paralinguistic, verbal, nonverbal, and discourse parameters and, over the years, became elaborated and refined to account for more and more contextual caveats (see Gallois, Ogay, & Giles, 2005, for an account of its history). Beyond communication, the theory has been welcomed in other social science handbooks, texts, and encyclopedias; despite its predominance in neo-positivistic inquiries, CAT has been an interpretive resource in various traditions within sociolinguistics, such as the ethnography of language. CAT has also been featured across many different languages. Moreover, it has been invoked across a range of between-group contexts and has been the springboard for an array of satellite theories in other communicative domains, such as second language acquisition (see Shepard, Giles, & Le Poire, 2001). Consequently, CAT has become recognized more broadly as "one of the most influential behavioral theories of communication" (Littlejohn & Foss, 2005, p. 147) and, as such, its empirical literature relating to verbal and nonverbal communication has been reviewed on a number of occasions (e.g., Giles & Ogay, 2006).

Main Features of the Theory

ACCOMMODATIVENESS

Although notions of "accommodation" have separate meanings in different theoretical terrains, in CAT accommodation is a process concerned with how we can both reduce and magnify communicative differences between people in interaction. Accommodation is considered one of the main routes to achieving the former—and it does so by enhancing interpersonal similarities and, thereby reducing uncertainties about the other. The effect of converging toward or "approximating" another has been shown to increase liking for the converger, enabling him or her to be seen as more competent and credible (e.g., Aune & Kikuchi, 1993). A common experience for many readers would be traveling abroad and seeing the delight of your waitperson when saying "Hello," "Thank you," "Please," and "Good-bye" in the waitperson's language.

Convergence can occur across a wide range of communicative dimensions. These include switching to the other's language or dialect (as above), or assuming the same level of the other's interruptions, speech rate, posture, and so forth (e.g., Li, 2001). These adjustments can be labeled as upward or downward when the communicative features have value connotations. "Upward convergence" is when a speaker adopts another's more prestigious accent, whereas "downward convergence" is when a speaker adapts to match another's more parochial, colloquial, or stigmatized speech pattern—for example, when physicians replace medical jargon with lay words and explanations when speaking with their patients. Accommodation can be manifest in ways other than convergence, as we take into account the other's conversational needs and goals (see Jones, Gallois, Callan, & Barker, 1999). Important here would be the ability to accommodate what is called another's "interpretive competence," that is, the other's ability to comprehend, or whether the other has had any experience with the topic or event being discussed. An example here would be a Briton (who has some knowledge of baseball) slowly explaining to an American (who has no knowledge of cricket) the game of cricket, using their shared knowledge of baseball as a foundation.

Indeed, convergence plays a crucial role in CAT to the extent that accommodative acts are often a function of the social power a target-other is perceived to possess. Others with low power are accommodated less frequently than others with high power. For example in male-female encounters, women, in general, will accommodate males more than vice versa (Namy, Nygaard, & Saureteig, 2002), while vendors in a market will accommodate more to their clientele than shoppers will to them (e.g., van den Berg, 1986). In a similar vein, Gregory and Webster (1996) described how Larry King, the host of a popular American TV news talk show on CNN, adapted the pitch of his voice as a function of his guests' status (e.g., he would converge toward President Clinton). When it came to guests that were held lower in social esteem (e.g., Vice President Dan Quayle), these lower-esteem guests accommodated more to King than King did to them. More generally, people will converge to others they find socially rewarding. For instance, Green and Murachver (in press) found that males converged more toward the language style of a physically attractive woman than they did toward a less attractive woman.

Another important feature of CAT is that people will accommodate subjectively to where they believe others to be communicatively rather than where they actually are in any objective, measurable sense (Thakerar, Giles, & Cheshire, 1982). However, the subjective and objective need not always be in accord, leading to the potential for miscommunication. Common instances of this are where social stereotypes associated with another's apparent or presumed group memberships (e.g., elderliness) may lead to faulty expectations about the other's competence and characteristics. In this instance, one may overaccommodate an older person by becoming extremely deferential and polite, or by touching them, slowing down speech rate, and enunciating loudly. For those elders who do not resonate to the way they have been so characterized, such miscarried accommodations (irrespective of, say, any actual nurturing intent) can be perceived as patronizing and demeaning, whereas perhaps for more frail elders it can be construed as empathic and being helpful. Related people can accommodate another fully—as when one converges exactly the 100-word-a-minute speaking rate of another, or partially—when one converges from a 50-word-a-minute rate to a more-rapid 75 words a minute. For varying situations, there are optimal levels of accommodation because people, while appreciating that their respect and admiration are being sought by such means, do not like to feel that they can be easily and so absolutely matched.

NONACCOMMODATIVENESS

Given the benefits of accommodating to others, this communicative process can almost be regarded as a conversational rule and an integral component of communicative competence and social skills. Indeed, work from another independent, theoretical frame on mimicry has claimed that "when people interact with each other, there in a nonconscious tendency to match each other's behavior" (van Baaren, Horgan, Chatrand, & Dijkmans, 2004, p. 453). That said, CAT's attention has also been drawn to conditions where not only does this not emerge, but where the complete converse is embraced. A case in point that relates to the opening of this chapter would be a teen text messaging a mother in that would be indecipherable to her. As implied above, being **non**accommodated to from a socially significant other does not usually excite a recipient's affection! Such nonaccommodativeness can message that one's respect and liking is not being sought, thereby rendering some damage to self-esteem, with unfavorable evaluations following for the nonaccommodator. The negative consequences attending lack of accommodation can, however, be reduced under extenuating circumstances, such as a presumed inability to speak the other's language, to understand their slang, and so on.

Again, nonaccommodative practices come in different forms, too. It can be manifest in "speech maintenance" where the speaker sustains a consistent communicative stance from person to person, irrespective of who the latter may be, so as to maintain an aura of authenticity. On other occasions, people can be **under**accommodative in that they do not attend or listen to another's needs: They have their own egocentric agendas. Among the most nonaccommodative positions would be where a speaker diverges by using a more or less prestigious accent (upward and downward divergence, respectively) or even switches languages. It, too, can vary from partial to full divergence, and can be triggered by dislike for or mistrust of another—and is usually met with negative and even derogatory responses. In an experimental set-up in South Africa, Dixon, Tredoux, Durrheim, and Foster (1994) found that so-called colored suspects (that is, suspects of mixed racial heritage) who diverged from a white interrogator by use of a Cape Afrikaans accent were judged more guilty of a crime than those who converged toward the interrogator's accent.

Divergence has been considered most in interpersonal encounters where interactants feel they are representing different groups, cultures, and communities with which they strongly affiliate, and where their in-group language or communication style is a fundamental dimension of their social identity. For instance, given the importance of speaking French to a Quebecois' identity, a separatist from this Canadian province might emphasize his or her French accent when talking to a monolingual English-Canadian. CAT has drawn from social identity theory (Tajfel, 1978). Members of different ethnic groups often accentuate their identities by diverging from one another—not only in dialect or language, but also in their distinctive nonverbal and dress styles—in pursuit of a positive social identity. This divergence can be particularly intense if people feel their identity is threatened and that the other group has historically and illegitimately discriminated against them. Indeed, if a person accommodates an out-group member in such situations, observers could attribute that person as being a cultural traitor.

From all this, it should be clear that while accommodation is often positively received, it need not always be so. Some members of certain national groups (reputedly, for example, the French and the Japanese) feel their language is so unique to their culture and impossible to learn by outsiders that they may not take kindly to foreigners' use of their own tongues, even if done with nativelike proficiency (Ross & Shortreed, 1990). By the same token, divergences are not always negatively perceived: indeed, they made be deemed mandatory and valued (as above) by in-group peers. In other situations, divergence may be adopted strategically in order to correct a communicative stance in another such as by slowing down in order to recalibrate an overly fast talker who is providing new information at such a fast pace that the hearer cannot absorb it comfortably. In yet other situations, objectively coded divergence could be positively perceived as speech complementarity. This could be when a romantically inclined male accentuates his manliness by adopting a deeper pitch and when a female, in tandem, accentuates her femininity by adopting a softer voice.

SYMMETRICALITY

Note that across all these outcomes, accommodation and nonaccommodation can be mutual, reciprocated, symmetrical, or asymmetrical (see Gallois & Giles, 1998). When they are symmetrical and accommodative, interpersonal relations should be particularly strengthened, but when they are mutually nonaccommodative, interpersonal relations are likely to become hostile and conflicted. An interesting feature of CAT is that communicators can adopt both accommodative and nonaccommodative stances with the same person in an attempt to convey contrastive identities. Zilles and King (2005) showed how immigrant German women in Brazil could use language features that accommodated host language features, yet at the same time could emphasize their linguistic origins.

Conceptualization of Communication in the Theory

In the 1980s (e.g., Thakerar et al., 1982), CAT began to take propositional forms that became increasingly more complex and, arguably, more demanding on readers. Consequently, subsequent reviews took on a more discursive tone (e.g., Giles & Noels, 1998). With a view that perhaps this had not assisted in conveying the thrust and essence of the theory for a while, Giles, Willemyns, Gallois, and Anderson (2007) crafted four key principles of accommodation that convey how communication is conceptualized within CAT. Given that the theory is supported in naturalistic and laboratory-contrived settings as well as in the media, the author believes that the four principles apply equally well to interpersonal communication in other new technology settings, such as e-mail (Thomson, Murachver, & Green, 2001) and messages left on a telephone answering system (Buzzanell, Burrell, Stafford, & Berkowitz, 1996). These principles follow:

- Speakers will, up to an optimal level, increasingly accommodate the communicative patterns believed characteristic of their interactants the more they wish to
  - ○ signal positive face and empathy;
  - ○ elicit the other's approval, respect, understanding, trust, compliance, and cooperation;
  - ○ develop a closer relationship;
  - ○ defuse a potentially volatile situation; or
  - ○ signal common social identities.

- When attributed (typically) with positive intent, patterns of perceived accommodation increasingly and cumulatively enhance recipients'
  - self-esteem;
  - task, interactional, and job satisfaction;
  - favorable images of the speaker's group, fostering the potential for partnerships to achieve common goals;
  - mutual understanding, felt supportiveness, and life satisfaction; and
  - attributions of speaker politeness, empathy, competence, benevolence, and trust.

- Speakers will (other interactional motives notwithstanding) increasingly **non**accommodate (e.g., diverge from) the communicative patterns believed characteristic of their interactants, the more they wish to signal (or promote)
  - relational dissatisfaction or disaffection with and disrespect for the others' traits, demeanor, actions, or social identities.

- When attributed with (usually) harmful intent, patterns of perceived **non**accommodation (e.g., divergence) will be
  - evaluated unfavorably as unfriendly, impolite, or communicatively incompetent; and
  - reacted to negatively by recipients (e.g., recipients will perceive speaker to be lacking in empathy and trust).

These principles are readily converted into testable hypotheses in concrete situations (see Giles et al., 2007). In addition, there exist schematic models of the accommodation process (see for example, Shepard et al., 2001) that underscore visually the theory's reflexive character. That is to say, accommodative acts are not merely determined by psychological mechanisms (such as divergence arising out of perceiving oneself to be a member of this or that group), communication patterns can also shape these cognitive and affective mechanisms in the first place (as when perceiving another diverging from oneself triggers and makes salient one's social identity). Thus, while the author contends that accommodation is driven by interpersonal motives of gaining social acceptance and building social connections, ultimately leading to solid relationships and even life satisfaction, the author also contends the converse flow of forces coexists. Hence, job satisfaction can lead to seeing others as accommodating, while seeing others as accommodating can just as easily lead to job satisfaction; inevitably, transactive cycles of such relationships exist.

Uses of the Theory

INTERPERSONAL AS INTERGROUP COMMUNICATION

A feature of CAT is its capacity to account for compelling processes not usually accountable under the rubric of interpersonal communication, yet which are fundamental to it. Many years ago, Tajfel and Turner (1979) introduced the distinction between encounters (even dyadic ones) that were either "interindividual" or "intergroup." The former were interactions that are based solely on the personal characteristics of the parties involved (e.g., their personalities and moods) and not at all dependent on their respective social category memberships. Hence, accommodation-nonaccommodation in these cases would be toward or away from the idiosyncratic communication attributes of the other. Intergroup encounters were the converse, and so accommodation-nonaccommodation would be pitched vis-à-vis the other's social category memberships (sexual orientation, gang, religion, political membership, and so on). Tajfel and Turner regarded this class of interactions as constituting and actually defining a major proportion of all the interpersonal situations we encounter. Even intimate communication between married couples—in the context of this gendered institution—can be usefully understood in intergroup terms (as in talk about who is continually doing the cleaning, caring for children, cooking, shopping, and so on). Likewise, a friend confiding openly and privately about contrasting sororities, professors, or engineering majors would also constitute intergroup talk.

Rather than construe these as opposite poles of a single interactional continuum, a number of scholars (e.g., Giles & Hewstone, 1982) felt it prudent to represent conversational possibilities as located along two orthogonal continua: interindividual (high low) and intergroup (high low). This lends the possibility of encounters being construed as high on both dimensions, or as a movement within the same conversation from, for example, interindividual to intergroup. An illustration of this would be the occasion when a man discloses to his mother that he is gay. Their relational history dictates that interindividual salience would be high, with the mother dealing with her son as the unique person she has known and loved since birth. At the same time however, her son's homosexuality will be pertinent, potentially shaping the encounter in many important ways. In sum, interpersonal communication that is triggered by social identities is fashioned by different processes (e.g., stereotyping and social differentiation) and message strategies from the processes molded by interindividual ones. CAT absorbs and blends such diversity in interpersonal encounters (Gallois & Giles, 1998).

PHASES OF RELATIONAL DEVELOPMENT

Accommodative processes have never been systematically explored in terms of the stages of relational development and dissolution. In fact, most work on CAT (as the foregoing attests) has focused on initial interactions between strangers during the acquainting process, or in role-related situations where accommodation regularly occurs for all the beneficial reasons specified above. But what of more developed relationships, where such functions have already largely been met? There are just a few studies that are relevant that underscore the value of sustaining accommodative practices. Harwood (2000) showed that closeness in and satisfaction with the grandparent-grandchild relationship from the perspectives of both participants was predicted by the extent to which they perceived the other to be accommodative (e.g., by listening to and talking about topics the other enjoys).

Another study has examined implicit relational development (through coding a composite of 32 language variables) by videotaping people talking with those of the same sex and opposite sex, as well as people talking with their spouse (Fitzpatrick, Mulac, & Dindia, 1995). Both men and women shift from their own gender-preferential styles of language to that of the other when they move from same-sex to opposite-sex strangers, and shift again when they converse with their spouses. The researchers found that highly sex-typed males adapted their speech little across these conversations, that women converged most when talking to a male stranger, and that men accommodated most to their wives. Regarding the latter, the authors commented that "the magnitude of this shift is striking" and that "for women, the initial leap from the extremes of the female-preferential style occurs when speaking to any man, husband, or stranger" (p. 35).

The participants in the Fitzpatrick and colleagues (1995) study were happily married. In contrast, Robertson and Murachver (2006) interviewed victims and perpetrators who were involved in abusive relationships, some of whom had been incarcerated. They found that those who had been psychologically abusive with their partners were much more likely to accommodate an interviewer who adopted negative language forms such as disagreeing and swearing, but less likely to reciprocate an interviewer who assumed more facilitative language forms (e.g., expressed empathy and compliments). It is a common adage—and one often heard at marital ceremonies—that relationships have to be continually worked on. CAT operates on the assumption that managing accommodative practices and dilemmas per se, and especially when one's partner is perceived to veer in nonaccommodative directions, might be an important ingredient in long-term relational satisfaction-dissatisfaction. Jamie Pennebaker (personal communication, April 16, 2007) has data indicating that relational attachment versus nonattachment in heterosexual romantic student-couples can be predicted by how much grammatical convergences (e.g., of adjectival and pronoun usages) were evident in their conversations three months earlier.

Strengths and Limitations of the Theory

For the most part, critiques of CAT have been favorable and empirical work spawned by CAT has appeared in many journals across different disciplines, with a number of journal special issues being devoted to CAT-inspired studies (e.g., Coupland & Giles, 1988). West and Turner (2007) stated that "there is no doubt that the theory is heuristic and has lasting scholastic value" (p. 547), noting that it has not been subject to much scholarly criticism. Many of CAT's strengths have been alluded to already: CAT's capacity to interface; microlinguistic and macrosocietal boundaries; interpersonal and intergroup tensions; and short-term and long-term outcomes.

Four of CAT's limitations are pinpointed here. First, we have little understanding regarding which particular communicative feature(s) will be accommodated to or differentiated from, or when and why that would happen. Second, and as discussed above, we do not yet understand the dynamics of how accommodative-nonaccommodative practices are adopted throughout the history of interpersonal relationships. Third, we are limited in our understanding of when accommodation directly causes certain interpersonal outcomes, and when it works indirectly. As CAT stands currently (see Principles 1 and 2), it favors direct paths, yet Buller and Aune (1992) showed that complying with someone's request for assistance was predicted by how much they perceived the relationship as close. This perception, in turn, was predicted by how accommodating (in terms of speech rate) the requester had been to them. Put another way, the relationship between accommodation and compliance was indirect. Similarly, people's perceptions of police officers' accommodative practices promote trust in them that, itself, predicts compliance with their instructions (e.g., Hajek et al., 2006). Clearly, more sophisticated mediational (as well as more reflexive and dialectical) models of CAT are begging to be conceptualized and tested. Fourth, the thorny issue of when accommodation and nonaccommodation strategies are consciously versus nonconsciously invoked (i.e., when they are automatic or ritualized) has yet to be studied within CAT.

Directions for Future Research and Applications

The limitations just outlined necessarily segue into and drive future empirical directions and, clearly, other theoretical questions can be raised, only a couple (one interpersonal and one intergroup) of which can be ignited here. For instance, as well as examining how and why we accommodate to certain degrees and with what consequences, it would be important to connect with other theoretical frameworks that might help us understand how people negotiate the kinds and levels of accommodations they make in discourse (see the grounding model of Kashima, Klein, & Clark, 2007). In addition, given the surge of recent interest in interpersonal relations for understanding the success (or not) of intergroup contact programs (e.g., Wright, Brody, & Aron, 2005), how do accommodative processes play into the behavioral dramas of such ongoing contact? Acknowledging that multiple interpersonal goals are involved, how can people effectively manage dilemmatic interpersonal communication when the other is, wittingly and or unwittingly, being inappropriately accommodative?

This last question moves us into applied issues, a terrain CAT has engaged many times. The theory has been used in different legal, medical, clinical, health, law enforcement, and criminal settings (see Giles, Coupland, & Coupland, 1991; Giles et al., 2007). A challenge for CAT as well as each of us on a practical day-to-day basis is how people manage their accommodative-nonaccommodative resources, while trying to balance their personal needs or pulls for authenticity and integrity, while acknowledging the pushes of social interdependence. Finally, and returning to our starting point, how we accommodate and fashion meaningful interpersonal communication with the socially different generations that follow us in a value- and technologically-changing world is possibly our most demanding quest.

Note

1. I would like to thank two anonymous reviewers for their helpful comments on a prior draft of this chapter, and would especially like to thank Dawn Braithwaite for her comprehensive and invaluable feedback.

References

Aune, R. K., & Kikuchi, T. (1993). Effects of language intensity similarity on perceptions of credibility, relational attributions, and persuasion. *Journal of Language and Social Psychology, 12,* 224–237.

Buller, D. B., & Aune, R. K. (1992). The effects of speech rate similarity on compliance: Application of communication accommodation theory. *Western Journal of Communication, 56,* 37–53.

Buzzanell, P. M., Burrell, N. A., Stafford, R. S., & Berkowitz, S. (1996). When I call you up and you're not there: Application of communication accommodation theory to telephone answering machine messages. *Western Journal of Communication, 60,* 310–336.

Coupland, N., & Giles, H. (Eds.). (1988). Communicative accommodation: Recent developments. *Language and Communication, 8*(3 & 4), 175–327.

Dixon, J. A., Tredoux, C. G., Durrheim, K. & Foster, D.H. (1994). The role of speech accommodation and crime type in attribution of guilt. *Journal of Social Psychology, 134,* 465–473.

Fitzpatrick, M. A., Mulac, A., & Dindia, K. (1995). Gender-preferential language use in spouse and stranger interaction. *Journal of Language and Social Psychology, 14,* 18–39.

Gallois, C., & Giles, H. (1998). Accommodating mutual influence in intergroup encounters. In C. A. Bennett & M. T. Palmer (Eds.), *Progress in communication sciences* (pp. 135–162). Stanford, CA: Ablex.

Gallois, C., Ogay, T., & Giles, H. (2005). Communication accommodation theory: A look back and a look ahead. In W. Gudykunst (Ed.), *Theorizing about intercultural communication* (pp. 121–148). Thousand Oaks, CA: Sage.

Giles, H., Coupland, J., & Coupland, N. (Eds.). (1991). *Contexts of accommodation.* New York: Cambridge University Press.

Giles, H., & Hewstone, M. (1982). Cognitive structures, speech, and social situations. *Language Sciences, 4,* 187–219.

Giles, H., & Noels, K. (1998). Communication accommodation in intercultural encounters. In J. Martin, T. Nakayama, & L. Flores (Eds.), *Readings in cultural contexts* (pp. 139–149). Mountain View, CA: Mayfield.

Giles, H., & Ogay, T. (2006). Communication accommodation theory. In B. B. Whaley & W. Samter (Eds.), *Explaining communication: Contemporary theories and exemplars* (pp. 293–310). Mahwah, NJ: Erlbaum.

Giles, H., & Powesland, P. F. (1975). *Speech style and social evaluation.* London: Academic Press.

Giles, H., Willemyns, M., Gallois, C., & Anderson, M. C. (2007). Accommodating a new frontier: The context of law enforcement. In K. Fiedler (Ed.), *Social communication.* (pp. 129–162). New York: Psychology Press.

Green, J., & Murachver, T. (in press). Does greater attraction lead to greater convergence? A test of communication accommodation theory. Under review.

Gregory, S. W., & Webster, S. (1996). A nonverbal signal in voices of interview partners effectively predicts communication accommodation and social status predictions. *Journal of Personality and Social Psychology, 70,* 1231–1240.

Hajek, C., Barker, V., Giles, H., Louw, J., Pecchioni, L., Makoni, S., & Myers, P. (2006). Perceptions of police-civilian encounters: African and American interethnic data. *Journal of Intercultural Communication Research, 35,* 161–182.

Harwood, J. (2000). Communicative predictors of solidarity in the grandparent-grandchild relationship. *Journal of Social and Personal Relationships, 17,* 743–766.

Jones, E. S., Gallois, C., Callan, V. J., & Barker, M. (1999). Strategies of accommodation: Development of a coding system for conversational interaction. *Journal of Language and Social Psychology, 18,* 123–152.

Kashima, Y., Klein, O., & Clark, A. E. (2007). Grounding: Sharing information in social interaction. In K. Fiedler (Ed.), *Social communication* (pp. 27–78). New York: Psychology Press.

Kuznia, R. (2006, March 5). One school, two worlds. *Santa Barbara New-Press,* pp. A1, 18–19.

Li, H. (2001). Cooperative and intrusive interruptions in inter- and intracultural dyadic discourse. *Journal of Language and Social Psychology, 20,* 259–284.

Littlejohn, S. W. (1999). Theories of human communication (6th ed.). Belmont, CA: Wadsworth.

Littlejohn, S. W., & Foss, K. A. (2005). *Theories of communication* (8th ed.). Belmont, CA: Wadsworth.

Namy, L. L., Nygaard, L. C., & Saureteig, D. (2002). Gender differences in vocal accommodation: The role of perception. *Journal of Language and Social Psychology, 21,* 422–432.

Robertson, K., & Murachver, T. (2006). Intimate partner violence, linguistic features and accommodation behavior of perpetrators and victims. *Journal of Language and Social Psychology, 25,* 406–422.

Ross, S., & Shortreed, I. M. (1990). Japanese foreigner talk: Convergence or divergence? *Journal of Asian Pacific Communication, 1,* 135–145.

Shepard, C. A., Giles, H., & Le Poire, B. A. (2001). Communication accommodation theory. In W. P. Robinson & H. Giles (Eds.), *The new handbook of language and social psychology* (pp. 33–56). New York: Wiley.

Tajfel, H. (Ed.) (1978). *Differentiation between social groups.* London: Academic Press.

Tajfel, H., & Turner, J. C. (1979). An integrative theory of intergroup conflict. In W. C. Austin & S. Worchel (Eds.), *The social psychology of intergroup relations* (pp. 33–53). Monterey, CA: Brooks/Cole.

Talking tips. 2005. Retrieved October 11, 2005, from http://homeworkhelp.aol.com/leapfrog?id=20050531163709990001.

Thakerar, J., Giles, H., & Cheshire, J. (1982). Psychological and linguistic parameters of speech accommodation theory. In C. Fraser & K. R. Scherer (Eds.), *Advances in the social psychology of language* (pp. 205–255). Cambridge, UK: Cambridge University Press.

Thomson, R., Murachver, T., & Green, J. (2001). Where is the gender in gendered language? *Psychological Science, 12,* 171–175.

Thurlow, C. (2007). Fabricating youth: New-media discourse and the technologization of young people. In S. Johnson & A. Ensslin (Eds.), *Language in the media: Representations, identities, ideologies* (pp. 213–233). London: Continuum.

van Baaren, R. B., Horgan T. G., Chatrand, T. L., & Dijkmans, M. (2004). The forest, the trees, and the chameleon: Context dependence and mimicry. *Journal of Personality and Social Psychology, 86,* 453–459.

van den Berg, M. E. (1986). *Language planning and language use in Taiwan: A study of language choice behavior in public settings.* Taipei, Taiwan: Crane.

West, R., & Turner, L. H. (2007). *Introducing communication theory: Analysis and application* (3rd ed.). New York: McGraw-Hill.

Wright, S. C., Brody, S. M., & Aron, A. (2005). Integroup contact: Still our best hope for improving intergroup relations. In C. S. Crandall & M. Schaller (Eds.), *Social psychology of prejudice: Historical and contemporary issues* (pp. 143–164). Seattle: Lewinian Press.

Zilles, A. M. S., & King, K. (2005). Self-presentation in sociolinguistic interviews: identities and language variation in Panambi, Brazil. *Journal of Multicultural and Multilingual Development, 9,* 74–94.

13

Conversation Analysis Theory

A Descriptive Approach
to Interpersonal Communication

Jenny Mandelbaum[1]

onversation Analysis (CA) Theory offers an observation-based descriptive theory of communication (or, more specifically for CA, talk and other conduct in interaction) with implications for the study of interpersonal communication. A primary aim of CA is to lay out the basic sense-making practices and regularities of interaction that form the basis for everyday communication, in both informal and professional settings. CA uses field recordings of conversation and other kinds of talk and embodied conduct in interaction as data, and builds systematic descriptions of the mechanisms that make human conduct possible. Taken together, these descriptions constitute a theory of communication. The key evidence for determining the relevance of these descriptions to communicators' lived experience is found in communicators' displayed orientations—displayed in the unfolding conduct itself—to the described practices. In this way, CA builds theory empirically.

Purpose and Meta-theoretical Assumptions

Originated by Harvey Sacks in collaboration with Emanuel Schegloff and Gail Jefferson, CA is grounded in Goffman's view that social interaction is an autonomous, self-contained domain of human conduct that is of central importance to the social world (e.g., Goffman, 1983). CA's focus on the structures and reasoning processes of everyday interaction is also built on insights from Garfinkel's (1967) ethnomethodology, which emphasizes the orderly procedures of everyday social conduct, and sees that orderliness as accomplished by its participants. Crucially for CA, Garfinkel proposed that description of human social conduct consists of descriptions of the procedures used by communicators to produce and interpret their social world.

A key feature of CA Theory is that the accounts it develops attend to the integrity of particular episodes of interaction (Schegloff, 2005). That is, rather than theory being guided by disciplinary concerns, the concerns and orientations of interactants, displayed in the practices they use to communicate, shape discovery. This derives from the assumption that conversation, like other aspects of social life, has its own orderliness, and thus what is organizationally consequential is that which is oriented to by the participants themselves, rather than that which is particularly of interest to the researcher.

The purpose and meta-theoretical assumptions of CA are based on the empirically grounded belief that description of observed phenomena constitutes a theory of human conduct. This can best be understood by examining a specimen of the sort with which conversation analysts usually work. The following transcription is typical of the kind that conversation analysts construct as a guide to audio- and videotape recorded interaction. The audio tape of this brief phone call is available at http://www.scils.rutgers.edu/~jennym/audio/stalled-128k.mp3. Using the key below, the eye quickly becomes attuned to decoding the symbols while listening to the tape-recorded data. This set of transcription conventions, developed by Gail Jefferson (2004), is widely used by researchers studying interaction in a number of fields.

Transcription Key:

?	indicates rising intonation (not necessarily a question) [**Line 1**]	
,	indicates "continuing" intonation [**Line 2**]	
.	indicates falling intonation (not necessarily end of sentence) [**Line 5**]	
:	indicates that preceding sound is extended or "stretched" [**Line 3**]	
[&]	mark beginning and ending of overlap [**Line 4**]	
·hh	marks an audible inbreath [**Line 8**]; **hhh** marks audible outbreath [**Line 12**]	
__	underlining shows a sound which is stressed [**Line 8**]	
(0.2)	indicates amount of silence in 10ths of seconds [**Line 9**]	
(h)	indicates laughter within words [**Line 18**]	

Excerpt 1

0		Ring
1	Marcia:	Hallo?
2	Donny:	'lo Marcia,
3	Marcia:	Yea [:h]
		[ ]

4	Donny:	[('t's D]onny.
5	Marcia:	Hi Donny.
6	Donny:	Guess what.hh
7	Marcia:	What.
8	Donny:	·hh My ca:r is sta::lled.
9		(0.2)
10	Donny:	(and) I'm up here in the Glen?
11	Marcia:	Oh::.
12	Donny:	hhh
13	Donny:	A:nd.hh (0.2) I don' know if it's: po:ssible, but
14		hhh see I haveta open up the ba:nk.hh
15		(0.3)
16	Donny:	a:t uh: (.) in Brentwood?hh=
17	Marcia:	=Yeah:- and I know you want- (.) en I whoa- (.) and I would, but-
18		except I've gotta leave in about five min(h)utes.=
19	Donny:	[=Okay then I gotta call somebody else.right away.
		[
20	Marcia:	[(hheh)
21	(.)	
22	Donny:	Okay?=
23	Marcia:	=Okay [Don]
		[ ]
24	Donny:	[Thanks] a lot.=Bye-.
25	Marcia:	Bye:.

Conversation analysts approach these data inductively with the aim of discovering their unfolding, participant-produced organization, by listening to them carefully turn-by-turn (or watching them, in the case of videotaped data). Repeated replayings of the data, accompanied by inspection of the transcript, yield observations about possible conversational practices and structures. These observations are then tested against many other conversations. In the brief moments of interaction that make up this phone call, we see encapsulated a rich array of conversational phenomena that provide the bedrock structure of conversational interaction (e.g., turn taking, action sequence organization, and repair organization, each addressed in more detail below), as well as beginning and ending a conversation, word selection, and so on. We also see a number of actions produced using interactional practices that can also be employed in other environments (e.g., seeking help and refusing to help; these practices are also explained in more detail below). Once a possible phenomenon or action has been identified, large numbers of instances are collected from tape-recorded conversations and analyzed to determine that phenomenon's regularities of use (including descriptions of occasions for use; design features, or "composition" of the phenomenon; and placement within its turn and sequence, or "position"). Thus CA is thoroughly empirical, building theories of interaction on a descriptive foundation of observation and analysis of particular instances of naturally occurring interaction. We will return to the specifics of this conversation later in the chapter, as a resource for instantiating aspects of CA Theory.

Main Features of the Theory

Three main features of CA Theory are centrally relevant to this discussion. First, CA relies on the understanding that "talk is action." For CA, what is most important about talk is that it is used by communicators to do things. Second, CA has found that "action is structured," consisting of collections of stable practices. Third, CA treats "action as locally organized." I address each of these in turn.

TALK IS ACTION

Key to an understanding of the CA approach to interpersonal communication is the observation that to understand communication one has to understand that "talk is in the first place action." That is, when someone says something, they are not only or even primarily describing (Austin, 1962), or transmitting information (Mokros & Deetz, 1996), or "making meaning." Rather, they are doing something (Heritage, 1984). In Excerpt 1, when Donny says to Marcia, "My car is stalled" (Line 8), he is not simply describing a current circumstance or transmitting information. In fact, Marcia could hear him to be making a request by reporting a problem. This is so because he is employing a practice for "doing requesting." Particulars of the local environment, such as intonation, what precedes and follows an utterance (e.g., in this case that it is preceded by "Guess what" and "What,"), and so on, shape how exactly an utterance is understood. Importantly, how it is understood will be revealed (to the speaker and to us as analysts) in how it is responded to (perhaps immediately next, but sometimes over an ensuing course of turns). Initially, in Excerpt 1, there is no response (which is itself noteworthy, given the relevance of a response), and Donny continues to provide details of the problem. Then in

Line 17 we see that Marcia may in fact have heard Donny to be reporting trouble so as to seek help from her when she says "and I know you want—and I whoa—and I would." Thus reporting problematic circumstances in the way that Donny does here may constitute a practice for doing an action—the action of showing that a request may be on its way (leaving it to the recipient to infer this), rather than making the request overtly.

ACTION IS STRUCTURED

Second, CA research has shown that "action is structured." The structures of conversation allow communicators to, among other things, coordinate their talk so that speakers take turns rather than talking simultaneously; coordinate their actions with others in order to build patterned sequences of action (such as a request sequence or a "how-are-you" sequence); repair errors and other troubles in speaking, understanding, or hearing; and open and close conversations. These basic organizational systems are communicators' solutions to the practical challenges of talking together (and getting things done through talking together), and are of fundamental importance to interpersonal communication, since each of them instantiates the interactive character of interpersonal communication that requires communicators to "work together." For instance in Excerpt 1, we see how "turn taking" can be managed: mostly, turns are taken with minimal gap or overlap between them. This is the arrangement that predominates in conversation (Sacks, Schegloff, & Jefferson, 1974) and it is this organization that allocates (and constrains) opportunities to participate in interpersonal communication. But note how in Lines 3–4 there is an overlap when Donny produces a self-identification at the earliest possible point at which Marcia's "Yeah" in Line 3 indicates to him that she may not have recognized him. Coming in at this earliest possible point (noticeable as a variant on "normal" turn-taking practices) is a way for Donny to enact "being in a hurry." This example shows how the set of context-free (that is, reproducible on any relevant occasion), yet context-sensitive (that is, adapted specifically to the local particulars of a situation), practices that constitutes the turn-taking system provides a basis for conversation, and how that basis can be relied on in the production of actions. Importantly, rather than being a mechanistic set of rules everyone follows unconsciously, the organization of turn-taking forms an "interpretive framework" for understanding action.

Interactants can build courses of actions through a series of turns that hangs together with bonds that are tighter than mere chronology, such that one action makes specially relevant a particular kind of next action. This is known as "action sequence organization." An instance of this can be seen in Lines 6–7 of Excerpt 1, where Donny's "Guess what" makes specially relevant an immediate next response such as "What" from Marcia. The "what" would be noticeably absent if Marcia did not produce it right away. Furthermore, "Guess what" indicates that, given a forwarding response from Marcia, Donny will produce another, related action—the delivery of news. Thus Line 6 actually begins to prepare a slot for Donny to produce news, if given the go-ahead by Marcia. (See Schegloff, 1995, for further discussion.) In addition, Donny projects the kind of response that Marcia could give to his next action by indicating before that action's production that what he will say next should be inspected for its news-worthiness. The building of an interlinked sequence of actions constitutes a process for communicators to work together in predictable ways to construct a recognizable course of action—in this case the announcement of some news as a possible request for help, and the relevance of its reception as news or as a request for help, or both. A basic conversational pattern for accomplishing this type of connection between actions (and the turns through which they are produced) such as that between "Guess what?" and "What?" has been descriptively named the "adjacency pair" (Schegloff, 2007b).

Another recurrent challenge that communicators face is how to deal with the inevitable troubles in speaking, hearing, or understanding that occur in communication. When a speaker says something that is not heard or understood, the speaker has a set of practices for fixing the problem, and the recipients have a set of practices for prompting the speaker to fix it, if the speaker does not do so without prompting first. The practices of "conversational repair" (e.g., Schegloff, Jefferson, & Sacks, 1977) provide ways of fixing problems of this kind. In Excerpt 1 we see instances of conversational repair when Marcia cuts off the progress of her talk in Line 17 saying "and I know you want—." This repair practice provides her with a method for restarting her turn. Here doing so can be used to claim that she may know what Donny wants, and to convey willingness, without actually stating what it is she takes it he wants, or making her failure to help overt. Thus repair can be used by a speaker simply to fix a problem in speaking, but sometimes doing so can also accomplish another interpersonal action.

The regular practices of turn taking, sequence organization and repairing trouble are among the wide array of orderly practices that constitute all conversations, and provide a bedrock for sociality. The description of these basic systems constitutes an observation-based descriptive theory of fundamental features of interpersonal communication. The particular ways in which turns are taken, sequences are patterned, repairs are made, and so on, organize interpersonal communication such that violations of these orderly practices can provide for the recognizability of various interpersonal actions. We saw this above with Donny's overlap in Line 4, where a "violation" of the practices of turn taking was a way of enacting "being in a hurry." Lerner (2004) showed that overlap also can be produced in ways that achieve solidarity. Crucially, you could not have the recognition of a "violation" such as simultaneous talk without a turn-taking system for speaking in conversation that shows that—ordinarily—turns at talk are produced one at a time with minimal gap or overlap.

ACTION IS LOCALLY ORGANIZED

Finally, from a CA perspective, as the above discussion indicates, communication is "locally organized." There are two important components of CA theorizing regarding what is meant by "local." First, with regard to what is "relevantly" local for interactants, CA utilizes a particular sense of "context." For CA, contexts are not "buckets" that shape and constrain communication (Drew & Heritage, 1992). Rather, context is "produced" and "enacted" by interactants' actions, in addition to shaping and constraining those actions. Interaction is thus both "context-shaped" and "context-renewing" (Drew & Heritage). Interactional practice is viewed as a domain that is relatively autonomous from traditional constituents of social structure such as gender, race, power, socioeconomic status, and so on. It is not that CA denies these constituents' existence or potential influence. Rather, CA emphasizes the importance of attending to their relevance and demonstrable impact on the current interaction (or "procedural consequentiality"; Schegloff, 1987) at any given moment. Thus for CA (as for the participants in the conversation), the focal action in Excerpt 1 is getting help (for Donny), and turning Donny down (for Marcia). Issues such as relationship or identity, which some interpersonal communication scholars might take to shape and control the interaction, for CA may be produced in and through the particular ways in which Donny seeks help and Marcia refuses to help. (See Mandelbaum & Pomerantz, 1991, for an extended discussion of this issue.)

Second, immediately preceding talk is a prevalent resource relied on by interactants for determining what a prior speaker may be doing in a given utterance. The action that a current turn may be doing may be shaped by features of "turn taking" that immediately precede it, or by features of "sequence organization," among other possibilities. For instance, as noted above, Marcia hears Donny's announcement at Line 8, "My car is stalled" in the context of his "Guess what" in Line 6. Furthermore, it is produced in the slot just after the opening of the conversation, where the reason for the call is normally produced (Schegloff, 1986). Its position here in the call, and just after the "guess what–what" adjacency pair prepares a slot for Marcia to hear whatever is produced next as her "big" news. The various features of the position of this news inform answers to the question every participant must ask of every turn—"Why that now?" In this sense, "adjacency" becomes an important concept for researchers to unpack, as it is for interactants also, in determining what is relevantly local.

Conceptualization of Communication in the Theory

For CA, communication consists of actions constructed by communicators out of talk and body behavior. As noted above, communication is regarded as a (necessarily) publicly available constitutive process, rather than as a vehicle for message transmission or meaning-making. Communication is regarded as the central resource for the enactment of all aspects of social life. Whereas CA began as an attempt to study the "orderliness" of everyday life, with taped conversations providing merely a conveniently preserved sample (Sacks, 1984), it rapidly became apparent that conversation itself is central to social life. Schegloff referred recurrently in his work to talk-in-interaction as the primordial site of sociality (e.g., Schegloff, 1987). CA's view of communication as a means for constituting action is consonant with recent moves in interpersonal communication theory to study relationships as constituted via communication (Duck, 1994; Goldsmith & Baxter, 1996). That is, rather than social structure and individual variation, and so on, being seen as "independent variables with discursive consequences" for communication in relationships (Hopper & Chen, 1996, p. 10), communicators also shape, construct, or "do" relationships through their communication. CA provides tools for documenting the practices through which this is accomplished, offering a dynamic conceptualization of relationships and identities, and positioning communication as a central mechanism for producing both relationships and identities. Particular ways of talking can shape and constrain relationships and identities, and changing those ways of talking can reshape them.

Uses of the Theory

CA studies proceed inductively, as noted above. This has resulted in a body of work that springs from analysts' observations of the natural world of interaction (with a careful focus on preserving the integrity of the interactional occasion as it was produced by and for"interactants"; Schegloff, 2005) rather than from systematic attempts to pursue the disciplinary concerns of interpersonal communication theory. In focusing on the structures, actions, and reasoning practices that constitute everyday and institutional talk-in-interaction, a body of CA work describes particulars of how communicators construct and manage their interpersonal relationships. Pomerantz and Mandelbaum (2005) note that "interactants maintain incumbency in complementary relationship categories, such as 'friend-friend,' 'intimate-intimate,' or 'father-son,' by engaging in conduct regarded as appropriate for incumbents of the relationship category and by ratifying appropriate conduct when performed by the co-interactant" (p. 160). That is, there is a variety of practices in and through which interactants enact incumbency in particular relationship categories. These practices show how "being in a relationship" is interactively constructed, since they reveal particular rights and obligations that relationship members enact vis-à-vis one another. For instance, Drew and Chilton (2000) and Morrison (1997) found, in studying calls between family members and friends, that a recurrent activity in these calls was inquiries that attended to what was known about the other person's schedule, and to problems experienced by the other person or their significant others (e.g., "How was the drive?"). Inquiries of this kind (which Morrison calls "tracking questions") were followed by a report of the relevant activities (e.g., "Just fine"), thus ratifying the claim of legitimate concern about and access to these events in the other's life, and then responded to with a display of understanding and interest in the report (e.g., "Good"), and further elaboration by the party of whom the inquiry was made. This work indicates that one set of practices associated with enacting "being in a relationship" involves how knowledge about one another is managed, invoked, and deployed.

Raymond and Heritage (2006) note that "there can be direct links between the identities of participants and the rights and responsibilities associated with those identities that are directly implicated in practices of speaking" (p. 681). They call this the "epistemics of social relations," and present a case study to show how particular ways of talking provide for claiming knowledge in such a way as to enact "having grandchildren." They show, for instance, how the interlocutor will defer to the "actual" grandparent's knowledge of the children through small features of talk, such as producing claims about the grandchildren as questions rather than as declaratives. These are examples of seen but unnoticed features of relationships that can be discovered empirically through systematic examination of actual cases of recorded interaction.

The "epistemics of social relations" is a critical nexus of interpersonal communication that is ripe for further investigation. Additionally, this work demonstrates that just because one "is" a grandparent (or incumbent of any other relationship or identity category) does not mean that such status is relevant on a given occasion. Rather, practical interactional steps must be taken by communicators to invoke the category's relevance (and all of its associations; Sacks, 1992) for any particular occasion. This then leads to the observation that, for practical purposes, incumbency in a relationship is not some entity that one "has," but rather is something that one "does" through communication. We "do" being a grandparent, grandchild, parent, female, boyfriend, girlfriend, married, and so on. Furthermore, CA uses its analytic tools to spell out the tacit yet relied-on knowledge that interactants draw on in dealing with one another in enacting these and other identities. A long-standing debate in the field of interpersonal communication concerns its "distinctive" character (Berger, 2005). Almost any action in conversation can have interpersonal consequences as a by-product. However in research of the kind illustrated here, CA has begun to describe practices that are particular to interpersonal communication; practices that seem to be fundamental to enacting connectedness in a relationship.

Strengths and Limitations of the Theory

Many of CA Theory's strengths can also be considered limitations, and derive from the fact that CA proceeds inductively. That is, the descriptions that CA builds are grounded in features of field recordings of naturally occurring communication, to which analysts can show interactants are demonstrably oriented. This provides interpersonal communication with a new sense of "local."

A strength of CA is that in focusing on that which is demonstrably relevant to and procedurally consequential for interactants, it avoids treating a communicator as "a judgmental dope of a cultural or psychological sort" in Garfinkel's (1967, p. 67) terminology. That is, an interaction order that is coherently structured to manage the procedural challenges inherent in interacting together is independent of individual and even cultural variation. While it can be deployed to enact or construct individuals qua individuals, and to enact individual goals, it is not the individuals' judgments, psyches, or cultures that shape its basic organization. Actors' circumstances are in fact shaped and altered by their actions (Heritage, 1995, p. 392). Thus the findings of CA that are relevant to interpersonal communication offer descriptions of the organization of the natural world of relationships and identities, and emphasize documented orientations that are manifested and deployed in interaction. As a result, conversation analytic work tends to take a bottom-up approach to society in general, and to relationships in particular. That is, the influence of societal institutions (ranging from marriage and family to medical, legal, corporate, or governmental, for instance) is recognized, but understood to be consequential for communication only inasmuch as it is demonstrably enacted and oriented to by communicators (Drew & Heritage, 1992; Schegloff, 1987). This has further consequences: First it becomes possible to spell out the communication practices through which concepts important to interpersonal communication are enacted in and through talk, such as gender (Hopper & LeBaron, 1998), culture (Hopper & Chen, 1996), or relationships (Pomerantz & Mandelbaum 2005), by analyzing interactional moments where these are demonstrably oriented to by interactants. Second, it provides a liberating view of relationships (one that places communication at the center): they are not produced by social structures or individual psychologies, but rather by communicators in interaction. If this is the case, then unsatisfactory or dysfunctional relationships can be reconstructed by the members of those relationships in different ways through communication. A consequence of this stance of CA Theory is that it deemphasizes the role of individual psychological drives on the one hand, and macrosocietal structures on the other. While some consider this to be a strength of the approach, others consider it a limitation. (However, see Kitzinger, 2005, for CA work that shows the relationship between the sequential organization of talk at the microlevel of interaction and the macrosocial structure of heteropatriarchy that communication reproduces by examining the interactional practices through which "family" is enacted.)

Another result of an inductive discovery process is that, in addition to the more expectable findings about the practices through which relationships are enacted and maintained, serendipitous findings can be made. For instance, while investigating laughter, Jefferson, Sacks, and Schegloff (1987) discovered the specifics of how the use of an obscenity, and uptake of it or resistance to it, can be ways of constituting intimacy. A disadvantage of the inductive process (with an emphasis on taking into account the integrity or the organic whole of the data) is that it may prohibit straightforward pursuit of disciplinary goals (see Schegloff, 2005).

Finally, the single-minded focus on describing interaction practices has meant that CA focuses on particulars, rather than on aggregates. It is important to note, however, that CA uses large collections of instances of a particular phenomenon in order to develop a description that is both context sensitive and context free; because of this, descriptions of practices are based on aggregates of single cases. However little attention has been paid to measuring outcome variables. For instance, issues such as satisfaction are not examined often, although some CA work in the medical context has examined this (e.g., Robinson & Heritage, 2006).

Directions for Future Research and Applications

The CA stance that relationships and identities are things that we "do" via communication rather than things that we "have" is strongly generative of future investigations and applications. As noted above, research on the basic mechanisms in conversation for producing and enabling interpersonal communication provides opportunities for documenting matters that have previously been addressed theoretically, or addressed using recollected occurrences.

Another intersection between traditional interpersonal communication and CA Theory is with regard to CA's focus on when and how particular membership categories are employed in interaction. What are the rights, entitlements, and obligations associated with them? Work in this domain began with Sacks (1992), and has been pursued by Schegloff (e.g., 2007a), Kitzinger (e.g., 2005), and others. This is a rich domain for spelling out both the communication practices in which and through which locally relevant identities are enacted and managed, and the interpersonal actions pursued through their enactment and management.

CA Theory provides for interpersonal communication research to start with accounts of actual practices, or "how" questions, and use answers to these questions to explore "why" questions, or questions about motivation, in a grounded fashion. For example, in Excerpt 1 above, analysis of "how" the action of requesting help is done could lead to grounded speculation about "why" Donny asked for help in this way (e.g., he asks in a way that minimizes imposition on Marcia, by putting her in the position to volunteer to help). Continued basic research examining how countless social actions are produced by communicators should result in further grounded insights about why they produce these actions.

Some CA work has recently taken a critical turn, and has been used to lay out, for instance, the practices of heteronormativity (Kitzinger, 2005). This suggests that future work in which CA is used to examine interpersonal communication could address other inequities produced through communication. By examining these particulars, we could describe in detail the communication practices that constitute a fully democratic relationship.

In these ways, in addition to laying out the particulars of interaction as a discreet domain in its own right, CA's description-based theory provides for both further amplification of important directions in traditional interpersonal communication and the breaking of new ground in our understanding of phenomena central to interpersonal communication that can be discovered in the seen but unnoticed interactional details that make up all relationships.

Note

1. I am grateful to Gene Lerner, Jeff Robinson, and Leslie Baxter for their extensive recommendations, and to Celia Kitzinger and Galina Bolden for their suggestions on earlier drafts of this chapter.

References

Austin, J. L. (1962). *How to do things with words.* Cambridge, MA: Harvard University Press.

Berger, C. (2005). Interpersonal communication: Theoretical perspectives, future prospects. *Journal of Communication, 55,* 415–447.

Drew, P., & Chilton, K. (2000). Calling just to keep in touch: Regular and habitualised telephone calls as an environment for small talk. In J. Coupland (Ed.), *Small talk* (pp. 137–162). Harlow, UK: Pearson Education Limited.

Drew, P., & Heritage, J. (1992). Analyzing talk at work: an introduction. In P. Drew & J. Heritage (Eds.), *Talk at work* (pp. 3–65). Cambridge, MA: Cambridge University Press.

Duck, S. (1994). *Meaningful relationships: Talking, sense, and relating.* Thousand Oaks, CA: Sage.

Garfinkel, H. (1967). *Studies in ethnomethodology.* Englewood Cliffs, NJ: Prentice-Hall.

Goffman, E. (1983). The interaction order. *American Sociological Review, 48,* 1–17.

Goldsmith, D., & Baxter, L. (1996). Constituting relationships in talk: A taxonomy of speech events in social and personal relationships. *Human Communication Research, 23,* 87–114.

Heritage, J. (1984). *Garfinkel and ethnomethodology.* Oxford, UK: Polity Press.

Heritage, J. (1995). Conversation analysis: Methodological aspects. In U. M. Quasthoff (Ed.), *Aspects of oral communication* (pp. 391–418). Berlin, Germany: De Gruyter.

Hopper, R., & Chen, C. (1996). Language, cultures, relationships: Telephone openings in Taiwan. *Research on Language and Social Interaction, 29,* 291–313.

Hopper, R., & LeBaron, C. (1998). How gender creeps into talk. *Research on Language and Social Interaction, 31,* 59–74.

Jefferson, G. (2004). Glossary of transcript symbols with an introduction. In G. H. Lerner (Ed.), *Conversation analysis: Studies from the first generation* (pp. 13–31). Amsterdam: John Benjamins.

Jefferson, G., Sacks, H., & Schegloff, E. (1987). Notes on laughter in the pursuit of intimacy. In G. Button & J. Lee (Eds.), *Talk and social organisation* (pp. 152–205). Avon, UK: Multilingual Matters.

Kitzinger, C. (2005). Heteronormativity in action: Reproducing the heterosexual nuclear family in out-of-hours doctor's calls. *Social Problems, 52,* 477–498.

Lerner, G. H. (2004). Collaborative turn sequences. In G. H. Lerner (Ed.), *Conversation analysis: Studies from the first generation* (pp. 225–256). Amsterdam: John Benjamins.

Mandelbaum, J., & Pomerantz, A. (1991). What drives social action? In K. Tracy (Ed.), *Understanding face-to-face interaction: Issues linking goals and discourse* (pp. 151–167). Hillsdale, NJ: Erlbaum.

Mokros, H. B., & Deetz, S. (1996). What counts as real? A constitutive view of communication and the disenfranchised in the context of health. In E. B. Ray (Ed.), *Communication and the disenfranchised: Social health issues and implications* (pp. 29–44). Hillsdale, NJ: Erlbaum.

Morrison, J. (1997). *Enacting involvement: Some conversational practices for being in relationships.* Unpublished doctoral dissertation, Temple University, Philadelphia, PA.

Pomerantz, A., & Mandelbaum, J. (2005). A conversation analytic approach to relationships: Their relevance for interactional conduct. In K. Fitch, & R. Sanders (Eds.), *Handbook of language and social interaction* (pp. 149–171). Mahwah, NJ: Erlbaum.

Raymond, G., & Heritage, J. (2006). The epistemics of social relations: Owning grandchildren. *Language in Society, 35,* 677–705.

Robinson, J. (2006). Managing trouble responsibility and relationships during conversational repair. *Communication Monographs, 73,* 137–161.

Robinson, J. D., & Heritage, J. (2006). Physicians' opening questions and patients' satisfaction. *Patient Education and Counseling, 60,* 279–285.

Sacks, H. (1984). Notes on methodology. In J. M. Atkinson & J. Heritage (Eds.), *Structures of social action: Studies in conversation analysis* (pp. 21–27). Cambridge, UK: Cambridge University Press.

Sacks, H. (1992). *Lectures on conversation: Vol 1–2* (G. Jefferson, Ed.). Oxford, UK: Blackwell.

Sacks, H., Schegloff, E. A., & Jefferson, G. (1974). A simplest systematics for the organization of turn-taking for conversation. *Language, 50,* 696–735.

Schegloff, E. A. (1986). The routine as achievement. *Human Studies, 9,* 111–151.

Schegloff, E. A. (1987). From micro to macro: Contexts and other connections. In J. C. Alexander, B. Giesen, R. Munch, & N J. Smelser (Eds.), *The macro-micro link* (pp. 207–234). Berkeley: University of California Press.

Schegloff, E. A. (1995). Discourse as an interactional achievement III: The omnirelevance of action. *Research on Language and Social Interaction, 28,* 185–211.

Schegloff, E. A. (2005). On integrity in inquiry . . . of the investigated, not the investigator. *Discourse Studies, 7,* 455–480.

Schegloff, E. A. (2007a) A tutorial on membership categorization. *Journal of Pragmatics, 39,* 462–482.

Schegloff, E. A. (2007b). *Sequence organization in interaction: A primer in conversation analysis I.* Cambridge, UK: Cambridge University Press.

Schegloff, E. A., Jefferson, G., & Sacks, H. (1977). The preference for self-correction in the organization of repair in conversation. *Language, 53,* 361–382.

14

Expectancy Violations Theory and Interaction Adaptation Theory

From Expectations to Adaptation

Cindy H. White

My initial interest in Expectancy Violations Theory (EVT) was sparked by the following question: When unexpected things happen, what determines if we see the event as a surprise or a disappointment? It seemed to me that a key difference was how the event related to what we expected, which influenced how we interpreted the event. For instance, I once had a new coworker whom I thought of as rather distant and standoffish; he was older than me and we appeared to have little in common. As a result, I did not talk much with him and knew little about him. One day after a departmental dinner we both attended he brought me a pound of a special type of rice that had been served at the meal that I had particularly enjoyed. His actions definitely violated my expectations. After that, I saw his distant behavior differently, and I began to interact with him differently.

One theoretical perspective that helps to explain how we interpret and react to these types of situations is EVT. Although following norms and conforming to expectations often seems like the best way to make social interaction work smoothly, Judee Burgoon's early work on the theory proposed that there are circumstances where violating norms is advantageous (Burgoon, 1978; Burgoon, Stacks, & Woodall, 1979). Specifically, initial tests of the theory explored how violations of personal space were interpreted in conversation and considered how characteristics of the communicator who engaged in a violation influenced those interpretations. Since its inception, EVT has been expanded and modified to address a wider range of behaviors, to articulate the influences that determine whether or not a violation will be seen as positive or negative, and to explain interaction responses to violations of expectations. In fact, the most recent extensions of many ideas from EVT are found in Interaction Adaptation Theory (IAT), a conceptual framework that helps to explain and predict how communicators manage to coordinate interaction behavior and how adaptation forms the foundation for effective relationships (Burgoon, Stern, & Dillman, 1995).

Purpose and Meta-theoretical Assumptions

EVT is a post-positivistic theory that seeks to explain and predict how communicators assess behavior that deviates from expectation and how they respond communicatively to such violations. The theory focuses heavily on nonverbal aspects of interaction but has been used to analyze a range of communication behaviors and contexts. For instance, EVT has been used to test how individuals perceive one another in laboratory settings (Burgoon et al., 1979) and to determine if customers who violated expectations of salespeople might be treated more favorably than custumers who did not violate expectations (Burgoon & Aho, 1982). IAT is similar in its orientation but more directly addresses behavioral responses to unexpected behavior. Both theories follow a hypothetico-deductive approach, which means they utilize a set of concepts (such as expectancies, communicator characteristics, violations) to posit specific predictions about the outcomes of interaction. The goal of the theories is to provide a framework that allows researchers to posit hypotheses and to test specific predictions across different interaction contexts. In the next section, I describe the concepts central to EVT and then discuss how these ideas have been incorporated into IAT.

Main Features of the Theories

EXPECTANCY VIOLATIONS THEORY

Expectancies. Fundamental to EVT is the construct of interaction expectancies. "Expectancy in the communication sense denotes an enduring pattern of anticipated behavior" (Burgoon, 1993, p. 31). EVT proposes that our expectations are influenced by three key factors: the communicator, the relationship, and the context in which the interaction occurs. Communicator characteristics include salient features of an interaction partner, such as gender, age, personality, and communication style. Relationship factors include things such as the degree of familiarity between partners or the equality of status between interaction partners. Contextual elements include aspects of the environment that might define how individuals should communicate in a particular situation, such as the formality of the setting or the nature of the task. Thinking back to the situation I described at the beginning of the chapter, it is easy to see how the age and gender of my coworker, lack of familiarity (we had not worked together long), and the work setting all impacted my expectations for interaction.

Expectancies may be related to the behaviors that are appropriate for a situation or particular group, or they may reflect what we know to be the typical behavior of a specific individual. Burgoon (1993) noted that expectancies can refer to what we anticipate will occur (predictive expectancies) or to what is desired or preferred (prescriptive expectancies). In many circumstances, these two types of expectancies are aligned, but they are not always synonymous. For instance, in the situation with my coworker, my predictive expectancy (based on my perception) was that he would be distant and perhaps not easy to work with, but my prescriptive expectancy was that coworkers should be warm and easy to work with. Burgoon and Ebesu Hubbard (2005) argued that EVT "assumes that expectancies . . . entail both a predictive and prescriptive component" (p. 151). By incorporating both types of predictions, the theory provides an opening for considering how violations of expectations are interpreted.

Violation valence. EVT proposes that when someone violates our expectations, we are forced to make sense of what is happening, and thus we shift our focus a bit to try to figure out what his or her behavior means. Within the theory, this process is explained in the following way. When an expectancy violation occurs, arousal is heightened. Heightened arousal initiates cognitive appraisals related to (a) the meaning of the violation and (b) the evaluation of the positive or negative value of the violation (violation valence). Initial versions of the theory proposed that violations create physiological arousal, but later work has suggested that the process need not involve this type of activation. Rather, arousal is described as an orienting response that involves "directing some attention away from the topic at hand and toward the violator and violation" (Burgoon, 1993, p. 35).

The evaluation we make of the violation is described in EVT as the valence of the violation and refers to the positivity or negativity of the meaning we assign to the violation. Some interaction behaviors carry clear social meaning, and so their valence, in a given context or relationship, is relatively clear. For instance, the negative meaning of an obscene gesture is usually not in doubt and would be considered a negative violation. By the same token, most partners in a romantic relationship would see an unexpected warm embrace on returning home as a positive violation. EVT predicts that a violation that has a positive valence will typically lead to better interaction outcomes than a non-violation. A violation that has a negative valence will typically lead to worse interaction outcomes than simply meeting expectations. The valence of a violation determines whether it will be better to do what is expected or to deviate from the norm. However, some interaction behaviors, such as the use of conversational distance, may be more ambiguous in meaning. When this is the case, EVT proposes that the reward value of the person violating expectations is a key factor in determining the valence of the violation.

Communicator reward value. People possess characteristics that influence the extent to which we find interacting with them rewarding. Individuals who are physically attractive, powerful, or highly competent are typically seen as more rewarding than those who do not have any (or all) of those characteristics. EVT suggests that assessments of these positive or negative attributes moderate our evaluations of violations, particularly when the meaning of a violation is open to interpretation. When a rewarding communicator interacts at a closer than expected distance, for example, we are likely to evaluate the violation positively, but when the same distance is adopted by a communicator who is not rewarding, we are likely to evaluate the violation negatively.

Extension of EVT to patterns of interaction. Many of the predictions from EVT relate to evaluations of an interaction partner or outcome. However, EVT has also attempted to address the following question: When someone violates our expectations, how do we respond to them in interaction? Studies that have used EVT to predict behavior in interaction have generated mixed results (e.g., Burgoon & Hale, 1988). For instance, Floyd and Voloudakis (1999) examined expectancy violations by friends during conversations in the lab. Based on EVT, they predicted that reduced involvement and pleasantness would be a negative violation of expectations since friends are expected to be at least moderately involved and pleasant with one another. They hypothesized that friends would compensate decreased partner involvement by increasing their own involvement in an attempt to draw the friend back up to more comfortable levels. They found, however, that decreased intimacy was generally reciprocated. Although EVT has been successful in broadening our understanding of the impact of expectancies on perceptions of interaction, it has been limited in its ability to predict behavioral adaptation that occurs in interaction. In response to this limitation, Burgoon, Stern, and Dillman (1995) developed IAT, a framework that builds on many of the principles of EVT but that focuses more fully on behavioral responses in interaction.

INTERACTION ADAPTATION THEORY

IAT proceeds from the assumption that adaptation in interaction forms the foundation of our relationships with one another and that adaptation is communicative, signaling both interactants and observers about the nature of the relationship between communicators. Adaptation refers to nonrandom patterns of behavior that occur in response to the interaction behavior of another (Burgoon et al., 1995). These patterns are often described in terms of whether the response reflects a matching or reciprocal behavior of a partner (called reciprocity) or whether the response involves behavior that appears to offset or compensate for the behavior of a partner (called compensation). For instance, I was recently talking with a friend who was excited about a job offer she received. Because of her excitement, her speech was quick and animated. I was immediately caught up in her excitement, reciprocating her speech rate and vocal animation. However, when we had talked previously about a job offer that fell through, I had tried to offset her behavior by remaining upbeat nonverbally and talking about future prospects: I tried to compensate for her disappointment (although I do not know how successful I was at the time). IAT proposes that we are predisposed to adapt to others in interaction because adaptation helps to fulfill survival needs by aligning ourselves with others. However, IAT also suggests that social factors (such as status) as well as personal preferences influence whether we reciprocate or compensate in interaction. IAT begins by identifying a range of factors that influence what we need, expect, and desire from another communicator in a particular situation.

Requirements, expectations, and desires. The factors that influence our initial interaction in a situation are referred to as the requirements, expectations, and desires (RED) that an individual holds as that individual begins an interaction. IAT incorporates the idea that some aspects of interaction are driven by basic biological needs related to approach-avoidance. These needs may influence our actions in fundamental and relatively unconscious ways and are referred to as requirements (R). Our expectations (E) for a situation reflect primarily social factors such as social or situational norms, as well as knowledge we may have of another's behavior based on past interactions. Desires (D) are highly personalized and reflect things such as one's personality and other individual differences. IAT notes that R, E, and D are interdependent and often cannot be fully distinguished. Initially, Burgoon and colleagues (1995) proposed that requirements, expectations, and desires were ordered hierarchically so that requirements superseded expectations in determining adaptation and expectations superseded desires. However, research by Floyd and Burgoon (1999) revealed that desires may play a key role in patterns of interaction, so the relative importance of each RED factor may vary depending on the situation.

Interaction position and actual behavior. The composite of requirement, expectation, and desire factors reflects what is referred to as an individual's interaction position (IP). "The IP represents a net assessment of what is needed, anticipated, and preferred as the dyadic interaction pattern in a situation" (Burgoon et al., 1995, p. 266). The IP for a specific individual helps predict how an individual will interpret a specific interaction situation and what that individual is likely to do initially in interaction. The IP is useful conceptually because it can be contrasted with actual behavior displayed by an interaction partner to help us predict responses in interaction and thus patterns of behavior.

The behavior enacted by a partner is referred to in IAT as actual behavior. IAT predictions focus on how an individual responds to the actual behavior of another person. The theory offers two basic predictions about behavioral responses, which are derived from examining the relationship between interaction position and actual behavior. "If IP is more positively valenced than A [actual behavior], then the anticipated interpersonal pattern is divergence, compensation, or maintenance. . . . Conversely, if A [actual behavior] is more positively valenced behavior than IP, then the anticipated interpersonal pattern is convergence, matching, and reciprocity" (Burgoon & Ebesu Hubbard, 2005, p. 163).

An example seems warranted here: let me draw from my own experience. As a teacher, I sometimes have conversations with students about poor performance on exams. How I feel about each interaction is influenced by a number of factors, such as my need for affiliation or cooperation that day (R). I also have some general expectations about how students should respond to grade feedback as well as expectations about specific students based on their prior actions in my class (E). In addition, I have general desires for such interactions, such as a preference for people who are open and those who are willing to take responsibility for their actions (D). One student in particular comes to mind. Her contributions to class led me to believe that she was a serious student capable of very good work, so I was concerned that she would be upset when she came to my office after performing poorly on an exam. My IP predicted that her behavior would be emotionally laden and rather negative; before she arrived, I felt myself bracing for an interaction where I hoped to be able to help her get past being upset about the exam. However, when she came to my office, she was quick to point out that she had been very busy right before the exam for our class and had not studied in the way she typically might for a test. As we reviewed her exam, she was upbeat and optimistic, already able to identify how she could improve her understanding of the material. As we ended our conversation, she told me she was sure she would do better on the next test (and sure enough, she did). According to IAT, her actual behavior (A) was clearly more positively valenced than my IP. As a result, I easily reciprocated her positive tone and engaging interaction style.

Another example also readily comes to mind. A student who had not performed well on prior work and often missed class arrived at my office. Although I expected that she would be concerned about her grade, I assumed she realized before the test that she was not doing well in the course. I thought we might strategize ways to ensure that she passed the class. When the student arrived, she quickly became aggressive, arguing that the test was unfair and that no student could be expected to adequately answer the questions. I had to work hard in this interaction to maintain my composure and to remain calm with this student (I hope I was). I felt that doing so was important to managing the conversation and keeping us on track so we could talk about what she might do. According to IAT, although I may not have been consciously aware of it, this was a situation where A was more negatively valenced than IP, so I maintained my behavior (and compensated her behavior to some extent) to offset her actions and to try to achieve my goal of talking about what she could do to improve her grade. These examples demonstrate the way that IAT extends several components of EVT to provide a framework for understanding how communication is responsive to interaction goals as well as to the behavior of others in interaction.

Conceptualization of Communication in the Theories

An important aspect of EVT is its attention to the interpretation of behavior in interaction. Although some behaviors have clear social meanings (e.g., certain gestures), other behaviors convey different messages depending on the context in which they are displayed and the relationship between partners. For instance, close proximity in conversation can be associated with displays of affection or of dominance. Thus, communication is assumed to involve some interpretation of the actions of another. Early on, EVT focused on cognitive appraisal and communicator reward, so that communication was positioned in the individual's assessment of a situation. Later EVT work has considered communicative responses to expectancy violations. IAT is a theory of interaction that explains how communicators respond to one another and assumes, at some level, that interaction is adaptive and coconstructed. In sum, while IAT attends to cognitive aspects of communication (in RED), interaction is central to the theory, and the goal of the theory is to predict how communicators will respond to one another in interaction. Burgoon and colleagues (1995) described EVT and IAT as theories that were conceptualized in order to explain behavior that is communicative in nature, which means they are primarily "mindful, intentional and symbolic" (p. 11), in contrast to theories that focus on biological or habitual behaviors in interaction.

Uses of the Theories

Because expectations influence our experience of virtually all interactions, EVT and IAT have been applied to a number of different interpersonal communication contexts. Three important contexts of application for the theories have been (a) the study of nonverbal behavior during conversation, (b) expectations and patterns of interaction in intimate relationships, and (c) the influence of expectations or adaptation on the detection of deception. Perhaps the most developed application of the theory has been to the study of nonverbal behaviors such as conversational distance, immediacy, and conversational involvement. One reason nonverbal behavior has been of interest is that researchers wanted to better understand how we make sense of nonverbal cues. For instance, the television show *Seinfeld* included a funny episode on the "close talker" whose interaction style made everyone uncomfortable. But, what determines if we see another person's close proximity as an intrusion into our personal space or rather as a sign of interest or involvement in the conversation? Burgoon (1978) and Burgoon and colleagues (1979) tested the impact of conversational distance violations in the laboratory. Confederates adopted conversational distances that either met expectations or were closer or farther than would have been expected, given the situation. Generally, these studies demonstrated that high-reward communicators were perceived most positively by their interaction partners when they violated expectations (by being either closer or farther from the partner than would be the norm) than when they met expectations. Low-reward communicators were perceived most positively when expectations were met. These findings suggested that communicator reward value played an important role in assessing violations. Moving out of the laboratory, Burgoon and Aho (1982) conducted three field experiments that examined how salespeople responded to conversational distance violations by confederates who posed as customers, and whose reward value was manipulated by modifying dress, behavior, and stated purchase goal (a large or small purchase). They found that violations did heighten awareness of behavior and that the reward value of the confederate influenced salesperson reactions to violations. The findings were complex, however, and suggested that a number of factors (like gender and behavioral norms) impact responses to violations. It is important to note that these initial tests, by focusing on conversational distance, created a situation in which the meaning of the violation was ambiguous, particularly in interactions with strangers. Conversational distance, by itself, may be difficult to interpret, so it may be particularly amenable to the influence of communicator reward value.

Acknowledging this, Burgoon and Hale (1988) examined the impact of immediacy behavior—a set of nonverbal cues that includes distance, lean and body orientation, eye contact, and openness of posture—on interaction between friends and strangers. Burgoon and Hale reasoned that since moderate levels of immediacy are the norm for interactions in the laboratory, high and low immediacy would be seen as expectancy violations. In addition, they thought that whether the interaction partner was a friend or stranger provided a natural way to operationalize communicator reward value. Based on EVT, they predicted that decreased immediacy would be seen as a negative violation for both friends and strangers and would lead to less positive interaction outcomes than conforming to expectations. Increased immediacy was predicted to function as a positive violation for friends since immediacy is desirable in friendship but as a negative violation for strangers since high immediacy should be disconcerting and unpleasant. Their predictions for decreased immediacy were supported, but they found that increased immediacy was typically seen as a positive violation that led to more positive outcomes than meeting expectations for both friends and strangers. Their research revealed that as sets of nonverbal cues are enacted, the meaning of behavior becomes clearer and the valence of the violation is not as readily moderated by communicator reward value.

Although initial EVT research focused on evaluations of behavior, later work highlighted the fact that expectancies (and expectancy violations) impact what individuals actually "do" during interaction with a partner. To assess this, Burgoon, LePoire, and Rosenthal (1995) examined how expectancies and actual behavior influenced evaluations and behavioral responses in interaction. In an experiment, they induced preinteraction expectancies, preparing participants to expect specific levels of conversational involvement from an interaction partner. They found that expectancies influenced evaluations of the partner and behavioral responses in interaction, but also found that the key determinant of how participants communicated during the conversation was the behavior of the partner. For instance, individuals induced to expect high involvement from their partner but who then interacted with a partner who displayed low involvement tended to reciprocate the low involvement in interaction. However, these individuals rated their partners as more involved than individuals who experienced similar involvement but who had not been induced to expect high involvement. Thus, expectancies influence perceptions of a partner's behavior, but communication behavior during interaction plays a key role in determining how individuals react to violations during conversation. Additional testing of IAT further supports this conclusion—both expectations and interaction behavior matter (Floyd & Burgoon, 1999; LePoire & Yoshimura, 1999).

A second context of application for EVT and IAT has been the study of expectancies and patterns of interaction in intimate relationships. In ongoing relationships, expectancies play a key role in creating a sense of shared perspective and connection between partners. One thing that makes close relationships satisfying is that we can rely on (e.g., expect) our partners to show interest and immediacy in interaction with us. But it is also possible for close relationship partners to develop negative expectations of one another, and those negative expectations play a key role in producing relationship dissatisfaction. The application of EVT to romantic relationships has been important because, as Guerrero, Jones, and Burgoon (2000) explained, understanding patterns of behavior in relationships can provide "insight into the spirals of positive and negative behavior that can either enhance or destroy relationships" (p. 326). In an initial test of EVT in relationships, Kelley and Burgoon (1991) asked marital partners to report on expectations for intimacy in the relationship, and then later assessed whether those expectancies had been met, exceeded (a positive violation), or not met (a negative violation). The highest levels of satisfaction were found in relationships where a positive violation had occurred and the lowest levels in relationships where a negative violation had occurred.

Guerrero and Burgoon (1996) posited that attachment style would impact how individuals responded to unexpected increases or decreases in nonverbal intimacy from a romantic partner. An individual's attachment style reflects the extent to which the individual seeks intimacy from others and desires validation within the relationship. They found a general pattern of reciprocity for increased intimacy. Both reciprocity and compensation occurred in response to decreased intimacy, and this seemed to be influenced by an individual's attachment style. Individuals with a preoccupied attachment style—a style that leads individuals to seek excessive intimacy and validation from others—were found to most strongly reciprocate increased intimacy and to compensate decreased intimacy, as compared to other attachment styles. Guerrero and Burgoon suggested that this reflects preoccupied partners' strong desires for intimacy. In contrast, individuals with a dismissive attachment style—a style that leads individuals to see themselves positively but to be dismissive of the value of others—also showed strong reciprocity for increased involvement and compensation for decreased involvement. The authors argued that this finding may reflect dismissive individuals' strong expectations that others will like and value them. Guerrero and colleagues (2000) further examined how romantic partners respond to unexpected changes in intimacy. They found that while partners tended to nonverbally reciprocate decreased intimacy, they also utilized verbal repair strategies designed to determine why the decrease in intimacy had occurred.

Afifi and Metts (1998) pointed out that research on expectations in relationships has often focused on relational transgressions (such as infidelity), which has led to the conclusion that expectancy violations in relationships are negative. When they examined the impact of a range of relational expectancy violations on uncertainty, they found that violations can be positive or negative. For instance, an unexpected gift from a romantic partner may be an important indicator of the partner's depth of feeling and definition of the relationship. Afifi and Metts found that expectancy violations were important for defining relationships; negative violations increased uncertainty about the relationship and positive violations decreased uncertainty about the relationship (see Knobloch, Chapter 10, this volume, for further discussion of uncertainty reduction). Their work highlights the way expectancy violations can help to define the nature of the relationship, since the positive violations they identified often clarified the level of intimacy felt by the partner. Another extension of EVT to relationships comes from Beavan (2003) who examined sexual resistance as an expectancy violation, comparing dating relationships and cross-sex friendships. She found that daters saw sexual resistance as more negatively valenced and more unexpected than cross-sex friends, but friends found sexual resistance to be more relationally important because it highlighted the definitional boundaries of cross-sex friendship.

Although little work on relational communication has utilized IAT, Burgoon and colleagues (1995) noted that personal relationships often highlight one of the most interesting questions that IAT could address: why do we sometimes respond to a partner's communication in ways that do not align with how we know we should or what is best for the relationship? IAT may help to explain why IPs become solidified and how changes in IP or in actual behavior might serve to alter problematic patterns of behavior. In sum, EVT and IAT provide a useful lens for examining communication in relationships.

A third application of EVT and IAT has been in the area of interpersonal deception research. In the study of deception, two key issues have been partly illuminated through the application of EVT and IAT. First, how do individuals detect deception and what role do expectations (particularly expectations of truthfulness) play in detection? Second, given that deception is an interactive process, how does behavior during interaction influence what deceivers do and what partners perceive? Aune, Ching, and Levine (1996) examined whether expectations of violations influenced awareness of deception; they found some support for EVT in that attributions of deceptive behavior were strongest for communicators low in social or physical attractiveness. Levine, Anders, Banas, Baum, Endo, Hu, and Wong (2000) compared EVT and three other models of norm violations to assess how violations of expectations influenced attributions of truthfulness. They found that unusual behavior was more likely than normative behavior to be viewed as deceptive, and this effect was not influenced by the fact that some communicators had been led to expect unusual behavior. Additionally, they argued that their results indicate that unusual behavior is likely to be seen as deceptive, regardless of expectations. However, because the unexpected behavior displayed in their study was quite unusual (it included things such as doing exercise stretches and appearing to watch an invisible insect fly around the room), it is difficult to determine the generalizability of their results. Nevertheless, the extension of EVT as a means to test attributions of deception is useful because prior research on EVT primarily examined perceptions of social attractiveness. In another study, White and Burgoon (2001) used IAT to predict patterns of reciprocity and compensation in deceptive and truthful interactions. Their results demonstrated that differences in the IPs of deceivers and truth-tellers influenced initial behavior displays, with deceivers showing more concern for self-presentation than truth-tellers and displaying lower initial involvement. However, both truth-teller and deceiver behaviors were impacted by the behavior of the interaction partner. Thus, these results support the IAT contention that the actual behavior of a partner in interaction strongly influences the behaviors displayed in interaction.

Strengths and Limitations of the Theories

Both EVT and IAT demonstrate the value of programmatic research. EVT addresses one of the most intriguing questions about human interaction: How much do our expectations impact our perceptions and responses to situations? The predictions of EVT have been modified as research has demonstrated that expectations are complex and that although they do impact perceptions of interaction, they do not override what occurs in actual interaction. IAT offers a more complete account of patterns of interaction that occur between communicators. The concept of an IP complicates the idea of expectancies: it provides a way to consider how expectancies are influenced by personal preferences and biological responses to interaction. Also, by focusing on patterns of interaction, IAT brings the behavior of communicators squarely into focus, providing a strong imperative for communication researchers to pay attention to what actually transpires in interaction rather than just relying on perceptions of communicators or impressions of observers.

The limitations of EVT are primarily related to its ability to predict patterns of interaction. Burgoon and colleagues (Burgoon et al., 1995; Burgoon & Ebesu Hubbard, 2005) articulated two shortcomings of EVT. First, EVT does not explain what would be expected when communicator reward value and behavior valence are at odds. For example, what happens when a low-reward communicator engages in a positive violation? Second, EVT does not provide a complete framework for understanding behavioral adaptation in interaction. It generally seems to underestimate the patterns of reciprocity that are evident in most interactions. For instance, although reduced involvement is dispreferred by most communicators in social situations, it is often reciprocated to some extent. When I am communicating with someone who displays less involvement than I might like, even if I want to offset that person's behavior and try to elicit more involvement, I am likely to reciprocate the behavior to some extent by decreasing my own involvement. This suggests that there are complex ways in which partners' interaction behaviors influence what occurs in interaction.

EVT is also silent on whether the valence of a behavior or the valence of the communicator is more important when the two are incongruent. IAT addresses these limitations by noting that the elements that are represented in the IP are expected to be hierarchical in their influence, so that the basic biological pull of reciprocity is expected to exert influence in most interactions. Additionally, the concept of an IP provides a way to consider how individual desires influence perceptions of behavior and interaction. Perhaps the biggest limitation of IAT is that there is only limited empirical evidence supporting the predictions of IAT about adaptation in interaction. Determining whether it can assess the relative importance of various components within the IP and identifying the situations under which compensation is most likely to occur will be a key test for IAT.

Directions for Future Research and Applications

EVT and IAT have the potential to help us better understand communication in a range of contexts, but they seem particularly well positioned to help us understand two additional areas of communication: intercultural communication and family interaction. Burgoon and Ebesu Hubbard (2005) argued that because expectancies are central to interaction in all cultures, EVT is applicable to cross-cultural interactions, although whether a violation will be positively or negatively valenced must be understood within the cultural frame of the individual experiencing the violation. They noted that both EVT and IAT can provide insight into intercultural communication patterns because they help us understand how expectations influence willingness to engage in intercultural interaction and interpretations of behaviors that are likely to be outside of our typical range of experience. This is a fruitful area for future research.

Although EVT has been used to study romantic relationships, it has not been applied to family communication. Research on family functioning indicates that overly rigid patterns of interaction are typically problematic in relationships (Burgoon et al., 1995). IAT provides a framework for understanding why communicators may lapse into problematic patterns of behavior, although they would prefer to avoid them. These two areas of research demonstrate where EVT and IAT may help researchers understand a wide variety of contexts ranging from situations where uncertainty is high and expectations are based on stereotypical knowledge, to circumstances where interaction is strongly patterned and based on intimate knowledge of the other.

References

Afifi, W. A., & Metts, S. (1998). Characteristics and consequences of expectation violations in close relationships. *Journal of Social and Personal Relationships, 15,* 365–392.

Aune, R. K., Ching, P. U., & Levine, T. R. (1996). Attributions of deception as a function of reward value: A test of two explanations. *Communication Quarterly, 44,* 478–486.

Beavan, J. L. (2003). Expectancy violation theory and sexual resistance in close, cross-sex relationships. *Communication Monographs, 70,* 68–82.

Burgoon, J. K. (1978). A communication model of personal space violations: Explication and an initial test. *Human Communication Research, 4,* 129–142.

Burgoon, J. K. (1993). Interpersonal expectations, expectancy violations, and emotional communication. *Journal of Language and Social Psychology, 12,* 30–48.

Burgoon, J. K., & Aho, L. (1982). Three field experiments of the effects of conversational distance. *Communication Monographs, 49,* 71–88.

Burgoon, J. K., & Ebesu Hubbard, A. S. (2005). Cross-cultural and intercultural applications of expectancy violations theory and interaction adaptation theory. In W. B. Gudykunst (Ed.), *Theorizing about intercultural communication* (pp. 149–171). Thousand Oaks, CA: Sage.

Burgoon, J. K., & Hale, J. L. (1988). Nonverbal expectancy violations: Model elaboration and application to immediacy behaviors. *Communication Monographs, 55,* 58–79.

Burgoon, J. K., LePoire, B. A., & Rosenthal, R. (1995). Effects of preinteraction expectancies and target communication on perceiver reciprocity and compensation in dyadic interaction. *Journal of Experimental Social Psychology, 31,* 287–321.

Burgoon, J. K., Stacks, D. W., & Woodall, G. W. (1979). A communication model of violations of distancing expectations. *Western Journal of Speech Communication, 43,* 153–167.

Burgoon, J. K., Stern, L. A., & Dillman, L. (1995). *Interpersonal adaptation: Dyadic interaction patterns.* New York: Cambridge University Press.

Floyd, K., & Burgoon, J. K. (1999). Reacting to nonverbal expressions of liking: A test of interaction adaptation theory. *Communication Monographs, 66,* 219–239.

Floyd, K., & Voloudakis, M. (1999). Affectionate behavior in adult platonic friendships: Interpreting and evaluation expectancy violations. *Human Communication Research, 25,* 341–369.

Guerrero, L. K., & Burgoon, J. K. (1996). Attachment styles and reactions to nonverbal involvement changes in romantic dyads: Patterns of reciprocity and compensation. *Human Communication Research, 22,* 335–370.

Guerrero, L. K., Jones, S. M., & Burgoon, J. K. (2000). Responses to nonverbal intimacy change in romantic dyads: Effect of behavioral valence and degree of behavioral change in nonverbal and verbal reactions. *Communication Monographs, 67,* 325–346.

Kelley, D. L. & Burgoon, J. K. (1991). Understanding marital satisfaction and couple type as functions of relational expectations. *Human Communication Research, 18,* 40–69.

LePoire, B. A., & Yoshimura, S. M. (1999). The effects of expectancies and actual communication on nonverbal adaptation and communication outcomes: A test of interaction adaptation theory. *Communication Monographs, 66,* 1–30.

Levine, T. R., Anders, L. N., Banas, J., Baum, K. L., Endo, K., Hu, A.D.S., & Wong, N.C.H. (2000). Norms, expectations, and deception: A norm violation model of veracity judgments. *Communication Monographs, 67,* 123–137.

White, C. H., & Burgoon, J. K. (2001). Adaptation and communicative design: Patterns of interaction in truthful and deceptive conversations. *Human Communication Research, 27,* 3–27.

15

Face Theory

Goffman's Dramatistic Approach to Interpersonal Interaction

Sandra Metts and William R. Cupach

E rving Goffman (1922–1982) was an influential and prolific scholar whose work continues to inform contemporary views of social interaction. As a sociologist, Goffman was not so much interested in the psychology of individuals as in the ways that symbolic systems enable them to coordinate interactions. In Goffman's (1967) words, his goal was to understand the answer to this question: "What minimal model of the actor is needed if we are to wind him up, stick him in amongst his fellows, and have an orderly traffic of behavior emerge?" (p. 3). This description of human interaction may seem somewhat unhuman, but Goffman was trying to make it clear that, no matter what unique characteristics people may have in their psychological identity, all people have a social self, a public image, or—as Goffman called it—a "face," that we display during interaction. If you have ever been nervous about a job interview, a speech, or a first date, or if you have ever spilled your coffee, stumbled as you walked down the hall, or said something stupid, you realize that your public self or face is socially constructed, and that losing it is a typically human concern.

Purpose and Meta-theoretical Assumptions

The purpose of Goffman's Face Theory is to help us understand two important aspects of interaction: (a) why and how people construct their public images, and (b) the strategies people use to maintain or restore their own or others' images if those images are lost or threatened. This goal is consistent with the meta-theoretical assumptions of the interpretivist paradigm. Indeed, the concept of public image, or face, as socially constructed is deeply embedded within the broader interpretivist perspective known as Symbolic Interactionism.

The fundamental premise of Symbolic Interactionism is that the routine interactions we engage in every day are not spontaneous creations of our own making. Rather, they are "symbolic enactments" that reflect our knowledge of the cultural rituals that allow people to coordinate their behavior and generate meaning. We all recognize that words and many nonverbal behaviors are symbols that do not resemble their referent, and that generate meaning only in context. For example, we can say, "My dog's name is Lady," or, "That lady is a dog." The meaning for the symbols "dog" and "lady" depend on the sequential ordering within the sentence and the interaction context of their expression.

Importantly, for Goffman "expressive elements" beyond words and nonverbal signals are also symbolic. The meanings of these other elements are learned by children through socialization, in much the same way that verbal language is learned. Why do we speak more politely to a person of higher status? Goffman would say we do so because status is a feature of a person's role and role is part of the system that guides our behavior and gives it meaning during interaction. If we chose to speak with a person of higher status just as we speak to a close friend, and the other person accepted that role definition and responded at the same level, his or her status would no longer constrain our behavior. However, Goffman would be quick to add that when the interaction occurs again in a different context (or "frame") we might recognize that showing deference to the other person's status is expected. We see this often among students and faculty who may have engaging and informal interactions outside the classroom but who reassume the student-teacher demeanor within the context of class.

Finally, a key feature of Symbolic Interactionism, and the basis of Goffman's Face Theory, is that even the private "self" is to a large degree a symbolic construction. As Goffman (1967) said, "Universal human nature is not a very human thing. By acquiring it, the person becomes a kind of construct built up not from inner psychic propensities but from moral rules that are impressed upon him from without" (p. 45). To illustrate, consider an infant who has not yet been socialized to an understanding of "self." This infant does not experience embarrassment, envy, jealousy, pride, or shame. In other words, a self that emerges from and acts within social structures, existing apart from the physical body, does not yet exist. The only self that exists is a composite of basic drives for food, security, and comfort. Eventually, these drives will be embedded within a social framework that guides the infant's expression and gives the drives symbolic meaning.

We now turn to a more detailed discussion of Face Theory with a particular focus on the dramaturgical metaphor that underlies it.

Main Features of the Theory

Goffman used the metaphor of interaction as "drama" in order to illustrate how and why face is constructed, maintained, and lost. For Goffman, interaction is like a performance in a play in the sense that people are like actors who deliver their lines, wear costumes, and use props that are appropriate to each scene. Although this may sound manipulative, contrived, or artificial, consider that you dress for class, bring your notebook and pen, and greet other students with pleasant comments even when you would rather be home in your "sweats."

Goffman's most explicit description of the dramaturgical metaphor is found in his book *Presentation of Self in Everyday Life* (1959), in which he described the coordinated interactions found in institutions such as hospitals or mental care facilities, workplaces, and in public contexts such as restaurants. He studied the mechanisms by which "teams" (e.g., hospital staff [nurses and doctors] or restaurant staff [hostesses, servers, and cooks]) were able to structure their actions in such a way so as to perform their roles. Goffman also applied his insights to "social teams" such as families and groups of friends. Based on his observations, Goffman (1959) argued that the process of social interaction manifests features similar to those found among actors who prepare themselves to perform on stage, deliver their performances, and receive acceptance by the audience. Specifically, he stated that a person's performance is "all the activity of a given participant on a given occasion that serves to influence in any way any of the other participants" (p. 22). In short, a performance is designed, consciously or unconsciously, to create an impression for others of who we are—an idealized self that fits appropriately into the requirements of the context. This pattern of actions that we use to create the impression is called a "part" or "routine." The other people in the situation contribute to the performance by serving as an audience, observers, or as coparticipants.

Furthermore, Goffman (1959) referred to a front region (or front stage) and a back region (or backstage). The "front region" is where the performance takes place; it contains the "expressive equipment" that an individual may use during the performance. Thus, it consists of both the "setting" (e.g., living room, classroom, restaurant, and the furniture or items within) and the "personal front" of the performer (including (a) appearance (e.g., clothing, sex, age, hair style, and racial characteristics), and (b) manner (e.g., looks, posture, facial expressions, bodily gestures) that give clues about the role the performer might play (e.g., aggressive, meek, friendly, and so on). The "back region" is the place where the props for performance are stored and where preparation for performance can be conducted. For most of us, the back region in our lives is our home or our office where we prepare ourselves to perform "on stage" in the presence of others at work, in the classroom, or at social events. We are not much concerned when a close friend stops by our house unannounced because he or she is part of the cast, so to speak, but a relative stranger arriving unannounced would evoke the awkwardness that an actor feels when an audience member enters the back stage and sees him or her "out of character."

Goffman did not explicitly use the terms "stage" and "performance" in his essay "On face-work: An analysis of Ritual Elements in Social Interaction" (1967), but he implicitly developed the dramaturgical perspective. When he described the practices of ordinary conversation and the normative order within these events, Goffman used the concept of "face," which he defined as the "positive social value a person effectively claims for himself" (p. 6). Our face is a type of performance, in that we present an image of our "self" through our appearance, our messages, and our actions that we believe will give the impression that we are competent and worthy social interactants.

In what Goffman (1967) called an "expressive ritual," interactants generally support each other's face presentation. We do so in part because we realize that if we do not cooperate in the protection of others' face, we cannot expect that they will cooperate in the protection of ours. In addition, we realize at some level that other people, like ourselves, are emotionally attached to their face. When face is accepted and validated, people feel good; when it is called into question, they feel bad. Thus, the general rules of "self-respect" and "considerateness" lead us to act in ways that maintain our own face and to cooperate in the maintenance of others' face. Importantly, this agreement is a working model for any given interaction. We may or may not actually be expressing or accepting some sincere, heart-felt expressions of self, but we give a ritualistic acknowledgement to the proffered images so that we can continue interaction.

Of course, Goffman (1967) also recognized that sometimes "incidents" occur and that the ordinary state of "being in face" could be disrupted, with the interaction becoming awkward or being derailed. He described two general types of "losing face." First, a person may "be in wrong face" when some type of information or some action discredits the image that he or she is putting forth. An example of being in wrong face are those occasions when people are expected to (and present themselves as able to) demonstrate competence at an activity such as giving a speech, but they fumble for words. Another example is when people are on a date and fail miserably at small talk, humor, and even simple social manners. Second, a person may "be out of face" when he or she is not able to put forth an image that is expected (even required) in a specific interactional context. Examples of being out of face are those occasions when people are at a loss as to how to act or what to say, as when a person who is married is sitting in a bar showing affectionate behaviors to a person other than the spouse, and a coworker who knows the spouse approaches the table.

Whatever the particular situation, when we lose face we become flustered, are embarrassed, or even "shamefaced." We realize that we cannot continue to present the image we had constructed as legitimate or appropriate. When these incidents occur, we use "face-work" to maintain the integrity of our own face or support the face display of others. When the incident is relatively minor, we try to remain poised (to not be flustered by our own embarrassment) and might use humor or a self-deprecating remark so that others will realize we are basically competent. Usually, other people laugh and support our face by saying, "Oh, you're not an idiot," or "I do things like that all the time." However, when face loss is more serious and disruptive, people rely on a ritualistic or scripted type of message exchange to restore face and reconstitute the interaction. Because these "moves" as Goffman (1967) called them, are deeply embedded within a culture's communication practices, we present them in more detail in the following section.

Conceptualization of Communication in the Theory

Goffman (1959) distinguished the concept of message from the broader construct of communication. His notion of message is not particularly remarkable in that he recognized "verbal messages" (i.e., signs that are given) and "nonverbal messages" (i.e., signs that are given off). We are generally more conscious of and in control of our verbal messages than of our nonverbal messages, although some nonverbal signs can also be used intentionally to convey an aspect of our proposed identity. Importantly, because we assume that verbal messages are more likely to be used with conscious intent, we often take information from nonverbal displays as more trustworthy than verbal displays and as evidence of whether or not the claim to a certain role or identity is legitimate. Beyond this notion of what constitutes a message, however, Goffman moved more directly into his unique rendering of Symbolic Interactionism when he discussed communication.

To fully appreciate Goffman's conceptualization of communication, it is helpful to compare it to the prominent views of his time. From the late 1950s through the 1970s, the common view of interpersonal communication stemmed largely from psychology where communication and self-disclosure were virtually synonymous. For example, Jourard's book, *The Transparent Self: Self-disclosure and Well-being* (1964), advocated an authentic and uncalculated openness about our feelings, wants, and needs as a vehicle to good physical and psychological health.

Goffman's view of communication is quite different. He (1967) stated, "I assume that the proper study of interaction is not the individual and his psychology, but rather the syntactical relations among the acts of different persons mutually present to one another" (p. 2). If we unpack this statement a bit, its meaning can be more fully appreciated. A syntactical relation is an ordering based on rules for structure. For example, in English the syntax of a sentence refers to word order as in "John hit the ball," rather than "ball the hit John." The first is meaningful as a sentence (apart from the content), whereas the second is not. What Goffman wanted his readers to understand is that communication consists of ordered sequences of messages between people, and that the only way that communication as an activity (apart from meaning) can occur is when these sequences unfold in a coordinated, rule-abiding pattern of exchange. When these conditions are met, interactants carry off their performances and maintain their face.

When these sequences are threatened or disrupted, individuals engage in a "preventive" or "corrective" process that in essentially a "pause" in the interaction to allow participants to realign their message sequence. For example, to prevent a disruption, speakers will avoid certain topics that might threaten their own or another person's face, or they will show respect for another person's position on an issue and offer disagreement in an indirect, face-saving way. We use civil inattention to appear that we have not noticed something embarrassing to another person, or we use polite deception when someone asks us to join them in a social activity but we don't want to go because we don't enjoy their company (e.g., "Oh, I wish I could go, but I have other plans").

When a disruption cannot be avoided and one or more participants lose face, an incident has occurred and the interaction order is in a state that Goffman (1967) called ritual disequilibrium. When a disruption occurs, efforts must be made to reestablish a satisfactory order. If the incident is a relatively inconsequential matter, then a simple interchange of two symbolic moves will suffice: "Excuse me. I'm sorry," and, "Certainly. No problem." However, when the incident is more complex, a longer sequence is necessary. According to Goffman (1967), interactants will use four ritualistic moves to restore order. These constitute the remedial interchange: (a) a challenge to "call attention to the misconduct" (spoken or implied), (b) an offering to show others that the offending person recognizes that his or her behavior violated expectations for maintaining face of self and others (e.g., by apologizing, downplaying the severity of the offense, or referring to extenuating circumstances), (c) an acceptance of the offering as sufficient to reestablish order and restore face, and (d) a thanks from the offending person that others have accepted and "forgiven" his or her poor performance. Sometimes one pass through the sequence is sufficient; at other times, it might take several passes.

Interestingly, Goffman argued that even the one aspect of human expression that might seem to be exempt from ritual control—the expression of emotion—is functionally very much a part of the ritual or syntactic order. When referring to sadness (at another's face loss) or anger (when our own face has been threatened), Goffman (1967) explained that "these emotions function as moves, and fit so precisely into the logic of the ritual game that it would seem difficult to understand them without it. . . . In fact, spontaneously expressed feelings are likely to fit into the formal pattern of the ritual inter-change more elegantly than consciously designed ones" (p. 23).

In sum, Goffman viewed communication as strategic in the sense that mes-sages are used to construct, maintain, and restore the organizational system of interaction that allows participants to enact their identities or conduct their performances. This is not to say that people are consciously aware of their intentions to manage interaction at all times or that people do not sometimes abuse the ritual courtesies afforded them by manipulating impressions for their own gain. It is simply to say that communication is the essential element in what Goffman called the "orderly traffic" of social behavior.

Uses of the Theory

Among the many facets of interpersonal communication to which Goffman's ideas have been applied, the occurrence of embarrassment has received the most systematic treatment. As Miller (1996) noted, Goffman's "rich descrip-tion of flustered actors and audiences trying to regain their poise and reestab-lish their scripts drew attention to understudied phenomena and helped prompt the first empirical studies of embarrassment in the 1960s. Goffman was, in many respects, the progenitor of modern embarrassment research" (pp. 111–112). Goffman (1967) did not consider embarrassment to be inher-ently inimical or counterproductive. Indeed, he realized that the actual display of embarrassment (blushing, being flustered, and the like) is constructive inso-far as it allows actors to convey that they are competent enough to recognize that the moral order has been breached, and that it requires restoration. Indeed, those who show some chagrin after committing a breach are viewed more favorably than those who do not (e.g., Semin & Manstead, 1982). As Goffman (1967) remarked, "the person who can witness another's humiliation and unfeelingly retain a cool countenance himself is said in our society to be 'heartless,' just as he who can unfeelingly participate in his own defacement is thought to be 'shameless'" (pp. 10–11).

Throughout his writings, Goffman illustrated a number of specific remedial moves, both preventive (e.g., tact) and corrective (e.g., accounts and apolo-gies), designed to counteract embarrassing and otherwise offensive incidents. As noted above, he carefully delineated the remedial interchange. He did not, however, systematically categorize the types of "offerings" that actors might employ. Consequently, one focus of subsequent research has been to elaborate the different ways in which embarrassed actors and observers repair embar-rassing incidents (for reviews, see Cupach & Metts, 1990, 1994; Miller 1996). This research indicates that, in addition to offering "apologies," actors and observers provide "accounts" that explain untoward actions. Accounts include excuses, which minimize responsibility (e.g., "It's not your fault," "I was held up in traffic"), and justifications, which minimize seriousness of the offense (e.g., "It's not as bad as you are making it out to be," "I did it to teach you a lesson"). An actor or observer can use "remediation" by attempting to physically repair damage (e.g., cleaning up a spill or replacing a broken vase). "Humor" (e.g., joking about one's ineptness or faux pas) is also common in relatively mild incidents. "Avoidance" is usually thought of as a preventive strategy, but it can be corrective, as well (e.g., ignoring a faux pas so as not to draw more attention to it, or fleeing the scene). Finally, "aggressive actions" (e.g., insult, criticism, or retaliation) are sometimes used by actors who are seriously offended. In such cases they are motivated to defend and repair their own face at the expense of the offender's face.

Because face reflects "situated" identity, the appropriateness of various remedial strategies depends on the nature of the event. Several studies have assessed this connection. Humor and remediation, for example, are more likely to be employed in response to a loss of comportment (Metts & Cupach, 1989), but less likely when experiencing empathic embarrassment (Cupach & Metts, 1992). Aggression, on the other hand, is more likely to be employed by an actor who is the recipient of teasing, ridicule, or criticism (Cupach & Metts, 1992; Sharkey & Stafford, 1990).

Goffman clearly recognized that embarrassment was not the only consequence of an incident; participants can also feel annoyed, angered, and offended, among other things. Accordingly, some researchers have studied social predicaments more generally, without focusing on the element of embarrassment. Hodgins, Liebeskind, and Schwartz (1996), for example, solicited participant accounts to hypothetical victims of face-threatening predicaments. Among numerous other results, they found that perpetrators gave lengthier and more face-saving accounts to friends than they did to acquaintances, and that they gave more face-saving accounts to high-status versus low-status victims.

In an effort to more directly assess the face implications of moves within the remedial interchange, researchers are beginning to assess directly the extent to which various challenges, offerings, and evaluations are perceived to be relatively face-threatening or face-saving. Manusov, Kellas, and Trees (2004) observed friendship dyads in which one person elicited and the other person provided an account for a failure event experienced by the accounter. Both the accounter and the elicitor completed measures of the extent to which their own behavior was attentive to the other's face, and the other's behavior was attentive to their own face. Among their numerous findings, both elicitors and accounters perceived that offerings of concessions and refusals were less attentive to the elicitor's face than were excuses. When examining challenges, accounters perceived more face attentiveness when there was no verbal challenge than when there was a direct question or rebuke, or an indirect or open question.

We close this section by reviewing two investigations that illustrate the diversity of contexts to which Goffman's concept of face-work extends. In one example, Cavanagh, R. E. Dobash, R. P. Dobash, and Lewis (2001) employed Goffman's conceptualization of remedial face-work to investigate how men who were violent toward their intimate female partners made sense of and characterized their violence. The authors conducted in-depth interviews with Scottish men who had been convicted of violent domestic offenses, as well as with their victimized partners. They found that violent men employed remedial strategies to minimize the repercussions of morally offensive behavior. "In seeking to make the meaning of a violent act more 'acceptable,' men deploy strategies for managing the meanings they attach to violence. They also seek to impose these meanings upon the women they abuse" (p. 700). Men used various forms of accounts, including "denial" (e.g., "I wouldn't say I was violent," "I don't remember"), "shifting blame" (e.g., "It's her fault," "Everybody around here was brought up that way"), "minimization" (e.g., "It doesn't happen every week," "She only had a little bit of blood on her face"), and "reduced competence" ("I'm not violent when I'm sober," "I can't help it. I have a bad temper"). In addition to offering accounts, men "apologized; expressed remorse; sometimes cried; promised to change; assured their partner that the violence would never happen again; and offered gifts—sometimes very lavish" (p. 707). Because elaborate apologies generally are accepted, they can "be used to disconnect one violent incident from another, thereby ensuring that violence is not seen as a feature of the relationship but rather as fragmented incidents detached from the relationship" (p. 708). Finally, the authors observed men using the remedial device of requests, which in this context could sometimes be considered demands (e.g., "I asked to her to stop nagging me, but she kept it up"). In this way, men shifted their responsibility for violence to the partner by rationalizing that the partner did not comply with their request. Cavanagh and colleagues (2001) contended that understanding this type of "exculpatory discourse" could be important in fashioning focused intervention designed to alter the meaning men ascribe to their violent behavior, and to modify their dysfunctional identity as a relational partner.

In a very different investigation, Brackett (2000) argued that the sometimes pejorative connotations of romance novels (whether conveyed by nonreaders or as misperceived by the readers themselves) would lead romance-novel readers to protect their identities in social situations by using face-saving strategies. She interviewed a small number of female romance-novel readers about their experiences, and identified several preventive and corrective strategies they employed to protect their identities. Preventive strategies included concealing the novel when in public, sometimes by using a nondescript book jacket, and by criticizing bad romance novels and shallow romance readers. This latter strategy is intended to diminish the ammunition of romance novel critics. Corrective strategies included making claims regarding the intellectual value of romance novels (such as providing insights and tidbits of useful information), and by emphasizing that the books were merely one source of leisure or escape, not something through which the readers lived a fantasy life. Brackett also found a separation strategy (e.g., "I'm not anything like the typical reader of romance novels") that could be used in both preventive and corrective situations. "Readers use separation strategies to distance themselves from the stereotypical image of both the readers and the books. This is a way to decrease their chances of stigma by association." (p. 355). Brackett admitted that it is unclear to what extent romance novel readers actually experience criticism from others or if they are reacting to self-criticism. Regardless, she concluded, "the source of the face threat may not be as important as the skills that the actor employs to nullify it" (p. 357).

Strengths and Limitations of the Theory

Undoubtedly, the most enduring contribution of Goffman's work, particularly his dramaturgical approach to face and face-work, is his comprehensive analysis of the routine and ordinary traffic of social interaction. As Burns (1992) said of Goffman, "he made clear what was previously unclear, pointed to the significance of things that had been regarded as of little or no consequence, and disentangled what was previously an indiscriminate muddle" (p. 6).

Goffman's Face Theory meets the criteria of a good theory. First, it has a broad "scope" and explains phenomena that occur frequently or in a wide range of circumstances. In this chapter, we have focused only on the dramaturgical elements of Goffman's work, but even amid this selective range it is apparent that his work has implications for understanding virtually all aspects of interpersonal communication. We could never communicate unless the numerous, diverse, and complex aspects of our individual personalities were selectively organized into a coherent unit appropriate for the needs of the circumstances— i.e., the performance, role, or face that Goffman discussed. Moreover, we could never exchange the simplest greeting, let alone initiate or maintain personal relationships, without implicit (ritualized) rules to guide our understanding of the actions that we and others are performing.

A second strength of Goffman's dramaturgical perspective is its "heurism." When a theory is "heuristic," it stimulates continued research in an area. Goffman's influence on subsequent scholars interested in social interaction has been enduring and widespread. Space does not permit a description of these many applications, but they range from ritual teasing at coed wedding and baby showers (Braithwaite, 1995), to public use of cell phones (Humphreys, 2005), conflict management (Oetzel, Ting-Toomey, Yokochi, Masumoto, & Takai, 2000), negotiating identities when developing intercultural relationships (Imahori & Cupach, 2005), and cross-cultural communication (Holtgraves,

1992). Indeed, a second-generation rendering of face and face-work underlies a prominent theory of interaction known as Politeness Theory. As evident in Chapter 19 of this volume, the research in this area alone is extensive.

Paradoxically, however, sometimes the strengths of a theory are the source of its limitations. In the case of Goffman's work, his scope is so broad that it causes the theory to be weak on the criterion of "parsimony." When a theory is parsimonious, it is "economical" in how it is expressed: it is direct and concise. Goffman's description of the elements and processes of social interaction is not parsimonious. His initial rendering of his dramaturgical perspective, for example, required an entire book, *The Presentation of Self in Everyday Life* (1959).

Directions for Future Research and Applications

Despite the broad heuristic power of Goffman's work, an area that has not received the attention we might expect from communication scholars is his notion of "social skill," which he also refers to as tact, savoir faire, or diplomacy. We believe that Goffman's ideas could be usefully employed to provide a fresh perspective on the construct of interpersonal communication competence (Spitzberg & Cupach, 2002). Given his focus on the ritual order of interaction, an individual's communication competence would be evidenced by the successful enactment of social roles and the facilitation of others' enactments. Drawing on the analogy of a card game, Goffman suggested that one aspect of our identity (our role or face) is like the hand we are dealt. The other aspect of our identity, however, is the skill with which we play that hand.

These skills are not easily catalogued and vary as much in degree as in kind. Goffman (1967) illustrated the dilemmas with which each actor must grapple:

> Too little perceptiveness, too little *savoir-faire*, too little pride and considerateness, and the person ceases to be someone who can be trusted to take a hint about himself or give a hint that will save others embarrassment. . . . Too much perceptiveness or too much pride, and the person becomes someone who is thin-skinned, who must be treated with kid gloves, requiring more care on the part of others than he may be worth to them. Too much *savoir-faire* or too much considerateness, and he becomes someone who is too socialized, who leaves the others with the feeling that they do not know how they really stand with him. (p. 40)

We do not have the luxury in this venue to elaborate these ideas, but we believe that they suggest a provocative alternative metaphor for interpersonal competence. Exploration of this approach could stimulate new conceptualization and measurement efforts in the area of interpersonal competence and social skills. Such efforts would hold promise not only for theory and research but ultimately for teaching and training individuals to develop perceptiveness, tact, effective face-work, and aplomb at playing the ritual game.

References

Brackett, K. P. (2000). Facework strategies among romance fiction readers. *Social Science Journal, 37,* 347–360.

Braithwaite, D. O. (1995). Ritualized embarrassment at "coed" wedding and baby showers. *Communication Reports, 8,* 145–157.

Burns, T. (1992). *Erving Goffman.* New York: Routledge.

Cavanagh, K., Dobash, R. E., Dobash, R. P., & Lewis, R. (2001). "Remedial work": Men's strategic responses to their violence against intimate female partners. *Sociology, 35,* 695–714.

Cupach, W. R., & Metts, S. (1990). Remedial processes in embarrassing predicaments. In J. A. Anderson (Ed.), *Communication yearbook 13* (pp. 323–352). Newbury Park, CA: Sage.

Cupach, W. R., & Metts, S. (1992). The effects of type of predicament and embarrassability on remedial responses to embarrassing situations. *Communication Quarterly, 40,* 149–161.

Cupach, W. R., & Metts, S. (1994). *Facework.* Thousand Oaks, CA: Sage.

Goffman, E. (1959). *The presentation of self in everyday life.* New York: Doubleday.

Goffman, E. (1967). *Interaction ritual: Essays on face-to-face behavior.* New York: Pantheon Books.

Hodgins, H. S., Liebeskind, E., & Schwartz, W. (1996). Getting out of hot water: Facework in social predicaments. *Journal of Personality and Social Psychology, 71,* 300–314.

Holtgraves, T. (1992). The linguistic realization of face management: Implications for language production and comprehension, person perception, and cross-cultural communication. *Social Psychology Quarterly, 55,* 141–159.

Humphreys, L. (2005). Cellphones in public: Social interactions in a wireless era. *New Media & Society, 7,* 810–833.

Imahori, T. T., & Cupach, W. R. (2005). Identity management theory: Facework in intercultural relationships. In W. B. Gudykunst (Ed.), *Theorizing about communication and culture* (pp. 195–210). Thousand Oaks, CA: Sage.

Jourard, S. M. (1964). *The transparent self: Self-disclosure and well-being.* New York: Van Nostrand Reinhold.

Manusov, V., Kellas, J. K., & Trees, A. R. (2004). Do unto others? Conversational moves and perceptions of attentiveness toward otherface in accounting sequences between friends. *Human Communication Research, 30,* 514–539.

Metts, S., & Cupach, W. R. (1989). Situational influence on the use of remedial strategies in embarrassing predicaments. *Communication Monographs, 56,* 151–162.

Miller, R. S. (1996). Embarrassment: Poise and peril in everyday life. New York: Guilford.

Oetzel, J. G., Ting-Toomey, S., Yokochi, Y., Masumoto, T., & Takai, J. (2000). A typology of facework behaviors in conflicts with best friends and relative strangers. *Communication Quarterly, 48,* 397–419.

Semin, G. R., & Manstead, A. S. R. (1982). The social implications of embarrassment displays and restitution behavior. *European Journal of Social Psychology, 12,* 367–377.

Sharkey, W. F., & Stafford, L. (1990). Responses to embarrassment. *Human Communication Research, 17,* 315–342.

Spitzberg, B. H., & Cupach, W. R. (2002). Interpersonal skills. In M. L. Knapp & J. Daly (Eds.), *Handbook of interpersonal communication* (3rd ed., pp. 564–611). Newbury Park, CA: Sage.

16

Information Manipulation Theory

Explaining How Deception Occurs

Steven McCornack

M ost adult Americans share at least some memory of President Bill Clinton's iconic act of deception. On January 26, 1998, Clinton hosted a press conference to rebut rumors of an affair with intern Monica Lewinsky. Clenching his fist angrily, Clinton declared, "I did not have sexual relations with that woman." Several months later, Clinton confessed that he had lied. Less familiar, however, is a similar instance of public doublespeak that occurred during the same time period. In 1998, then-Governor Roy Romer (Colorado) confessed to an extramarital affair with Betty Jane Thornberry, his former deputy chief of staff. Or did he? When asked by reporters if they'd had sex, Romer replied, "It's a very affectionate relationship." When pressed as to whether the word "affection" meant sex, Romer responded, "I'm not trying to define where affection ends and sex begins."

We often think of deception as the antonym of truth. Messages exchanged between communicators are presumed to fall into one of two categories: "truth" or "lie." Correspondingly, people are thought to be either "honest" or "dishonest." Thinking of communication as a simple dichotomy is comforting. It allows us to believe (among other things) that a wide behavioral gulf exists between truthtellers and liars. As a consequence, lies are believed to be distinguishable from truths in ways that allow us to "detect" them. All we have to do is identify the set of readily apparent characteristics that differentiate lies and liars from truths and truthtellers, and then maintain a vigilant watch for these attributes in our interpersonal dealings with others.

But the truth about deception is more complicated—and more interesting—than popular folk beliefs (McCornack, 1997). In everyday interactions, people rarely either tell the truth or a lie. Instead, people manipulate the information they share with others in complex and subtle ways, resulting in messages that are simultaneously somewhat honest and somewhat deceptive (McCornack, 1992). And when we focus our attention on "how" deception is accomplished, we find that people deceive in myriad ways (Metts, 1989; Turner, Edgley, & Olmstead, 1975). Occasionally people deceive by producing messages that are bald-faced lies: "I did not have sexual relations with that woman, Ms. Lewinsky." More commonly, people mislead by producing messages that manipulate information in other ways. For instance, Governor Romer's response to the reporter's query didn't share any false information. Instead, he used "irrelevance" and "vagueness" to veil his infidelity. He failed to answer the reporter's initial question directly, instead commenting on the relationship as a whole. He then presented the vague "I'm not trying to define . . . ," which left listeners guessing as to whether sex had occurred.

In this chapter, we examine the ways people manipulate information in the interpersonal communication messages they share with others. In doing so, we explore Information Manipulation Theory (IMT; McCornack, 1992), a theory designed to explain how people deceive and how people are deceived.

Purpose and Meta-theoretical Assumptions

We live in a culture that touts the importance of honesty. Our religions entreat us to be truthful, our courts require honesty pledges prior to testifying, and public figures and personal relationship partners are punished for prevaricating. At the same time, deception scholars (such as I) are fond of saying, "People who say they never lie are the biggest liars of all." By this, we mean that no one is honest—if by "honest" we mean someone who habitually discloses all of the truthful information that is relevant. Instead, most of our communication with others involves both the sharing of honest information and a certain degree of editing, "spinning," or outright distortion that makes our messages less than fully honest (McCornack, 1997; Metts, 1989; Turner et al., 1975). Think about it. You're walking hand in hand with your romantic partner, thinking how happy you are to be with him or her, when suddenly you spy an attractive passerby. As you surreptitiously steal a glance, your partner queries, "What are you thinking?" How do you respond? Honestly, by saying, "I was thinking about how happy I am to be with you, but then I started checking out the hottie over there"? Or do you deceive by deleting the second clause; saying something akin to, "I was thinking about how happy I am to be with you"? Likely, you will say the latter.

IMT is a theory describing and explaining how we do this—that is, how people play with information in honest and deceptive ways during interpersonal interactions. IMT blends into one theory three disparate meta-theoretical traditions: constructivism, positivism, and interpretive theory. The roots of IMT lie primarily in "constructivism," a branch of post-positivism suggesting that we each actively construct a view of the world that surrounds us, based on our perceptions. Because people's perceptual "constructions" necessarily differ (to some degree at least), so too will views of deception-related concerns such as "what needs to be said in order to be completely honest" and "what counts as a lie." What's more, from the constructivist perspective, all perceptual constructions of the world are fallible—that is, no one person has the only "correct" or "objective" view of reality.

At the same time, IMT shares the positivistic goal of providing a theoretical explanation of the underlying mechanisms responsible for deception (specifically, message design and inferential reasoning). And although IMT is a theory in its own right, it builds on prior theory from the interpretive tradition regarding conversational understanding suggested by philosopher H. Paul Grice (1989). Hence, to understand IMT, one must first understand Grice's arguments.

GRICE'S COOPERATIVE PRINCIPLE

In a series of lectures at Harvard in 1967, philosopher H. Paul Grice (1989) outlined the principles underlying how people understand communication. Grice noted that when we interact with others, we don't exchange a series of random and disconnected remarks. Instead, our interpersonal encounters "are characteristically, to some degree at least, cooperative efforts; and each participant recognizes in them, to some extent, a common purpose or set of purposes, or at least a mutually accepted direction" (p. 26). Grice argued that, in general, people follow the Cooperative Principle (CP): "Make your contribution such as is required, at the stage at which it occurs, by the accepted purpose or direction of the talk exchange in which you are engaged" (p. 26).

Grice specified four specific rules or "maxims" that together constitute what is "required" to fulfill the CP. (1) The "quantity maxim" relates to expectations regarding the amount of information that should be presented. During ordinary conversations, messages are assumed to be as informative as is required, given the demands of the situation. If you ask a romantic partner, "What did you do last night?" you typically will presume that the answer that follows will be fully informative—that is, that it shares with you all relevant information from the prior evening. If, at a later point, you discover that your partner spent much of the evening in a sexual tryst with a romantic rival—information your partner chose not to include in his or her original response—you likely will perceive your partner's message as having been decidedly uninformative (to say the least).

(2) The "quality maxim" relates to expectations regarding truthfulness. Communicators are expected to not share information they know to be false or for which they lack evidence. Just as you assume that a partner has told you everything that is relevant from a previous evening (quantity), you also assume that your partner is not telling you false information: for example, you assume your partner would not say, "I was at the library studying," when in fact she or he was out partying with friends.

(3) The "relation maxim" suggests that, during encounters, people will present messages relevant to the preceding discourse. Partners will answer questions when asked, present statements relevant to prior statements, and so forth.

(4) Finally, Grice argued for the "manner maxim," which he viewed "as relating not . . . to what is said, but rather to how what is said is to be said" (p. 27). This includes the expectation that people will avoid obscurity and ambiguity in their messages, and that they will present information in a brief and orderly fashion.

As is obvious to anyone who has ever had a conversation, people do not always abide by these maxims (Levinson, 1983). But Grice didn't envision these maxims—or the CP in general—as binding laws that people always follow. Instead, he envisioned that in most ordinary conversations people orient in a general fashion to these principles, such that "when talk does not proceed according to their specifications, hearers assume that, contrary to appearances, the principles are nevertheless being adhered to at some deeper level" (Levinson, p. 102).

CENTRAL ASSUMPTION OF IMT

The fact that we typically presume the communication of others to be informative, honest, relevant, and clear—that is, cooperative—makes us vulnerable to deception. Sometimes people produce messages that are less informative than is required, present false information, are irrelevant, or are overly vague, but design their messages in ways that the violation is not obvious. When this happens, deception results. Thus, the central assumption of IMT is that messages that are commonly thought of as "deceptive" derive from covert violations of Grice's conversational maxims (McCornack, 1992).

From the perspective of IMT, the production and presentation of deceptive messages can be considered a phenomenon in which speakers exploit the belief on the part of listeners that they (the speakers) are adhering to the principles governing cooperative exchanges. Deceptive messages are deceptive in that, while they constitute deviations from the principles underlying conversational understanding, they remain covert deviations. Listeners are misled by their belief that speakers are functioning in a cooperative fashion.

CENTRAL PURPOSES OF IMT

The central purposes of IMT are to identify the ways in which people manipulate information in the messages they produce (how speakers deceive) and to explain how deception functions (how listeners are deceived). Drawing on the arguments of Grice, IMT suggests that during interpersonal encounters listeners possess four types of expectations regarding the information transmitted to them by speakers: quantity, quality, relation, and manner. Thus, speakers can covertly violate any or all of these expectations in transforming the information they possess so as to deceive listeners (Galasinski, 1994). Put differently, at least four dimensions exist along which information can be varied in the production of deceptive messages: playing with the amount of information that is disclosed, presenting untruthful information, manipulating relevance of the message, and toying with the manner in which the information is presented.

IMT also provides an account of how exactly deceptive messages deceive. When presented with deceptive messages, listeners are misled in part by believing that the messages are cooperative—that is, that the messages are informative, truthful, relevant, and clear (McCornack, Levine, Morrison, & Lapinski, 1996). Listeners also are misled because when they receive a deceptive message they often presume additional information that simply is not true (Jacobs, Dawson, & Brashers, 1994). For example, consider the case mentioned above, where a romantic partner spends the evening with a rival. When you ask your partner what she or he did the previous evening, your partner tells you, "I watched a movie" (true) "at home" (true) and "went to bed early" (true). What your partner does not tell you is that she or he watched the movie with a romantic rival, after which they both went to bed early. This deceptive message is a quantity violation, in that while the information it presents is truthful, it leaves out information most of us would consider essential—namely, the fact that these activities were shared with a rival.

Now consider how this message deceives. On receiving this message, you presume that your partner has been fully informative—a presumption that is incorrect. But you also likely go on to presume additional false information, such as "my partner did not have sex with someone else last night" and "my partner was alone throughout the entire evening." Thus, deceptive messages deceive others both by getting them to falsely believe that messages are fully cooperative and by fostering belief in additional false information.

Main Features of the Theory

At the heart of IMT is the notion that four dimensions exist along which people routinely manipulate information in the communication messages they design (Levine, 1998). This suggests that, on the broadest level, people can produce one of five messages in any situation: a message that discloses all of the relevant information for the situation (a fully cooperative message), or messages involving manipulations of quantity, quality, relation, or manner. To illustrate these options in detail, we examine a case study, and the messages that might result. Imagine you have been dating "Terry" for nearly three years, and that you feel very close and intimate toward him or her. Because Terry goes to a different school upstate, the two of you have agreed to date other people. Nevertheless, you feel jealous and possessive toward Terry. You see Terry only occasionally, but you call each other every Sunday and talk for an hour. Unbeknownst to you, on Friday one of Terry's friends invites Terry to go to a party on Saturday, but it's a date party. Terry presumes you cannot visit for the weekend, so Terry asks someone from communication class, someone attractive. The two of them go to the party and end up having a great time together. Throughout Saturday, however, you call Terry but get no response. Worried, you drive upstate on Sunday. Arriving at Terry's doorstep, you tell Terry, "I decided to drive down for the day and surprise you. I tried calling you all day, but kept getting your voice mail. What were you doing last night?"

COOPERATIVE MESSAGES

One message option Terry faces in this situation is to disclose all of the information that is relevant to your query, in an informative, truthful, relevant, and clear fashion: "I'm sorry to have worried you. Please don't be mad or jealous, but I went to a date party with someone else I'm interested in, and we had a lot of fun. I didn't ask you because I didn't think you could make it down. If you think we need to talk about our agreement to date other people, let's do it." Although this message is by almost any standard "completely honest," it also is extremely rare. Studies document that most people faced with the Terry scenario do not produce messages of this sort, but that they instead create messages involving manipulations of information (McCornack, 1992).

QUANTITY VIOLATIONS

The most common way people manipulate information is through violating quantity—that is, by producing messages that are less informative than is required. For example, Terry might reply, "I'm sorry to have worried you. I went to a party and had a lot of fun." Although the information presented in this message is truthful, relevant, and clear (Terry did "go to a party" and "had a lot of fun"), it leaves out the most critical pieces of relevant information: namely, that the party **was a date party**; that Terry **went with someone else**; and that **this person is someone in whom Terry is interested**. On receiving this message, you would be deceived if you believed it to be fully cooperative. You also would be deceived to the degree to which you presumed additional, false information (e.g., "Terry went to the party alone," "The party wasn't a date party," and so on.).

QUALITY VIOLATIONS

Although quantity violations are the most common form of deceptive message (Turner et al., 1975), they are not the most common message people think of when they consider "deception." Instead, when people think of deception, they typically think of "bald-faced lies"—manipulations of quality. For instance, Terry might have said, "I'm sorry to have worried you. I wasn't feeling well, so I turned my cell phone off and went to bed early. I'm feeling better now, though. It must have a 24-hour flu bug or something." This message is deceptive in that it presents false information that will lead to false beliefs in your mind (e.g., "Poor Terry! How awful to have spent the evening alone and ill.").

RELATION VIOLATIONS

A third way people play with information when communicating is through presenting messages that are irrelevant, given the preceding talk. Such attempts appear to be the rarest form of deception (McCornack, 1992), largely because it is difficult to make such manipulations "covert." By definition, when you fail to relevantly respond to what has just been said, your partner likely will notice. For example, Terry might have said, "Why didn't you tell me you were coming!? I know you get paranoid sometimes, but driving all the way up here just to check up on me is a bit ridiculous, don't you think? How would you like it if I paid a sneak visit to you and acted like a jerk by asking you what you had been doing!?" When people violate relation, they often take this type of approach—assuming that the best defense is a good offense—creating messages that call into question the validity of the previous query, thus shutting down the topic for further discussion.

MANNER VIOLATIONS

A fourth way people manipulate information is through "manner violations"—producing messages that are vague or ambiguous. For instance, Terry might have said, "I'm sorry to have worried you. I was really busy with some stuff last night, so I turned my phone off." In this case, Terry uses the vague "really busy with some stuff" to veil the events of the evening. Of course, similar to violations of relation, violations of manner are difficult to covertly render. If you're paying close attention to Terry's response, you're likely to wonder what exactly is meant by "really busy" and "some stuff," and ask Terry additional questions about it.

COMPLEX COMBINATIONS

Although we have focused our attention on relatively straightforward examples (the five message types discussed above), people also mix and match the information they manipulate in the same message. Consider this response from Terry, one that meets the requirements of quantity, but then "spins" the meaning of the information by adding additional false information, violating quality: "Well, on Friday a friend of mine invited me to a party for Saturday night. I really wanted to go, but unfortunately we had to have a date. I would have asked you, but figured you couldn't make it up, so I asked someone from class who I also have been interested in to go with me. We went to the party together and had a lot of fun at first, but then it got kind of boring, and all I could think about was how much I missed you. Please don't feel threatened by this." In this message, Terry abides by quantity, disclosing that the party was a date party, the party was attended with someone else in whom Terry is also interested, and that a lot of fun was had. But Terry also attenuates this message by adding false information, thus violating quality. The "fun" was experienced only at first, after which it got kind of boring and all Terry could think about was how much Terry missed you—all information that is false.

Conceptualization of Communication in the Theory

Communication is the central vehicle through which we exchange meaning with others. But from the perspective of IMT, this exchange of meaning is not accomplished through the production and presentation of messages that are either truths or lies. Instead, most of the messages we present to others in daily communication involve some form of information control or "manipulation." Consider the findings from one of the most influential early studies of deception, conducted by Turner and colleagues (1975). They had respondents record "important" conversations with a relationship partner over a two-week period, and then revisit these conversations. Respondents were asked to assess each message they had presented in the conversation in terms of whether it was "honest" (fully informative, truthful, relevant, and clear) or whether it controlled (manipulated) information. They found that only 38.5% of messages presented in important conversations did not involve information manipulation; that is, 61.5% of messages involved information manipulation of some type. In addition, when they analyzed entire conversations, not a single instance was found of an encounter in which every message presented by a person was honest.

IMT shares the view documented by Turner and colleagues (1975) that deceptive communication is ubiquitous. Rather than social realities and relationships being fostered and maintained through unbridled honesty, people almost constantly control the information they share with others. As famed sociologist Erving Goffman (1967) expressed it, personal and professional relationship harmony "tends to be based not on agreement of candidly expressed heart-felt evaluations but on a willingness to give temporary lip service to judgments with which participants do not really agree" (p. 11).

Uses of the Theory

During interpersonal encounters, people typically don't produce truths or lies. Instead, people have available to them a multitude of options for how they can play with information in their messages, and they exercise these options on a routine basis. The fact that information manipulation occurs as a regular part of everyday interaction suggests at least two significant practical implications that help us to better understand interpersonal communication. First, rather than being an unusual form of action typified by readily identifiable behavioral characteristics, deception is an interpersonal constant. In its typical form, deception occurs as a spontaneous type of contextual problem solving. Questions and comments arise during interaction that we (or our partners) realize are problematic—messages that obligate us to share information that will be hurtful, will present us or others in an unfavorable light, or that may permanently damage relationships. In response, we spin, play with, control, and manipulate information. Rather than saying "Yes, I had sex with my assistant," we say, "I'm not trying to define where affection ends and sex begins."

Second, because deception typifies much of interpersonal communication, and because it commonly is accomplished through the subtle and complex weaving together of information, we cannot reasonably hope to detect the "lies" of others (McCornack, 1997). People play with information routinely, casually, and frequently, in ways designed to lead others away from the full truth (DePaulo, Kashy, Kirkendol, Wyer, & Epstein, 1996). And the most common way in which people do this—quantity violations—does not involve the presentation of any false information at all, but instead involves the simple excising out of particular pieces of truth perceived as problematic. No evidence exists to suggest that such messages are readily "detectable"—that is, distinguishable from their "truthful" counterparts (McCornack, 1997). Consequently—and expressed in the bluntest possible terms—people should abandon the goal of "catching others' lies." Put differently, the most practical thing one can do in dealing with deception in our lives and relationships is to trust people until proven wrong.

Strengths and Limitations of the Theory

IMT was the first theory to suggest that deceptive messages can best be described by examining the multiple dimensions along which information is manipulated, rather than by labeling them as categorical types (e.g., "truths," or "lies"). This is perhaps the greatest strength of IMT: it provides scholars and laypersons who are interested in accurately capturing the richness of messages with a descriptive framework for detailing how exactly information is manipulated in messages. It also was the first perspective to suggest exactly how deceptive messages deceive—through the exploitation of listener beliefs in speaker cooperativeness, and the establishment of false beliefs in listeners' minds.

At the same time, two significant challenges confront IMT. First, in its original form, IMT neglected to present a set of testable and potentially falsifiable predictions regarding deception and deceptive message design. Because of this shortcoming, IMT can best be thought of as a "fledgling theory-in-progress" rather than as a fully developed theory.

Second, the bandwidth of deceptive messages accounted for by IMT is somewhat narrow, at least when compared with the myriad ways people deceive others. Consider the following example. Several years ago, a female friend of mine, who I'll call Susan, was having an affair. Susan's best friend at the time was a woman I'll call Jane; Susan had told Jane all about the affair. One afternoon, following a picnic shared with Susan's husband, her friend Jane, and several mutual friends, Susan's husband (with no advance warning whatsoever) remarked to Susan, "I get the impression Jane thinks you've been cheating on me." With lightning speed, Susan responded with, "Jane knows if I ever did anything like that I would tell her." In fact, this message was absolutely true—Susan **had** cheated and **had** told Jane in detail about it. By the standards of IMT, this message was as informative as was required in the context (given her husband's preceding message); it was truthful, relevant, and clear. But my friend used this message to trigger a deceptive inference on the part of her husband, namely "I haven't cheated on you." Because of its focus on information manipulation, IMT doesn't readily encompass such messages—that is, deception that occurs through knowing and exploiting how our intimate partners think, without any notable "information manipulation" in the message itself.

Directions for Future Research and Applications

Laypersons and scholars alike often think of deception as a traitlike quality that exists inside messages, rather than as something that is constructed within the heads of perceivers and deceivers based on their perceptions of messages. Messages are presumed to be either intrinsically "honest" or "dishonest," in turn, message honesty and dishonesty is presumed to be an attribute that is not just detectable, but a universal constant that everyone perceives in the same ways. Arguably the most exciting and provocative line of future work related to IMT is that which calls these presumptions into question. Specifically, research examining cross-cultural perception of information manipulation suggests wide disparity in perception of information manipulation and corresponding perceptions of deceptiveness. These differing perceptions derive from cultural differences in views of politeness, and how messages best should be constructed so as to maintain face—the positive social self we present to others during interaction (Goffman, 1967). For example, McCornack and colleagues (1996) found that respondents in the United States (most of whom were Euro-American), consistently viewed messages involving information manipulation as more deceptive than as completely disclosive, "cooperative" messages. But Yeung, Levine, and Nishiyama (1999), examining perceptions among Chinese respondents in Hong Kong, found that although messages manipulating quality and messages manipulating relation were perceived as deceptive, messages manipulating quantity and messages manipulating manner were not. Lapinski and Levine (2000) found that for respondents in Hawaii (most of whom were of Asian descent), perceptions of dishonesty stemming from information manipulation depended largely on the perceived motivation behind the message. Specifically, quantity manipulations performed in order to save one's own face were judged significantly more deceptive than manipulations of quantity enacted for the benefit of others. As Lapinski and Levine (2000) concluded, the same message may be viewed as polite and face saving when told for the benefit of others, but devious and conniving when told for the benefit of self.

To conclude, IMT provides us with a rich framework for exploring the oftentimes subtle and complex ways in which people manipulate information during interpersonal encounters. In doing so, it reminds us that messages rarely are truths or lies, and instead typically fall somewhere in between these poles. Rather than suggesting that we are all "liars," such a perspective reminds us that the fabric of social interaction is maintained not through unbridled and unmediated disclosure, but through the careful crafting of messages designed to present information we believe best serves our needs and relationships.

226 ■ Discourse/Interaction-Centered Theories of Interpersonal Communication

References

DePaulo, B. M., Kashy, D. A., Kirkendol, S. E., Wyer, M. M., & Epstein, J. A. (1996). Lying in everyday life. *Journal of Personality and Social Psychology, 70,* 979–995.

Galasinski, D. (1994, July). *Deception: Linguist's perspective.* Paper presented at the International Communication Association convention, Sydney, Australia.

Goffman, E. (1967). *Interaction ritual: Essays in face-to-face behavior.* Garden City, NY: Anchor Books.

Grice, P. (1989). *Studies in the way of words.* Cambridge, MA: Harvard University Press.

Jacobs, S., Dawson, E., & Brashers, D. (1994, November). *Information manipulation theory: A replication and assessment.* Paper presented at the annual meeting of the Speech Communication Association, New Orleans, LA.

Lapinski, M. K., & Levine, T. R. (2000). Culture and information manipulation theory: The effects of self construal and locus of benefit on information manipulation. *Communication Studies, 51,* 55–74.

Levine, T. R. (1998). Modeling the psychometric properties of information manipulation ratings. *Communication Research Reports, 15,* 218–225.

Levinson, S. C. (1983). *Pragmatics.* New York: Cambridge University Press.

McCornack, S. A. (1992). Information manipulation theory. *Communication Monographs, 59,* 1–16.

McCornack, S. A. (1997). The generation of deceptive messages: Laying the groundwork for a viable theory of interpersonal deception. In J. O. Greene (Ed.), *Message production: Advances in communication theory.* Mahwah, NJ: Erlbaum.

McCornack, S. A., Levine, T. R., Morrison, K., & Lapinski, M. (1996). Speaking of information manipulation: A critical rejoinder. *Communication Monographs, 63,* 83–91.

Metts, S. (1989). An exploratory investigation of deception in close relationships. *Journal of Social and Personal Relationships, 6,* 159–179.

Turner, R. E., Edgley, C., & Olmstead, G. (1975). Information control in conversations: Honesty is not always the best policy. *Kansas Journal of Sociology, 11,* 69-89.

Yeung, L. N. T., Levine, T. R., & Nishiyama, K. (1999). Information manipulation theory and perceptions of deception in Hong Kong. *Communication Reports, 12,* 1–11.

17

Interpersonal Deception Theory

Purposive and Interdependent Behavior during Deception

Judee K. Burgoon and David B. Buller

D eception is ubiquitous. Humans dissemble about everything, from whether they are irritated with their partner, to how qualified they are for a job, to their intentions to exercise. When construed broadly to include not just bald-faced lies but also omissions, equivocations, hedges, and the like, deception occurs in one-third or more of all conversations, with people averaging two lies per day (DePaulo, Kashy, Kirkendol, Wyer, & Epstein, 1996). This state of affairs stands in contrast to the presumption in most encounters that others will be truthful (Grice, 1989). Deception, then, shadows every walk of social life, and with important consequences.

In this chapter, we present a theory that examines deception through the lens of interpersonal communication. Interpersonal Deception Theory (IDT; Buller & Burgoon, 1996; Burgoon & Buller, 2004) can be contrasted with more psychologically oriented models, such as the leakage hypothesis (Ekman, 1985) or four-factor theory (Zuckerman, DePaulo, & Rosenthal, 1981), in that it focuses less on inward psychological and involuntary autonomic responses (e.g., fear reactions) and more on outward social factors such as the communicative interplay between sender and receiver. IDT emphasizes those aspects that are voluntary and intentional and includes in the model individual and social factors that influence deception and suspicion displays, the interaction patterns between deceiver and deceived, and the outcomes of credibility and detection accuracy. The original theory presented a large number of assumptions and propositions (testable statements). A brief overview of them is presented here.

Purpose and Meta-theoretical Assumptions

IDT is a post-positivistic theory, with an interconnected set of general state-ments predicting and explaining the background circumstances, processes, and outcomes of interpersonal deception. It is based on assumptions about the strategic, interactive, and evolving nature of interpersonal communication and deception that provide the groundwork for the theory's propositions. IDT takes a bird's-eye view and attempts to present a macrolevel explanation of the most important features of a deceptive episode, as understood from a com-munication perspective (e.g., communicators' natural tendencies to match conversational patterns), rather than focus on a single microlevel causal mech-anism (e.g., fear of being detected). Some of these communication features are neither original with IDT nor limited solely to deception.

A core assumption underpinning IDT is that deception is no different from other forms of communication, in that humans are goal-oriented, adaptive creatures. Their communication—whether it be truthful or deceptive—is intended to satisfy a host of goals such as presenting oneself favorably to others, managing the expression of feelings and emotions in a socially accept-able way, maintaining relational harmony, easing conversational flow, and per-suading others to accept one's ideas and proposals. Both sender and receiver in any communication exchange have multiple goals in force, which means that communication is naturally an adaptive give-and-take between individuals as they each seek to achieve their own goals. Though many of the functions of human communication become routinized early on and operate at a low level of awareness, they still represent deliberate action. Because deception is by def-inition an intentional act, IDT underscores that it should be characterized as strategic, meaning that perpetrators of deceit pursue various tactics to achieve their communication goals, to be seen as credible, to have their duplicity accepted as truth, and to evade detection.

Another core assumption is that information management is fundamental to communication. People may choose to hide, distort, misrepresent, obfus-cate, or avoid transmitting information in their communication by manipulat-ing the veracity, completeness, directness, relevance, and personalization of their messages (Burgoon, Buller, Guerrero, Afifi, & Feldman, 1996). Deceivers must manage not only the central message, usually verbal, which conveys the deceptive content, but also the accompanying language and nonverbal behav-iors intended to evade detection and bolster credibility. Notwithstanding the assumption that deceptive episodes are fraught with intentional actions, another assumption is that deceptive displays may also include unintended actions, usually nonverbal, that inadvertently reveal the sender's deceptive intent or the true state of affairs (Ekman & Friesen, 1969). These include dif-ferent cognitive and emotional responses (e.g., heightened arousal, negative affect, and cognitive effort) than truthtellers display (Johnson, Barnhardt, & Zhu, 2004; Vrij, Fisher, Mann, & Leal, 2006).

A third key assumption in IDT is that receivers are active participants in deceptive episodes who influence their time course and ultimate outcomes. Receivers are active information processors whose "antennae" are tuned into the actions of senders; who experience greater cognitive difficulty, unpleasantness, and vigilance when their suspicions are aroused; who provide various forms of feedback to senders that can range from acceptance to skepticism to outright disbelief; and who themselves can actively and strategically adapt their own communication styles as their suspicions wax and wane.

These assumptions (and several others) are the "drivers" for IDT. They answer many of the "why" questions regarding what deceivers and their targets think and do.

Main Features of the Theory

IDT attempts to explain how senders and receivers engage in the process of deceiving and detecting deception while immersed in a conversational exchange where the goals of the parties may not always mesh. Consider, for instance, a married couple arguing about a husband's penchant for gambling. In response to his denials that he has a gambling problem, the wife may take a new tack on how she questions him about his whereabouts. In turn, he may become more evasive in how he answers her. Ultimately, whether she uncovers the truth—and whether or not each party regards the conversation as successful— will be governed by the combination of senders' actions, receivers' reactions, and the interplay between them.

The propositions in IDT cover the entire process of deceptive communication and must be understood in conjunction with one another and with the assumptions. The first two propositions are general statements intended to identify key contextual and relationship factors in which all deceptive episodes are enmeshed. The first are features of the communication context—interactivity and task demands. Interactivity refers to whether message exchange is interdependent (a given message is connected to prior messages), takes place in real time, and has multiple verbal and nonverbal channels available (among other factors). Task demands concern whether or not participants are engaged in a conversation that is mentally or emotionally difficult to conduct. The second calls attention to the relationship between sender and receiver as a significant influence on what participants think and do.

> Proposition 1. Context features of deceptive interchanges that systematically affect sender and receiver cognitions and behaviors are the interactivity of the medium and the demands of the conversational task.

Proposition 2. Relational features of deceptive interchanges that systematically influence sender and receiver cognitions and behaviors are familiarity and relationship valence.

The husband, should he choose to deceive his wife about his gambling, can capitalize on the availability of social cues in full audiovisual contexts (e.g., face-to-face conversations between the married couple) to present himself in the most appealing fashion and keep telltale indicators of deceit in check. Comparatively, more telltale signs would be available for her to detect if the couple just exchanged e-mails. The husband might also choose a real-time (synchronous) form of communication such as the telephone to foster a sense of closeness and trust with his wife and to reduce chances of detection that would be present with different-time (asynchronous) communication. However, synchronous communication has its drawbacks. The husband has to produce messages on the fly, with less time to plan, rehearse, or edit messages, so he risks greater detectability. The demands of the task and the wife's familiarity with how her husband dissembles must also be factored in. Telling a white lie about whether the wife's new outfit makes her look overweight is easy. Trying to hide substantial gambling losses is much more challenging and requires more finesse. In addition, more is at stake (if the couple values the marriage). As for the matter of familiarity, people in close relationships know each other's history, values, daily routines, and usual communication styles. Deceivers can capitalize on this knowledge to construct plausible messages. Detectors can also use this information to unmask lies, but usually the advantage in this cat and mouse game goes to deceivers.

Context and relationship factors not only influence how a deceptive episode unfolds and with what consequences but also receivers' and deceivers' cognitive-affective states.

Proposition 3. Interactive contexts and positively toned relationships are associated with higher expectations that a sender is truthful.

Proposition 4. The more receivers expect truthfulness and the more they are familiar with the deceivers or deceptive behavior, the less deceivers fear detection.

Because of their strong attachments and positive feelings for one another, marital partners often give each other the benefit of the doubt. Thus, the wife may accept as truthful the husband's claims that he gambles only infrequently or loses only small amounts. At the same time, the attachment and emotions can cause the husband to become anxious when deceiving, particularly when he knows his wife expects him to tell the truth and when he fears that she knows him well enough to recognize irregularities in his communication.

The next set of propositions concerns behavioral displays. Proposition 5 formalizes the belief that communication (and therefore also deception) includes both strategic (intentional) and nonstrategic (unintentional) elements. Propositions 6 through 10 predict how these behavioral patterns are altered over time, depending on whether or not the communication context is interactive, whether the relationship is a familiar one and positively or negatively toned, the deceiver's motives and social skills, and the suspicions of the receiver. The full reasoning behind these and subsequent propositions can be found in Buller and Burgoon (1996) and Burgoon and Buller (2004).

> Proposition 5. Deceivers engage in both strategic and nonstrategic activities. Strategic activity includes managing information content of messages, associated nonverbal behavior, and overall image. Nonstrategic activity reveals arousal, negative or dampened affect, depressed involvement, and impaired speech.

> Proposition 6. Interactive contexts heighten strategic activity and lessen nonstrategic activity over time.

> Proposition 7. Deceiving for self-gain prompts more strategic activity and nonstrategic behavior than deceiving for the benefit of others.

> Proposition 8. The more receivers expect truthfulness, the less deceivers are motivated to behave strategically.

> Proposition 9. Greater familiarity prompts more strategic and nonstrategic activity by senders.

> Proposition 10. Skilled communicators display more strategic activity and less nonstrategic activity than less skilled communicators.

To illustrate, the gambling husband's choice of strategies will be affected by whether or not he is deceiving primarily for his own benefit (Proposition 7): to preserve his reputation (an identity goal), to maintain marital harmony (a relational goal), and to continue his gambling unabated (an instrumental goal). It is easier, for example, to tell a lie if the purpose is to protect the other person rather than oneself. When deceiving for his own gain, the husband's likely first gambit will be concealment—omitting any reference to his gambling in his accounts of his whereabouts or activities—rather than outright lying because lies are more difficult to keep straight, are more easily uncovered by those who are familiar with his history and day-to-day routines (e.g., the wife rather than a neighbor; Proposition 9), and will have a more devastating impact on his image and relationships if found out. He will take advantage of family and coworkers' expectations for truthfulness to accept whatever he says (Proposition 8). Contrary to what might seem intuitive, he will have an easier time bringing any nervousness and speech dysfluencies under control if he perpetrates the deception in a face-to-face conversation with his wife rather than in an exchange of voice-mail messages (Proposition 6). He will also do better at keeping nonstrategic behavior in check if his targets are trusting, do not know him, and are unschooled in the ways of deception (Propositions 8 and 9), and if he is a skilled communicator (Proposition 10).

Propositions 11–14 call attention to four factors that should influence judgments of a sender's credibility and the accuracy of deception detection. The same factors that enable senders to engage in strategic activity—interactivity, truth bias, and sender skill—should result in senders being seen as credible and evading detection. In addition, the more senders adhere to "normal," expected communication patterns, the more they should be seen as credible and evade detection of deception. Conversely, receivers will have a better prospect of detecting deception if communication occurs through some noninteractive medium (such as e-mail), if receivers lack a truth bias, and if senders are unskilled communicators who display unusual behaviors.

> Proposition 11. Receivers are more likely to judge senders as credible when the context is interactive, when receivers have high truth biases, and when senders are skilled communicators.
>
> Proposition 12. Receivers are less likely to detect deception when the context is interactive, when receivers have truth biases, and when senders are skilled communicators.
>
> Proposition 13. Receivers are less likely to judge senders as credible when sender communication deviates from expected patterns.
>
> Proposition 14. Receivers are more likely to detect deception when sender communication deviates from expected patterns, when receivers are familiar with sender information and behavior, and when receivers have strong decoding skills.

These propositions suggest that the deck is stacked against the wife discovering her husband's duplicity about his gambling problem, because she is likely to be predisposed toward believing him, especially if she has no cause to suspect a gambling problem, and if he is skilled at communicating (Propositions 11 and 12). The husband will do well if he conforms to normal conversational patterns that are typical of the couple's interaction styles (Propositions 13 and 14). If he strays from his usual pattern of interacting with her—say, by becoming taciturn or overly effusive or expressive—she is bound to become suspicious.

Suspicion is a critical component of deceptive episodes. The next propositions speak directly to the role of suspicion in the process, positing that suspicious receivers adjust their communication patterns and, in doing so, often alert senders to their skepticism. And, just as nondeceptive communication entails senders attending and adapting to feedback from the receivers, deceivers are expected to pick up on receivers' suspicions and modify their messages to be more believable.

> Proposition 15. Suspicion evokes changes in both strategic and nonstrategic behavior by receivers.
>
> Proposition 16. Senders perceive suspicion when it is present such that (a) deviations from expected receiver behavior and (b) receiver behavior signaling disbelief,

uncertainty, or the need for additional information increase sender perceptions of suspicion.

Proposition 17. Suspicion (perceived or actual) evokes changes in both strategic and nonstrategic behavior by senders.

According to these propositions, the wife's suspicions can actually make it even more difficult to detect her husband's deceptions, especially if she reveals her suspicions by probing or appearing surprised or incredulous (Proposition 15). Her husband should pay close attention to the wife's behaviors as he lies and make strategic adjustments to bolster the believability of his communication if she signals disbelief (Propositions 16 and 17).

Once the conversation is under way, sender and receiver cognitions and behavioral patterns fluctuate in response to behaviors enacted by each other. The next two propositions underscore that this process is a dynamic and adaptive one.

Proposition 18. Deception and suspicion displays change over time.

Proposition 19. Reciprocity is the dominant interaction adaptation pattern between senders and receivers during interpersonal deception.

Consider what happens if the suspicious wife indirectly questions her husband about the work he was purportedly doing at the office the night before, when he was in fact at a local casino. He may evade by talking instead about what other people were working on. Suppose she then shifts to a more direct approach, asking if he stopped at the casino last night. He may try to stonewall about his whereabouts by omitting the critical detail of stopping off at the casino. If she escalates to a more direct accusation, he may reciprocate with a stronger assertion that he has not been gambling. If she persists, he may fabricate a story about his whereabouts. If she does not buy that story, she may respond with anger, to which he may respond in kind with angry indignation. Thus, the deceptive exchange will change in character over the course of the conversation (Proposition 18). Because deceptive exchange is embedded within normal conversational patterns, one of the most prevalent being the tendency for relational partners to reciprocate one another's interaction patterns, each person's manner of communicating typically will beget similar (reciprocal) verbal and nonverbal behaviors from the spouse (Proposition 19).

The last propositions concern the final outcomes of deceptive interactions—receivers' judgments of believability and senders' perceptions of success. Final receiver beliefs and decoding skills, and the sender's most recent communication are influential in these outcomes.

Proposition 20. Final sender credibility and receiver detection accuracy are functions of (a) final receiver cognitions (suspicion, truth biases), (b) receiver decoding skill, and (c) final sender behavioral displays.

Proposition 21. Sender-perceived deception success is a function of perceived suspicion and final receiver behavioral displays.

With the ongoing interplay between husband and wife, it follows that judgments should also change. Judgments of credibility and detection accuracy depend more on what happens at the end than at the beginning or middle of an interaction, and how strong the receiver's decoding skills are. If a wife is not good at reading nonverbal signals, or if the husband has resolved her suspicions over time and has put forth a believable demeanor by interaction's end, she will not detect his deception and he will judge himself to be a success. For instance, the husband could take advantage of the tendency to reciprocate by resorting to affectionate teasing rather than anger when confronted, cajoling his wife into responding with similar shows of affection that would reestablish her trust and thus mislead her into concluding that he does not have a gambling problem, even if she was not sure at earlier times in the conversation.

We have tested these propositions in a 15-year series of studies. It supports many of the propositions, including the influence of the interpersonal relationship between receivers and senders (Buller, Burgoon, White, & Ebesu, 1994), conversational demands on senders (Buller, Strzyzewski, & Hunsaker, 1991), strategic and nonstrategic behavior by senders and receivers (Burgoon & Buller, 1994), interactivity (Burgoon, Buller, & Floyd, 2002), medium of communication (Zhou, Burgoon, Twitchell, & Nunamaker, 2004), motivation by senders (Burgoon & Floyd, 2000), senders' social skills (Burgoon, Buller, Guerrero, & Feldman, 1994), suspicion by receivers (Burgoon, Buller, Ebesu, Rockwell, & White, 1996), evolution in behavioral displays over time (Burgoon, Buller, White, Afifi, & Buslig, 1999), reciprocity of behavior between senders and receivers (Burgoon, Stern & Dillman, 1995), senders' reactions to perceived suspicion (Burgoon, Buller, Dillman, & Walther, 1995) and judgments by senders and receivers at the end of an interaction (Burgoon, Buller, & Guerrero, 1995).

Conceptualization of Communication in the Theory

Our repeated emphasis on conceptualizing communication as a joint creation of sender and receiver, as interactive, evolving, and achieving several aims simultaneously may seem strange to communication students who consider these qualities to be truisms. But, many other theories of deception at least implicitly consider communication to be unidirectional—a sender delivers a message to a receiver who judges its veracity (Ekman & Friesen, 1969; Zuckerman et al., 1981) (e.g., the husband responds to questions about his gambling habit and the wife simply decides if the answers are believable). Our assumption that both parties pursue various strategies during interaction calls attention to the goal-directed nature of communication. People may not be routinely manipulative or fully cognizant of their actions, but they are not simply reactive organisms. Conversational behavior is influenced by a host of cognitive and behavior factors—goals, expectations, and knowledge of the partner (husband or wife); interpretations and evaluations of conversational behavior; social skills; the conversational context; and the relationship (long-term marriage). It is cognitively demanding to engage in conversation, and the demands can escalate when one decides to deceive or suspects deceit. These demands ebb and flow based on the messages, conversational goals, and clarity of meaning. Participants will necessarily be selective information processors who conserve and direct cognitive resources toward the interaction and information processing tasks. This means that husband and wife will not remain fully vigilant about the other's behaviors. Interpersonal communication is organized by normative expectations—the expectations for honesty and reciprocity being basic. Expectations can and are violated, and conformity or deviation from normal patterns is recognized and influences interpretations. Finally, all messages are judged on credibility.

Uses of the Theory

IDT can serve as a lens for modeling interpersonal communication and highlighting those variables and processes that are especially significant. Whether deceiving or telling the truth, people try to manage the content of their messages, their nonverbal behaviors, and their overall style so that they are believed. IDT's account of how this is accomplished pertains to truthful as well as deceptive episodes. The same is true for other IDT principles: that communication evolves; that people adapt to their conversational partners; and that their success in being understood and believed is influenced by their own feelings, thoughts, and actions (thereby their relationship), and the conversational context, including the communication medium. IDT predicts that deceivers capitalize on people's trust in one another's truthfulness, just as truthtellers do. In fact, a major objective of deceivers is to create a normal-appearing demeanor, relying on people's truth biases and their unwitting assistance in building a believable story line. In other words, deceptive episodes are characterized by the same kinds of adaptation and reciprocity as occur in nondeceptive interpersonal communication. IDT underscores the importance of understanding any interpersonal encounter as one of mutual influence and change.

A central feature of IDT is its emphasis on interactivity. Much of the work on this principle aims to understand how the interplay between sender and receiver influences both participants' sense of involvement, connection, and common ground; judgments of one another's believability; and performance in face-to-face and mediated forms (e.g., telephone, e-mail, blogging) of interpersonal interaction (e.g., Burgoon, Bonito, Ramirez, Kam, Dunbar, & Fischer, 2002). Here again, the principle of interactivity generalizes beyond deception to other interpersonal exchanges.

Strengths and Limitations of the Theory

IDT was first published in a special issue of *Communication Theory* in which two critiques were invited (DePaulo, Ansfield, & Bell, 1996; Stiff, 1996). Stiff raised definitional issues as to how "interpersonal" and "interactive" should be defined, and advocated that deception be approached as a persuasive activity, a proposal consistent with the premise in IDT that deception is strategic. DePaulo and colleagues faulted IDT for incorporating several processes rather than simply one mechanism to explain the totality of the communication phenomenon. IDT's assumptions and definitions move it beyond mere synthesis to a set of systematically connected propositions that allows understanding, prediction, and explanation of a wide range of conversational behavior. Admittedly, IDT does not have a single causal or generative mechanism, but neither does interpersonal communication. This complexity is a strength.

Theories such as IDT are useful in the scientific inquiry of human behavior if they make predictions that can be submitted to testing and if the hypotheses to be tested can, in principle, be disconfirmed. IDT makes testable claims and ones for which the evidence could turn out to be nonsupportive. For instance, a prediction such as "deceptive displays change over time" can be falsified by evidence that deception displays are fairly unchanging and consistent over time or are more stable than truthful displays. That said, IDT is pitched at a more abstract level and some of the proposition wordings would benefit from greater precision. For example, the original proposition on how suspicion is manifested in behavior was vague and could not generate a prediction that could be falsified. Our reworded version (Proposition 15) implies that suspicious receivers will differ from nonsuspicious ones by exhibiting both strategic responses (e.g., adoption of various questioning strategies) and inadvertent ones that betray their suspicion.

Also, some of the propositions (e.g., 1 and 2) are generic statements that are intended to highlight variables that must be attended to when explaining deception. For example, Proposition 18—"Deception and suspicion displays change over time"—might seem self-evident and therefore difficult to falsify. Implied in the extant deception literature has been the claim that behavioral signatures of deception will be the same no matter at what point they are observed in an interaction. Whether deceivers adapt their behaviors is one of the few substantive IDT claims with which others have taken issue (Levine &

McCornack 1996).This important prediction of IDT has in fact been tested and supported (Stiff, Corman, Krizek, & Snider, 1994; White & Burgoon, 2001). The substance of other propositions deserves further scrutiny. There are some with which we ourselves might take issue, and we welcome discussions and tests of the specific claims.

Directions for Future Research and Applications

Apart from evaluating specific propositions, one recent direction for IDT research has been extension to new technologies and media. The notion of interactivity is being tested in terms of what verbal and nonverbal deception displays characterize forms of media that are proximal (e.g., face-to-face) versus distal (e.g., e-mail), media-rich (audiovisual) versus media-lean (audio only), synchronous (in real time) versus asynchronous (delayed response), and recoverable (reviewable) versus nonrecoverable (not reviewable). How new media affect deception detection is also being investigated.

On the application front, IDT is being used to guide the development of technologies for automatically detecting deception and hostile intent. Many language features can be automatically extracted from transcribed text using parsers, artificial intelligence approaches to data mining, and classification software. Many nonverbal visual features can be automatically identified from videotaped images using computer vision techniques. These are being tested for their ability to discriminate truth from deception or suspicious from trustworthy conduct, with an eye toward including them in computer software that can be used by law enforcement and security screeners. The same behavioral signatures are being incorporated into training on deception detection in such contexts as forensic auditing, border protection, and criminal investigations. As more insight is garnered into how deception is conducted under different circumstances, greater understanding of how people engage generally in interpersonal communication will emerge.

References

Buller, D. B., & Burgoon, J. K. (1996). Interpersonal deception theory. *Communication Theory, 6*, 203–242.

Buller, D. B., Burgoon, J. K., White, C., & Ebesu, A. S. (1994). Interpersonal deception: VII. Behavioral profiles of falsification, equivocation, and concealment. *Journal of Language and Social Psychology, 13*, 366–396.

Buller, D. B., Strzyzewski, K. D., & Hunsaker, F. G. (1991). Interpersonal deception: II. The inferiority of conversational participants as deception detectors. *Communication Monographs, 58*, 40.

Burgoon, J. K., Bonito, J. A., Ramirez, A., Kam, K., Dunbar, N., & Fischer, J. (2002). Testing the interactivity principle: Effects of mediation, propinquity, and verbal and nonverbal modalities in interpersonal interaction. *Journal of Communication, 52,* 657–677.

Burgoon, J. K., & Buller, D. B. (1994). Interpersonal deception: III. Effects of deceit on perceived communication and nonverbal behavior dynamics. *Journal of Nonverbal Behavior, 18,* 155–284.

Burgoon, J. K., & Buller, D. B. (2004). Interpersonal deception theory. In S. Seiter, & R. H. Gass, (Eds.), *Perspectives on persuasion, social influence, and compliance gaining* (pp. 239–264). Boston: Allyn & Bacon.

Burgoon, J. K., Buller, D. B., Dillman, L., & Walther, J. (1995). Interpersonal deception: IV. Effects of suspicion on perceived communication and nonverbal behavior dynamics. *Human Communication Research, 22,* 196.

Burgoon, J. K., Buller, D. B., Ebesu, A., Rockwell, P., & White, C. (1996). Testing interpersonal deception theory: Effects of suspicion on nonverbal behavior and relational messages. *Communication Theory, 6,* 243–267.

Burgoon, J. K., Buller, D. B., & Floyd, K. (2002). Does participation affect deception success? A test of the interactivity effect. *Human Communication Research, 27,* 503–534.

Burgoon, J. K., Buller, D. B., & Guerrero, L. K. (1995). Interpersonal deception: IX. Effects of social skill and nonverbal communication on deception success and detection accuracy. *Journal of Language and Social Psychology, 14,* 289–311.

Burgoon, J. K., Buller, D. B., Guerrero, L. K., Afifi, W., & Feldman, C. (1996). Interpersonal deception: XII. Information management dimensions underlying deceptive and truthful messages. *Communication Monographs, 63,* 50–69.

Burgoon, J. K., Buller, D. B., Guerrero, L. K., & Feldman, C. M. (1994). Interpersonal deception: VI. Viewing deception success from deceiver and observer perspectives: Effects of preinteractional and interactional factors. *Communication Studies, 45,* 263–280.

Burgoon, J. K., Buller, D. B., White, C. H., Afifi, W. A., & Buslig, A.L.S. (1999). The role of conversational involvement in deceptive interpersonal communication. *Personality and Social Psychology Bulletin, 25,* 669–685.

Burgoon, J. K., & Floyd, K. (2000). Testing for the motivation impairment effect during deceptive and truthful interaction. *Western Journal of Communication, 64,* 243–267.

Burgoon, J. K., Stern, L. A., & Dillman, L. (1995). *Interpersonal adaptation: Dyadic interaction patterns.* New York: Cambridge University Press.

DePaulo, B. M., Ansfield, M. E., & Bell, K. L. (1996). Theories about deception and paradigms for studying it: A critical appraisal of Buller and Burgoon's interpersonal deception theory and research. *Communication Theory, 6,* 287–296.

DePaulo, B. M., Kashy, D. A., Kirkendol, S. E., Wyer, M. M., & Epstein, J. A. (1996). Lying in everyday life. *Journal of Personality Social Psychology, 70,* 979–995.

Ekman, P. (1985). *Telling lies.* New York: Norton.

Ekman, P., & Friesen, W. V. (1969). Nonverbal leakage and clues to deception. *Psychiatry, 32,* 88–106.

Grice, H. P. (1989). *Studies in the ways of words.* Cambridge, MA: Harvard University Press.

Johnson, R., Jr., Barnhardt, J., & Zhu, J. (2004). The contribution of executive processes to deceptive responding. *Neuropsychologia, 42,* 878–901.

Levine, T. R. & McCornack, A. S. (1996). A critical analysis of the behavioral adaptation explanation of the probing effect. *Human Communication Research, 22,* 575–588.

Stiff, J. B. (1996). Theoretical approaches to the study of deceptive communication: Comments on interpersonal deception theory. *Communication Theory, 6,* 289–296.

Stiff, J. B., Corman, S., Krizek, B., & Snider, E. (1994). Individuals' differences and changes in nonverbal behavior: Unmasking the changing faces of deception. *Communication Research, 21,* 555–581.

Vrij, A., Fisher, R., Mann, S., & Leal, S. (2006). Detecting deception by manipulating cognitive load. *Trends in Cognitive Sciences, 10,* 141–142.

White, C. H., & Burgoon, J. K. (2001). Adaptation and communicative design: Patterns of interaction in truthful and deceptive conversations. *Human Communication Research, 27,* 9–37.

Zhou, L., Burgoon, J. K., Twitchell, D., & Nunamaker, J. F., Jr. (2004). Automating linguistics-based cues for detecting deception in text-based asynchronous computer-mediated communication. *Group Decision and Negotiation, 13,* 81–106.

Zuckerman, M., DePaulo, B. M., & Rosenthal, R. (1981). Verbal and nonverbal communication of deception. In L. Berkowitz (Ed.), *Advances in experimental social psychology* (pp. 1–59). New York: Academic Press.

18

Narrative Theories

Making Sense of Interpersonal Communication

Jody Koenig Kellas

Throughout the course of living everyday events, people tell stories about them. People build and communicate their relationships, cultures, and identities, in part, through the stories they tell. Thus, narratives and storytelling are consequential sites for theorizing interpersonal communication. Research on personal narratives has merited and received a great deal of attention over the past two decades within a variety of disciplines including communication, psychology, sociology, sociolinguistics, English, folklore, and anthropology. Despite the growing interest in narratives and the common reference to narrative theory in interpersonal and family communication research, however, there is no single narrative theory that guides communication research generally or interpersonal communication research specifically. In fact, few narrative approaches are called narrative theories at all. Despite this, there are several theoretically rich frameworks, perspectives, and bodies of research on narrative that are advanced in the interdisciplinary body of narrative research. Indeed, some scholars choose to use the term narrative theorizing, rather than narrative theory, because, although narrative approaches provide a common theoretical framework, most have not yet advanced consistently into formal theories tested in particular communication contexts (P. Japp, personal communication, April 27, 2007). Some communication scholars have begun to advance narrative theories specific to interpersonal contexts (see Langellier & Peterson's [2004] Narrative Performance Theory), and the task of integrating the research on narrative has been approached elsewhere for various purposes (e.g., Bochner, 2002; Langellier, 1989; Ochs, 1997). Few attempts, however, have been made to integrate the vast and diverse literature on narrative and storytelling in ways that highlight the applicability of narrative theories to research on interpersonal communication and personal relationships (for exceptions see Bochner, and Langellier), nor in ways that represent a picture of narrative theories across paradigms. This chapter, therefore, offers a review of narrative theories, perspectives, and research traditions across paradigms that might enable such a focus and offer some clarity for how students and scholars of interpersonal communication may situate narrative in their research projects, their understanding of personal relationships, and their use and development of narrative theory.

Purpose and Meta-theoretical Assumptions

Despite the diversity of narrative scholarship, most, if not all, research that grounds itself in narrative inquiry proposes to highlight the ways in which humans make sense of and construct their identities, relationships, and lives. First, stories help us make sense of our lives. According to Bochner (2002), "The act of telling [stories] is a process of interpretation in which the teller and listener collaborate in sense-making" (p. 81). Narrative emplotment helps individuals organize lived events—many of which are messy, multivocal, complicated, or confusing—into more manageable packages that make sense in the context of their lives and relationships. For example, Lucy and Jake might tell and retell the story about the birth of their first child when friends and family ask them to do so. Although they experienced the joy of welcoming a healthy and happy baby boy, Jesse, to the world, the birth itself was wrought with complications. Narrative theorizing would allow scholars to investigate the content of their story, how telling it helps them to make sense of the whirlwind of activities surrounding Jesse's birth, and how they might make sense of it in light of the sociohistorical and cultural context (i.e., master narratives) of childbirth in American society.

Many relational stories, such as Lucy and Jake's, also help people construct their individual and relational identities. Thus, a second purpose of narrative theories is to interrogate the ways in which stories construct, confirm, reject, or negotiate those identities. For example, Reese (1996) investigated the extent to which the story that a mother tells her child about his or her birth influences her child's self-understanding. Moreover, when Lucy and Jake tell the story of Jesse's birth, they construct their relationships by casting themselves as characters in and tellers of the story in relation to one another. Thus, despite its diversity, most narrative theorizing concerns the sense-making and identity-building functions of narratives and storytelling.

Paradigmatically, the lion's share of research on narrative in communication grounds itself in interpretive and critical paradigms of research (Bochner, Ellis,

& Tillman-Healy, 1997). Many of the scholars who have taken an interpretive or critical "narrative turn" (Bochner, 2002, p. 78) rejected the notion of narrative as a "fixed and stable communication phenomenon," as well as "the possibility of generalizing about the human condition" (Mumby, 1993, pp. 2–3), and thus positioned quantitative social science outside the narrative realm (Bochner). Communication scholars interested in how narratives function interpersonally may benefit from examining narrative theory across all three paradigms, however, for at least two reasons: First, communication researchers from post-positivist, interpretive, and critical paradigms all conduct narrative research, yet a division between paradigms has prevented a review that integrates the study of narrative or narrative theory across paradigms. Second, an examination of narrative from various paradigms may provide the richest understanding of how narrative operates at the level of interpersonal communication and therefore how it offers a means for explaining how we can theorize narratives in and about personal relationships, specifically.

Main Features of the Theories

Based on the variety of narrative theories, the terminology used for its core concepts has become somewhat clouded. Often, the terms "narrative" and "story" are used interchangeably. Other scholars, however, provide distinct definitions for each concept (e.g., Ochs, 1997). In general, researchers view narrative more broadly than they view story. For example, researchers who conceive of narrative ontologically tend to use the word "narrative" to refer to a global frame through which to understand human behavior, interpretation, and history (e.g., Fisher, 1989). Others, however, view narrative as encompassing both large- and small-level communicative practices. Ochs explained that "the term 'narrative' is used either in a narrow sense to specify the genre of story or in a broad sense to cover a vast range of genres, including not only stories, but also reports, sports and news broadcasts, plans, and agendas among others" (p. 189). Ochs's overview recognizes the complexity associated with the many forms of narrative, but it also supports the general consensus in the literature that narrative is a broader and more gestalt concept than is story. Returning to our example, scholars might use the term "master narrative" to situate Lucy and Jake's birth story in the larger narrative landscape of what it means to have a baby in American society. Alternatively, the term "narrative" might be used to encapsulate the many stories and chronicles of events surrounding Jesse's complicated birth.

The term "story," on the other hand, is used most generally to describe the recounting of some noteworthy event and may be described as a genre of narrative in Ochs's (1997) framework. The term "story" is often used to describe an individually constructed discourse unit. Stories typically include plotlines with beginnings (e.g., "Lucy was three weeks away from her due date and we were out at a baseball game, so we were really surprised when her contractions started in the third inning!"), middles (e.g., "All of a sudden the whole mood of the room changed. The doctors got quiet and focused and they stopped smiling. I knew something was wrong.") and ends (e.g., "When Lucy finally had Jesse in her arms and I could finally wrap my arms around both of them, I knew everything would be OK."). Whereas stories summarize relational events and may act as representations of relational culture, "storytelling" is a process central to the construction and reflection of that culture. From an interpersonal perspective, researchers might be interested in "jointly told stories," that is, the collaborative constructions through which people recount events by assigning plot, character, and setting in a way that helps them make sense of and give meaning to the event(s) and to the relationship in which they are told. Lucy and Jake might jointly tell this story to family and friends, making the storytelling a collaborative effort that requires them to negotiate their meanings about the event and their relationship through the interactive accomplishment of the telling. The reference to narrative theory in the literature tends to be gestalt, encompassing research on narratives, stories, or storytelling.

Finally, most narrative inquiry acknowledges "temporality" as a feature of narratives and stories, noting both the temporal nature of plot and sequence as well as the dynamic processes by which stories are told and retold over time, making them fluid, evolving constructions (e.g., Bochner, 2002; Ochs, 1997; Ricoeur, 1981). Thus, Lucy and Jake's stories about the birth of their first child might change over time based on new experiences, such as the less-complicated birth of their second child.

Conceptualization of Communication in the Theories

In his foundational article, David Maines (1993) positioned narrative, first and foremost, as a communicative phenomenon and one that deserves more focus, attention, and expertise from those who ground themselves in the study of symbolic meaning-making. Despite this, narrative theory is currently advanced and applied in personal-relationships research across other disciplines more than it is advanced and applied in communication. Moreover, much narrative theory and research focuses on master narratives or individual stories, rather than on the communicative features of storytelling. Although I argue below that theorizing about narrative and stories informs our understanding of interpersonal communication, I also contend that interpersonal narrative theorizing needs to attend more closely to the telling of stories. Focusing on storytelling builds on Langellier and Peterson's (2004) projects of situating narrative in a communication approach to storytelling, but adds to these projects by building bridges across traditional paradigmatic divides. The remainder of this section reviews how research from four different perspectives of narrative inquiry might inform an understanding of narratives, stories, and storytelling in and about personal relationships.

NARRATIVE AS ONTOLOGY

At the broadest level of abstraction, scholars in communication and other fields view narrative ontologically. That is, narrative constitutes our way of being in the world and is conceived as knowledge set against social and historical backgrounds. Fisher's (1989) Narrative Paradigm, for example, argued for the importance of studying narrative by asserting that people are inherently storytelling beings, or "authors and co-authors who creatively read and evaluate the texts of life and literature" (p. 18). He rejected the notion of narrative as story and instead argued that all human communication and knowledge is interpretable and should be theorized as narrative. Others (e.g., Bruner, 1990) argued further that humans make sense of the things that happen to them in terms of narrative features (i.e., by mapping plot, sequence, agency onto the events in their lives so that they are easier to understand). Viewing narrative from this perspective would mean analyzing all of Jake and Lucy's interactions at the time of the birth as narratives themselves, or arguing that Lucy and Jake understand the disconnected set of complicated events better by assigning narrative properties to them. Importantly, narrative at this level does not focus on the story (e.g., Jesse's birth story), but rather focuses on the narrative nature of human interaction and sense-making. By viewing humans as storytellers and human communication as narrative, interpretable, and assessed against a larger historical context, scholars like Fisher and Bruner established narrative as the way that humans exist within, and make sense of, the world.

Bochner and his colleagues (1997) were among the few communication researchers to connect ontological approaches to narrative within personal relationship research. They offered such a link by conceiving of personal relationships—and the research about them—as narrative in nature. Whereas Fisher (1989) argued that all human communication may be interpreted as narration, Bochner and his colleagues interpreted all research as narrative by introducing the concept of evocative narrative and the Autoethnography Perspective: narrative research in which the authors and their experiences become the object of research and in which these data are seen as stories of personal relationships. From this perspective, researchers use their own personal experience as an interpretive story in which they make themselves the subjects and their experiences the data of research. Combined, ontological approaches to narrative and storytelling provide theoretical backing for understanding narratives as inseparable from the ways in which we exist within, interpret, and understand personal relationships.

NARRATIVE AS EPISTEMOLOGY

Narrative as epistemology refers to theory and research that are concerned with narrative as the form of analysis. Orbuch (1997) distinguished among three types of narrative research in which storied accounts may be conceived: (a) the object of inquiry, (b) the means of inquiry, and (c) the product of inquiry. Approaches that adopt narrative as epistemology parallel in many ways the latter two of these types. First, some communication researchers invoke the term narrative theory when, in fact, they are using narrative methods to understand some other communication phenomenon; in other words, narrative is the means of collecting data about something beyond the story. For example, researchers might conduct in-depth semistructured interviews in which many stories, such as Lucy and Jake's, about pregnancy and birth arise. Because of the rich, narrative descriptions that emerge during the interviews, the scholars might situate their research in narrative terms. Second, other researchers view research reports themselves as narrative constructions. In other words, when researchers publish scholarly articles, they are essentially providing narrative accounts of the research process (Bochner, 2002). For these scholars, narrative is the product of inquiry (Orbuch).

Other researchers reject the notion that narrative as epistemology constitutes narrative theory, arguing that in order to be called narrative inquiry or theorizing, the research must have narratives, stories, or storytelling as its primary focus or foci (see Reissman, 1993). Ultimately, as Reissman pointed out, the possibilities for analyzing narrative are vast, and narrative analysis can attend to all three functions of language: (a) the ideational or referential meaning of what is said, (b) the textual, or the structure, syntax, and semantics of stories, or (c) the interpersonal, or the role of the relationship between speakers. Research that adopts these foci, including the content, structure, and interactive features of stories, are reviewed below.

NARRATIVE AS INDIVIDUAL CONSTRUCTION

Researchers who study narrative as individual construction collect and describe stories from individuals about themselves, their families, or their personal relationships. The research described at this level tends to examine either the structure or the content of personal relationship stories. Several researchers examine narratives from a structural perspective. Labov and Waltesky (1967), for example, developed a typology for characterizing a fully formed narrative. Such narratives include (a) an abstract that foregrounds the story with an overall summary, (b) an orientation that sets the scene and introduces characters, (c) complicating actions that describe the central events of the story, (d) a resolution that concludes the events, and (e) a coda that wraps the narrative up and often provides a moral to the story. Similarly, Gergen and Gergen (1987) established rules for what constitutes a well-formed relationship narrative, and Koenig Kellas and Manusov (2003) examined break-up stories for narrative completeness. Studies of narrative structure assign a value to the means of constructing stories. In other words, the ability to organize a narrative according to socially acceptable criteria assumes importance. This is evidenced by the focus on "fully" and "complete" narratives and by the assertion that the absence of these narrative qualities may compromise the story coherence and the narrator's status as a storyteller and even as a competent person (Labov & Waletsky, 1967; Polanyi, 1985). The value-laden nature of story structure highlights the importance of the narrator's audience; however, research that focuses on narrative structure generally does little to analyze the audience's participation in the storytelling process.

Narrative research that focuses on the thematic content of stories does so in order to understand the ways in which individuals have constructed their individual and relational identities or made sense of relational events. For example, Vangelisti, Crumley, and Baker (1999) analyzed the themes of stories that individuals told about their "real" and "ideal" families in order to better understand their standards for family relationships.

Finally, inquiry on narrative as individual construction investigates the links between story structure and content and the functions stories serve for individuals and relationships, such as individual and relational health. For example, researchers might analyze the themes associated with birth stories (like Lucy and Jake's), how women communicate an emerging sense of mothering identity in these stories, or how the theme and organization of such stories helps to predict participants' satisfaction with their marriages and families. Although the predictive nature of this research may contradict interpretive and critical approaches to narrative inquiry, much of the extant interpersonal communication research on storytelling emerges from studies at this level of conceptualization. Because of this, the research on narrative as individual construction and its functions are reviewed later in this chapter in the section on how narrative theories have been used in interpersonal communication research.

NARRATIVE AS RELATIONAL PROCESS

Finally, a small body of narrative inquiry conceives of narrative relationally. Storytelling at this level is not simply an individual construction. Instead, the focus is on how audience members or relational partners negotiate the story itself or the history and "reality" of their relationship together. Thus, inquiry that views narrative as relational process focuses on the "storytelling," both as an act of performance, or way of "doing" relationships, and as a collaborative process of joint storytelling between relational partners.

Scholars engaging in narrative theory as performance focus on the ways in which people tell stories and thereby "do" relationships. For example, in their Narrative Performance Theory, Langellier and Peterson (2004) focused on col-laborative storytelling among family members "as one of the many possible strategies for doing family and reproducing family culture" (p. 34). With this theory, they concentrated on the dual sense in which storytelling is both per-formance (i.e., something a family does) and performative (the doing of story-telling that constitutes and forms the family). Specifically, Langellier and Peterson analyzed the division of narrative labor as three generations of Franco-American women jointly told family stories and found that women differed across generations in the ways that they told the stories, made sense of them, listened to each other, and facilitated the storytelling.

Conversation analysts also focus on the study of narrative and the accom-plishments that narrators and audience members achieve when they negotiate the telling of a story. For example, Polanyi (1985) found that the point of a story about fainting on the subway had to be narratable, interesting to the audience, and interactively accomplished in ways that could affect the reputa-tion of the teller as a good storyteller and as a competent member of society. Mandelbaum (1987) examined how "withs" (relationships) are interactively achieved in public through storytelling by examining the ways in which two potential tellers approach, forward, and ratify each other's versions of a shared story. As these examples illustrate, conversational storytelling as performance focuses on microanalytic approaches to assessing narrative labor, how stories emerge naturally in conversation, how "problems" are dealt with in interaction, and how people "do" (accomplish) certain things in storytelling interaction.

Narrative inquiry also focuses on joint storytelling processes across rela-tionships. Bochner and his colleagues (1997) supported the need to look at stories as relational: "Storytelling is not only the way we understand our rela-tionships, but also the means by which our relationships are fashioned" (p. 310). In other words, joint storytelling functions not only as a way to reflect about relationships but also affects the reality of how relational partners and their audiences view these relationships. Storytelling, in part, constitutes rela-tionships, and extant research supports this view (e.g., Buehlman, Gottman, & Katz, 1992; Koenig Kellas, 2005; Veroff, Sutherland, Chadiha, & Ortega, 1993).

Because of the focus on the ways in which relational members together con-struct their relationships, jointly told stories in and about relationships can be seen as significant processes of interpersonal and relational communication across a variety of personal contexts, such as families, romantic relationships, and friendships. Storytelling emerges as particularly relevant to interpersonal communication theorizing: it represents the communicative manifestation of stories, and the investigation of jointly told stories at the relational level offers a dynamic and interactive portrait of storytelling in and about relationships. More research on narrative from an interpersonal communication perspective should focus on theory-building and research on storytelling, since it explicitly positions narrative as communication (Langellier & Peterson, 2004). The research at this level, although understudied, is also consequential because it indicates that jointly told stories are associated with individual and relational outcomes such as reported relational satisfaction and family functioning (e.g., Koenig Kellas, 2005; Veroff et al., 1993). Joint storytelling perspectives are further reviewed in the next section.

Uses of the Theories

The organizational typology of narrative literature advanced above acknowledges the potential for theories from different paradigms to inform our understanding of interpersonal communication. If we are to continue to build narrative theory, however, we will benefit from examining research that has already concentrated on the functions of narrative in and about personal relationships. Several studies, such as those reviewed within this section, focus specifically on how individuals' stories lead to certain outcomes or accomplish general and particular functions such as communicating identity, coping with loss, and predicting psychological health and relational qualities.

RESTORYING IDENTITY AND LIVES

Theorizing on life stories and narrative therapy offer examples of how telling the stories of one's life may help to socially construct identity as well as how to revise those identities in ways that benefit our psychological and relational well-being. Life story research examines the individual stories that people construct over time that allow them to create, understand, communicate, and evaluate a sense of self (Linde, 1993). Sociolinguists, like Linde and psychologists such as McAdams (1997) have used life stories to understand how people socially negotiate the coherence, or believability, of their identities through the stories they tell. McAdams's Personal Myth Theory suggests that people have the ability to restory their lives when their current stories are unproductive or debilitating. This echoes narrative therapists' focus on "restorying," which is the belief that multiple interpretations exist for the events of our lives, and that stories provide people with a means for creating new interpretations and for improving their understanding of their lived experience. Although those who examine life stories and narrative therapy claim that story coherence must be socially negotiated, this body of research does little to examine the communicative processes associated with telling them. The ways in which individuals socially negotiate their storied identities is an area ripe for interpersonal communication theorizing.

COPING WITH LOSS AND TRAUMA

The literature on the outcomes of accounts (stories) for failed relationships, loss, and trauma also attests to the potentially positive functions of stories. For example, Harvey, Orbuch, and Weber (1992) proposed a Stress Response Model for account-making and theorized that storytelling about relational loss allows account-makers to achieve a better self-esteem, engage in emotional purging, establish a sense of control, and search for closure and understanding (Weber, Harvey, & Stanley, 1989). Pennebaker's (1997) Inhibition/Confrontation Framework and years of empirical research suggested that ruminating about traumatic experiences is far less healthy than writing or telling stories about them. In their study on stories of relationship dissolution, Koenig Kellas and Manusov (2003) examined the relationship between the completeness of a break-up story and adjustment to the dissolution process. They found that individuals who provided coherent and sequential narratives were more adjusted than those who did not. Their results also indicated that individuals with complete stories reported higher self-esteem than those with less complete stories. These studies indicate that stories can serve a healing function. In fact, Sedney, Baker, and Gross (1994) warned that the absence of stories may limit family communication and emotional relief from difficult events.

PREDICTING RELATIONAL QUALITIES AND PSYCHOLOGICAL HEALTH

Another small but growing line of research in interpersonal and family communication examines the relationships that exist between narrative content, process, and individual and relational outcome variables. Vangelisti and colleagues (1999), for example, found that people who told family stories about togetherness, care, humor, reconstruction, and adaptability were more satisfied with their families than people whose stories contained themes of hostility, divergent values, chaos, personality attributes, and hostility.

Moreover, researchers in psychology and communication studies have examined the ways in which couples' and families' joint storytelling helps to predict important relationship outcomes, such as satisfaction, functioning, and divorce. Psychologists have interviewed newly married couples and investigated the ways in which joint storytelling about how the couple met, fell in love, and got married related to marital satisfaction and predicted divorce. For example, in their studies of oral histories, Buehlman and colleagues (1992) found that couples who glorified the struggle of difficult times were less likely to divorce than couples who described their relationship in chaotic terms. In the Early Years of Marriage project, Veroff and colleagues (1993) focused on storytelling processes and found that couples who differed in their joint story-telling style were less satisfied than couples who told the story in a similar style. Recently, communication researchers have begun to examine the implications of joint storytelling for identity construction and family functioning. Koenig Kellas and Trees (2006) identified a set of four interactional sense-making behaviors relevant to joint storytelling in families: (a) "engagement" (involve-ment and warmth), (b) "turn-taking" (dynamism and distribution of turns), (c) "perspective-taking" (acknowledgment and confirmation of others' per-spectives), and (d) "coherence" (organization and degree of collaboration or jointness). Of these, perspective-taking significantly predicted family satisfac-tion, cohesion, adaptability, and overall functioning in family triads telling a family identity story (Koenig Kellas, 2005). Moreover, families who considered themselves to be storytelling families and who told stories often were signifi-cantly more satisfied and functional than families who were not storytelling families. This finding and the others that highlight the positive functions of narratives and storytelling in interpersonal interactions further position nar-rative inquiry as consequential to our understanding of interpersonal commu-nication and may have implications for theory building about narratives in interpersonal communication.

Strengths and Limitations of the Theories

Narrative theorizing has the potential to help us understand how people com-municatively construct their individual and relational identities, make sense of the world and their interpersonal interactions, cope with loss, restory unpro-ductive concepts of self and others, and explain relational qualities and out-comes such as satisfaction, well-being, and divorce. With the potential to affect and reflect so many aspects of interpersonal communication, communication researchers ought to harness extant research and continue to build narrative theory.

The breadth and diversity, however, function as both strengths and limita-tions of narrative theories. Because there is no one narrative theory to under-stand interpersonal communication, and because there is at the same time such a breadth of research on narrative inquiry across disciplines, much of the current research on storytelling in relationships is ironically atheoretical. Although this research is useful for understanding storytelling behavior, it would benefit from theoretical conclusions to help explain, predict, and control communication behavior in post-positivist research, guide rich interpretations of individual or relational meaning-making in interpretive research, and reveal and evaluate injustice in critical research.

Directions for Future Research and Applications

Narrative inquiry in interpersonal communication and related fields currently operates from a positivity bias. Most of the research cited above references the positive outcomes of narrative approaches or interpersonal storytelling. However, as critical researchers have already noted, stories have the potential to isolate individuals (e.g., family members; Langellier & Peterson, 2004) as well as to reify traditional master narratives (e.g., heterosexual accounts of meeting, falling in love, and getting married). Thus, narrative inquiry and theory building need to interrogate not only the positive functions of narrative and storytelling but also need to examine the ways in which stories disconfirm, belittle, reject, reify stereotypes, or hurt individual and relational members. For example, we might investigate how master narratives for personal relationships—such as marriage, child-bearing, or family development—impact the interpersonal communication of individuals in marginalized relationships, such as homosexual couples, child-free couples, or members of stepfamilies. Additional research should also focus more attention on the interactive features and functions of storytelling as a relational process and in naturally occurring settings. Moreover, a focus on the potentially negative processes and functions of joint storytelling, such as how partners manage the difficulties of narrative discrepancy or conflicting versions of a story, merits attention.

Building narrative theory in interpersonal communication research has implications in several applied settings, such as family therapy, couples counseling, doctor-patient communication, corporate training programs, textbooks on personal relationships, and other instructional approaches to understanding and improving interpersonal communication. By focusing on narrative as relational communication, we may draw from across paradigms, provide a more complete picture of narrative inquiry, situate narrative in an interpersonal communication domain, and examine narratives and stories as one of the primary ways we symbolically constitute our lives—a belief common across paradigms. Such an approach necessitates a focus on narratives as relational, joint, and interactive; it necessitates a focus on talk; and it begs for additional research and theory-building on the narrative construction of our lives.

References

Bochner, A. P. (2002). Perspectives on inquiry III: The moral of stories. In M. L. Knapp & J. A. Daly (Eds.), *Handbook of interpersonal communication* (3rd ed.; pp. 73–101). Thousand Oaks, CA: Sage.

Bochner, A. P., Ellis, C., & Tillman-Healy, L. M. (1997). Relationships as stories. In S. Duck (Ed.), *Handbook of personal relationships: Theory, research and interventions* (2nd ed.; pp. 307–324). New York: John Wiley & Sons.

Bruner, J. (1990). *Acts of meaning.* Cambridge, MA: Harvard University Press.

Buehlman, K. T., Gottman, J. M., & Katz, L. F. (1992). How a couple views their past predicts their future: Predicting divorce from an oral history interview. *Journal of Family Psychology, 5,* 295–318.

Fisher, W. R. (1989). *Human communication as narration: Toward a philosophy of reason, value, and action.* Columbia: University of South Carolina Press.

Gergen, K. J., & Gergen, M. M. (1987). Narratives of relationships. In R. Burnett, P. McGhee, & D. Clarke (Eds.), *Accounting for relationships* (pp. 269–288). London: Methuen.

Harvey, J. H., Orbuch, T. L., & Weber, A. L. (1992). Introduction: Convergence of the attribution and accounts concepts in the study of close relationships. In J. H. Harvey, T. L. Orbuch, & A. L. Weber (Eds.), *Attributions, accounts, and close relationships* (pp. 1–18). New York: Springer-Verlag.

Koenig Kellas, J. (2005). Family ties: Communicating identity through jointly told stories. *Communication Monographs, 72,* 365–389.

Koenig Kellas, J., & Manusov, V. (2003). What's in a story? The relationship between narrative completeness and tellers' adjustment to relationship dissolution. *Journal of Social and Personal Relationships, 20,* 285–307.

Koenig Kellas, J., & Trees, A. R. (2006). Finding meaning in difficult family experiences: Sense-making and interaction processes during joint family storytelling. *Journal of Family Communication, 6,* 49–76.

Labov, W., & Waletsky, J. (1967). Narrative analysis: Oral versions of personal experience. In J. Helm (Ed.), *Essays on the verbal and visual arts: Proceedings of the 1966 annual spring meeting of the American Ethnological Society* (pp. 12–44). Seattle: University of Washington Press.

Langellier, K. M. (1989). Personal narratives: Perspectives on theory and research. *Text and Performance Quarterly, 9,* 243–276.

Langellier, K. M., & Peterson, E. E. (2004). *Storytelling in daily life: Performing narrative.* Philadelphia: Temple University Press.

Linde, C. (1993). *Life stories: The creation of coherence.* New York: Oxford University Press.

Maines, D. R. (1993). Narrative's moment and sociology's phenomena: Toward a narrative sociology. *Sociological Quarterly, 34,* 17–37.

Mandelbaum, J. (1987). Couples sharing stories. *Communication Quarterly, 35*(2) 144–170.

McAdams, D. P. (1997). *The stories we live by.* New York: The Guilford Press.

Mumby, D. K. (1993). *Narrative and social control: Critical perspectives.* Thousand Oaks, CA: Sage.

Ochs, E. (1997). Narrative. In T. van Dijk (Ed.), *Discourse as structure and process* (pp. 185–207). London: Sage.

Orbuch, T. L. (1997). People's accounts count: The sociology of accounts. *Annual Review of Sociology, 23,* 455–478.

Pennebaker, J. W. (1997). *Opening up: The healing power of expressing emotions.* New York: The Guilford Press.

Polanyi, L. (1985). *Telling the American story.* Norwood, NJ: Ablex.

Reese, E. (1996). Conceptions of self in mother-child birth stories. *Journal of Narrative and Life History, 6,* 23–38.

Reissman, C. K. (1993). *Narrative analysis.* London: Sage.

Ricoeur, P. (1981). Narrative time. In W. J. T. Mitchell (Ed.), *On narrative* (pp. 165–186). Chicago: University of Chicago Press.

Sedney, M., Baker, J. E., & Gross, E. (1994). "The story" of a death: Therapeutic considerations with bereaved families. *Journal of Marital and Family Therapy, 20,* 287–296.

Vangelisti, A. L., Crumley, L. P., & Baker, J. L. (1999). Family portraits: Stories as standards for family relationships. *Journal of Social and Personal Relationships, 16*(3), 335–368.

Veroff, J., Sutherland, L., Chadiha, L., & Ortega, R. M. (1993). Newlyweds tell their stories: Predicting marital quality from narrative assessments. *Journal of Marriage and the Family, 55,* 317–329.

Weber, A. L., Harvey, J. H., & Stanley, M. A. (1989). The nature and motivations of accounts for failed relationships. In R. Burnett, P. McGhee, & D. D. Clarke (Eds.), *Accounting for relationships: Explanation, representation, and knowledge* (pp. 114–133). London: Methuen.

19

Politeness Theory

How We Use Language to Save Face

Daena J. Goldsmith

In the 10 years that Jean and Pat have been friends, Jean cannot recall a time when it was so difficult to know what to say, how to say it, or whether to say it at all. Six months ago, Pat was diagnosed with a health problem, and her doctor told her to lose 20 pounds. Nothing has worked so far—crazy diets, contraptions purchased online, even hypnosis! Jean wants to talk with Pat about this problem, and thinks Pat should join a nearby exercise club and start working out. Pat's doctor said flat out, "Pat, get off the couch and into the gym!" But Jean knows weight is a sensitive topic, especially for Pat, and especially now, when Pat is feeling frustrated by spending a lot of money on things that have not worked. It could also sound pushy, and Jean is not in much of a position to hand out advice, not having set foot in a gym since required P.E. class in high school.

Brown and Levinson's (1987) Politeness Theory helps answer several questions about this example. Why is it challenging for Jean to give advice to Pat in this situation? What features of Pat and Jean's relationship and of the particular situation might make it more or less difficult to give advice? Is there a way for Jean to advise Pat that will minimize some of the risks?

Purpose and Meta-theoretical Assumptions

Brown and Levinson (1987) are sociolinguists who observed that in everyday interaction, we sometimes say what we mean directly, but that we also often beat around the bush instead. For example, we could say, "Get me a drink" but often we express that request in a way that sounds less blunt (e.g., "Hey bud, could ya get me a cold one while you're up?") or we hint around (e.g., "I'm parched!"). Brown and Levinson also observed that the features of language that people used for these purposes were present in three quite different languages (English spoken in Britain and the United States, Tzeltal spoken in Chiapas, Mexico, and Tamil spoken in the Tamilnadu region of India). They reasoned that there must be some fundamental social principles that explain why people around the globe would have developed these linguistic features. Why don't we just say what we mean, in the most direct, efficient way possible all the time? How do you explain when and how we depart from directness and how those departures are interpreted? Politeness Theory answers these questions. It describes the various language forms we use and social conditions related to the use and interpretation of these language forms.

Politeness Theory is a rational model (O'Keefe, 1992). It directs our attention to how features of language are interpreted in social contexts and explains why we see recurring patterns of language structure, use, and inference. The theory makes predictions about patterns and interpretations of language use (resembling a post-positivistic approach), but instead of explaining individual message production, it focuses on message design and interpretation in relation to social structure (resembling interpretive approaches).

Main Features of the Theory

FACE AND FACE-THREATENING ACTIONS

Politeness Theory begins with Goffman's (1967) concept of "face" (see Metts and Cupach, Chapter 15, this volume). Brown and Levinson (1987, p. 61) defined "face" as "the public self-image that every member wants to claim for himself [or herself]." There are several noteworthy features of this concept. First, face is public. It is the "you" that can be observed in your actions rather than the "you" that exists in your mental self-concept. Second, face is social. Your success in acting out a particular image depends on others picking up on what you are doing and acting in ways that are more or less compatible. Third, face is claimed. It can be lost, saved, or sustained by the actions people take in a particular interaction. Finally, face is something we want. Brown and Levinson further specified positive and negative face wants. Positive face wants involve having our social image accepted and approved by the others in the interaction. Negative face has to do with the rights and respect that are due our image. We resent it when people impose on us inappropriately or fail to show the proper deference or respect.

In every interaction, our face is on the line—we are always enacting some public self-image. Many of our ordinary, everyday actions have the potential to threaten our own or another person's face. For example, questioning someone else's actions, disagreeing, or interrupting can all threaten another person's positive face wants for approval, whereas asking someone to do something, or reminding someone of an obligation, can threaten that person's negative face wants for respect and freedom of action. In Jean and Pat's scenario, face concerns may be one reason why Jean feels concerned about discussing Pat's weight loss and advising Pat to join a health club. Talking about Pat's weight problem threatens an image of Pat as a healthy person who does not have to worry about what to eat, and as a person who can set a goal and meet it. It may also stir up concerns about physical attractiveness. Pat is 20 pounds overweight whether Jean and Pat talk about it or not; the face threat comes from discussing it.

These threats to Pat's image as healthy, effective, and physically attractive are examples of positive face threats. Pat likely wants an image that includes these desirable social attributes and wants Jean's communication to support that image. Advising Pat to join a health club illustrates additional face threats. The advice would recommend doing something effortful. In addition to the practical imposition on Pat's time and resources, the advice also threatens Pat's freedom to make up her own mind and to not have others tell her what to do. These impositions constitute negative face threats. Positive face threats might arise if Pat takes the advice as criticism of previous actions (diet, weight loss devices, hypnosis) or feels it implies that she had not already thought of this obvious solution.

If Jean and Pat end up talking about Pat's weight, each person's actions will be relevant to face—they will be claiming face and they may be threatening or saving face. What Jean says and how, and Pat's response and self-presentation, will shape the public self-image each person claims. Will Jean come across as a concerned and caring friend, or as a bossy, hypocritical busybody? Will Pat seem like a pathetic couch potato or a confident, determined individual fighting a battle shared by many other people?

POLITENESS STRATEGIES

Consider the following options Jean might pursue in advising Pat to join a gym:

1. "Pat, join Gym for Life."

2. "Hey Pat, I know how hard you've been working at this weight loss thing and you got me thinkin' I should be doin' somethin' too. Let's join that gym that's on the way home from work. I'll pay for a trial pass if you'll go with me."

3. "Look, I know I'm about the last person to give health advice, but I wondered if maybe you'd considered possibly, you know, joining a gym? There's that one at 42nd and Taylor that's close and cheap. Up to you of course, whatever you think."

4. "You won't believe who I saw coming out of Gym for Life—Chris Beason! Chris has lost so much weight that I almost didn't know who it was."

5. Jean could say nothing, and keep her advice to herself.

How do these options differ? As you read these options, do you imagine a different kind of relationship between Jean and Pat? Are they close friends or not so close? Does one of them more often take the lead than the other? Do some of these options sound more like something women friends would say versus what men might say? How does Jean seem—Confident? Careful? Concerned? How does Pat come off—Easy-going? Easily angered? Competent?

Politeness Theory gives a detailed description of the various ways language can be used to save another person's face when one commits a "face-threatening action" (FTA). The first option above illustrates the "bald on record" strategy. Notice that this option involves saying the FTA—in this case, the advice to join the gym—explicitly or "on the record." There is nothing else said, which is what makes it "bald."

Options 2 and 3 are also on record because they explicitly state the idea of Pat joining the gym. However, the wording of the advice and other things that are said tone down the face threat of advising. Option 2 uses "positive face redress" to compensate for face threat by playing up the solidarity between Jean and Pat. Jean "claims common ground" by using informal language, pointing out commonalities between the two of them, recognizing Pat's efforts, and assuming that Pat knows which gym it is. Jean also "presents them as cooperators" by offering to join the gym together and giving reasons to persuade Pat. Finally Jean "recognizes some of Pat's wants" by offering to pay for the trial offer. Notice how these strategies give approval and acceptance and act as though the closeness and similarity between Jean and Pat makes it all right to give advice. Option 3 uses "negative face redress" to mitigate face threat by being respectful. Jean "avoids presuming" too much by using questions and hedges. Jean "avoids sounding coercive" by giving Pat the option not to act and by minimizing how imposing the advice would be. Jean "communicates a desire not to impinge" by apologizing. Finally, Jean "explicitly addresses wants for freedom" by saying Pat does not have to do it and stating it's Pat's decision. In contrast to positive face redress, these strategies are deferential, toning down forcefulness and keeping a careful distance.

Option 4 does not actually give advice. On record, Jean tells a story about Chris; if advising occurs, it is between the lines or "off record." Pat may nonetheless infer the advice—why else is Jean mentioning it?—particularly if Jean has previously mentioned joining this particular gym, or if Chris has the same health condition as Pat, or if the statement comes up in a discussion of Pat's weight loss attempts. If Pat thinks joining the gym is a good idea, it is possible for this to look like Pat's idea and not a directive from Jean (e.g., imagine Pat responding by saying, "You know, I've been thinking about joining that gym myself."). Alternatively, if Pat resents being advised, Jean could always say, "I wasn't giving you advice. I was just talking about Chris." Thus, off record strategies protect face by leaving room to maneuver. Face is public, so it matters whether or not the FTA is on the public record. However, off record strategies risk a failure to draw the intended inference (e.g., Pat really does think this is just a story about Chris and does not consider Jean's idea about joining the gym).

A final option is, of course, to decide that an FTA is just too risky and to withhold comment altogether, as in Option 5.

A major contribution of Politeness Theory is to help us hear how nuances of language can create an overall impression—of the speaker, the hearer, the action, and the relationship. These linguistic features are sometimes used to define relationships and identities even when there is no face threat and speakers sometimes blend and sequence different strategies. Drawing attention to these different strategies helps us understand how these processes work and can also help us consider our options in challenging situations. Which option should Jean select?

SOCIAL CONDITIONS THAT SHAPE POLITENESS

Brown and Levinson (1987) wrote that the five options range from least polite (bald on record) to most polite (do not do the FTA). Three features of social situations shape what politeness strategy will be most appropriate: "power," "distance," and "rank." Power (P) refers to the degree to which one person can impose his or her plans and self-evaluation on another (e.g., are the two people peers, or does one person have more control or status than the other?). Distance (D) includes both closeness and social similarity (e.g., are the two people strangers from different walks of life or close friends of the same age, race, and sex?). "Rank" (R) refers to culturally defined understandings of how different FTAs are (e.g., for many Americans, advice about weight loss is more sensitive than advice about finding a good airfare).

The combination of P, D, and R affects the "weight" (degree of face threat) in a situation. When there is greater weight, choose a more polite strategy (Options 4 or 5); when there is less weight, choose a less polite strategy (Option 1 or 2). If we are not polite enough, we could come across as rude and insensitive. But if we are too polite, we might not get our point across or we might make our action seem more face threatening than it is. Imagine your best friend (equal P, low D) said to you, "Excuse me, I would never ask except that I'm really in a horrible bind and I'll be grateful to you for life. Could I use your pen for a minute?" (low R). You might feel frustrated that your friend is wasting time beating around the bush, you might think your friend is being sarcastic, you might wonder if your friend thinks you are unlikely to comply or thinks your relationship is fragile, or you might just think your friend is weird. Effective communication entails choosing the right amount of politeness for the situation. We not only use P, D, and R to select a face strategy, but we also use them to infer what another person is trying to do and why.

We can use P, D, and R to guess what Jean is likely to do, or speculate as to which option Pat would find most appropriate. Jean and Pat are friends, which suggests D may be low, and we could probe further the closeness and similarity of their friendship. American friends are often equal in power, but we might get a finer grain on P by asking, "Does one person call the shots more often than the other? Is one friend dependent on the other? Do they have different areas of expertise?" Finally, we can consider R, how threatening the advice is (compared to other actions like ordering, requesting, or enforcing an obligation, but also compared to other kinds of advice, such as the difference between advice on different topics). In this example, P and D might lead us to expect friends would use a less polite strategy (e.g., Option 1 or 2) for giving advice. Because R is high, however, Jean might decide to handle this particular advice more carefully (e.g., Option 3 or 4). As you can see, there is no precise calculus for determining when we might choose Option 2 versus Option 3 versus Option 4, but P, D, and R do help us model some of the social considerations involved in choosing or evaluating a politeness strategy. It can also help us to think comparatively. For example, how are Jean's options different from what Pat's doctor said?

Conceptualization of Communication in the Theory

Politeness Theory views communication as a rational, social, cooperative activity. "Rational" might suggest individuals formulating goals in their minds and then thoughtfully choosing how to pursue them. However, I am inclined to agree with O'Keefe (1992), who pointed out that Politeness Theory says little about cognitive structures but has a lot to say about linguistic and social structures. The theory is rational in the sense that it describes a set of principles for reasoned judgment about communication rather than a description of what goes on cognitively when we open our mouths to speak.

Politeness Theory focuses on socially shared assumptions and reasoning principles that underlie communication. It gives a functional explanation for why languages have certain features and for how people can arrive at shared understandings of those features. For example, if Jean uses positive redress to advise Pat to join the gym, Jean may have various personal motives: Jean may intend to help Pat, or promote the cause of physical fitness, or sound smart, or get Pat out of the house so Jean can have time alone, and so on. Jean may use positive redress out of sincere fellow feeling for Pat or out of a manipulative desire to succeed. Politeness Theory is not useful for probing these personal, internal motivations. It is useful, however, for seeing how it is that we recognize that advice has been given (i.e., that Jean intended to tell Pat to do something that Pat might not have otherwise done) and how giving advice with positive face redress presents different self-images and relationships than alternative ways of speaking.

Politeness Theory also presumes a cooperative motivation to honor face. This assumption works in many of our mundane interactions. It is important to clarify that the kind of cooperation assumed involves coparticipating in interaction (i.e., we assume that others desire to communicate information, that they are attempting to be relevant and not deceptive, and so on). As in a game of soccer or a court of law, it assumes that there is agreement on the fundamental rules of the game, even though players may compete or oppose one another in what they do and say.

Uses of the Theory

Politeness Theory has been employed to study diverse issues of interest to scholars and laypeople alike, such as how a crew member's politeness when he or she speaks to a pilot might contribute to aviation accidents (Linde, 1988), how students talk with their instructors about a disappointing grade (Sabee & Wilson, 2005), how young people resist an undesired request for sex (Afifi & Lee, 2000), how elderly people respond to patronizing advice from a younger person (Hummert & Mazloff, 2001), and how anesthesiologists handle workplace conflict (Jameson, 2004).

Politeness Theory has been interpreted in at least three distinct ways within the communication field and related disciplines (Goldsmith, 2007). Probably the most common use of the theory within the communication discipline has been to predict behavior. Typically, researchers present respondents with different kinds of situations that vary in P, D, or R, and then test to see what politeness strategy people will produce. For example, Baxter (1984) asked students to imagine they were working on a group project and had to ask a group member to redo his or her part of the project. Different versions of the scenario varied with how well the students knew one another, whether the speaker was a group leader or just a member, and whether the rewrite involved much or little effort. Studies in this tradition have found partial support for the effects of P, D, and R on choice of polite strategy. Requests are the FTA most often studied; power has tended to be the best predictor of how politely a speaker will make a request, whereas distance has not been consistently predictive (Goldsmith). In some studies, respondents choose the most polite strategies with those they know least well, whereas in other studies, respondents choose the most polite strategies with those they know best.

Other scholars have used Politeness Theory to predict how behavior will be evaluated. For example, Carson and Cupach (2000) found that when managers reprimanded an employee, the managers were perceived as fairer and more competent when they used redress instead of when they made the reprimand bald on record. Like studies predicting strategy use, studies predicting how strategies are interpreted have found partial support for the theory. The predicted order of politeness strategies (i.e., bald on record will be seen as less polite than redress, which will be less polite than off record) does not always hold. Under some circumstances, more direct strategies are seen as more polite, for example (Goldsmith, 2007).

Some scholars have concluded that prediction is problematic because our actions and evaluations are so dependent on features of the people interacting, their relationship, and the situation in which they find themselves. Instead, these scholars use Politeness Theory to help us see how general social processes enable social actors to act and interpret one another's actions in particular situations. Politeness Theory helps us identify politeness phenomena and understand the processes that lead to our diverse, creative, situated, and often unpredictable use of politeness in everyday situations (Craig, Tracy, & Spisak, 1986). For example, Aronsson and Rundstrom (1989) showed how pediatricians were typically polite to parents but could direct bald on record statements to a child. For example, one doctor said to the mother of an allergic child, "But then it's best to avoid cats, or what would you say?" but said to the child, "WHAT?! You SHOULD NOT do that." Concepts from Politeness Theory (P, D, R, politeness strategies) were used to examine distinctive features of pediatric consultations, including interactional sequences among three people. In the example above, the bald on record statement from an authoritative adult to a child provides a way to clearly tell the mother what not to do without threatening her face.

Strengths and Limitations of the Theory

Politeness Theory is widely cited across many academic disciplines. The theory was originally published as a book chapter in 1978; by 1987, the theory had generated enough research and controversy to justify rereleasing it as a stand-alone book with a section summarizing and responding to other scholars. Book-length treatments of Politeness Theory exist (e.g., Ting-Toomey, 1994; Watts, 2003). Here I will summarize a few major themes.

One ongoing controversy concerns the cross-cultural relevance of the theory. Brown and Levinson (1987) proposed universal social principles that underlie the linguistic practices of particular cultures. They said that face wants and rational action to protect one another's face are common to humans everywhere. Cultures vary, however, in how P and D are distributed across social relationships and how R is distributed across social actions. This variability in how P, D, and R take shape accounts for cultural difference. For example, Brown and Levinson suggested that if members of one culture seem to be "warm, easy-going, and friendly" (p. 243) compared to other cultures, it may be because they often use positive redress to deal with FTAs and that, in turn, may be because they may be part of a culture in which there is little emphasis on power differences, or in which there is great emphasis on closeness and similarity, or in which few actions are viewed as particularly face threatening. Some say this explanation does not adequately represent diverse cultural beliefs and practices (e.g., Ting-Toomey, 1994; Watts, Ide, & Ehlich, 1992). For example, in some cultures, face and politeness may be less a matter of individual strategic choice than of normative behavior to fit into the social group. Some cultures place little emphasis on negative face wants for individual freedom and privacy (Bargiela-Chiappini, 2003).

Another point of contention is how politeness strategies are conceptualized. The data on which the theory was based tended to be single speech acts; the theory said little about combinations or sequences of speech acts. Try to imagine Options 1 through 5 above in a conversation. Would you combine elements of different options? Would what came before and after these acts influence how you reacted to them? Goldsmith (2000) found bald on record advice to a friend to be less face threatening if the advice was solicited, suggesting that Option 1 might seem more appropriate and Option 5 might seem quite rude if either one followed Pat saying, "Do you think I should join a gym?" Likewise, the theory focuses on verbal communication and scholars have remarked on the importance of nonverbal communication for facework and politeness (e.g., Trees & Manusov, 1998).

Several theorists have proposed modifications to Politeness Theory to improve its conceptualization of FTAs and politeness strategies. For example, Wilson, Aleman, and Leatham (1998) modeled how participants in an interaction use contextual information to draw inferences about one another's goals and implied face threats. Lim and Bowers (1991) reconceptualized positive and negative face into wants for fellowship, competence, and autonomy and proposed that different types of face-work are needed to honor these distinct face wants. K. Tracy and Baratz (1994) suggested that the cumulative effect of the many proposed revisions ought to call into question the continued usefulness of Politeness Theory. They call for case studies that examine the relevance and form of face concerns in particular contexts.

Despite these controversies, Politeness Theory remains an influential theory and it has a central role in other communication theories, including communication privacy management theory (see Petronio & Durham, Chapter 23, this volume) and message design logic theory (O'Keefe, 1997).

One of the theory's greatest strengths is its bold, ambitious scope. The theory draws together an incredibly wide range of language features into one comprehensive lens and then, having focused our attention on these subtle features of talk, Brown and Levinson (1987) explain how these are responsible for fundamental concerns such as how we perceive others' images, how power and intimacy are negotiated in relationships, and how there come to be communication differences between genders, cultures, and other social groups. By proposing a parsimonious set of concepts, taking a strong stand on their interrelationships, and making explicit statements about what is and is not universal about human communication, the theory has prompted many tests and refinements and directed attention to studying how language forms build social life.

The theory is especially useful to communication scholars as a normative model of strategic communication (Goldsmith, 2007; O'Keefe, 1992; Wilson et al., 1998). Many communication theories are variable analytic attempts to find the determinants of what people will say or do (and this has been a prominent interpretation of Politeness Theory, too). In contrast, Politeness Theory can direct our attention to normative judgments of what people should say and do, if they wish to be seen as appropriate and effective. It focuses our attention on dilemmas of interaction and on the creative and constructive ways people use language to enact identities and relationships as they pursue tasks such as requesting, advising, or criticizing.

Directions for Future Research and Applications

By now, you may have noticed a recurring bifurcation of approaches to Politeness Theory, between those who seek prediction and those who seek interpretation. Not surprisingly, then, directions for future research differ, depending on one's scholarly goals. One future direction concerns extensions and refinements of Politeness Theory. For example, in my own research, I have examined how judgments of face threat are influenced by the content of statements (and not just the linguistic form) and the sequence in which a FTA occurs (Goldsmith, 1999, 2000). Wilson and Kunkel (2000) showed how revisions to Brown and Levinson's (1987) theory enabled them to predict how FTAs would be perceived and what kinds of reason-giving redress speakers would use to mitigate these threats.

Another direction for future research is to understand how concerns for face and resources for face-work take shape in particular social and cultural contexts. For example, K. Tracy and her colleagues examined these issues in academic colloquia (K. Tracy & Baratz, 1994) and calls to 911 (S. Tracy & K. Tracy, 1998). Research comparing face concerns and face-work resources across cultures is also an important area of study.

O'Keefe (1997) proposed that the logic embedded in Politeness Theory is but one way people have of reasoning about messages. She proposed other message design logics that undergird individuals' production and evaluation of messages, directing our attention to the possibility of individual differences in polite behavior and its interpretation.

A final direction for future research concerns understanding the relationship between politeness and impoliteness, and between researchers' concepts and judgments by laypeople. Bald on record strategies are still attempts to be polite, used when urgency or low weight of an FTA justifies a lack of politeness. In contrast, intentional efforts to be disagreeable, rude, and insulting entail a different, though perhaps parallel, set of strategies (e.g., Culpepper, Bousfield, & Wichmann, 2003). Furthermore, what we mean by politeness in everyday conversation does not correspond neatly to the definition of politeness in the theory. Watts (2003) for example, developed an alternative framework for capturing these evaluations.

Let's return to Jean and Pat one last time. Does Politeness Theory offer them any help? It helps explain why the situation is challenging. We sometimes assume that if we are close to someone, we ought to be able to speak our minds openly and directly. When we have difficulty doing so, we may doubt our own skill and psychological health or the strength of our relationship. Several theories and much research suggest this assumption is flawed, but nonetheless we sometimes feel bad when it is hard to say something to someone we care about. Politeness Theory reminds us that directness is not always desirable and helps us pinpoint what it may be about the situation that is difficult: Pat's image as a socially desirable person capable of making changes and taking care of her own health, as well as Jean's image as someone who understands their relationship and does not overstep boundaries, who is sensitive to others, and who has certain rights and responsibilities in a relationship.

Politeness Theory can also help us think of a range of ways we might go about saying the same thing, and the relative advantages and disadvantages of each. If Jean is too direct, Pat may feel criticized and bossed around, but if Jean is too indirect, Pat may not grasp the suggestion. Using positive redress—the language of solidarity—could build on the closeness of their relationship to mute any possible criticism Pat might feel and to justify why Jean does have an interest in directing Pat's behavior. Using negative redress—the language of deference—acknowledges the sensitive nature of the topic and tones down what might otherwise sound harsh or pushy. Hints and ambiguity could leave both friends with the option of ignoring the advice or of taking it without having to acknowledge that one person told the other what to do.

Let me conclude by encouraging you to observe how Politeness Theory may apply in your own everyday life. First, it might explain recurring difficulties in some of your relationships. For example, can it help you understand what it is about a rude coworker that you find so off-putting or how interactions with your instructor from a different culture create frustration for you both? Second, Politeness Theory might help you think about alternative ways of pursuing your goals. Are you bald on record when it might be more effective for you to be more polite? Do you too often rely on off record strategies that do not get your point across? Does overreliance on negative redress strategies make you sound less powerful, or do positive redress strategies come across as too familiar? Politeness Theory may also give you a way to explain communication differences and clarify your intentions if you were to problem solve with someone you care about. Finally, even in the absence of communication problems, Politeness Theory can help you appreciate the finely tuned variations in our speech that convey our images of self and other, construct our relationships, and conduct our interpersonal business.

References

Afifi, W. A., & Lee, J. W. (2000). Balancing instrumental and identity goals in relationships: The role of request directness and request persistence in the selection of sexual resistance strategies. *Communication Monographs, 67,* 284–305.

Aronsson, K., & Rundstrom, B. (1989). Cats, dogs, and sweets in the clinical negotiation of reality: On politeness and coherence in pediatric discourse. *Language and Society, 18,* 483–504.

Bargiela-Chiappini, F. (2003). Face and politeness: New (insights) for old (concepts). *Journal of Pragmatics, 35,* 1453–1469.

Baxter, L. A. (1984). An investigation of compliance-gaining as politeness. *Human Communication Research, 10,* 427–456.

Brown, P., & Levinson, S. C. (1987). *Politeness: Some universals in language usage.* New York: Cambridge University Press.

Carson, C. L., & Cupach, W. R. (2000). Facing corrections in the workplace: The influence of perceived face threat on the consequences of managerial episodes. *Journal of Applied Communication Research, 28,* 215–234.

Craig, R. T., Tracy, K., & Spisak, F. (1986). The discourse of requests: Assessment of a politeness approach. *Human Communication Research, 12,* 437–468.

Culpepper, J., Bousfield, D., & Wichmann, A. (2003). Impoliteness revisited: With special reference to dynamic and prosodic aspects. *Journal of Pragmatics, 35,* 1545–1579.

Goffman, E. (1967). *Interaction ritual.* Garden City, NY: Anchor Books.

Goldsmith, D. J. (1999). Content-based resources for giving face-sensitive advice in troubles-talk episodes. *Research on Language and Social Interaction, 32,* 303–336.

Goldsmith, D. J. (2000). Soliciting advice: The role of sequential placement in mitigating face threat. *Communication Monographs, 67,* 1–19.

Goldsmith, D. J. (2007). Brown and Levinson's politeness theory. In B. Whaley & W. Samter (Eds.), *Explaining communication: Contemporary theories and exemplars* (pp. 219–236). Mahwah, NJ: Erlbaum.

Hummert, M. L., & Mazloff, D. C. (2001). Older adults' responses to patronizing advice: Balancing politeness and identity in context. *Journal of Language and Social Psychology, 20,* 167–195.

Jameson, J. K. (2004). Negotiating autonomy and connection through politeness: A dialectical approach to organizational conflict management. *Western Journal of Communication, 68,* 257–277.

Lim, T., & Bowers, J. W. (1991). Facework: Solidarity, approbation, and tact. *Human Communication Research, 17,* 415–450.

Linde, C. (1988). The quantitative study of communicative success: Politeness and accidents in aviation discourse. *Language in Society, 17,* 375–399.

O'Keefe, B. J. (1992). Developing and testing rational models of message design. *Human Communication Research, 18,* 637–649.

O'Keefe, B. J. (1997). Variation, adaptation, and functional explanation in the study of message design. In G. Philipsen & T. L. Albrecht (Eds.), *Developing communication theories* (pp. 85–118). Albany, NY: SUNY Press.

Sabee, C. M., & Wilson, S. R. (2005). Students primary goals, attributions, and facework during conversations about disappointing grades. *Communication Education, 54,* 185–204.

Ting-Toomey, S. (1994). *The challenge of facework: Cross-cultural and interpersonal issues.* Albany, NY: SUNY Press.

Tracy, K., & Baratz, S. (1994). The case for case studies of facework. In S. Ting-Toomey (Ed.), *The challenge of facework: Cross-cultural and interpersonal issues* (pp. 287–305). Albany, NY: SUNY Press.

Tracy, S. J., & Tracy, K. (1998). Rudeness at 911: Reconceptualizing face and face-attack. *Human Communication Research, 25,* 225–251.

Trees, A. R., & Manusov, V. (1998). Managing face concerns in criticism: Integrating nonverbal behaviors as a dimension of politeness in female friendship dyads. *Human Communication Research, 24,* 564–583.

Watts, R. J. (2003). *Politeness.* Cambridge, UK: Cambridge University Press.

Watts, R. J., Ide, S., & Ehlich, K. (1992). *Politeness in language: Studies in its history, theory, and practice.* Berlin, Germany: Mouton de Gruyter.

Wilson, S. J., Aleman, C. G., & Leatham, G. B. (1998). Identity implications of influence goals: A revised analysis of face-threatening acts and application to seeking compliance with same-sex friends. *Human Communication Research, 25,* 64–96.

Wilson, S. J., & Kunkel, A. W. (2000). Identity implications of influence goals: Similarities in perceived face threats and facework across sex and close relationships. *Journal of Language and Social Psychology, 19,* 195–221.

20

Speech Codes Theory

Traces of Culture in Interpersonal Communication

Gerry Philipsen

S peech Codes Theory was developed to apply to all contexts, modes, and
settings of communicative conduct. The empirical cases—and surveys and
experiments—on which it is built are drawn from studies of interpersonal,
organizational, public, and communal communication (Philipsen, 1992, 1997,
2003; Philipsen, Coutu, & Covarrubias, 2005). However, Speech Codes Theory
has a particular relevance to interpersonal communication, which relevance I
delineate in this chapter. I define "interpersonal communication" as the production and interpretation of messages between or among two or more people,
when those messages are concerned, explicitly or implicitly, with the persons'
selves and the persons' relationships with each other.

Purpose and Meta-theoretical Assumptions

The principal assumption of Speech Codes Theory that I apply here to interpersonal communication is that whenever people engage in interpersonal
communication there are traces of culture woven into their messages. Traces
of culture appear in many forms, verbal and otherwise. The subset of traces of
culture that I will be concerned with here are those that can be discerned in
words that pertain to communicative conduct, and premises that link two or
more words, at least one of which pertains to communicative conduct, in a
general statement of belief or value. Such traces include not only the words
and premises that are immediately observable in the messages produced in

interpersonal communication but also the meanings and significance they have for the people who use and experience them.

The purpose of Speech Codes Theory, in this context, is to help discern, interpret, and explain the meaning and force of cultural traces, in particular instances of interpersonal communication.

TRACES OF CULTURE IN INTERPERSONAL COMMUNICATION

To illustrate what I mean by interpersonal communication and by "discern," "interpret," and "explain the meaning and force of cultural traces" in instances of it, I present two vignettes and provide a brief commentary on each of them.

A Norwegian woman complained to an interviewer that her husband will never stand up to his mother when she tries to interfere with the couple's independence. The husband says he believes in "peace at any price" (*fred for enhver pris*), but the wife says she believes that sometimes the price is too high.

What does peace mean in this vignette? Why does the concept of peace at any price, usually used in the context of negotiations between nations over armed conflict, seem to have such importance to the Norwegian man, who uses it to justify his refusal to talk about important topics with his mother? Although his wife believes that the price she is paying for peace is too high, she says she understands the reasoning behind his statement. What, for these interlocutors, is the meaning and force of the man's insistence on not talking bluntly with his mother?

This first vignette is drawn from a program of research conducted and reported by a Norwegian anthropologist, Marianne Gullestad, who studies Norwegian culture. One part of her project is her study of a series of Norwegian words and expressions that she found were used "with frequency and intensity" (1992, p.142) when some Norwegians talk about "interpersonal relations." The two Norwegian words that Gullestad focuses on are *fred* ("peace") and *ro* ("quiet"). She shows that when Norwegians use *fred* in talking about interpersonal relations, they do not express its primary meaning in Norwegian, "absence of war," but rather one of its many secondary meanings, particularly the sense of being "free from disturbances from others." In such contexts they use *ro* to refer to "a state of mind characterized by wholeness and control" (p. 146). To be free from disturbances from others, that is, to "find peace," is, according to the logic that Gullestad formulated, necessary for the achievement of the desired state of personal "wholeness and control." Thus "peace," she said, is often sought at any price, and is used as a justification for avoiding contact with others.

Gullestad (1992) used her study of *fred* and *ro*, along with an examination of several other Norwegian words, to construct a Norwegian "code" (pp. 103, 170) of "social relations" (p. 147). An important part of this code can be summarized by the following principles:

1. "A certain social distance (peace) creates good social relations";

2. For an individual human being, "control of self is especially important" and is "especially connected to peace in its meaning of 'quiet' (*ro*)";

3. As "guidelines for action," one should strive to be "whole, balanced, and safe by not involving oneself too much and by avoiding open personal conflicts. People who do not understand a little hint ought to be avoided" (p. 147).

I think Gullestad regarded this as one part, not the whole, of a Norwegian code of interpersonal relations. Given that her comments extended to communicative conduct (explicitly, in Point 3, with her reference to "not involving oneself too much," "avoiding open personal conflicts," and the importance of understanding "a little hint"), I regard it as part of a Norwegian code of communicative conduct.

With just this much of the code that Gullestad provided in the principles in the preceding paragraph, we can return to the vignette, perhaps with a greater understanding of the meanings of *fred* and *ro* to the Norwegian husband and of the weight of the expression for him of *fred for enhver pris*. Specifically, we find in Gullestad's (1992) work evidence that some Norwegians consider "peace" crucial not just to "good social relations" but also to keeping oneself "whole, balanced, and safe" (p. 147). That is, Gullestad showed how some Norwegians speak about various ways of communicating as being crucial not only to interpersonal life, but also to their very sense of self.

An American university student recalls that when he was nine years old his parents divorced and his father was given weekly visiting rights. On the days that the boy spent with his father, the father insisted that they "communicate" about their "relationship." The father's efforts became burdensome to the boy, who wished his father had just taken him to a baseball game.

What do "communicate" and "relationship" mean to the people who participated in this second vignette? Why does the boy resist "communication," for which one American dictionary gives as the first sense, "the transfer of meaning"? Why would the father think that he and his son would have to communicate, over and over, about their "relationship," which presumably is a biological one of father and son? Is not the relationship of father and son immutable? What, for man and boy, is the force of the man's insistence that he and his son "communicate" about their "relationship"?

During the period of time that Marianne Gullestad was working with Norwegian materials to formulate a Norwegian code of interpersonal relations, my colleagues and I in the United States, as well as other U.S. scholars, were working to formulate an American code of interpersonal relations. As Gullestad did in Norway, we studied the way that Americans used some of the key terms of this code. Tamar Katriel and I began this process of discovering an

American code by tracing the appearance of "communication" in some American speech about interpersonal life. One of our earliest findings was that, as with the Norwegian usage of "peace" in speech about interpersonal relations, much American usage of "communication" in speech about interpersonal relations did not suggest its primary dictionary meaning, but rather something that carries a good deal more moral freight. We glossed the meaning of this situated usage as "close, open, supportive speech," with "close," "open," and "supportive" being terms that we also had to interpret (Katriel & Philipsen, 1981, p. 309). This definition was not in any dictionary, but was warranted by the way people actually used the word "communication."

We also found in our early study (Katriel & Philipsen, 1981) that when Americans used the word "communication" in speech about interpersonal relations, they used it along with several other words we established as part of an American cultural vocabulary of interpersonal relations. Words we presented in 1981 include "relationship," "self," "work," and "feedback." Later studies provide detailed ethnographic interpretations of "commitment" (Quinn, 1982), "relationship" (Rosenthal, 1984), and "honest" (Carbaugh, 1988). See also Bellah, Madsen, Sullivan, Swidler, and Tipton (1985), Philipsen (1992, 1997), and Philipsen, Horkley, and Huhman (1999), for treatments of these words and their meanings as cultural words in this American code of communicative conduct.

Just as Gullestad (1992) found evidence for a Norwegian premise that "a certain social distance (peace) creates good social relations" (p. 147), we found evidence for the widespread and significant use by Americans of a premise that communication is necessary for a relationship (Katriel & Philipsen, 1981). We used "What we need is communication" in the title of our article to represent an attitude expressed often by many of our respondents in discussing their relationships.

Here is a more recent expression of the premise we reported in 1981. Hollandsworth (1995), a columnist in an American magazine, wrote about interpersonal relations in romantic situations: "Most women aren't satisfied in a relationship until they find a man who's truly communicative—a man who doesn't hesitate to discuss his feelings, desires, and anxieties" (p. 7). With regard to "relationship," the statement's use of "satisfied in" suggests that a "relationship" can be more or less satisfying, that is, "satisfaction" is a variable associated with "relationships." Two other popular writers wrote at this time that "when communication breaks down, your relationship is headed for danger" (Bilicki & Goetz, 1995, p. 60), suggesting that a "relationship" is something that not only can vary, but that it is fragile, susceptible to "breakdown." With regard to the word "communicative," which is a form of the word "communication," Hollandsworth implied with his use of the word "truly" that there is a true (and false) variety of communicative, and that in the true variant the "man" must "not hesitate" to engage in the speech activity of "discussion" (presumably a give and take of talk) about some specific topical areas—his "feelings," "desires," and "anxieties" (Hollandsworth, p. 7). These authors, writing in popular magazines, suggested a belief that "communication" and "relationship" are linked to each other in important ways; they thus echo Katriel and Philipsen's (1981) report of the widespread and significant American use of the premise that "communication is necessary for a relationship."

With just this much of the code that Katriel and I, and others, have provided in work on an American code, we can return to the American vignette, perhaps with a greater appreciation of the meanings of "communication" and "relationship" to the father, and of the weight that the premise that "what we need is communication" (for "our relationship") carried for him. Although in some codes it would be unthinkable for a "relationship" to "break down" because one of the parties to it seems less than "satisfied" with it, this is the sort of talk that the American father was presumably exposed to, in his face-to-face interactions as well as in the popular media. (See, especially, Philipsen, 1992, chap. 5, for a treatment of the correlation of face-to-face and mediated talk about "communication" and "relationships.")

SPEECH CODES

In interpreting the meanings and explaining the force in these vignettes of words and premises about communicative conduct, I suggested that the people mentioned in them used a code to produce, interpret, and evaluate their own and others' communicative conduct. I used my understanding of those codes to interpret and explain the communicative conduct of the people who used them. What sort of codes are these? I refer to them as "speech codes," which I define as follows: Speech codes are historically situated and socially constructed systems of words, meanings, premises, and rules about communicative conduct. The word "speech" in "speech codes" is a shorthand term, a figure of speech, standing here for all the possible means of communicative conduct that can be encountered in a given time and place. The word "code" in "speech codes" refers to a system of words, meanings, premises, and rules that people use as a resource to talk about, interpret, and shape communicative conduct. These senses of speech and of code, when placed together in the term speech code, establish a definition of a speech code as a historically situated and socially constructed system of words, meanings, premises, and rules that people use to talk about their own and others' communicative conduct.

In 1992, I set forth a prototypical version of a theory of speech codes, with four empirically grounded principles about their nature, their functioning in communicative conduct, and how to discover and describe them. In 1997, I made a formal statement of Speech Codes Theory, with five empirically grounded propositions. In the latest version of the theory, Philipsen and colleagues (2005) expanded the theory to six propositions, responded to published criticisms of it, and clarified further the nature of the construct of code in it. In the paragraphs that follow I describe the main features of the theory, and the six speech codes propositions.

Main Features of the Theory

The first descriptive generalization is that everywhere there is a distinctive culture, there will be found a distinctive speech code. This was illustrated in the brief juxtaposition of (some elements of) Norwegian and American speech codes, with the suggestion that the Norwegian code gives greater endorsement than does the American to interpersonal communication that is indirect and respectful of personal boundaries, while the American code gives greater endorsement than does the Norwegian to directness of communication and a more changeable self. These are two among many accounts of speech codes that have been analyzed contrastively.

The second descriptive generalization is that every individual will encounter multiple speech codes during a lifetime. Thus, although a Norwegian or an American might use the codes I have described here, these individuals presumably can—and do—draw on other codes that are used in their social environments. Gullestad (1992) and Philipsen (1992) provided book-length treatments of the societies in which they studied the codes they reported; both cases showed evidence of more than one code being used in these societies.

The third descriptive generalization is that in every speech code the words, meanings, premises, and rules pertaining to communicative conduct are systematically linked with words, meanings, premises, and rules pertaining to the nature of persons and the nature of social relationships. This is illustrated here for the Norwegian code in the linkage between indirectness of communication, and the preservation of the well-being of a bounded person. It is illustrated here for the American code in the linkage between openness, and the strength of interpersonal relationships. The import of this generalization is that whenever people engage in interpersonal communication, and use words and premises pertaining to communicative conduct, they bring into the discussion words and premises that carry cultural traces that are always linked, for their meaning and significance, to words and meanings pertaining to notions of self or of interpersonal relations.

These three generalizations are, respectively, Propositions 1, 2, and 3 of Speech Codes Theory.

Speech Codes Theory posits a way to discover and describe traces of culture in communicative conduct. It does this through Proposition 5 of the theory, that the words, rules, and premises of a speech code are inextricably woven into communicative conduct (Philipsen et al., 2005). The import of Proposition 5 is that it tells one where to look (and listen) for traces of culture—that is, it tells one to look at (and listen to) communicative conduct, and to search therein for the use of a cultural code or codes. It also tells one what to look (and listen) for there, with a specification of a series of ways to discover traces of culture in speaking— for example, to search for the use of words or phrases about communicative conduct (e.g., "a little hint") and premises that include at least one word about communicative conduct (e.g., "communication is necessary for a relationships").

Speech Codes Theory posits a way to interpret and explain observed communicative conduct. In the presentation and examination of the two episodes presented above, I illustrated how speech codes, once discovered and described, can be used to interpret and explain communicative conduct, for example by showing the cultural meaning of the concept of peace and its importance to a Norwegian man in guiding his communicative conduct with his mother and his wife, and by showing the cultural meaning of the concepts of communication and relationship to an American man and the sense of imperative he felt to "communicate" so as to prevent a "breakdown" of the "relationship" with his son.

There are two propositions involved here. Proposition 4 of the theory says that the significance of particular communicative acts is contingent on the speech codes that people use to interpret them—that is, if someone observed a husband refusing to speak up to his mother in defense of the rights of his wife and himself as a couple, the not speaking up would be heard differently if interpreted in the terms of the Norwegian code than it would in the terms of the American code, as these codes were described above. Proposition 6 of Speech Codes Theory says that people use speech codes not only to interpret communicative conduct, but also to evaluate it (as good or bad) and to explain (that is, justify or account for) it.

Speech Codes Theory is an empirical theory. Each of its six propositions was built on a foundation of empirical evidence. Most of that empirical evidence consists of ethnographic studies of speech codes in particular times and places and the comparative analysis of such studies. Gullestad's studies of Norwegian communicative conduct (1992) and the research of Katriel and Philipsen (1981), Philipsen (1975, 1976, 1986, 1992), Carbaugh (1988), Coutu (2000), and others into American communicative conduct are examples of such ethnographic work that provides an empirical account of a speech code in a particular time and place: Norway and the United States, respectively. Philipsen and Carbaugh (1988) and Philipsen (2003) cited a large body of speech codes research conducted in many societies and many languages throughout the world, a fund of research on which Speech Codes Theory is based.

Speech Codes Theory is a dynamic theory. It is subject to change on the basis of new evidence or the rethinking of old evidence. For example, in each of the second and third published versions of the theory (Philipsen, 1997;

Philipsen et al., 2005) one proposition was added based on a reconsideration of existing research or the consideration of new research, in each case leading to a data-based expansion of the number of propositions. (Coutu, 2000, was instrumental in driving the addition of Proposition 2.) Furthermore, each proposition in the theory is stated so that it can be disconfirmed by new evidence or a rethinking of old evidence.

Conceptualization of Communication in the Theory

I define "communication" as the production and interpretation of messages between or among two or more people. There is a commitment in the ethnographic research through which speech codes are discovered and described to pay attention to whatever the people one is studying take communication to be. This requires that the researcher be open to considering a variety of phenomena as falling within the domain of communication that the researcher might otherwise rule out: e.g., considering plants, trees, the wind, or other nonhuman and nonanimal phenomena as potentially part of the communication process. At the same time, if there are no boundaries whatsoever as to what counts as communicative, it is difficult to say what precisely would or would not be included in a speech code, and it is in that spirit that in this exposition of Speech Codes Theory I have presented working definitions of communication and of interpersonal communication.

Uses of the Theory

There are two ways that Speech Codes Theory provides an understanding of interpersonal communication. One is that it provides a perspective on a feature of interpersonal communication in all societies and cultures. The other is that it provides an approach to discerning cultural traces wherever they appear in particular instances of interpersonal communication and to interpreting the meaning and force of those instances for the people who produce and experience them. I will elaborate on each of these points briefly.

First, earlier in this chapter I presented two vignettes of interpersonal communication, one in Norway and one in America. These vignettes were interpreted by reference to what the people in the vignettes said and, by reference in each case, to a large body of research into the cultural background of the people described in them. In each case, an illustration was provided of the idea that when people engage in interpersonal communication there are traces of culture in their messages about their selves and their relations to each other. Furthermore, the analysis of these vignettes showed that one place these traces appeared was in culturally distinctive words and premises pertaining to communicative conduct. Finally, the analysis of these vignettes showed that, where culturally distinctive words and meanings pertaining to communicative conduct appeared, they appeared not only on their own terms but in premises that link them to culturally distinctive words and meanings for a state of personal well-being or a state of interpersonal relations. The large body of speech codes research, conducted in many languages and many societies, shows that what I illustrated here for Norwegian and American interpersonal communication is true in many other places, including but not limited to Colombia, Finland, Germany, Israel, Mexico, and Spain (see Philipsen, 2003). Speech Codes Theory takes these findings from many cultures and generalizes them to formulate a property of interpersonal communication in all times and places. That property is that when words for and premises pertaining to communicative conduct appear in interpersonal communication there will be traces of culture present in them, and that these traces will bear culturally distinctive meanings and significance.

Speech Codes Theory can help the participants in, or observers of, interpersonal communication to understand the cultural significance of particular instances of the theory. There are three ways the theory does this. First, it helps a person discern that a speech code is being used in someone's interpersonal messages, e.g., by directing attention to words and premises about communicative conduct that are used in those messages. Second, it helps a person interpret the meanings of words about communicative conduct by tracing their use in relation to other words and meanings that co-occur with those words about communicative conduct. Third, it helps to explain why people say what they say in interpersonal messages by showing how, in the premises they use, they link their notions about ways of communicating to their notions about personal well-being and good social relations.

Strengths and Limitations of the Theory

Speech Codes Theory has several strengths as a theory that help to interpret and explain interpersonal communication. First, it specifies several propositions about the nature, discovery, and use of speech codes in interpersonal communication. Second, those propositions are grounded in a substantial fund of evidence gathered through experiment and experience in the study of speech codes. Third, Speech Codes Theory provides several ways to help participants in interpersonal communication understand what they and their fellow interlocutors are saying about themselves and their relationships.

Speech Codes Theory is limited in that it applies to a narrow, albeit an important, dimension of interpersonal communication. That dimension is culture. The theory does not account for personal codes or for universal behavioral tendencies. Thus, it is a theory that is complementary to other theories that provide sharply focused ways to discern, interpret, and explain interpersonal communication.

Directions for Future Research and Applications

I see three clear areas for future research and application of Speech Codes Theory in interpersonal communication. First, researchers should examine whether participants in interpersonal communication are aware of the use of speech codes by themselves and their interlocutors. As indicated above, we have a great deal of information, across many societies, that suggests that everywhere there is interpersonal communication the participants produce and interpret messages in part through the use of culturally distinctive words and premises pertaining to communicative conduct. When participants do the producing and interpreting, how aware are they that they are using a particular cultural code? For example, when someone talks with a friend, lover, spouse, or relative about their relation to each other, and uses such words as "peace," "quiet," "communication," or "relationship," is that person aware that he or she is speaking not naturally but culturally, that is, in the terms of a distinctive cultural code?

When someone repeats a version of the statement that "communication is necessary for a relationship," has that person considered whether things other than "communication" might be just as or more important? For example, is "communication" more important, or even as important, to a romantic or marital "relationship" as, say, carefulness in the making and keeping of romantic or marital vows, self-sacrifice in consideration of the other's well-being in the escalation of a romantic relationship, or fidelity to a partner? Textbooks in interpersonal communication tend to carry several pages, sometimes whole chapters, on the topics of self-disclosure and the negotiation of selves, but in many cases do not even mention such topics as the speech acts of promising or of making a vow. Additionally, can "relationships" end or break down? If so, what is the notion of relationship that is therefore implied? Cannot relationships be constituted on the basis of blood or the making of vows, and can blood be negotiated? Does awareness that one is using a particular code, say the American code discussed in this chapter, extend to the idea that in using this particular code one is emphasizing one set of moral and ethical commitments over others?

Second, researchers should examine the key terms and premises of the American code of "communication" that is referred to in this chapter. Several different key words in this code have been discerned and interpreted, including "communication," "close," "open," "supportive," "work," "self," "relationship," "commitment," and "honesty." What we do not know is how these and other words fit together into an American cultural system of symbols and meanings pertaining to communicative conduct. This American code is important to Americans and to anyone who wants to understand those Americans who use it, and yet there is little in the way of a systematic tying together of the diverse studies, each of which reveals something important about contemporary American life, but all of which, when put together into a comprehensive synthesis, would provide an important understanding of both America and the important speech code found in America.

Third, researchers should examine what is the force, if any, that speech codes have on the thought and conduct of people who use those codes. Proposition 5 of Speech Codes Theory implies that just because someone uses a speech code does not mean that the person's thought is restricted or shaped by that use, or that the person's communicative conduct is determined by the terms of the code. At the same time, there is a great deal of evidence that such codes indeed do have some shaping influence on the thought and conduct of those who use them. The question of cultural and linguistic determinism is a classic and enduring one. The more elaborated development elsewhere of Proposition 5 suggests several important lines of research that need to be pursued before we have a satisfactory understanding of the force of speech codes.

References

Bellah, R., Madsen R., Sullivan, W., Swidler, A., & Tipton, S. (1985). *Habits of the heart: Individualism and commitment in American life.* Berkeley: University of California Press.

Bilicki, B. & Goetz, M. (1995, April). What went wrong in the first place? *Woman's Own*, 60.

Carbaugh, D. (1988). *Talking American: Cultural discourses on DONAHUE.* Norwood, NJ: Ablex.

Coutu, L. M. (2000). Communication codes of rationality and spirituality in the discourse of and about Robert S. McNamara's *In Retrospect. Research on Language and Social Interaction, 33,* 179–211.

Gullestad, M. (1992). *The art of social relations: Essays on culture, social action and everyday life in modern Norway.* New York: Oxford University Press.

Hollandsworth, S. (1995, May/June). 7 things you must know about a man before you get involved with him. *American Woman, 7,* 30.

Katriel, T., & Philipsen, G. (1981). "What we need is communication": "Communication" as a cultural category in some American speech. *Communication Monographs, 48,* 302–317.

Philipsen, G. (1975). Speaking "like a man" in Teamsterville: Culture patterns of role enactment in an urban neighborhood. *Quarterly Journal of Speech, 61,* 13–22.

Philipsen, G. (1976). Places for speaking in Teamsterville. *Quarterly Journal of Speech, 62,* 15–25.

Philipsen, G. (1986). Mayor Daley's council speech: A cultural analysis. *Quarterly Journal of Speech, 72,* 247–260.

Philipsen, G. (1992). *Speaking culturally: Explorations in social communication.* Albany, NY: SUNY Press.

Philipsen, G. (1997). A theory of speech codes. In G. Philipsen & T. L. Albrecht (Eds.), *Developing communication theories* (pp. 119–156). Albany, NY: SUNY Press.

Philipsen, G. (2003). Cultural communication. In W. Gudykunst (Ed.), *Cross-cultural and intercultural communication* (pp. 33–52).Thousand Oaks, CA: Sage.

Philipsen, G., Coutu, L., & Covarrubias, P. (2005). Speech codes theory: Restatement, revisions, and response to criticisms. In W. Gudykunst (Ed.), *Theorizing about intercultural communication* (pp. 55–68). Thousand Oaks, CA: Sage.

Philipsen, G., Horkley, N., & Huhman, M. (1999). *"Communication" as a keyword in American culture.* Unpublished paper.

Quinn, N. (1982). "Commitment" in American marriage: A cultural analysis. *American Ethnologist, 9,* 775–798.

Rosenthal, P. (1984). *Words and values: Some leading words and where they lead us.* New York: Oxford University Press.

PART III

Relationship-Centered Theories of Interpersonal Communication

C hapters in the third and final part of the book share a relationship-centered approach to interpersonal communication. As a group, these theories center on understanding the role of communication in developing, sustaining, and terminating social and personal relationships. Communication scholars have been an integral part of an interdisciplinary and international group of researchers dedicated to the scientific study of personal relationships, an effort that kicked into gear in the late 1980s. Most of the scholars in this section of the book are active members of the International Association for Relationship Research (IARR), which includes members from disciplines including communication studies, family studies and child development, gerontology, psychology, and sociology (although we would note that many other scholars in the present volume are active in this association). What is unique about Part III is that the theories cohere around the context of personal relationships rather than around individual message production or processing, or discourse and interaction, as we saw in Parts I and II, respectively.

There are nine theories represented in this part of the book. Six of the nine theories were developed by scholars who identify professionally with the communication studies discipline: Affection Exchange Theory, Communication Privacy Management Theory, Relational Communication Theory, Relational Dialectics Theory, Relationship Stages Theories, and Social Information Processing Theory. Attachment Theory and Social Exchange Theories were developed in psychology and have been used extensively in that discipline and in several others. Critical Feminist Theories are truly interdisciplinary, growing out of disciplines including women's studies, philosophy, law, cultural studies, and English.

Akin to the chapters in Part II, the chapters in Part III represent the breadth of meta-theoretical perspectives. Five of the nine theories spring from post-positivism: Affection Exchange Theory, Attachment Theory, Relational

Communication Theory, Social Exchange Theories, and Social Information Processing Theory. Common to these theories is the goal of explanation and prediction of patterns among communication variables. For those theories developed both from inside and from outside communication studies, the theorists presume an objective reality and cause-and-effect or functional patterns that can be discovered via scientific observation. In fact you will notice that some of these authors talk about their theories as scientific theories. For example, in their chapter on Affection Exchange Theory, Floyd, Judd, and Hesse explain that the theory "is a scientific theory. Its principal purpose is to explain why human beings communicate affection to each other, and with what consequences." Clearly you can see the authors' goals fitting into the post-positivist paradigm.

A second clear fit is that of Critical Feminist Theories into the critical paradigm. In her chapter, Julia Wood weaves together critical feminist theories, which seek to uncover, question, and transform patriarchal ideologies by which some persons become dominant and others silenced. Critical feminist theorists focus on issues of sex and gender and the cultural practices and structures that shape the lives and relationships of women and men in ways that promote (in)equality.

The last three chapters are more challenging to categorize. At first glance, Relational Dialectics Theory seems to fit best into the interpretive metatheoretical discourse, because the theory focuses on how meanings are locally and socially constructed and sustained through communicative activities. Some of the researchers using this theory have worked in the interpretive paradigm, seeking to understand how social realities are produced and maintained via the communication of relational partners, families, and groups. Yet, as Baxter and Braithwaite point out in their chapter, Relational Dialectics Theory replaces a focus on individual subjectivity with a focus on discourse, and challenges the bias toward consensus that often characterizes the interpretive approach. Finally, as we saw in Part II of this volume, some theories defy categorization into one meta-theoretical discourse. Sometimes it is because theories originate in one paradigm and are adopted and studied by researchers in another tradition. We believe that is the case with Communication Privacy Management Theory. This theory originates from the communication studies discipline, which stems originally from research on self-disclosure begun in social psychology. The theory has been used by post-positivistic researchers interested in predicting and explaining boundaries and the regulation of revealing and concealing private information in dyadic, family, group, or organizational systems. Petronio and Durham rightly point out that the theory also has been used by interpretive scholars to understand the process of boundary regulation in various contexts. In terms of Relationship Stage Theories, the authors argue for their roots in post-positivism with more recent approaches also sharing assumptions of the interpretivist paradigm.

As with the chapters in Parts I and II of the book, the chapters in Part III also can be woven together with additional themes beyond paradigmatic membership. Several of the chapters emphasize how individuals produce and process messages, and thus could just as easily be grouped with the chapters in Part I were it not for their explicit focus on the context of personal relationships. Included in this grouping are Attachment Theory, Social Exchange Theory, Communication Privacy Management Theory, and Social Information Processing Theory. Other theories in this section display a focus on discourse and interaction patterns, including Relational Communication Theory, Relational Dialectics Theory, and Relationship Stage Theories.

Two of the theories—Affection Exchange Theory and Attachment Theory—provide examples of theories that draw on bioevolutionary arguments, although in different ways. These theories stand in stark contrast to theories that argue in favor of reality being socially constructed, not biologically (and thus universally) predisposed: Critical Feminist Theories, Relational Dialectics Theory, and selectively, the Relationship Stage Theories.

Two of the chapters are explicitly focused on how relationships change over time: Relationship Stage Theories and Social Information Processing Theory. Other theories address relationship change more obliquely, including Relational Dialectics Theory and Relational Communication Theory. Other theories focus on factors that motivate individuals to enter into, sustain, and terminate relationships, including Affection Exchange Theory, Attachment Theory, and Social Exchange Theory.

Taken together, the chapters in this section of the book focus more narrowly than the chapters in the first two parts of the book. Whereas those chapters focus on face-to-face communication more generally, the chapters in this section share an interest in answering questions regarding why and how personal relationships form and function.

21

Affection Exchange Theory

A Bio-Evolutionary Look at Affectionate Communication

Kory Floyd, Jeff Judd, and Colin Hesse

M any interpersonal relationships are initiated and maintained through the exchange of affectionate behaviors, such as hugging, kissing, hand holding, or by saying "I love you." Indeed, expressions of affection often serve as turning points that advance relational development. Affectionate communication contributes not only to the health of relationships, however, but also to the health of the people in them. Why humans engage in affectionate behavior, and why it is associated with these benefits, are among the questions addressed by Affection Exchange Theory (AET). This chapter will describe the purpose and assumptions of AET and delineate its basic principles. It will also identify how AET conceptually defines communication, and will review some of the research that has used AET to increase understanding of personal relationships. Finally, it will address the theory's strengths and limitations, and offer suggestions for future research and applications.

Purpose and Meta-theoretical Assumptions

AET is a scientific theory. Its principal purpose is to explain why human beings communicate affection to each other, and with what consequences. Paradigmatically, the theory fits most closely within the post-positivist tradition. AET's fundamental assumptions are grounded in neo-Darwinian thought, particularly insofar as they suppose that (a) procreation and survival are both superordinate human goals, (b) communicative behaviors can serve one or both of these superordinate goals even in nonevident ways, and (c) individuals need not be conscious of the evolutionary goals their behaviors serve.

Undergirding these are two fundamental assumptions. The first such assumption is that humans, like other living organisms, are subject to the principles of natural selection and sexual selection. As articulated by Darwin in 1859, these include the notion that heritable characteristics or tendencies that advantage an organism with respect to procreation or survival will be "selected for," ensuring their greater representation in succeeding generations. The second fundamental assumption is that human communicative behavior is only partially subject to the willful control of the communicator. Evolved adaptive tendencies, as well as physiological influences (such as those of hormones), affect communicative behavior in ways that are not necessarily evident to the conscious self. AET thus assumes that communication is affected not only by socially constructed influences (such as gender roles or cultural norms) but also by influences that are grounded in biology and evolutionary adaptation.

Main Features of the Theory

AET begins with the proposition that "the need and capacity for affection are inborn" (Proposition 1). That is, humans are born both with the ability and with the need to feel affection, which is defined as an internal state of fondness and intense positive for a living target. This proposition has two important implications, the first of which is that humans need not learn to feel affection, but that both the ability and the need to experience affection are innate. The second implication is that the need for affection is fundamental in the human species, which implies benefits when it is met and negative consequences when it is unfulfilled.

The second proposition of AET is that affectionate feelings and "affectionate expressions are distinct experiences that often, but not always, covary" (Proposition 2). Here, the theory differentiates between the emotional experience of affection and the behaviors through which affection is made manifest. This distinction is consequential for two reasons. First, humans have the ability to experience affection without expressing those feelings. One may have affectionate feelings for another, for instance, but fail to express them out of fear of rejection or out of deference to the social constraints of the context. Second, humans can express affection without feeling it, which humans often do in the service of politeness norms. These expressions can also serve ulterior motives, such as acquisition of a favor.

The third and perhaps most important proposition is that "affectionate communication is adaptive with respect to human viability and fertility" (Proposition 3). This is the heart of AET, the proposal that receiving and conveying affectionate expressions contributes to survival and procreation success. More specific subpropositions identify two principal causal pathways through which affectionate communication serves these superordinate goals. One is that affectionate behavior promotes the establishment and maintenance of significant pair-bonds, increasing access to material resources (such as food or shelter) and emotional resources (such as attention or social support) that help sustain life. The other is that engaging in affection communication portrays oneself to potential mating partners as a viable partner and a fit potential parent. The idea here is that conveying affection to a romantic partner can denote the emotional capacity and commitment necessary to be a loving mate and a responsible parent.

AET further provides that, because the motivations of survival and procreation are so fundamental, the experiences of feeling and exchanging affection covary with physiological characteristics governing immune system strength, stress, and reward. This subproposition addresses the question of why giving and receiving affection within a positive interpersonal relationship (such as a friendship or marriage) is so physically rewarding (and likewise, why failing to receive it is so physically aversive). Because these behaviors contribute to survival and procreation, it is adaptive that they would be physically pleasurable (much as eating, sleeping, or having sex are usually physically pleasurable experiences).

Not all affectionate behavior enhances survival and procreation, however. Within the wrong relationships or in the wrong contexts, affectionate communication can inhibit these motivations. AET thus proposes that "humans vary in their optimal tolerances for affection and affectionate behavior" (Proposition 4), and that "affectionate behaviors that violate the range of optimal tolerance are physiologically aversive" (Proposition 5). Floyd and colleague (1997; Floyd & Burgoon, 1999) were among the first to speculate that, although affectionate behavior is normatively positive, it can in fact produce quite negative outcomes under certain circumstances. Receiving an affectionate touch from a stranger, for instance, not only violates norms for appropriate social behavior but can also initiate a negative emotional and physiological response (i.e., a stress response). This is in contrast to the positivity typically associated with the exchange of affection, but is expected (according to AET) in situations in which the affectionate behavior may inhibit one's survival or procreation motivation.

Conceptualization of Communication in the Theory

AET conceptually defines only "affectionate" communication, rather than communication in general, although some broader concepts about communication can be derived from its approach. In the theory, "affectionate communication" is defined as encompassing those behaviors that encode feelings of fondness and intense positive regard, and are generally decoded as such by their intended receivers. Although forms of affection display are largely shaped by cultural norms and constrained by contextual demands, it is the presentation (whether accurate or not) of an affectionate emotion that qualifies a behavioral expression as affectionate.

Floyd and Morman's (1998) tripartite model of affectionate behavior adds conceptual clarity by distinguishing among three forms of affection display. The "verbal" communication of affection consists of spoken or written affectionate expressions such as, "I love you," or "You mean so much to me." The "direct nonverbal" communication of affection includes nonlinguistic or paralinguistic behaviors that denote affection within the relationship or speech community in which they are used; in North America, these include behaviors such as hugging, kissing, or holding hands. Finally, "indirect nonverbal" communication is composed of behaviors that connote affection through the provision of social or material support. These may include things like helping with a task or lending the use of a car. Unlike with verbal and direct nonverbal expressions, the affectionate message in indirect nonverbal expressions is ancillary to the behavior itself and is consequently less overt.

As noted above, AET conceives of affectionate communication as a behavior that is affected by both socially constructed and evolutionarily derived influences, and that is only partially under the conscious control of the communicator. These assumptions are not necessarily limited to affectionate communication, per se, so although AET does not conceptualize other forms of communication, the theory would apply these conceptual principles to communicative behavior in general.

Uses of the Theory

Since AET was originally proposed in 2001 (Floyd, 2001), nearly 20 different tests of the theory have been conducted to help understand processes of interpersonal communication better. Many of these tests belong to one of two general categories: those that have focused on which relationships are more affectionate than others, and those that have focused on the mental and physical health benefits of being affectionate. Findings from both groups of studies are reviewed in the following section.

AFFECTIONATE COMMUNICATION AND RELATIONSHIPS

AET proposes that affectionate communication serves as a resource that can contribute both to the survival and to the reproductive success of those who engage in it. As Hamilton (1964) originally proposed, reproductive success involves contributing one's genetic materials to future generations. Thus, individuals can achieve reproductive success not only by having children of their own, but also by ensuring the survival of others who carry their genes, such as nieces, nephews, or cousins. Importantly, personal relationships vary in terms of their level of genetic relatedness; humans share more genes in common with parents than grandparents, for instance, and more with siblings than with cousins. Consequently, some personal relationships are more important than others to genetic reproduction.

If this notion is true, and if affection is a resource that contributes to survival (as AET proposes), then certain relationships should be more affectionate than others. This hypothesis has been tested in several family relationships that vary systematically in their levels of genetic relatedness. For instance, Floyd and Morman (2002) found that men were more affectionate with their biological sons than with their stepsons, and Floyd and Morr (2003) reported that adults were more affectionate with their siblings than with their siblings-in-law. Both of these findings support alternative, nonevolutionary explanations. For example, most fathers likely feel emotionally closer to their biological sons than their stepsons, because they have known their biological sons longer. As a result, variables such as closeness or relationship duration could account for the difference in affectionate behavior observed between these two relationship types. However, both of these studies ruled out numerous competing explanations. Specifically, the differences in affectionate behavior between biological sons and stepsons, and between siblings and siblings-in-law, could not be accounted for by differences in closeness, duration of the relationship, how far apart participants lived, how often they saw each other, or other plausible explanations. Even when all of these variables were controlled, the relationships still differed systematically in their levels of affectionate behavior in the ways that AET predicted.

Although most parents would likely report being equally affectionate with all of their children, AET hypothesizes instead that parents give more affection to the children who are the most likely to produce offspring themselves (although the theory does not suggest that parents do this consciously). The explanation is that parents have greater reproductive success when their children reproduce than when they do not, making it evolutionarily adaptive to invest the greatest resources in children with the greatest reproductive potential. Several things may inhibit reproductive probability, including sterility or the inability to attract a mate. Homosexuality also inhibits reproductive probability; two studies have shown that fathers give more affection to their heterosexual sons than to their homosexual sons (Floyd, 2001; Floyd, Sargent, & Di Corcia, 2004).

AFFECTIONATE COMMUNICATION AND HEALTH

A large body of research already shows that receiving affectionate behavior (especially affectionate touch) is beneficial to physical and mental health. (For an extensive review, see Floyd, 2006a.) One of the innovative aspects of AET, however, is its proposition that individuals can also reap health benefits by "giving" affection to others. Specifically, AET provides that expressing affection reduces the body's susceptibility to stress and activates its hormonal reward systems, which have sedative and analgesic effects.

Testing these ideas has involved two specific types of studies. The purpose of the first type has been to identify the health parameters that are reliably associated with affectionate behavior. These efforts began with Floyd's (2002) demonstration that highly affectionate people are advantaged, relative to less-affectionate people, on a host of mental health measures. In this study, under-graduate students were each given a pair of identical questionnaires with the instruction to give one of the questionnaires to "the most affectionate person you know" and the other to "the least affectionate person you know." The questionnaires measured self-esteem, general mental health, social engagement, life satisfaction, and susceptibility to depression and stress. Floyd found that the highly affectionate people scored more positively than their less-affectionate counterparts on all of these measures, and a later study showed that these associations remained statistically significant even when the amount of affection people received from others was controlled (Floyd, Hess, Miczo, Halone, Mikkelson, & Tusing, 2005).

Despite their potential importance, these findings were limited by the use of self-report measures. This is particularly problematic for measures such as susceptibility to stress, since some forms of stress occur outside of conscious awareness. Testing AET's ideas more directly has required the measurement of objective markers of health, such as hormonal activity and blood chemistry. In one study, Floyd (2006b) reported a strong positive association between trait affection level (i.e., how affectionate an individual typically is with others) and 24-hour variation in the adrenal hormone cortisol, which helps regulate the body's response to stress. Substantial 24-hour variation signals a healthy ability to respond to stress, whereas minimal variation indicates suppression of the stress response. In another study, Floyd, Hesse, and Haynes (2007) reported that higher levels of affectionate behavior were associated with lower blood pressure and healthier average blood glucose levels.

Working from these associations, the second type of study has sought to ascertain causal relationships between affectionate behavior and health outcomes. In one such study (Floyd et al., 2007), participants took part in a series of stress-inducing laboratory activities designed to elevate their blood cortisol levels. Afterward, they were randomly assigned to one of three groups. Those in the experimental group were asked to think of the most significant person in their lives and to write a letter to that person in which they expressed their love and affection for that person. In one of the control groups, participants were asked only to think about the most significant person in their lives but not to communicate their feelings, and in the other control group, participants were instructed only to sit quietly. If expressing affection fortifies the body's ability to respond to stress, as AET predicts, then cortisol levels should return to their baseline values more quickly for those in the experimental group than for those in the other groups, and that is what occurred. Current experimental work in our laboratory is examining whether increasing nonverbal affectionate behavior in romantic relationships can reduce serum cholesterol, and initial results show significant promise (e.g., Floyd, Mikkelson, Hesse, & Pauley, 2007).

Strengths and Limitations of the Theory

Like all theories, AET enjoys certain strengths and endures certain liabilities. Among the most important strengths of AET is simply that it is the first comprehensive theory about affectionate communication. As a consequence, it is able to explain a wide range of findings identified by studies conducted within different theoretic traditions (see Floyd, 2006a). An additional strength is that AET answers higher-order questions about affectionate communication, such as why human beings are affectionate in the first place. Although other theories have been able to answer lower-order questions, such as when people are likely to reciprocate affectionate expressions, AET provides a conceptually broader and grander view of how affectionate communication contributes to important, enduring human motivations related to survival and procreation. A third strength, implied in the previous section, is that AET's hypotheses have enjoyed substantial empirical support—not only in the areas of family relationships and health but also in nonverbal communication (Floyd & Ray, 2003) and persuasion (Floyd, Erbert, Davis, & Haynes, 2006).

The most consequential limitation of the theory is the lack of detail it presently offers regarding the pathways through which affectionate communication contributes to physical health. Generalized pathways are delineated, including the body's systems for reward and stress response, but these provide only broad bases for hypothesizing specific physiological effects. Research has yet to discover, for instance, which particular hormones, chemical messengers, or immune system attributes are the most directly responsible for the benefits that affectionate behavior can bring, so the theory provides only general guidance on these questions. As research in this area matures, it will facilitate greater precision in the theory's predictive ability.

Some may regard AET's relative lack of attention to social learning as an additional limitation, insofar as the theory fails to specify the cultural, political, economic, or environmental variables that account for the most variance in affectionate behavior. These omissions were intentional—not because AET conceives of these sources of variance as inconsequential, but because it adopts a bioevolutionary approach that privileges the explication of evolutionary and physiological causes over socially constructed ones. This necessarily limits AET's predictive ability, however, just as exclusively social learning theories are similarly limited.

Directions for Future Research and Applications

The exchange of affection is such a fundamental relational activity that its study offers much promise for understanding and improving the human condition. As noted above, one of the most important directions for future research and application relates to the improvement of mental and physical health. As experiments identify how affectionate communication is associated with immunocompetence, stress management, mental and emotional regulation, and other aspects of well-being, these findings may aid in the development of behavioral (nonpharmacological) interventions that could serve as ancillary treatments for physical and mental disorders. This research is still in its infancy, but its promise is substantial.

AET's explication of the relationship between affectionate behavior and reproduction also has potential application in the understanding and prevention of sexual assault. To the extent that rape and other forms of sexual assault occur within familiar relationships, they may be preceded by insincere affectionate expressions intended to persuade the victim that sexual interaction is warranted. Indeed, in a survey of more than 1,000 American college students, Floyd and colleagues (2006) found that individuals reported "initiating sexual activity" as among the most common reasons why they had expressed insincere verbal affection to others. With respect to understanding and preventing sexual assault, the important question is not why one person would use an affectionate expression to coax another into sexual interaction, but why such a strategy would prove successful. The explanation offered by AET is that it is evolutionarily adaptive for humans to attend to affectionate expressions as signals of another's potential fitness as a mate and parent. Thus, receiving an affectionate expression that is believed (by the recipient) to be sincere will be sufficiently persuasive, in many instances, to allow ill-advised or otherwise unwanted sexual interaction.

These are two arenas in which AET provides not only clear and testable predictions, but also useful applications. Future research in these and other areas will further illuminate the many aspects of human life touched by the communication of affection.

References

Floyd, K. (1997). Communicating affection in dyadic relationships: An assessment of behavior and expectancies. *Communication Quarterly, 45,* 68–80.

Floyd, K. (2001). Human affection exchange: I. Reproductive probability as a predictor of men's affection with their sons. *Journal of Men's Studies, 10,* 39–50.

Floyd, K. (2002). Human affection exchange: V. Attributes of the highly affectionate. *Communication Quarterly, 50,* 135–152.

Floyd, K. (2006a). *Communicating affection: Interpersonal behavior and social context.* Cambridge, UK: Cambridge University Press.

Floyd, K. (2006b). Human affection exchange: XII. Affectionate communication is associated with diurnal variation in salivary free cortisol. *Western Journal of Communication, 70,* 47–63.

Floyd, K., & Burgoon, J. K. (1999). Reacting to nonverbal expressions of liking: A test of interaction adaptation theory. *Communication Monographs, 66,* 219–239.

Floyd, K., Erbert, L. A., Davis, K. L., & Haynes, M. T. (2006). *Human affection exchange: XVI. An exploratory study of affectionate expressions as manipulation attempts.* Unpublished manuscript, Arizona State University, Tempe, AZ.

Floyd, K., Hess, J. A., Miczo, L. A., Halone, K. K., Mikkelson, A. C., & Tusing, K. J. (2005). Human affection exchange: VIII. Further evidence of the benefits of expressed affection. *Communication Quarterly, 53,* 285–303.

Floyd, K., Hesse, C., & Haynes, M. T. (2007). Human affection exchange: XV. Metabolic and cardiovascular correlates of trait expressed affection. *Communication Quarterly 55,* 19–94.

Floyd, K., Mikkelson, A. C., Hesse, C., & Pauley, P. M. (2007). Affectionate writing reduces total cholesterol: Two randomized, controlled trials. *Human Communication Research, 33,* 119–142.

Floyd, K., Mikkelson, A. C., Tafoya, M. A., Farinelli, L., La Valley, A. G., Judd, J., Haynes, M. T., Davis, K. L., & Wilson, J. (2007). Human affection exchange: XIII. Affectionate communication accelerates neuroendocrine stress recovery. *Health Communication, 22,* 123–132.

Floyd, K., & Morman, M. T. (1998). The measurement of affectionate communication. *Communication Quarterly, 46,* 144–162.

Floyd, K., & Morman, M. T. (2002). Human affection exchange: III. Discriminative parental solicitude in men's affection with their biological and non-biological sons. *Communication Quarterly, 49,* 310–327.

Floyd, K., & Morr, M. C. (2003). Human affection exchange: VII. Affectionate communication in the sibling/spouse/sibling-in-law triad. *Communication Quarterly, 51,* 247–261.

Floyd, K., & Ray, G. B. (2003). Human affection exchange: IV. Vocalic predictors of perceived affection in initial interactions. *Western Journal of Communication, 67,* 56–73.

Floyd, K., Sargent, J. E., & Di Corcia, M. (2004). Human affection exchange: VI. Further tests of reproductive probability as a predictor of men's affection with their sons. *Journal of Social Psychology, 144,* 191–206.

Hamilton, W. D. (1964). The genetical evolution of social behavior. I & II. *Journal of Theoretical Biology, 7,* 1–52.

22

Attachment Theory

A Communication Perspective

Laura K. Guerrero

S arah, Elizabeth, and Maria get together to chat about life, love, and their recent divorces. As they talk, it becomes clear that each woman is coping with her divorce differently. Even though Sarah's divorce was finalized a year ago, she is not at all interested in dating. Instead, she throws herself into her career, wanting to prove to herself and her ex-husband that she is self-sufficient. After trying to stop the inevitable, Elizabeth finally signed the divorce papers. She finds herself clinging to her children and her sister, and hoping to find someone new because she hates being alone. Maria also hopes for a new love interest, but is too afraid of being hurt again to pursue any new romantic possibilities. She would rather be alone than risk rejection.

Why are Sarah, Elizabeth, and Maria reacting so differently to their divorces? Attachment theory provides a framework for understanding their reactions, as well as more general differences in people's communication. This chapter advances a communication perspective on Attachment Theory. Throughout this chapter, I show that communication plays a central role in Attachment Theory—as a cause, consequence, and reinforcing agent of attachment, and as a mediator between attachment and relationship quality.

Purpose and Meta-theoretical Assumptions

The original purpose of Attachment Theory was to understand how parent-child interaction affects personality development (Ainsworth & Bowlby, 1991). The theory has been applied to a variety of relationships across the life span,

295

including those between parents and children, friends, romantic partners, and siblings. Ainsworth and Bowlby noted that Attachment Theory has always "been eclectic, drawing on a number of scientific disciplines, including developmental, cognitive, social, and personality psychology, systems theory, and various branches of biological science, including genetics" (p. 340). Since the mid-1980s, the theory has also been widely used by social psychologists, family scholars and clinicians, and, to a lesser extent, by communication researchers. Attachment theorists have also used various empirical research methods, ranging from detailed observations and interviews to questionnaires and laboratory experiments. Thus, Attachment Theory is a social scientific theory that crosses disciplinary and methodological boundaries.

Bowlby's (1969, 1973) original theorizing on attachment was consistent with three general assumptions that many attachment scholars still embrace today. The most fundamental of these assumptions is that humans have an innate propensity for forming attachments with others, beginning in infancy and continuing throughout one's life. Bowlby's observations of institutionalized children led him to conclude that deprivation of maternal affection has aversive consequences on children, which persist across the life span. When separated from their mothers, children often moved from showing distress to becoming detached. The longer the separation, the more likely children were to exhibit detached, antisocial behavior. To help explain his observations, Bowlby turned to ethological research, which showed similar patterns of behavior among various animals, including baby birds and monkeys (Ainsworth & Bowlby, 1991). Bowlby concluded that attachment is a critical, innate component of human behavior that serves a protective function throughout one's life. This belief is consistent with two other basic assumptions of Attachment Theory: (a) attachment is a product of both biological forces and social interaction in one's environment, and (b) the attachment system, which includes cognition, emotion, and observable behavior, is activated when humans need protection or experience distress, or both.

Main Features of the Theory

One feature that sets Attachment Theory apart from other theories is that it examines cohesive patterns of cognition, emotion, and behavior across the life span. In addition, the theory explains how people develop different attachment styles, as well as how those attachment styles can be modified. These features, and the main concepts in Attachment Theory, are captured in five principles that help illuminate the relationship between attachment and communication.

The first principle is that early interaction with caregivers leads to security (or insecurity), which sets the stage for personality development and later attachments. Ainsworth's research (e.g., Ainsworth, Blehar, Waters, & Wall, 1978) investigated how children become securely attached to caregivers, and how children who are insecurely attached use defense mechanisms. Her research utilizing in-home observations and interviews followed by the strange situation experiment (which involved exposing 1-year-old children to an unfamiliar environment) provided a foundation for research on attachment styles. Secure children responded to the strange situation by becoming somewhat distressed on initial separation, but then by adapting to the environment and being happy when the caregiver returned. Avoidant children were indifferent when the caregiver departed and returned. Finally, anxious ambivalent children were particularly distressed when the caregiver departed and both angry and relieved when she returned. Hazan and Shaver's (1987) work showed that these three attachment styles also characterize adult attachments in love relationships.

A second principle guiding Attachment Theory is that working models of self and others combine to create an attachment style. Working models are cognitive schemata that represent one's experiences interacting with others. The model of self reflects the degree to which a person has a positive versus a negative image of self. The model of others reflects how rewarding (or unrewarding) a person perceives relationships to be. Based on these working models, Bartholomew and Horowitz (1991) described four distinct attachment styles for adults: secure (positive model of self and others), dismissive (positive model of self and negative model of others), preoccupied (negative model of self and positive model of others), and fearful (negative model of self and others). Secures are self-sufficient and comfortable with intimacy. They desire a balance of autonomy and closeness within their relationships. Dismissives are fiercely independent, sometimes to the point of shunning others to prove they can cope on their own. They dislike relying on others and are uncomfortable with closeness. Personal goals and activities are prioritized over relationships. Preoccupieds are exactly the opposite—they crave intimacy and put a much higher premium on close relationships than personal activities. They also cling to their relationships because they worry that their partners will abandon them. Finally, fearful individuals have usually been hurt or rejected in past relationships, so they are afraid of getting close to others even though they would like the security of a close relationship.

A third principle is that people with different attachment styles vary in terms of perceptions, emotional experiences, and communication, all of which influence the quality of one's relationships. Bartholomew (1993) contended that attachment styles affect how people think, feel, and behave in response to relational events. For example, Jang, Smith, and Levine (2002) examined how people with different attachment styles reacted when they discovered that their partners had deceived them. Secure individuals were likely to talk about the issue; dismissive individuals were most likely to terminate the relationship.

Bartholomew also described attachment as a style of social interaction that reflects the type and quality of relationship a person desires and expects based on working models of self and others. Similarly, Shaver, Collins, and Clark (1996) defined attachment styles as "relatively coherent and stable patterns of emotion and behavior [that] are exhibited in close relationships" (p. 25). A number of communicative behaviors have been found to vary as a function of attachment style, as will be described later in this chapter.

A fourth principle is that although attachment styles are relatively stable, they can be modified. The stability of attachment styles is attributed to at least two sources—that the foundation for personality development laid during childhood is strong, and that attachment styles are constantly reinforced when people engage in social behaviors that reflect perceptions of themselves and others. For example, if Sarah continues to isolate herself from others and focus almost exclusively on her career, she will reinforce the idea that she is self-sufficient and that she does not need a relationship to be happy. Changes in attachment style are often attributed to critical life events, such as divorce, death, or developing a healthy relationship. So Elizabeth may have been more secure before her divorce than after her divorce, and Maria might become more secure if she meets someone who patiently waits for her to get over her fear of rejection.

Finally, a fifth and relatively new principle is that attachment style can vary as a function of relationship type and relational partner. Research suggests that around 70% of adults perceive themselves to have a consistent attachment style, while 30% perceive that their level of security has fluctuated (e.g., Davila, Burge, & Hammen, 1997; Davila, Karney, & Bradbury, 1999). Critical life events, such as the divorces Sarah, Elizabeth, and Maria went through, have the power to activate the attachment system and modify a person's attachment style. Other researchers have shown that attachment styles vary on the basis of relationship type (Cozzarelli, Hoekstra, & Bylsma, 2000; Pierce & Lydon, 2001). So Maria might be afraid of being hurt in a new romantic relationship, but she might be secure in her relationships with friends and family.

Conceptualization of Communication in the Theory

As the principles summarized above suggest, communication occupies a central role in Attachment Theory. In fact, communication plays at least four roles in the attachment process, as shown in Figure 22.1 and described next.

COMMUNICATION AS A CAUSE OF ATTACHMENT STYLE

First, communication causes attachment styles to develop and change (see Line 1 in the figure). Young children tend to develop a secure attachment style

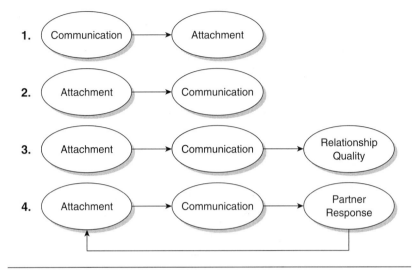

Figure 22.1   Connections between Communication and Attachment

when they have caregivers who are attentive, responsive, and sensitive to their needs. Children who are neglected or overstimulated by caregivers tend to become avoidant. Avoidance acts as a defensive mechanism that leads these children to become prematurely independent (in the case of neglect) or shuts down social interaction (in the case of overstimulation). Finally, young children are likely to develop an anxious ambivalent style when the caregiver provides them with inconsistent care. Children blame themselves for this inconsistency and experience a mix of emotions, including anxiety, when interacting with the parent (e.g., Ainsworth et al., 1978). Communication continues to function as a causal agent of attachment throughout the life span (Ainsworth & Bowlby, 1991). New social interactions with significant others modify existing models of self and others, and, consequently, one's attachment style. A young child who has been neglected by her parents may become more secure on making a few good friends. Conversely, a young man may have wonderful interactions with his family, but if he experiences hurt and frustration with dating partners, he might develop a fearful attachment in romantic relationships.

COMMUNICATION AS A CONSEQUENCE OF ATTACHMENT STYLE

Second, once an attachment style has developed, a person's communication reflects her or his perceptions of self and others (see Line 2, Figure 22.1). Take Sarah, Elizabeth, and Maria as examples. Sarah might turn down opportunities to date new men by saying, "I'm too busy with my career to get involved with anyone right now." Such a statement indicates that Sarah sees her personal ambitions as more important than establishing new relationships. Elizabeth, on the other hand, might complain to her sister or children that they are not "there for her" when she needs them, or that they do not "spend enough time" with her. These are classic preoccupied statements that reflect Elizabeth's need for self-validation and her fear of being alone. Finally, if Maria's friends manage to talk her into attending a social gathering, she might sit in the corner watching people rather than initiating conversation with someone she finds attractive. In each of these cases, the woman's communication (or in Maria's case, her lack of communication) is a "consequence" of her attachment style as well as her models of self and others. Models of self and others are also related to two basic dimensions of communication: how anxious versus confident a person appears, and how much a person avoids versus approaches social interaction, respectively.

COMMUNICATION AS A MEDIATOR OF
ATTACHMENT AND RELATIONSHIP QUALITY

Third, research suggests that secure individuals have a communication style that promotes healthy relationships (see Line 3, Figure 22.1). Considerable research shows that secure individuals report more relationship satisfaction and stability than individuals with other attachment styles (Feeney, Noller, & Roberts, 2000). Feeney and her colleagues theorized that attachment-style differences in communication help explain why secure individuals have more satisfying relationships. Research supports these claims, showing that conflict behavior (Feeney, 1994), self-disclosure (Keelan, Dion, & Dion, 1998), and emotional expression (Guerrero, Farinelli, & McEwan, 2007) help explain attachment-style differences in relational satisfaction. Thus, communication is the vehicle through which secure individuals develop and maintain successful relationships.

COMMUNICATION AS REINFORCING OF ATTACHMENT STYLE

Fourth, attachment styles are self-reinforcing because people communicate in ways that are consistent with their attachment styles, which then leads people to treat them in ways that reinforce their models of self and others (Bartholomew, 1993; see Line 4, figure 22.1). Secure individuals tend to display communication that reflects self-confidence and positive feelings toward others, leading people to respond positively to them. Interaction with an insecure person is often less enjoyable. Imagine being a friend of Sarah, Elizabeth, or Maria. How might you respond to their behavior? If Sarah rarely returned your phone calls because she was busy with work, you would probably reduce contact with her eventually. As a result, Sarah might learn to cope without her friends, reinforcing the dismissive notion that relationships are not as important as her own personal goals. If Elizabeth constantly called you to complain about her ex-husband and ask about any single men you know, you would probably start to pull away, which would fuel her preoccupied perception that other people do not value her as much as she values them. With Maria, you might get frustrated that she never wants to go new places and meet new people. Eventually Maria's behavior might isolate her from you and her other friends (who would probably stop inviting her to go out with them), and also prevent her from meeting any interesting new men.

Uses of the Theory

Research has shown that attachment is reflected in specific forms of interpersonal communication, including relational maintenance, conflict, intimacy, emotional expression, and social skill. The research in each of these areas is reviewed next.

MAINTENANCE AND CONFLICT BEHAVIOR

Engaging in maintenance behavior and being able to manage conflict constructively are two keys to a successful relationship. Several studies suggest that secures have an advantage in both these areas. Research suggests that secures use more prosocial maintenance behaviors, such as romance, shared activities, assurances, and positivity (being cheerful and optimistic) than do those with other attachment styles (Bippus & Rollin, 2003; Guerrero & Bachman, 2006; Simon & Baxter, 1993). Moreover, people tend to report less maintenance when they rate themselves as highly anxious or avoidant (Guerrero & Bachman). Secure individuals also engage in more problem solving and compromise during conflict episodes than do those with insecure attachment styles (Bippus & Rollin; Pistole, 1989). In contrast, people with avoidant attachment styles (dismissives and fearfuls) are most likely to use withdrawal and defensiveness in response to conflict, whereas preoccupieds are most likely to engage in demanding behavior, nagging, and whining (Creasey, Kershaw, & Boston, 1999; O'Connell-Corcoran & Mallinckrodt, 2000; Simpson, Rholes, & Phillips, 1996).

NONVERBAL AND VERBAL EXPRESSIONS OF INTIMACY

Individuals with positive models of others (secures and preoccupieds) exhibit more nonverbal and verbal intimacy than those with negative models of others (dismissives and fearfuls). In a study examining conversations between romantic couples, secure and preoccupied individuals displayed more facial and vocal pleasantness, interest, and attentiveness than did their dismissive and fearful counterparts (Guerrero, 1996). In another study involving conversations between romantic partners (Tucker & Anders, 1998), secure individuals were most likely to laugh, touch, smile, and show expressiveness and enjoyment. Avoidant individuals tended to display relatively low levels of smiling, expressiveness, and enjoyment. Anxious individuals displayed less enjoyment and expressiveness, suggesting that preoccupation may not always be associated with warm, expressive communication. Findings for self-disclosure follow a similar pattern. Secures engage in the most "appropriate and flexible patterns of self-disclosure" (Feeney et al., 2000, p. 198). Preoccupied individuals also engage in high levels of self-disclosure; however, their disclosure is sometimes inappropriate or indiscriminate (Mikulincer & Nachshon, 1991). The two avoidant styles of attachment—dismissive and fearful—are characterized by lower levels of disclosure (Feeney et al.).

EMOTIONAL EXPRESSION

Other research has identified attachment-style differences in the expression of specific emotions. In a study by Feeney (1999), anxious wives and husbands were less likely to express love, and avoidant husbands were less likely to express love, pride, or happiness. Studies focusing on jealousy suggest that secure individuals disclose jealous feelings, including anger, and respond to jealousy in ways that help maintain relationships (Guerrero, 1998; Sharpsteen & Kirkpatrick, 1997). Preoccupied individuals report relatively high levels of surveillance behavior, such as checking up on the partner, whereas fearful and dismissive individuals are most likely to deny jealous feelings and least likely to talk about jealousy in a constructive manner (Guerrero). Research on anger suggests that secure individuals are likely to express anger using negotiation or assertive communication, preoccupied individuals are likely to cope with anger through direct or passive aggression, and fearful individuals are likely to use passive responses when dealing with anger (Feeney, 1995; Guerrero et al., 2007). Similar findings have surfaced for sadness. Specifically, secure individuals are most likely to cope with sadness by seeking social support from others and engaging in positive activity that distracts them from their problems (Guerrero et al.).

SOCIAL SKILL

Secure individuals are the most socially skilled in terms of expressing themselves, responding appropriately to others, and providing comfort and social support to others (Kunce & Shaver, 1994; Simpson, Rholes, & Nelligan, 1992;

Weger & Polcar, 2002). In contrast, dismissive and fearful individuals have trouble expressing themselves and comforting others, preoccupied individuals are often viewed as overly sensitive and anxious, and fearful individuals tend to lack assertiveness (Anders & Tucker, 2000; Guerrero & Jones, 2003, 2005). Fearful individuals may be the least socially skilled of the four styles because their high levels of avoidance and anxiety keep them from initiating social interaction and developing interpersonal skills. In conversations with romantic partners, fearful individuals show signs of anxiety (e.g., a lack of fluency, long response latencies, and a lack of composure) as well as signs of avoidance (e.g., relatively far proxemic distancing and low levels of focus on the partner; Guerrero, 1996; Guerrero & Jones, 2005), suggesting that their negative models of self and others are indeed reflected in their behavior.

Strengths and Limitations of the Theory

During the last two decades, there has been an explosion of research on attachment-style differences in close relationships. The popularity of Attachment Theory can be attributed to some of the theory's strengths. Ironically, some of the limitations of Attachment Theory can also be traced to the rapid expansion and application of the theory.

Attachment Theory's strengths include its intuitive appeal, parsimony, applicability, generalizability, and multidisciplinary nature. Attachment Theory is intuitively appealing. People can relate to the four attachment styles and see themselves and others as fitting into these categories. The theory is parsimonious— the concept of attachment style represents the intersection of working models of self and others while also explaining coherent patterns of cognition, emotion, and behavior. Attachment-style differences have been found for a variety of perceptions, emotions, and behaviors. Thus, Attachment Theory is applicable to many aspects of relationship functioning. Attachment Theory is also generalizable to various relationships that occur throughout the life span. Another important strength of Attachment Theory is that it crosses disciplinary and methodological boundaries. The transdisciplinary nature of Attachment Theory has promoted dialogue among scholars from different fields, leading to a more comprehensive understanding of attachment processes.

Research on Attachment Theory has been limited by measurement problems and a focus on attachment as a personality variable. The rapid growth of research on Attachment Theory contributed to measurement problems. Research investigating attachment-style differences progressed more rapidly than work aimed at developing reliable and valid measures of attachment. As a result, researchers measure attachment using a variety of methods (e.g., having people check one of three or four categorical descriptions of attachment style, or having people rate themselves using continuous measures that tap into attachment-style dimensions such as anxiety, avoidance, trust, fear of intimacy, and relationships as secondary). This inconsistency in measurement makes it difficult to compare, contrast, and generalize findings from different studies. Another limitation of Attachment Theory research is that attachment style is often treated solely as a personality variable. This has led some communication scholars to argue that Attachment Theory is not a theory at all, but rather a glorified individual-difference variable. To fully appreciate the explanatory power of Attachment Theory, scholars need to move beyond looking at only attachment-style differences in communication, and to move toward understanding the broader role that communication plays in the attachment system.

Directions for Future Research and Applications

The current limitations of Attachment Theory research point to several directions for future research. For example, scholars need to contextualize attachment style in terms of relationship type. Scholars also need to better understand how ongoing interaction with significant others modifies attachment styles, how communication reinforces attachment style, and how and when communication mediates the association between attachment style and relationship quality. Research has also shown that partners' attachment styles interact to predict communication patterns (e.g., Guerrero & Bachman, 2006; Le Poire, Shepard, Duggan, 1999), so it is critical that more research focuses on how both partners' attachment styles influence communication.

More work on measurement also needs to be conducted. Currently, many attachment researchers examine two dimensions—anxiety and avoidance—which are thought to tap into working models of self and others, respectively. While these dimensions are important, they do not capture the unique features that characterize the four attachment styles. For example, knowing Elizabeth is high in anxiety and low in avoidance fails to provide information about how much she craves excessive intimacy and obsesses over her relationships. Knowing Maria is high in both anxiety and avoidance does not tell researchers how much she fears intimacy. Thus, the best system for measuring attachment may include gauging anxiety and avoidance, as well as characteristics unique to each style (such as preoccupation and fear of intimacy).

Attachment Theory also has important practical implications. Indeed, Bowlby hoped clinicians would use principles of Attachment Theory to help insecure people develop more positive models of themselves and others (Ainsworth & Bowlby, 1991). Communication consultants can apply Attachment Theory to help people develop more socially skilled styles of interaction that could help improve their models of self and others. Counselors and clinicians can also use Attachment Theory to help promote healthier relationships. Knowing partners' attachment styles may uncover potential problem areas. For instance, if a dismissive is paired with a preoccupied, issues related to autonomy and affection may likely surface. In addition, relational partners may be able to adjust their communication patterns to break cycles of reinforcement. Imagine how you could help Sarah, Elizabeth, and Maria develop more secure styles. You might entice Sarah to engage in interesting social activities that complement her personal goals. With Elizabeth, you might resist the impulse to pull away and instead listen to her problems and bolster her self-esteem. Finally, you might gradually introduce Maria to a wider circle of friends who make her feel comfortable in new social situations.

In sum, Attachment Theory provides a framework for understanding the role that communication plays in developing and modifying working models of self and others. The theory also highlights how these working models combine to produce attachment styles that are characterized by distinct patterns of cognition, emotion, and behavior. Communication reinforces attachment styles and mediates the relationship between attachment styles and relationship quality. Future research should investigate the many roles that communication plays in the attachment process, with attachment contextualized within various relationship types. Such research will promote a better understanding of the interplay between attachment and interpersonal interaction across the life span.

References

Ainsworth, M.D.S., Blehar, M. C., Waters, E., & Wall, S. (1978). *Patterns of attachment: A psychological study of the strange situation.* Hillsdale, NJ: Erlbaum.

Ainsworth, M.D.S., & Bowlby, J. (1991). An ethological approach to personality development. *American Psychologist, 46,* 333–341.

Anders, S. L., & Tucker, J. S. (2000). Adult attachment style, interpersonal communication competence, and social support. *Personal Relationships, 7,* 379–389.

Bartholomew, K. (1993). From childhood to adult relationships: Attachment theory and research. In S. Duck (Ed.), *Understanding relationship processes: Vol. 2. Learning about relationships* (pp. 30–62). Newbury Park, CA: Sage.

Bartholomew, K., & Horowitz, L. M. (1991). Attachment styles among young adults: A test of a four-category model. *Journal of Personality and Social Psychology, 61,* 226–244.

Bippus, A. M., & Rollin, E. (2003). Attachment style differences in relational maintenance and conflict behaviors: Friends' perceptions. *Communication Reports, 16,* 113–123.

Bowlby, J. (1969). *Attachment and loss: Vol 1. Attachment.* New York: Basic Books.

Bowlby, J. (1973). *Attachment and loss: Vol 2. Separation.* New York: Basic Books.

Cozzarelli, C., Hoekstra, S. J., & Bylsma, W. H. (2000). General versus specific mental models of attachment: Are they associated with different outcomes? *Personality and Social Psychology Bulletin, 26,* 605–618.

Creasey, G., Kershaw, K., & Boston, A. (1999). Conflict management with friends and romantic partners: The role of attachment and negative mood regulation expectancies. *Journal of Youth and Adolescence, 28,* 523–543.

Davila, J., Burge, D., & Hammen, C. (1997). Why does attachment style change? *Journal of Personality and Social Psychology, 73,* 826–838.

Davila, J. Karney, B. R., & Bradbury, T. N. (1999). Attachment change processes in the early years of marriage. *Journal of Personality and Social Psychology, 76,* 783–802.

Feeney, J. A. (1994). Attachment style, communication patterns, and satisfaction across the life cycle of marriage. *Personal Relationships, 1,* 333–348.

Feeney, J. A. (1995). Adult attachment and emotional control. *Personal Relationships, 2,* 143–159.

Feeney, J. A. (1999). Adult attachment, emotional control, and marital satisfaction. *Personal Relationships, 6,* 169–185.

Feeney, J. A., Noller, P., & Roberts, N. (2000). Attachment and close relationships. In C. Hendrick & S. S. Hendrick (Eds.), *Close relationships: A sourcebook* (pp. 185–201). Thousand Oaks, CA: Sage.

Guerrero, L. K. (1996). Attachment-style differences in intimacy and involvement: A test of the four-category model. *Communication Monographs, 63,* 269–292.

Guerrero, L. K. (1998). Attachment-style differences in the experience and expression of romantic jealousy. *Personal Relationships, 5,* 273–291.

Guerrero, L. K., & Bachman, G. F. (2006). Associations among relational maintenance behaviors, attachment-style categories, and attachment dimensions. *Communication Studies, 57,* 341–361.

Guerrero, L. K., Farinelli, L., & McEwan, B. (2007, November). *Attachment and relational satisfaction: The mediating effect of emotional expression.* Paper presented at the annual conference of the National Communication Association, Chicago.

Guerrero, L. K., & Jones, S. M. (2003). Differences in one's own and one's partner's perceptions of social skills as a function of attachment style. *Communication Quarterly, 51,* 277–295.

Guerrero, L. K., & Jones, S. M. (2005). Differences in conversational skills as a function of attachment style: A follow-up study. *Communication Quarterly, 53,* 305–321.

Hazan, C., & Shaver, P. (1987). Conceptualizing romantic love as an attachment process. *Journal of Personality and Social Psychology, 52,* 511–524.

Jang, S. A., Smith, S. W., & Levine, T. R. (2002). To stay or to leave? The role of attachment styles in communication patterns and potential termination of romantic relationships following discovery of deception. *Communication Monographs, 69,* 236–252.

Keelan, J. P. R., Dion, K. K., & Dion, K. L. (1998). Attachment style and relationship satisfaction: Test of a self-disclosure explanation. *Canadian Journal of Behavioural Science, 30,* 24–35.

Kunce, L. J., & Shaver, P. R. (1994). An attachment-theoretical approach to caregiving in romantic relationships. In K. Bartholomew & D. Perlman (Eds.), *Advances in personal relationships: Vol. 5. Attachment processes in adulthood* (pp. 205–237). Bristol, PA: Kingsley.

Le Poire, B. A., Shepard, C., & Duggan, A. (1999). Nonverbal involvement, expressiveness, and pleasantness as predicted by parental and partner attachment style. *Communication Monographs, 66,* 293–311.

Mikulincer, M., & Nachshon, O. (1991). Attachment styles and patterns of self-disclosure. *Journal of Personality and Social Psychology, 61,* 321–331.

O'Connell-Corcoran, K., & Mallinckrodt, B. (2000). Adult attachment, self-efficacy, perspective taking, and conflict resolution. *Journal of Counseling and Development, 78,* 473–483.

Pierce, T., & Lydon, J. E. (2001). Global and specific relational models in the experience of social interactions. *Journal of Personality and Social Psychology, 80,* 613–631.

Pistole, M. C. (1989). Attachment in adult romantic relationships: Style of conflict resolution and relationship satisfaction. *Journal of Social and Personal Relationships, 6,* 505–510.

Sharpsteen, D. J., & Kirkpatrick, L. A. (1997). Romantic jealousy and adult romantic attachment. *Journal of Personality and Social Psychology, 72,* 627–640.

Shaver, P. R., Collins, N., & Clark, C. L. (1996). Attachment styles and internal working models of self and relationship partners. In G.J.O. Fletcher & J. Fitness (Eds.), *Knowledge structures in close relationships: A social psychological approach* (pp. 25–61). Mahwah, NJ: Erlbaum.

Simon, E. P., & Baxter, L. A. (1993). Attachment-style differences in relationship maintenance strategies. *Western Journal of Communication, 57,* 416–430.

Simpson, J. A., Rholes, W. S., & Nelligan, J. S. (1992). Support-seeking and support-giving within couples in an anxiety-provoking situation: The role of attachment styles. *Journal of Personality and Social Psychology, 62,* 434–446.

Simpson, J. A., Rholes, W. S., & Phillips, D. (1996). Conflict in close relationships: An attachment perspective. *Journal of Personality and Social Psychology, 71,* 899–914.

Tucker, J. S., & Anders, S. L. (1998). Adult attachment style and nonverbal closeness in dating couples. *Journal of Nonverbal Behavior, 22,* 109–124.

Weger, H., & Polcar, L. E. (2002). Attachment style and person-centered comforting. *Western Journal of Communication, 66,* 64–103.

23

Communication Privacy Management Theory

Significance for Interpersonal Communication

Sandra Petronio and Wesley T. Durham

L auren was a 20-year-old college student who seemingly had everything. During her junior year, she was voted football Homecoming Queen, made exceptional marks in her classes, and had a "full ride" scholarship to the university she had always dreamed of attending. Life was good. However, during the summer between her junior and senior year of college, Lauren's dreams were altered. Immediately following her junior year, her college sweetheart broke off their romantic relationship. Surprised and broken hearted, Lauren began drinking and partying heavily, and found herself having a string of regrettable sexual encounters.

At the beginning of the fall semester of her senior year, Lauren and her college sweetheart rekindled their relationship. Lauren was as happy as she had ever been. However, as she did every fall, Lauren donated blood during the university's blood drive. Four weeks after donating blood, Lauren was notified that her blood had tested positive for HIV. The counselor told her that she needed to notify all individuals with whom she had had intercourse because they might have been exposed to the virus. Immediately, Lauren began to panic. She wondered how to tell her previous sexual partners, her parents, her friends, and more importantly her boyfriend.

Lauren's story indicates the tension and strain that can accompany managing private information. This story illustrates the complexity of privacy management and the need for a theoretical framework to help us understand the decisions we make, the way we think about privacy, and how we cope with privacy infractions. This chapter gives a brief introduction to a theory called Communication Privacy Management (CPM) developed by one of the authors, Petronio (2002). In this chapter, we discuss the purpose, principles, and value of CPM. CPM is a theory that assists researchers, students, and practitioners to grasp how individuals reveal and conceal private information.

Purpose and Meta-theoretical Assumptions

CPM is a grounded theory based on systematic research designed to develop an evidence-based understanding of the way people regulate revealing and concealing. In addition, on initially encountering CPM, it is helpful to leave previously held beliefs about disclosure behind. Unlike earlier theories, CPM views "disclosure" as the process of revealing private information, yet always in relationship to concealing private information. Since they are in a dialectical tension with each other, the way revealing and concealing take place is through a management system. This notion shifts the frame from focusing only on "self-disclosure" to a broader more comprehensive view that includes "private disclosures" capturing the elements of privacy and the process of disclosure. Thus, Petronio (2002), argued that "CPM makes private information, as the content of what is disclosed, a primary focal point" (p. 3). CPM also depends on the notion of boundaries to give us a way to conceptualize how people manage private information.

Unlike many theories that fit neatly within one particular methodological paradigm, CPM has proven to be a useful theoretical tool for interpretivists and post-positivists alike. This is largely because CPM was not developed as a methodological tool per se. From an interpretivist's perspective, human action is purposive and socially embedded; human actions are attributed meaning by others who interact from within that same web of meaning (Baxter & Babbie, 2004). CPM can be described as an interpretive theory insofar as human action, in this case the disclosure of private information, is purposive, rule driven, and interpreted by those participating in the disclosure event. On the other hand, CPM has also been used successfully to guide post-positivist research. According to Baxter and Babbie (2004), post-positivist research attempts to explain, predict, and control human behavior. For instance, Caughlin and his colleagues have effectively used CPM to guide post-positivist research on the correlation between topic avoidance and relational (dis)satisfaction (e.g., Caughlin & Afifi, 2004). Thus, this theory gives versatility to the choice of methodology because it has not been developed with a methodological objective as its guide. Instead, CPM theory offers principles and a prospective that allows many different types of methodologies to be used to test the viability of the theoretical proposals.

Main Features of the Theory

CPM is organized around six major principles. The first three principles are "assumption maxims" made about managing private disclosures that underpin CPM theory. The remaining three principles represent "interaction maxims" reflecting the way communicative interactions with others are regulated when revealing and concealing private information. We discuss the "assumption maxims" that underlie CPM theory in this section. In the next section, we talk about the "interaction maxims" found in CPM that guide communicative actions and reactions in managing privacy. In both this and the following sections, we introduce these principles and use situations such as Lauren's to help explain the ideas. The three principles that characterize the "assumption maxims" are (1) public-private dialectical tension, (2) conceptualization of private information, and (3) privacy rules.

PUBLIC-PRIVATE DIALECTICAL TENSION

CPM views the process of disclosure as inherently dialectical, meaning that when people disclose, they manage a friction—a push and pull—of revealing or concealing private information. In Lauren's story, we see that she feels compelled to selectively reveal her HIV status. Nevertheless, because of stigma and the dramatic nature of being HIV positive, at the same time she feels compelled to conceal that information. The simultaneous nature of wanting to tell and also wanting to conceal makes CPM theory necessary to understand how people navigate privacy.

look at (D)/ confront

CONCEPTUALIZATION OF PRIVATE INFORMATION

CPM argues that one way to conceptualize private information is in terms of a possession. In other words, private information is something you believe is rightfully yours—it belongs to you. Concurrent with the perception of ownership, is the assumption that if it is your private information, you have the right to control it. Thus, you believe you are entitled to disclose the information to others or keep it private depending on what seems the best choice for you. For example, if you find out that you have a genetic predisposition to a disease, you are likely to want to control who knows about this information. The predisposition is about you, thus it is private information about which you want to make disclosure decisions and over which you want to exercise rightful control.

This particular assumption of CPM has extended how we view the process of disclosure and privacy. According to Petronio (2002), "CPM uses the metaphor of boundaries to illustrate that, although there may be a flow of private information to others, borders mark ownership lines so control issues are easily understood" (p. 3).

PRIVACY RULES

Since we believe we own private information and have the right to control its disclosure, we need a means to regulate the flow of information that we define as private. CPM offers the concept of "privacy rules" to illustrate the way people make choices about dissemination to others. Privacy rules are developed using at least five criteria, including cultural criteria, gendered criteria, motivational criteria, contextual criteria, and risk-benefit ratio criteria (Petronio, 2002). These criteria are the backdrop for rule development, meaning that they provide guidelines for decisions that regulate the ebb and flow of private information. Each criterion makes a contribution to the development of privacy rules that people use to manage their boundaries. For example, cultural criteria are important because privacy often has a particular value in a society, ethnicity, or group. If a culture defines openness as a critical key to societal functioning, the tendency for people from that culture will be to embrace openness rather than secrecy.

Gender also plays a role in rule development. Men and women differ in the kind of privacy rules they use leading to divergent requirements for revealing or concealing. Women need to feel confident in their targets, whereas men need to feel confident that the situation is appropriate (Petronio, 2002). Besides culture and gender, rules are also predicated on motivations that people have for revealing or concealing. The context also plays a part, particularly as a catalyst for rule change. When people are divorced, it is likely that they do not use the same privacy rules to disclose with a former spouse that they used when married. Finally, people calculate risks against benefits to judge whether they should keep something private or reveal the information completely or partially.

Privacy rules are learned through socialization (Petronio, 2002). For example, when children are young, parents teach their children when it is or is not acceptable and appropriate to disclose information about the family. Within families, children may be socialized to uphold certain privacy boundaries. Parents might teach their children not to discuss issues such as income or political affiliations with others. As people join groups, organizations, and new families they also are instructed by others about the expected ways to manage privacy.

In other cases, privacy rules are acquired. For instance, junior faculty members who sit on search committees for faculty positions may not be familiar with the degree of privacy and confidentiality needed during the process. In order to compensate for this lack of familiarity, the chair of the search committee or the senior faculty members may go over the policies with the junior faculty member to ensure that the collectively held privacy rules are enforced and that confidentiality is maintained throughout the process.

Attributes of privacy rules can also be described by their properties. If certain privacy rules work well for us, they can become routine. When privacy rules do not work, we typically alter them to fit our needs. Take, for instance, the notion of "gossip." If you disclosed private information to someone in confidence but that person repeats the information against your wishes, you probably will not disclose personal information to that person again. Gossip, by definition, violates how a person wants to manage private information. Once it is discovered that someone has violated confidences, it is likely that a person would change the rules and conceal information from that person in the future.

Conceptualization of Communication in the Theory

In the previous section we discussed "assumption maxims" that underlie CPM theory. The dialectical and conceptual assumptions about privacy management give us the foundation for privacy management. The privacy rules reflect the decision criteria that people develop and use for choice making about disclosure or privacy. In this section, we illustrate why CPM is considered a communication theory. CPM is born out of a communication perspective and can be thought of as wholly a *communication* theory. Fundamentals of the theory and the tests of the principles are predicated on seeking an understanding about the domain of a communication phenomenon, using the knowledge about communication that largely comes from communication literature. As such, it is one of the first solidly positioned communication theories. Unlike earlier perspectives on disclosure, CPM makes the communicative process a central feature by taking into account both the recipient and the discloser. The three remaining principles representing the "interaction maxims" illustrate how CPM is, at its heart, a communication theory, born and bred. These principles are (4) shared boundaries, (5) boundary coordination, and (6) boundary turbulence.

SHARED BOUNDARIES

One of the most innovative and attractive features of CPM theory is the argument for a different way to think about the aftermath of disclosure. Petronio (2002) pointed out that once a person discloses private information, the action logically and fundamentally changes the nature of the information. In other words, the information no longer is solely owned by the discloser. "Sharing" was once used as a substitute phrase for disclosure, but in many ways

Petronio's conceptualization of sharing is more accurate. Thus, when you tell someone private information, you are making that person a co-owner or shareholder of the information. Together you create one mutual boundary around the information.

CPM explains that you can have many layers of privacy boundaries where shared information resides. For example, you can have dyadic privacy boundaries when only two people are co-owners, group boundaries, family privacy boundaries, organizationally private boundaries (i.e., proprietary information), and even societal private boundaries (i.e., information in the United States protected by the Department of Homeland Security). Because shared privacy boundaries make the calculus for boundary regulation more complex, Petronio (2002) proposed three boundary coordination operations, discussed below, that people use to synchronize regulating mutually held private information.

BOUNDARY COORDINATION

Boundary coordination operations refer to how individuals co-own and comanage private information. As previously mentioned, CPM does not view disclosure as a unidirectional communication process. Instead, disclosed private information affects both the discloser and the recipient of a disclosure. After people reveal private information, all involved parties become responsible for co-owning and comanaging the information. Petronio (2002) argued that boundaries must be coordinated through rules to have smooth interactions and viable outcomes for relationships. There are three processes involved in boundary coordination: regulation of boundary linkages, boundary ownership rights, and boundary permeability.

"Boundary linkages" represent alliances formed between a discloser and his or her recipients. Boundary linkages can occur in numerous ways. A discloser can target a particular recipient in order to reveal private information, or an unintended recipient can receive private information accidentally (Petronio, Jones, & Morr, 2003). For instance, if Lauren tells her boyfriend that she is HIV positive, but her boyfriend's roommate happens to overhear the disclosure, both men will know about her status. However, while Lauren might have intended to link her boyfriend into the privacy boundary around her status, she did not plan on the roommate finding out. He is an unintended recipient mistakenly linked into the boundary. As a consequence, the boyfriend's roommate may feel less responsibility to negotiate privacy rules about the information or might be less uncomfortable acknowledging he knows about her HIV status. Either way, Lauren may be less able to protect her information under these circumstances. Because Lauren does not have the ability to negotiate privacy rules that regulate the information, coordination is more difficult but actually more necessary.

"Boundary ownership" refers to the rights, privileges, and amount of responsibility for co-owners of private information. In the example above, Lauren discloses her HIV status intentionally to her boyfriend. Her boyfriend becomes a shareholder or stakeholder of the information. The complication of knowing is, no doubt, dramatic for him. Although he may think it is important to know, knowing about her status may also prove dilemmatic (Greene, Derlega, Yep, & Petronio, 2003; Petronio et al., 2003). This example illustrates that, although the role of recipient as a co-owner may be positive, it also may cause the confidant to experience conflict, particularly if the receiver is not able to cope with the information disclosed. With disclosures, confidants also frequently receive expectations for how the information should be handled. In our example, Lauren is likely to ask her boyfriend to keep her status confidential, perhaps even pleading with him to have the information remain between the two of them. Petronio (2002) argued that if the parameters dealing with private information are clear between the parties, then co-owners more aptly regulate access to the private information in a similar way. However, when these parameters are not clear, it is more likely that a co-owner will breach a rule about how the information should be comanaged. This discussion illustrates an underlying condition of smooth boundary coordination. In other words, when the parties involved are intentionally privileged and they negotiate rules (i.e., when they actually talk about their expectations), the rules they use to manage privacy allow for efficient and effective regulation of the information with fewer complications.

"Boundary permeability" refers to the amount of access or openness within a privacy boundary. As access to private information increases, boundaries become more permeable. Since boundary permeability signifies the level of access, thinner walls represent more access or openness so private information flows more easily. In opposition to this, thicker walls of the boundary represent less access or no access, as with secrets (Petronio, 2002). No doubt, Lauren intended for the information about her HIV status to remain within an impermeable privacy boundary with her boyfriend.

When boundaries are jointly coordinated, we see three ways that they are managed. First, collective boundaries can be managed in a "disproportionate" way: one person in the boundary discloses more private information than other recipients. The lopsidedness is predicated on the amount of disclosed information that one person may contribute to a mutually held privacy boundary. Sometimes when one person tells a great deal and the others tell very little, a power differential may occur. Knowing more about a person may lead to having the ability to exercise more control over the discloser. For example, when people are in need of health care they willingly disclose a great deal of private information, yet information is not typically reciprocated by the healthcare worker (Petronio & Kovach, 1997). Nonetheless, this situation results in healthcare workers knowing more about the patient than the patient knows about the healthcare workers. Typically, the latter may only use the information to help the former. However, the healthcare worker may also believe that he or she knows enough to make choices for the patient.

Second, collective boundaries can be managed in an "intersected" fashion: each member shares and co-owns information in equitable ways. Third, collective boundaries can be managed in a "unified" way: everyone is responsible for jointly held information. Unified boundaries are most often found in families, where personal information affects the group as well as the individual family member (Petronio, 2002). Although the aim is to achieve coordinated privacy boundaries, it is clear that this hope is often unattainable. Consequently, CPM theory offers a theoretical way to understand privacy management when there is boundary turbulence.

BOUNDARY TURBULENCE

To have smooth management when private information is co-owned, the comanagers must coordinate their actions. Often, due to incongruent expectations, misunderstandings of privacy parameters, or access rules, the handling of private information is conflicted. Take the example of Lauren, her boyfriend, and her boyfriend's roommate. Even if Lauren and her boyfriend keep her HIV positive status private, her boyfriend's roommate may not understand how the couple wants to manage that information. Consequently, if he reveals Lauren's HIV positive status to someone else, then he has given another person access to that private information and boundary turbulence is possible. There are many cases where turbulence occurs: in particular, privacy violations, dilemmas, and misconceptions about ownership contribute to boundary turbulence. We discuss research that investigates turbulence when we discuss applications of the theory.

Uses of the Theory

CPM is a dynamic theory that has been applied to explore a number of interpersonal communication issues. For example, researchers using CPM have studied: (a) stepfamily communication (Caughlin, 2002; Caughlin, Golish, Olson, Sargent, Cook, & Petronio, 2000; Durham, Braithwaite, Daas, Toller, & Jones, 2003; Golish & Caughlin, 2002), (b) marital communication (Petronio et al., 2003; Petronio & Jones, 2006; Petronio, 1994, 2000a, 2000b), (c) HIV disclosures to family members (Dindia, 1998; Greene, Parrott, & Serovich, 1993; Petronio, 2002; Yep, 2000), (d) child sexual abuse (Petronio, Reeder, Hecht, & Mon't Ros-Mendoza, 1996), and (e) family planning (Durham, in press;

Durham & Braithwaite, 2005). Turbulent conditions such as privacy dilemmas and disclosure processes represent important areas of research in interpersonal communication because of the intrinsically complex nature of privacy management within relational systems (Afifi, 2003; Caughlin, et al., 2000; Caughlin & Afifi, 2004; Petronio et al., 2003).

Studying turbulence gives us a way to decipher the unevenness of human interaction. Besides helping us understand the dynamics of relational systems, privacy dilemmas also highlight the recipient of disclosure. Emphasis on the confidant has been sparse in the research literature, yet CPM calls us to examine what happens to the receiver. Recently, researchers using CPM have taken a look at such issues as pregnant women and the unsolicited disclosive advice they receive from others (Petronio & Jones, 2006). CPM theory has also given us insights into how stepchildren feel caught between two families. They must manage information that they receive differently depending on which privacy rules prevail in different households, and they are concerned about regulating issues of loyalty (Afifi, 2003). We also can grasp the dilemma that physicians and their families face when they are embroiled in medical mistakes (Petronio, 2006). Furthermore, bereavement researchers have commented on the confusion that many recipients feel after an individual discloses information pertaining to the death of a child (Hastings, 2000; Toller, 2005). According to Hastings, although the recipients of particular disclosures may wish to provide support to bereaved parents, the recipients might not know how to provide it. Some disclosures might thus be perceived by recipients as burdensome; those recipients take on the role of the reluctant confidant for the discloser (Bergen & McBride, 2002).

The privacy rules that guide disclosures in marital interactions characterize a burgeoning area of privacy (Durham, in press; Morr, 2002). Interest in the rules that govern private disclosures between marital couples began in the mid- to late-1980s (Fitzpatrick, 1987). Several of the foundational lines of research articulate with the principles of CPM. In particular, Petronio (2002) noted that "Fitzpatrick's portrayal of marital couples helps to isolate a way to consider boundary coordination" (p. 150).

Petronio (2000a, 2000b) suggested that newlyweds often struggle with determining what private information they should disclose to one another as they develop privacy rules. Newlyweds go through a process of formulating acceptable levels of openness and closedness in their marriages; privacy rules are created through this process (Petronio, 2000b). Roloff and Ifert (2000) suggested that one of the most important determinants of successful boundary management might be how marital couples negotiate the disclosure of partner criticism. Withholding complaints has both positive and negative outcomes for marriages. By resisting the urge to criticize one's spouse, the individual may successfully avoid marital conflict; however, if spouses never verbalize criticism toward each other, then both spouses are unlikely to change the undesirable or damaging behavior of the other (Roloff & Ifert, 2000).

While some existing interpersonal communication research using CPM has focused on disclosures within particular relational forms (e.g., stepfamilies and marriages), some scholars have studied how certain life situations or events, such as HIV infection (Dindia, 1998; Greene et al., 1993; Petronio, 2002; Yep, 2000) are disclosed to social network members. CPM proposes that patterns of disclosures and privacy rules regulating boundary coordination can potentially shift when dramatic life events occur.

Using the theoretical lens of CPM helps us to understand that individuals who test positive for HIV suffer privacy dilemmas on multiple dimensions. For instance, a person who is HIV positive may wants to reveal his or her health status to others, as we saw with Lauren. The problem arises when the discloser is stigmatized when people learn of this health status. Often, the level of stigmatization is compounded by concomitantly revealing sexual preferences (Greene et al., 1993). Privacy rules, no doubt, change once a person finds out that he or she is HIV positive. Whereas before that discovery, partners would be more likely to have rules granting disclosure of private health information to each other, being HIV positive means that the partner is often the last to know (Greene et al., 2003). Privacy rules that hamper disclosure for whatever reason may also compromise the ability to gain social support from partners and friends (Yep, 2000). CPM proposes that privacy rules regulate linkages such as the selection of within-family confidants for people who are HIV positive.

Because CPM provides a frame for the interface of privacy and disclosure, it encourages us to think about the conditions of both revealing and concealing. The work on topic avoidance illustrates a privacy rule strategy that is used when we feel compelled to keep information protected within the privacy boundary. For instance, researchers have studied (a) topic avoidance and the role of the reluctant confidant within friendships (Afifi & Guerrero, 1998, 2000; Bergen & McBride, 2002), (b) the disclosure of information following the death of a child (Hastings, 2000), (c) the disclosure of pregnancy narratives (Petronio, 2000a; Petronio & Jones, 2006), and the revelation of childhood sexual abuse (Petronio et al., 1996).

People with all kinds of relational connections are linked into privacy boundaries or isolated from information (Petronio, 2002). Work by Caughlin (2002), helps us see the way people regulate privacy rules in voluntary relationships like friendships. Friendship relationships tend to have more lenient rules that guide disclosures than exist in involuntary, familial relationships. Afifi and Burgoon (1998) reported that cross-sex friends often avoid different topics more than do dating or married couples. Specifically, the management of privacy boundaries intersects the management of relationships, as witnessed in findings of Afifi and Burgoon (1998). In some cases, however, individuals experience boundary turbulence when they mistakenly reveal too much information or mistakenly withhold information from their friends. Consequently, relational problems can erupt because of turbulence in privacy management when individuals do not disclose enough (Petronio, et al., 1996) or when they disclose too much (Bergen & McBride, 2002).

CPM argues that one of the criteria on which privacy rules are predicated is the motivation for revealing or concealing private information. Some research has begun to understand the ways in which motivations impact choice to reveal or conceal. For example, Petronio and colleagues (1996), in their study of disclosure patterns for child sexual abuse victims, found that some of these children did not disclose information because they had been threatened by the perpetrators and were afraid to tell. Consequently, the children constructed a set of rules that were largely dependent on carefully managing their privacy boundaries. Such children only tell after they "hint around" first to see if they can trust the confidant, or they wait to see if someone talks to them first about their abuse. In other words, they wait to be given permission, and they select a setting where they feel safe. Caughlin and his colleagues have directly studied the link between motivations and privacy management within a CPM framework (Caughlin, 2002; Caughlin & Afifi, 2004; Golish & Caughlin, 2002). For instance, they found that relational dissatisfaction was moderated by an individual's motivations for avoiding disclosure of a topic (e.g., Caughlin & Afifi) suggesting that motivational criteria for decision making regarding revealing and concealing is a robust theoretical assumption. As CPM continues to be used and its propositions continue to be tested, we will begin to see elaborations of the theory and confirmations of those principles that have heuristic weight.

Strengths and Limitations of the Theory

CPM is a valuable theory containing significant strength. Unlike many previous theories adopted from other disciplines, CPM represents a theory explicitly grounded in and deriving from "communication." CPM is a theory of communication that helps us to understand how and why we reveal and conceal private information. In its short life, CPM has generated a plethora of research in a multitude of contexts across disciplines such as computer science, health, psychology, sociology, business, and government. In communication, CPM has been used primarily by researchers in interpersonal and family communication. However, as the other disciplines show us, CPM can be used to understand privacy and disclosure in contexts such as health care, education, and organizations. The greatest strength of CPM is its utility and heuristic value in both basic and applied research. CPM is a flexible theory that can both aid researchers in fully understanding the privacy expressiveness dialectic, and can be applicable to real world problems. Although there is much strength, we also recognize that CPM theory is very new. For its full effect to be known, CPM needs to grow and develop further. To do that, we need the continuous use of the theoretical principles to make adjustments to proposals that need refinement.

Directions for Future Research and Applications

The directions for future research using CPM theory are numerous. Balancing privacy and disclosure is not a task found only in our close personal relationships. Healthcare providers must both keep patient confidentiality and disclose their health information appropriately, for example to another health care provider. Coworkers share personal information to be held in confidence, but often they reveal. Educators attempt to balance immediacy with professional distance, but often they disclose too much about themselves to their students. CPM represents a theoretical perspective that allows us to better understand what individuals disclose, what they keep private, and how private information is handled among people. Future research needs to continue testing the viability of application. In addition, it is necessary to develop a diagnostic tool to help us understand the reasons turbulence occurs and a repair mechanism to teach us how to mend privacy breakdowns. As we have seen, the heuristic value of CPM for not only communication, but also many different disciplines, seems promising.

References

Afifi, T. (2003). "Feeling caught" in stepfamilies: Managing boundary turbulence through appropriate communication privacy rules. *Journal of Social and Personal Relationships, 20,* 729–755.

Afifi, W. A., & Burgoon, J. K. (1998). We never talk about that: A comparison of cross-sex friendships and dating relationships on uncertainty and topic avoidance. *Personal Relationships, 5,* 255–272.

Afifi, W. A., & Guerrero, L. K. (1998). Some things are better left unsaid II: Topic avoidance in friendships. *Communication Quarterly, 46,* 231–249.

Afifi, W. A, & Guerrero, L. K. (2000). Motivations underlying topic avoidance in close relationships. In S. Petronio (Ed.), *Balancing the secrets of private disclosures* (pp. 165–179). Mahwah, NJ: Erlbaum.

Baxter, L. A., & Babbie, E. (2004). *The basics of communication research.* Belmont, CA: Wadsworth.

Bergen, K. J., & McBride, M. C. (2002, February). *Becoming a reluctant confidant: Communication boundary management in close friendships.* Paper presented at the Western States Communication Association Convention, Long Beach, CA.

Caughlin, J. (2002). The demand/withdraw pattern of communication as a predictor of marital satisfaction over time. *Human Communication Research, 28,* 49–86.

Caughlin, J., & Afifi, T. D. (2004). When is topic avoidance unsatisfying? Examining moderators of the association between avoidance and dissatisfaction. *Human Communication Research, 30,* 479–513.

Caughlin, J., Golish, T. D., Olson, L., Sargent, J., Cook, J., & Petronio, S. (2000). Intrafamily secrets in various family configurations: A communication boundary management perspective. *Communication Studies, 51,* 116–134.

Dindia, K. (1998). "Going into and coming out of the closet": The dialectics of stigma disclosure. In B. M. Montgomery & L. A. Baxter (Eds.), *Dialectical approaches to studying personal relationships* (pp. 83–108). Mahwah, NJ: Erlbaum.

Durham, W. T. (in press). The rules-based process of revealing/concealing the family planning decisions of voluntarily child-free couples: A communication privacy management perspective. *Communication Studies.*

Durham, W. T., & Braithwaite, D. O. (2005, November). *Communication privacy management within the family planning trajectories of voluntarily child-free couples.* Paper presented at the National Communication Association Conference, Boston, MA.

Durham, W. T., Braithwaite, D. O., Daas, K. L., Toller, P. W., & Jones, A. C. (2003, November). *"I really didn't want to hear it": Stepchildren as reluctant confidants.* Paper presented at the National Communication Association Conference, Miami Beach, FL.

Fitzpatrick, M. A. (1987). Marriage and verbal intimacy. In V. Derlega & J. H. Berg (Eds.), *Self-disclosure: Theory, research, and therapy* (pp. 133–154). New York: Plenum Press.

Golish, T. D., & Caughlin, J. (2002). "I'd rather not talk about it": Adolescents' and young adults' use of topic avoidance in stepfamilies. *Journal of Applied Communication Research, 30,* 78–106.

Greene, K., Derlega, V. J., Yep, G., & Petronio, S. (2003). *Privacy and disclosure of HIV interpersonal relationships.* Mahwah, NJ: Erlbaum.

Greene, K., Parrott, R., & Serovich, J. M. (1993). Privacy, HIV testing, and AIDS: College students' versus parents' perspectives. *Health Communication, 5,* 59–74.

Hastings, S. O. (2000). Self-disclosure and identity management by bereaved parents. *Communication Studies, 51,* 352–369.

Morr, M. C. (2002). *Private disclosure in a family membership transition: In-laws' disclosure to newlyweds.* Unpublished doctoral dissertation. Arizona State University, Tempe, AZ.

Petronio, S. (1994). Privacy binds family interactions: The case of parental privacy invasion. In W. R. Cupach & B. H. Spitzberg (Eds.), *The dark side of interpersonal communication* (pp. 241–258). Hillsdale, NJ: Erlbaum.

Petronio, S. (2000a). The ramifications of a reluctant confidant. In A. C. Richards, & T. Schumrum (Eds.), *Invitations to dialogue: The legacy of Sidney Jourard* (pp. 113–132). Dubuque, IA: Kendall/Hunt.

Petronio, S. (2000b). The embarrassment of private disclosures: A case study of newly married couples. In D. O. Braithwaite & J. T. Wood (Eds.), *Case studies in interpersonal communication: Processes and problems* (pp. 131–144). Belmont, CA: Wadsworth.

Petronio, S. (2002). *Boundaries of privacy: Dialectics of disclosure.* Albany, NY: SUNY Press.

Petronio, S. (2006). Impact of medical mistakes: Navigating work-family boundaries for physicians and their families. *Communication Monographs, 73,* 462–467.

Petronio, S., & Jones, S. S. (2006). When "friendly advice" becomes privacy dilemma for pregnant couples: Applying CPM theory. In R. West & L. Turner (Eds.), *Family communication: A reference of theory and research* (pp. 201–208). Thousand Oaks, CA: Sage.

Petronio, S., Jones, S. S., & Morr, M. (2003). Family privacy dilemmas: A communication privacy management perspective. In L. Frey (Ed.), *Bona fide groups* (pp. 23–56). Mahwah, NJ: Erlbaum.

Petronio, S., & Kovach, S. (1997). Managing privacy boundaries: Health providers' perceptions of resident care in Scottish nursing homes. *Journal of Applied Communication Research, 25,* 115–131.

Petronio, S., Reeder, H., Hecht, M., & Mon't Ros-Mendoza, T. (1996). Disclosure of sexual abuse by children and adolescents. *Journal of Applied Communication Research, 24,* 181–199.

Roloff, M. E., & Ifert, D. E. (2000). Conflict management through avoidance: Withholding complaints, suppressing arguments, and declaring topics taboo. In S. Petronio (Ed.), *Balancing the secrets of private disclosures* (pp. 151–163). Mahwah, NJ: Erlbaum.

Toller, P. W. (2005). Negotiation of dialectical contradictions by parents who have experienced the death of a child. *Journal of Applied Communication Research, 33,* 46–66.

Yep, G. (2000). Disclosure of HIV infection in interpersonal relationships: A communication boundary management approach. In S. Petronio (Ed.), *Balancing the secrets of private disclosures* (pp. 83–95). Mahwah, NJ: Erlbaum.

24

Critical Feminist Theories

Giving Voice and Visibility to Women's Experiences in Interpersonal Communication

Julia T. Wood

In a book that is credited with launching the liberal branch of the second wave feminism in the United States, Betty Friedan (1963) called attention to what she called "the problem that has no name." Friedan saw that problem as having two parts. First, many middle class stay-at-home mothers felt frustrated and not completely fulfilled because their lives were restricted to home and family. Second, because the ideology of the time maintained that they were living the American dream, many of these women felt guilty for not being fulfilled and grateful.

Friedan (1963) did not leave the problem unnamed. Instead, she labeled it the feminine mystique—the ideology that being a full-time mother and homemaker was the ideal for women. That particular act of naming was pivotal in instigating the second wave of feminism. In naming something that was common in women's experience but unmarked in language, Friedan enacted a key feminist move—she gave voice to what had not been voiced, and, in so doing, she gave visibility and social standing to what had been invisible and thus had no social legitimacy (Spender, 1984a, 1984b). Friedan was neither the first nor last feminist to understand the importance of giving voice—not only to women's experiences, but also to the significance and meaning that women themselves attach to their experiences. Acknowledging and naming women's perspectives on their experiences is prerequisite to having those experiences and women's coding of them counted in cultural life. For example, until the term "sexual harassment" was coined, the English language had no adequate name for uninvited and unwelcome sexual attention that targeted women in the workplace and in educational contexts. Similarly, the term "marital rape" increased social and legal awareness that nonconsensual sex between spouses is wrong.

In this chapter, I discuss the process of women's voicing of their experiences, which is a key means by which Critical Feminist Theories contribute to interpersonal communication (Ardener, 1978; Rakow & Wackwitz, 2004; Spender, 1984a, 1984b). Specifically, I will focus on the crucial act of naming, which provides a vocabulary that is essential for recognizing, valuing, and—in some cases—challenging taken-for-granted aspects of interpersonal relationships.

Purpose and Meta-theoretical Assumptions

Critical Feminist Theories are subsets of two broader groups of theories: Feminist Theories, not all of which are critical, and Critical Theories, not all of which are feminist. I will provide an overview of Feminist Theories and Critical Theories as a basis for explaining the focus of Critical Feminist Theories and the assumptions that underlie them.

FEMINIST THEORIES

"Feminism" is defined as the belief that men and women are equal and should have equal respect and opportunities in all spheres of life—personal, social, work, and public. Central to Feminist Theories are two concepts. First, there is "gender," which is distinct from "sex." Sex is a biological category—male or female—that is determined genetically. Gender comprises social definitions of masculinity and femininity at specific historical moments and in specific cultural contexts. Put another way, gender is the social meanings attached to sex by others and ourselves as well as our ways of embodying—or refusing to embody—those social meanings. Gender influences expectations and perceptions of women and men, as well as the roles, opportunities, and material circumstances of women's and men's lives.

Judith Butler (1990, 1993) argued that gender comes into being as we perform it in everyday life. We simultaneously enact and produce gender through a variety of mundane, performative practices such as dominating or deferring in conversation, offering empathy or solutions when a friend expresses discomfort, and inviting others into conversations or maintaining a center-stage position in interaction. All of these practices communicate, embody, and confer an illusory naturalness on normative codes of masculinity and femininity. According to Butler, gender exists if and only if people act in ways that compel belief in the reality of masculinity and femininity.

A third central concept for Feminist Theories is "patriarchy," which is a system that reflects primarily the interests, perspectives, and experiences of men, as a group. Feminist theorists note that many cultures, including those in the West, were organized predominantly by white, ostensibly heterosexual men, who relied on their experiences, needs, values, preferences, interests, and perspectives to order social life. As a result, our social world is set up in ways that do not fully reflect women's or minorities' experiences, needs, values, preferences, interests, and perspectives.

Feminist theorists do not assume that men necessarily organized society in a deliberate effort to subordinate women and minorities. The point is that when Western cultures were established, men held positions of leadership, and women did not. Men's standpoint did not—in fact, could not—include many experiences typical for women, such as being on call for children 24 hours a day; feeling responsible for monitoring and tending to interpersonal dynamics; engaging in the thankless, repetitive drudgery of keeping a home clean; and doing all of the work to plan, prepare, serve, and clean up after meals (Galvin, 2006). More prominent in a male standpoint would be activities that men routinely enact—working outside of the home; engaging in competitive activities in the workplace and battlegrounds; and seeing the home as a haven graced by mannerly children, clean clothes, and well-prepared meals.

Patriarchy does not refer individual men's deliberate oppression of women. Allan Johnson (1997) explained that "'patriarchy' doesn't refer to me or any man or collection of men, but to a kind of society in which men *and* [emphasis in original] women participate" (p. 4–5). Agreeing, Dorothy Smith (1987) noted that patriarchy "is not a conspiracy among men that they impose on women. It is a complementary social process between men and women" (p. 34). Because patriarchy was set up a long time ago, it is a system that predates you, me, and others now living. If today we could organize society from scratch, we might choose a different model. But the patriarchal model is the one that we have inherited—modified in some ways (women are no longer men's property)—but still patriarchal.

CRITICAL THEORIES

Critical Theories aim to identify prevailing structures and practices that create or uphold disadvantage, inequity, or oppression, and to point the way toward alternatives that promote more egalitarian possibilities for individuals, relationships, groups, and societies. Unlike post-positivist theories, Critical Theories do not embrace explanation and control as primary goals. Instead, Critical Theories are centrally concerned with social change—with making a difference in how cultures operate and how those operations affect people in material and nonmaterial ways.

Scholars in the Critical Theory tradition ask how cultural structures and practices shape the lives of members of a culture and, conversely, how members' lives and activities shape cultural structures and practices. Critical theorists are particularly interested in analyzing the means by which dominant groups privilege their interests and perspectives as universal, that is, as representing an entire culture. At the same time, critical theorists want to understand how oppressed groups become empowered and, in some cases, how to change dominant patterns and perhaps the ideologies that underlie them.

Critical theorists are intensely interested in struggles between competing ideologies, or sets of ideas that organize groups' understandings of reality (Hall, 1986, 1989). For example, they ask how ideology defines the parameters and sites of struggle between dominant and nondominant races, middle-class and working-class people, heterosexuals and nonheterosexuals, and men and women. In each case, there is a dominant group and a less-powerful group or groups, and they participate in what Stuart Hall (1989) called the "theatre of struggle," which is an ongoing battle over whose voices, whose perspectives, and whose values gain a hearing and cultural legitimacy.

In focusing on ideological control, critical theorists trace how power is deployed and resisted. In doing so, many critical theorists pay attention to both formal kinds of power (e.g., laws that define who can marry) and informal kinds of power (e.g., everyday practices that communicate normative understandings of who is and who is not part of a family). This allows critical theorists to critique not only official forms of power such as laws, but also "tiny, everyday" practices (Foucault, 1984, p. 211) that reproduce and sustain particular ideologies and their attendant inequities. By studying how dominant and marginal groups enact and resist power, critical theorists aim to identify how cultures work and to challenge, disrupt, and remake cultural life so that it better reflects and represents the interests and perspectives of all who comprise it.

THE INTERSECTION OF FEMINIST AND CRITICAL THEORIES

When Critical Theories and Feminist Theories intersect, the result is theories that identify, critique, and seek to change inequities and discrimination, particularly those that are based on sex and gender (Dow, 1995; Dow & Wood, 2006; Wood, 1995). In other words, Critical Feminist Theories ask how cultural structures and practices shape women's and men's lives and communication practices, and conversely how women's and men's lives and communication shape cultural structures and practices. By extension, critical feminist theorists are particularly interested in understanding how women become empowered and, in some cases, how they change dominant patterns and perhaps the ideologies that underlie them.

Like other critical theorists, those who are feminist are keenly interested in how power is deployed and resisted. This concern leads many critical theorists to pay attention to both formal kinds of power (e.g., now-revoked laws that defined women as men's property) and informal kinds of power (e.g., male generic language that erases women by naming phenomena from men's and not women's perspectives). This allows critical theorists to analyze not only official forms of power such as laws, but also "tiny, everyday" practices (Foucault, 1984, p. 211) that reproduce and sustain inequitable roles and expectations for men's and women's behaviors, including their communication. Among these tiny, everyday practices are names and, equally important, the absence of names for experiences and perspectives that are more typical of women than of men.

Critical Feminist Theories identify, question, and seek to reform patriarchal ideologies that give rise to oppression, as well as the asymmetrical rights, opportunities, roles, and so forth. Note that the critique mounted by critical feminist theorists is not confined to matters of sex or gender inequality. Also part of the critique are efforts to devalue and oppress any groups that do not reflect the standpoint and interests of those who hold dominant positions in cultural life. The dominant masculinist and heteronormative ideology of Western culture produces a decidedly limited understanding of interpersonal relationships and the communication that generates and sustains them. Attending to neglected facets of interpersonal relationships and to existing perspectives that erase or misrepresent women's experiences in relationships are priorities of critical feminist theory and research.

Within the broad category of Critical Feminist Theories there are many specific schools of thought, such as Foucauldian, socialist and Marxist, performative, postcolonial, and psychoanalytic, not all of which are mutually exclusive theoretical camps. Obviously, a single short chapter cannot describe how all of these contribute to an understanding of interpersonal communication and relationships. For this reason, I will focus on a particular subset of the Critical Feminist Theories that highlight the importance of naming experiences from women's perspectives. This subset of theories include Muted Group, Co-cultural, and Standpoint Theories. Although these theories differ in some ways (see Muted Group Theory Excerpts, 2005), all three assume that social location has implications for experience, knowledge, language, and power. This shared assumption can be elaborated by identifying an additional four specific assumptions that inform and underlie this group of Critical Feminist Theories, to be discussed below.

UNDERLYING ASSUMPTIONS

The key assumptions of Critical Feminist Theories reflect the goals of identifying and challenging gender-based inequity, discrimination, devaluation, marginalization, and so forth. Among the assumptions that inform and guide Critical Feminist Theories are four that are particularly relevant to interpersonal communication and relationships: (a) In patriarchal cultures, women make up a subordinate group. (b) Because women, as a group, are subordinate in patriarchal cultures, some experiences, knowledge, and activities that are unique to, or more typical of, women are not represented in language or are represented in ways that do not reflect women's meanings for those experiences. (c) Women's experiences, knowledge, and activities merit respect and linguistic status, which are prerequisites to women's full inclusion in interpersonal, social, and political lives. (d) Voice is a key means of valuing and including women's experiences, knowledge, and activities in cultural life. The character and importance of these assumptions will become clearer as we explore the main features of Critical Feminist Theories.

Main Features of the Theories

POWER

Critical Feminist Theories focus keenly on power relations and linked issues such as the unequal status and privilege accorded to women compared to that accorded to men. Analyses of power relations have demonstrated that, as a group, men—particularly white, heterosexual, able-bodied men—are more likely than women, as a group, to hold positions of power in society, assume dominance in families, and exercise control in everyday interactions (Collins, 1986; Hartsock, 1983; Keller, 1985; Wood, 1994, 2006; also, see Wood, 2007 for a summary of research). According to critical feminist theorists, the greater power generally held by men is a primary reason that women's experiences, perspectives, and knowledge have been devalued, and that women's voices have been suppressed.

WOMEN'S EXPERIENCES, PERSPECTIVES, AND KNOWLEDGE

Arising out of attention to power relations and women's subordinate location within those relations, Critical Feminist Theories seek to raise awareness of women's experiences, perspectives, and knowledge, which historically have been less acknowledged and valued than men's experiences, perspectives, and knowledge. Highlighting the experiences, perspectives and knowledge that, at least historically, arise from women's location in social life leads to a focus on what Dorothy Smith (1987) called "everyday life." Traditionally, while men were in the boardrooms and on the war fronts, women were in the home and community where they assumed responsibility for the routine, everyday dynamics of life—caring for children, cleaning and maintaining a home, preparing meals, supporting schools, contributing time and effort to civic organizations, and so forth. According to prominent critical feminist theorists (Harding, 1991, 2004, 2006; Haraway, 1988; Hartsock, 1983; Ruddick, 1989), this enmeshment in everyday life cultivates a particular kind of consciousness that is sensitive to nuances of others' communication, responsive to feeling and need, and more focused on process than specific instrumental outcomes. In short, it is a kind of consciousness that is shaped by and attuned to the rhythms of everyday life.

Conceptualization of Communication in the Theories

Because communication is the principal way that we represent experiences, perspectives, and knowledge, communication is an important emphasis in Critical Feminist Theories. Often referred to by related terms such as "language" and "voice," communication is recognized as the primary means by which we express ourselves. In turn, communication—specifically, naming—is central to how we humans understand our experiences, thoughts, and feelings; convey those to others; and have those represented in the common language, and thus knowledge, of a culture. It follows that without names for experiences, thoughts, and feelings, we have less full knowledge of them and markedly less ability to share them with others.

Critical Feminist Theories offer two important views of communication. First, communication is understood as means of enacting power relations between people. Second, communication is a way to name phenomena and thereby render phenomena subject to notice, reference, and negotiation. By implication, phenomena that are not named are less noticeable, less acknowledged and valued, less available for reference, and less open to challenge and negotiation.

Use of the theories, like the feminist movement that informs them, is not restricted to the "ivory tower" (Dow & Wood, 2006). Instead, these theories aim for practical impact in the everyday world of personal and social relationships. As hinted above, a primary way this happens is through naming what has not been named, noticed, or valued. To illustrate this value of Critical Feminist Theories, I will briefly identify five phenomena common in women's experience of interpersonal life that once were not named, but that now have been named and thus brought into social awareness.

SEXUAL HARASSMENT

"Sexual harassment" is unwanted and unwelcome conduct of a sexual nature that interferes with performance in work and educational settings. Doubtlessly, sexual harassment has existed for centuries, yet it was not named until the 1970s (Wood, 1992). Until that time, people, primarily women, who endured unwanted sexualized behavior at work and in school had no way to name what happened to them. The language of their culture provided no language that named the practice as illegal, much less immoral. Victims of harassment could only resort to inadequate language such as "going too far," "being pushy," or "flirting," terms that do not begin to describe the character of sexual harassment and, furthermore, that do not mark it as wrong, immoral, and illegal.

DATE RAPE AND MARITAL RAPE

Like sexual harassment, date and marital rape are not new phenomena. However, naming these practices as criminal acts—rape—is new. Only toward the end of the twentieth century did most states adopt laws that specifically recognized nonconsensual sex between dates or spouses as the crime of rape. And only by naming nonconsensual sex in any context as a crime were the grievous violations recognized for what they are (Wriggins, 1998).

CONVERSATIONAL MAINTENANCE WORK

In 1978, Pamela Fishman gave a name to a phenomenon familiar to most women but unnamed until then. Her studies of interaction between men and women led Fishman to conclude that women do a lot of work to maintain conversations. They ask questions about others' activities and interests, pull others into conversation, and respond to what others say with comments and follow-up questions. Fishman's research (1978), as well as later research that confirmed her findings (Alexander & Wood, 2000; Dunn, 1999; Taylor, 2002), showed that women do far more of the work to keep a conversation going than do men. In coining the term "conversational maintenance work," Fishman gave a name to an activity that is vital to interpersonal communication.

SECOND SHIFT

Writing in 1989, sociologist Arlie Hochschild used the term second shift to name a phenomenon common in the lives of women who work outside of the home. The "second shift" is all of the housework, cooking, and childcare that women engage in after returning from a shift in the paid labor force. Hochschild (1989) reported that roughly 20% of men in dual-worker couples assume half of the work required to run a home and family. More recent studies (Galvin, 2006; for a summary, see Duck & Wood, 2006) have confirmed the persistence of inequity in responsibility for work in the domestic sphere. In naming this phenomenon as a form of work, the term second shift gives visibility to what had been invisible.

PSYCHOLOGICAL RESPONSIBILITY

The second shift involves more than concrete tasks such as fixing meals, bathing children, and vacuuming. In addition, it includes "psychological responsibility" (Hochschild, 1989), which is the responsibility to remember, plan, schedule, and so forth. For example, behind a prepared dinner sitting on a table are a number of generally unseen and unnoticed tasks such as considering household members' nutritional needs and dietary preferences, deciding on a menu, and shopping for the necessary ingredients.

Strengths and Limitations of the Theories

By most of the criteria routinely used to assess theories, Critical Feminist Theories fare well. They offer broad frameworks for studying and thinking about interpersonal relationships and the ways in which communication both shapes and reflects the dynamics of those relationships. They meet the criterion of utility or of pragmatism by heightening awareness of aspects of relationships that have little or no visibility within alternative theories. In limiting themselves to relatively few concepts (gender, power, dominance, and so forth), they meet the criterion of parsimony.

Finally, on the criterion of heurism Critical Feminist Theories clearly excel. They provoke original insight into interpersonal dynamics such as the second shift and psychological responsibility, and they spark critical perspectives on how relationships do and could operate. Even if we are uncomfortable with some of the issues and options highlighted by Critical Feminist Theories, they clearly challenge conventional ways of thinking and offer us new insights and choices as we go about the business of organizing relationships, thinking about how others organize theirs, and reflecting on the ways in which cultural structures and practices contour our personal and social relationships.

Two primary criticisms of the theories merit our attention. First, some scholars (Putnam, 1982) have expressed concern that the theories have limited ability to explain interpersonal communication because they (over)emphasize sex and gender while ignoring other influences on how people think, act, feel, and communicate. A second concern is that the theories have limited utility because they focus on a small subset of women—middle-class, Caucasian, able-bodied, heterosexual women—and their experiences. This criticism had greater legitimacy 20 or even 10 years ago than it does today. Influenced by postcolonial scholarship, feminist theorists increasingly recognize the diversity of women.

Directions for Future Research and Applications

Critical feminist theorizing will continue to evolve in ways that affect both academic study of relationships and our everyday experiences in relationships. From the outset, Feminist Theories have been practical, aiming to give us tools for understanding and shaping our personal and collective lives. As I have shown in this chapter, the act of naming, which reflects critical feminist theorists' attention to relationships between social location, knowledge, and voice, has had substantial impact on how people understand their experiences in relationships and, by extension, how they develop and sustain those relationships. We can now name dynamics such as the second shift and date rape. With naming comes consciousness of inequities that persist in private contexts, despite hard-won gains in equality between the sexes in the public sphere. In turn, consciousness of inequalities and the ability to reference them in communication enhance individuals' opportunities to make their relationships more fair, deliberate, and satisfying.

Awareness of inequities in relationships is a start, but it is not the ultimate goal. The vital aim of Critical Feminist Theories is to eradicate inequities so that people participate equally in relationships, and invest and benefit equitably from their interpersonal associations. This goal continues to motivate critical feminist theorizing. In the years ahead, theorists in this tradition will persevere in the important work of naming issues, dynamics, and experiences that help us recognize and work to overcome inequities in our relationships. This work will need to accommodate the ongoing changes in relationships such as breadwinner and homemaker roles becoming less distinct and less sex-linked, and family forms multiplying (Galvin, 2006). These and other changes will usher in new relationship dynamics and the potentials for new forms of inequity that Critical Feminist Theories will need to address if those theories are to have the influence in the future that they have enjoyed to date.

Critical Feminist Theories question not only normative understandings of the roles of men and women in relationships but also the interests that are and are not served by existing normative understandings of relationships and sex roles. Among the ways that Critical Feminist Theories have contributed to our understanding of interpersonal communication is the naming of experiences that are more common to women than to men that previously had not been named and thus had not had social legitimacy. Because naming is powerful, it alters both understandings of those relationships and the concrete, lived experiences that people have in their relationships.

In the future, interpersonal communication scholars may extend the theories' contributions by noticing and naming additional phenomena that are part of the too-often invisible gendered organization of relationships and cultural life.

In addition, scholars should be asking what kinds of communication reflect and sustain inequities in relationships and what kinds of communication cultivate or are present in equitable relationships.

References

Alexander, M. G., & Wood, W. (2000). Women, men and positive emotions: A social role interpretation. In A. H. Fischer (Ed.), *Gender and emotion: Social psychological perspectives* (pp. 189–210). New York: Cambridge University Press.

Ardener, S. (1978). *Defining females: The nature of women in society.* New York: Wiley.

Butler, J. (1990). Performative acts and gender constitution: An essay in phenomenology and feminist theory. In S. Case (Ed.), *Performing feminisms: Feminist critical theory and theatre* (pp. 270–282). Baltimore: Johns Hopkins University Press.

Butler, J. (1993). *Bodies that matter: On the discursive limits of "sex."* New York: Routledge.

Collins, P. H. (1986). Learning from the outsider within. *Social Problems, 23,* 514–532.

Dow, B. J. (1995). Feminism, difference(s), and rhetorical studies. *Communication Studies, 46,* 106–117.

Dow, B. J., & Wood, J. T. (2006). The evolution of gender and communication research: Intersections of theory, politics, and scholarship. In B. J. Dow & J. T. Wood (Eds.), *The handbook of gender and communication* (pp. ix-xxiv). Thousand Oaks, CA: Sage.

Duck, S., & Wood, J. T. (2006). What goes up may come down: Sex and gendered patterns in relational dissolution. In M. Fine & J. Harvey (Eds.), *Handbook of divorce and relationship dissolution* (pp. 169–187). Mahwah, NJ: Erlbaum.

Dunn, J. (1999). Siblings, friends, and the development of social understanding. In W. A. Collins & B. Laursen (Eds.), *Relationships as developmental contexts* (pp. 263–279). Mahwah, NJ: Erlbaum.

Fishman, P. M. (1978). Interaction: The work women do. *Social Problems, 25,* 397–406.

Foucault, M. (1984). *The Foucault reader.* P. Rabinow (Ed.). New York: Pantheon.

Friedan, B. (1963). *The feminine mystique.* New York: W. W. Norton.

Galvin, K. (2006). Gender and family interaction: Dress rehearsal for an improvisation? In B. Dow & J. T. Wood (Eds.). *The SAGE handbook of gender and communication* (pp. 41–55). Thousand Oaks, CA: Sage.

Hall, S. (1986). The problem of ideology—Marxism without guarantees. *Journal of Communication Inquiry, 10,* 28–44.

Hall, S. (1989). Ideology. In E. Barnouw et al. (Eds.), *International encyclopedia of communication* (Vol. 2, pp. 307–311). New York: Oxford University Press.

Haraway, D. (1988). Situated knowledges: The science question in feminism and the privilege of partial perspective. *Signs, 14,* 575–599.

Harding, S. (1991). *Whose science? Whose knowledge? Thinking from women's lives.* Ithaca, NY: Cornell University Press.

Harding, S. (Ed.). (2004). *The feminist standpoint theory reader: Intellectual and political controversies.* New York: Routledge.

Harding, S. (2006). *Science and social inequality: Feminist and postcolonial issues.* Urbana, IL: University of Illinois Press.

Hartsock, N. (1983). The feminist standpoint: Developing the ground for a specifically feminist historical materialism. In S. Harding & M. B. Hintikka (Eds.), *Discovering reality* (pp. 283–310). Boston: Ridel.

Hochschild, A., with Machung, A. (1989). *The second shift.* New York: Viking.

Johnson, A. (1997). *The gender knot: Unraveling our patriarchal legacy.* Philadelphia: Temple University Press.

Keller, E. (1985). *Reflections on science and gender.* New Haven, CT: Yale University Press.

Muted Group Theory Excerpts. (2005). *Women in Language, 28,* 50–72.

Putnam, L. (1982). In search of gender: A critique of communication and sex-roles research. *Women's Studies in Communication, 5,* 1–9.

Rakow, L., & Wackwitz, L. (Eds.). (2004). *Feminist communication theory: Selections in context.* Thousand Oaks, CA: Sage.

Ruddick, S. (1989). *Maternal thinking: Toward a politics of peace.* Boston: Beacon.

Smith, D. (1987). *The everyday world as problematic.* Toronto, Canada: University of Toronto.

Spender, D. (1984a). *Man made language.* London: Routledge.

Spender, D. (1984b). Defining reality: A powerful tool. In C. Kramarae, M. Schultz, & W. O'Barr (Eds.), *Language and power* (pp. 195–205). Beverly Hills, CA: Sage.

Taylor, S. (2002). *The tending instinct: How nurturing is essential for who we are and how we live.* New York: Times Books.

Wood, J. T. (1992). Telling our stories: Narratives as a basis for theorizing sexual harassment. *Journal of Applied Communication Research, 4,* 349–363.

Wood, J. T. (1994). *Who cares? Women, care and culture.* Carbondale, IL: Southern Illinois University Press.

Wood, J. T. (1995). Feminist scholarship and the study of personal and social relationships. *Journal of Social and Personal Relationships, 12,* 103–120.

Wood, J. T. (2006). Gendered power, aggression and violence in heterosexual relationships. In D. Canary & K. Dindia (Eds.), *Sex differences and similarities in communication* (2nd ed., pp. 397–411). Mahwah, NJ: Erlbaum.

Wood, J. T. (2007). *Gendered lives: Communication, gender, and culture* (7th ed.). Belmont, CA: Thomson Wadsworth.

Wriggins, J. (1998). Rape. In W. Mankiller, G. Mink, M. Navarro, B. Smith, & G. Steinem (Eds.), *The reader's companion to U.S. women's history* (pp. 612–614). New York: Houghton Mifflin.

25

Relational Communication Theory

A Systemic-Interactional Approach
to Interpersonal Relationships

L. Edna Rogers

The study of relationships has long fascinated scholars across the social sciences; this is increasingly true in the field of interpersonal communication. The increased interest in applying communication theories to relationship study coincided with a growing recognition of the intrinsic, intimate tie between communication and relationship, with communication seen as the formative process by which relational systems come into being. This view is prominent in a number of different theoretical perspectives and is a basic premise of Relational Communication Theory. The once somewhat radical idea of viewing relationships as "ongoing conversations" (Berger & Kellner, 1964, p. 3) is now more commonplace. The constitutive quality of communication has been echoed by others, such as in Duncan's (1967) well-known phrase, "We do not relate and then talk, but we relate in talk" (p. 249), or Sigman's (1998) emphasis that "a relationship is not an entity from which communication emanates, but a location in an ongoing behavioral stream" (p. 52).

The interwoven nature of communication and relationship also reflects the influence of the relationship on communication. Given this interconnection, the relational communication perspective views relationships as being enacted and formed through the relational members' communication processes, and, in turn, views the nature of the relationship produced as influencing the ongoing communication between the members. For understanding interpersonal relationships, these processes represent a central focus of Relational Communication Theory.

As a way of giving a more informal, visual representation of this perspective, relationships can be viewed as evolving "art forms" creatively performed by the participants in the ongoing movement of their communicative "dance." How we move in relation to one another via our communication behaviors forms the patterns that define our relationships in an ongoing flow of mutual influence. Analogous to dance steps, individual messages combine into sequences of recurring patterns of interaction that characterize the jointly produced relationship. Thus, individual message behaviors are an essential "part" in the creation of the interpersonal dance, but of central interest to relational communication are the coproduced, system-level patterns of the "whole" dance. The distinction between individual behaviors and system patterns is a basic feature of this theory.

Purpose and Meta-theoretical Assumptions

At the time this theory was developed, there were few process-centered theories of communication. As such, an overall goal was to apply an interactional approach to the study of relationships for acquiring new insights on the processes of communication and their associated influence on relationships. More specifically, the central purpose of Relational Communication Theory is to provide a theoretical and practical understanding of the processes of interrelating with others and how the participants' coenacted patterns of communication influence their relational lives.

The theoretical approach taken was founded on the legacy of Bateson's (1951) conceptual efforts in constructing a "new order of communication" (p. 209) that offered a process view of communication and relationships. This new order necessitated a reformulation of the traditional linear, reductionistic paradigmatic stance, to one that gave prominence to patterned relations over individual events and interrelatedness over unilateral cause. System and cybernetic theories further supported this view with their emphasis on patterns of organization, multilevel systems, and cyclic processes of interaction. Given this alternative view, the relational communication approach assumes that people interrelate with one another through their communication behaviors, that communication is a formative process, and that relational systems are formed through the mutually defined patterns of communication. Based on an observational approach to the study of interaction, the primary interest of Relational Communication Theory is to identify the interactive patterns that characterize different types of relational systems and the ramifications of these patterns. Of the three main paradigms described in this text that guide social science research, this approach falls within the general framework of post-positivism, but it is important to note that it is based on a probabilistic view of relational processes, not a deterministic one.

Main Features of the Theory

The theoretical stance of relational communication is rooted in the seminal writings of Bateson (1935, 1936). However, it was not until the publication of Watzlawick, Beavin, and Jackson's (1967) *Pragmatics of Human Communication* that these writings were brought to light. The authors of this influential text included central aspects of Bateson's work in their formulation of a systemic, interaction-based perspective of communication. The lines of thought drawn together in *Pragmatics* formed an integrated foundation for the theory of relational communication. The major features of this theory are based on the general principles of system theory and cybernetics, and the conceptual insights of Bateson.

System theory presented an overarching worldview—not of separate events, but of the interrelatedness of events. The organizing principles of system theory (von Bertalanffy, 1968) focus on the interconnection and integration of the system's component parts that form the larger systemic whole. The concept of interdependency is the most basic of the defining characteristics of a system. It refers to the mutual influence of the interrelated member parts that creates a system, such that a system is more than (i.e., different from) the sum of its parts. Interdependency is also the quality that forms the embedded hierarchical levels of systems within larger systems. Each of these system levels represents an integrated whole, and at the same time each is a part, or a subsystem, of the higher, encompassing system. Using the family as an illustration, a husband-wife relationship forms one system, a parent-child relation another. Each is a "whole" system, yet simultaneously a "part" of the larger family system. In turn, the family is a unified "whole" and, at the same time, "part" of the higher, extended family system.

The importance of the "part/whole" (Koestler, 1978) structuring of multi-leveled systems is that each level simultaneously influences and is influenced by the higher level. However, an important distinction is that each level has properties that are not present in other levels. Thus, an individual member of an interpersonal relationship does not represent the jointly produced characteristics of the larger system, just as with the dance metaphor, the individual dance steps do not depict the "whole" of the dance. The theoretical and research significance of this distinction is to recognize that different levels of analysis provide different types of information and insight. Thus, studies of single messages or individuals, as useful as these may be, do not provide a description of the larger relational system. In order to capture the codefined patterns of communication descriptive of relationships, a relational level of analysis is necessary, and represents a key feature of relational communication.

Cybernetics (Wiener, 1948), the study of communication feedback control processes, adds an essential quality to system theory. The focus of cybernetics is on how systems are regulated through the continuous flow of feedback information occurring within the system. From this perspective, systems are viewed as being maintained, modified, and changed by the circular processes of influence that emerge from and guide the members' communicative interactions with one another. The regulative properties of cybernetic systems are grounded within the ongoing dialectic oscillations of continuity and change in the process of maintaining systemic integration. These fluctuating dynamics reflect the adaptive interplay of the members' behaviors vis-à-vis one another. In this process, system members are continually engaged in giving off information about themselves and their relationships through the feedback loops of message exchange.

Cybernetic principles were instrumental in promoting a view of communication focused on process and its regulative function. In developing a process model of the family, Kantor and Lehr (1975) introduced the concept of "distance regulation" for describing the cybernetic orientation of the model. In their view, system members are continually informing one another through their communicative behaviors as to what constitutes appropriate distance within as well as outside the system. Their concept of distance captures the regulative processes at work in all relationships. From spatial to emotional concerns, the verbal and nonverbal behaviors of the relational members continually give off "distancing" information as to how far or how close they "stand" in relation to one another. For instance, when a mother calls her college student son and says, "I haven't heard from you for awhile," she is implying that he should keep in closer touch with her, and if the son replies with, "I'm really busy. I've got a bunch of finals and a paper to finish," he's expressing, at least at this time, a need for distance. But with the added comment, "Mom, I love you," everybody feels better, i.e., closer.

System and cybernetic perspectives laid the groundwork for the relational communication approach, with the more specific features resting on the conceptual work of Bateson (1935, 1936). From the beginning, his view of relationships was based on system thinking. In his approach, Bateson focused on identifying patterns of communication that progressively moved, in his words, toward "knowledge of the larger interactive system" (Bateson, 1972, p. 433). His conceptualization of the duality of message meaning is a basic starting point for describing how patterns of relationship are formed.

Bateson (1951) proposed that messages simultaneously offer two levels of meaning: a content meaning and a relational meaning. The content level provides information based on what the message is about, while the relational level provides information on how the message is to be interpreted. In line with the above distancing examples, the content information of the expression, "Where have you been? You're late," refers to time, but at the relational level the comment is typically interpreted as a form of disappointment or criticism regarding the other's lack of responsibility or concern. If the other responds with, "You're always so uptight. Just relax," the potential of a relational pattern of mutual blaming is put in place. If, however, the other responds with, "You're right. I'm really sorry," a different, softer definition of relational meaning is offered that is less likely to trigger a critical response. In light of these two levels of meaning, the content, or "what" is said, is always contextualized by the higher, meta-level relational meaning of "how" it is said. Content plays a part, but it is largely at the relational level that interactors indicate how they define the relation. Thus, in the ongoing exchange of relational meaning, system members codefine the patterns descriptive of their relationship.

To depict relational patterns, Bateson (1979) described the process as one of "double description." By analogy, he illustrated this process in this way: "It is correct (and a great improvement) to begin to think of the two parties in the interaction as two eyes, each giving a monocular view of what goes on and, together giving a binocular view in depth. This double description is the relationship" (p. 142). As two eyes in combination generate a binocular view, messages in combination generate patterns of communication, which in turn generate the larger evolving patterns of relationship.

The concepts of symmetry and complementarity described by Bateson (1979) represent two general patterns of communication based on the similarity or difference of the relational meaning of the messages exchanged. Symmetry refers to interaction sequences in which the participants' behaviors mirror one another, such as responding to a complaint with a complaint, or to a supportive message with support. In contrast, complementary patterns refer to sequences in which the behaviors are different but fit together, as in giving and accepting advice or asking and answering a question. Both symmetry and complementarity can take different forms, depending on the type and order of the messages exchanged. An argument between two friends over what movie to watch represents a competitive form of symmetry: when each wants to do whatever the other wants to do, a pattern of submissive symmetry results. With complementary patterns, if one person's suggestions are accepted by the other, a dominate/submissive type of complementarity is formed, but if a person's requests for help are refused, a submissive/dominate type results.

Bateson's (1979) approach for depicting patterns of relationships moves from the identification of communication patterns that are formed from the combination of messages with messages, as illustrated above, to successive combinations of patterns with patterns that form larger sequences of patterns that in turn provide a more holistic description of the relationship. The following examples illustrate some of these larger pattern configurations. For instance, interaction episodes that intermix symmetry and complementarity form an overall flexible pattern. Likewise, a mix of the two types of complementarity represents another relatively flexible pattern. It consists of a series of exchanges in which the members alternate between asserting themselves and accepting each other's suggestions or ideas, and represents one of the more harmonious relational patterns. However, rigid complementarity, as the term suggests, is a highly redundant, potentially stifling form of exchange. This pattern results when interactors repeatedly enact the same part in an ongoing sequence of complementarity—for instance, with one person asserting control and the other submitting to the first person's directives. In contrast, patterns of escalating competitive symmetry reflect an ongoing struggle over who will be in control of the relationship. With each exchange, the members disagree or reject the other's relational definition. Brief episodes of this pattern occur in most relationships, but repeated enactments of escalating symmetry are clearly indicative of a troubled relationship.

Symmetry and complementarity serve as prototypes for exemplifying the process of pattern formation. The progressive movement of identifying patterns of relationships through the evolving processes of communication gives meaning to Bateson's (1979) description of this approach as an ongoing "dialectic of process and form" (p. 194) with process influencing relational form, and relational form influencing the ongoing communication process.

The main features of Relational Communication Theory all revolve around the emphasis placed on interaction patterns. In brief, these features focus on the interdependency of system members, circular influencing processes of communication, the relational level of meaning of the messages exchanged, and the coproduced communication patterns descriptive of relationships.

Conceptualization of Communication in the Theory

At base, Relational Communication Theory conceptualizes communication as a social process, the life-giving essence of our humanness. It is the process through which we interrelate with others, mutually create social realities, and form relationships as well as self-identities. The theory's conceptual stance on the primacy of communication as a formative, constitutive process has already been described, and hopefully demonstrated. This conceptualization is in line with Sigman's (1995) emphasis on the consequentiality of communication—that is, communication is foremost a formative process in its own right, not simply a consequence of other factors.

Clearly, from the relational communication point of view, communication is not seen as a singular event, nor as something done "to" another person.

Rather, communication is a process of engaging "with" another person in an ongoing stream of dialogue. As such, communication rests not on one person or the other but within the interconnective process of engagement. From the beginning, the theoretical approach has been centered on the formative, relational qualities of communication, based on the premise that the mutually created patterns formed "do not lie within individual interactors, but rather exist between them" (Rogers & Farace, 1975, p. 222).

Uses of the Theory

Relational communication adds to an understanding of interpersonal communication by focusing directly on the communication processes of interrelating with others. The types of insights offered are described in the propositions generated by the theory and the methods used for examining these propositions.

A basic theoretical premise of Relational Communication Theory is the predicted relational functionality of relatively flexible patterns of interaction. Based on this supposition, it is proposed that more positive, viable interpersonal relationships will manifest patterns of communication that provide both sufficient mutual confirmation of the members' definitions of the relationship for relational predictability, and pattern modification for adapting to changing relational dynamics, situations, or contexts. The fluidity of pattern variation allows for the dialectic interplay of spontaneity and continuity, closeness and separateness, and other pattern oscillations that avoid the negative impact of stagnating or escalating patterns. Thus, the flexibility demonstrated in the members' enacted patterns of communication is predicted to be associated with positive relational outcomes.

In contrast, it is proposed that overly redundant, rigid patterns of communication offer less potential for negotiating relational differences or enacting alternative patterns for adapting to changing situations, and therefore less flexible patterns will be associated with more negative relational evaluations and outcomes. Furthermore, in negotiating problematic issues, members of rigidly structured systems are predicted to be particularly prone to reenacting the same communicative "dance steps," regardless of the ineffectiveness of those patterns. Thus, members will tend to increasingly become entrapped in patterns that work against them, and, over time, that work against the members' abilities to maintain the relationship.

Faced with similar problematic issues, the members of flexible systems are not predicted to be exempt from engaging in disruptive, ineffective patterns, such as rigid complementarity or escalating symmetry. When these occur, however, the members are predicted to more readily transition to enacting communication patterns that constrain and alter the continuation of potentially dysfunctional patterns. Given these proposed differences, well-functioning systems are predicted to evidence a fluidity of self-correcting communicative processes that counter potentially problematic relational tendencies. Conversely, these corrective processes are more likely to be lacking in rigidly structured systems. Within this general framework, additional propositions have been generated regarding specific types of communication patterns and their associated influence on relationships (Rogers & Escudero, 2004).

The use of relational communication for understanding interpersonal communication rests not only on the theoretical propositions but also on the ability to test these propositions with appropriately designed methods. To accomplish this, the relational communication control coding system was developed to describe the regulative function of messages that form different patterns of communication (Rogers & Farace, 1975). Based on the relational level of meaning, the coding system is designed to index the control implications of the messages exchanged. The control definition of each message is coded in terms of its grammatical form (e.g., assertion, question, talkover, and so on) and response mode relative to the previous speaker's message (e.g., support, nonsupport, extension, order, disconfirmation, and so on). Messages that assert a directive or firm definition of the relationship are coded as one-up control moves (↑), requests or acceptance of the other's relational definition are coded as one-down messages (↓), control leveling messages are coded as one-across moves (→).

For describing interaction patterns, the sequential combination of message control provides specific descriptions of different patterns of communication. Based on the definitions given earlier, complementary patterns are represented by opposite control messages of one-up and one-down (↑↓, ↓↑), and symmetrical patterns are based on similar control directions (↑↑, ↓↓, →→). An additional set, referred to as transitory patterns, is formed by the combination of one-across messages with one-up and one-down messages (→↑, ↑→, →↓, ↓→).

With the sequential combination of these patterns, larger patterns are formed. For instance, rigid complementarity is represented by a series of one-up and one-down messages with the same person consistently in the one-up position. Competitive escalating symmetry results from an ongoing exchange of one-up control messages.

As an example of how these procedures are applied, the following is a brief slice of interaction between a therapist (T) and a client (C).

Control Code

C: You mean you're just going to come in here and
tell me what to do.   ↑

T: No, I'm here to help explore what you do.   ↑

C: Explore, explore what! ↑
T: Your relationship with your wife. ↑
C: But . . . I don't know if . . . how can we do that? ↓
T: Well, how do you feel about her? ↓
C: I don't know. →
T: Try to answer. Describe your feelings toward her. ↑
C: I don't know if I can. →
T: What comes to mind when you think of her? ↓
C: Anger . . . and disappointment. ↑
T: Is it directed at you or her? ↓
C: At her. ↑

In mapping these sequences, the initial one-up control moves form a pattern of competitive symmetry that demonstrates a brief struggle for control of the therapy session. Then a transitory pattern based on a mix of one-across messages with the one-down and one-up messages moves the interaction into a transition phase that leads to a cooperative form of interaction between the client and therapist as indicated by the complementary pattern. In this way, the identification of the coproduced patterns provides a method for testing the predicted associations in different interpersonal relations.

Strengths and Limitations of the Theory

The strengths and limitations of any theory go hand in hand, such that each is the source of the other. In other words, for the phenomena under study, the focus of a theory draws boundaries as to what's included and what's excluded. The potential strengths of a theory stem from those aspects that are given attention, and the potential limitations stem from those that are not.

In this manner, the strengths of Relational Communication Theory lie in its interactional focus on communication. With this emphasis, the theory offers a point of view that is directly centered on an understanding of the interpersonal processes of communication. By focusing on process, the theory incorporates an essential quality of communication: a temporal dimension. As relational members communicate with one another, they do so over time. In attending to the sequential unfolding of communication and evolving pattern formations, important aspects of the temporalness of the interaction are taken into account. Process-centered theories, although limited in number, add to our knowledge of interpersonal communication by filling a theoretical space between the more numerous psychologically and sociologically oriented theories of communication. Perhaps most importantly, process-based theories emphasize the consequentiality of communication, which means that the explanatory quality of communication is brought up front in our theoretical models. Thus, rather than viewing communication as a consequent effect of other factors, we view communication as an explanatory source, in its own right, of other factors.

In addition, the focus on the relational level of communication captures the socialness of the interrelating process. A less formal way of expressing the inherent social quality of communication is that in our relationships, you and I both make a difference, but together we "are" the difference. An awareness of how we together, for better or worse, create our relationships through our communicative behaviors provides not only theoretical understanding but also practical insights on the inner workings of interpersonal relationships. A summarizing, overall evaluation of the theory's strength is the heuristic value of relational communication based on the amount of research generated by the application of the theory over the past 30 years. See Rogers and Escudero (2004) for a comprehensive research review.

The limitations of the theory, as suggested above, are based on those aspects not given priority. In attending to interaction systems, less attention is given to the individual members. To clarify the relational view, individual participants are seen as active agents that impute meaning, improvise, and choose the behaviors they enact. The influence of the individual on a relationship is such that it takes only one member to change his or her behavior, and thus to change the relationship. In these ways, the importance of the individual is not trivialized, but, at the same time, the individual is not privileged by a focus on relational patterns.

In particular, the members' interpretations, emotions, and feelings that emerge in the process of interacting are underrepresented. These have been given some attention by coding the nonverbal emotions displayed by the interactors during an interaction and by asking the participants to describe their relational satisfactions and disappointments, their understandings of one another, and so on, but typically these measures have been fairly global in nature. More recently, the participants' moment-to-moment emotional responses to each other's messages are being used to tap into these important features of the interaction process. Nevertheless, in view of the richness of the interrelating process, more could be included.

A related limitation is the central focus of the theory on the regulative, control dimension of communication. As basic as control dynamics are in all relationships, from early on in the development of the theory some scholars (Millar & Rogers, 1987) clearly recognized the necessity of including other dimensions, such as intimacy and trust, to extend the scope of the theory. These and other limitations have served to guide future directions for enhancing the theory.

Directions for Future Research and Applications

The directions considered as central for future research are not so much new directions as they are a continuation of previously envisioned areas in need of expansion. The past primary focus on dyadic systems provided the impetus to extend the application of the theory to larger relational systems. To move in this direction, Heatherington and Friedlander (1987) adapted the relational coding system to capture additional communication patterns that occur in relationships of three or more members. In multimember interactions, messages may have relational implications for more than one member. This occurs when one member's message is a direct response to another member, but indirectly defines the first member's relation with yet another member. For example, a message that expresses disagreement with Member A may indirectly support the view of Member B. Likewise, direct and indirect definitions result when Person 1 ignores Person 2's direct message by speaking to Person 3, or when Person 1 speaks to Person 2 about Person 3, and so on. The identification of these triadic sequences, along with the direct patterns of message exchange, more fully describe the interaction complexities of larger groups. These procedures have provided the basis for an extensive, ongoing program of research (Heatherington & Friedlander, 2004).

The inclusion of other relational dimensions in addition to control is an essential direction for future development. Present investigations of multiple dimensions give promise of the benefits of this research direction. Research based on the interactional processes of relational control and nonverbal affect (Escudero, Rogers, & Gutierrez, 1997) found that the analysis of each dimension added relational insight, but that it added more insight when the dimensions were analyzed in combination. The sequential analysis of conjointly coded control-affect message behaviors significantly expanded the descriptive and analytical power in identifying multiple pattern combinations and their impact on the relationships studied.

The investigation of different dimensions was extended in a recent study based on the inclusion of three simultaneously occurring facets of the participants' communication process (Heatherington, Escudero, & Friedlander, 2005). This research involved the combined investigation of relational control, the members' ongoing emotional response to partners' messages, and the cognitive construction of meaning expressed in the content of the messages. The conjoint analysis of these three dimensions, while analytically challenging, provided a more extensive systemic view of the members' relational dynamics.

In the studies just described, the dimensions included for expanding the relational communication perspective focused on the participants' views of the interaction process. Thus, this line of research also addresses the issue of giving more attention to the emotional and cognitive meaning of the individual members. Clearly, an integrated analysis of different dimensions offers a more comprehensive understanding of the interrelating process of communication and underscores the need to move in this direction.

Theories are typically seen as works in process, and this is the case with relational communication, with much accomplished and much to be done. Each of the directions outlined for future research will continue to advance the Relational Communication Theory and its emphasis on the value of studying interpersonal relationships from a communication perspective.

References

Bateson, G. (1935). Culture, contact and schismogenesis. *Man, 35,* 178–183.

Bateson, G. (1936). *Naven.* Cambridge, UK: Cambridge University Press.

Bateson, G. (1951). Information and codification: A philosophical approach. In J. Ruesch & G. Bateson (Eds.), *Communication: The social matrix of psychiatry* (pp. 168–211). New York: Norton.

Bateson, G. (1972). *Steps to an ecology of mind.* New York: Ballantine Books.

Bateson, G. (1979). *Mind and nature: A necessary unity.* New York: Bantam Books.

Berger, P., & Kellner, H. (1964). Marriage and the construction of reality: An exercise in the microsociology of knowledge. *Diogenes, 46,* 1–25.

Duncan, H. (1967). The search for a social theory of communication in American sociology. In F. Dance (Ed.), *Human communication theory* (pp. 236–263). New York: Holt, Rinehart & Winston.

Escudero, V., Rogers, L. E., & Gutierrez, E. (1997). Patterns of relational control and nonverbal affect in clinic and nonclinic couples. *Journal of Social and Personal Relationships, 14,* 5–29.

Heatherington, L., & Friedlander, M. (1987). *Family relational communication control coding system.* Unpublished coding manual, Department of Psychology, Williams College, Williamstown, MA.

Heatherington, L., & Friedlander, M. (2004). From dyads to triads, and beyond: Relational control in individual and family therapy. In L. E. Rogers & V. Escudero (Eds.), *Relational communication: An interactional perspective to the study of process and form* (pp. 103–129). Mahwah, NJ: Erlbaum.

Heatherington, L., Escudero, V., & Friedlander, M. (2005). Couple interaction during problem discussions: Toward an integrated methodology. *Journal of Family Communication, 5,* 191–207.

Kantor, D., & Lehr, W. (1975). *Inside the family: Toward a theory of family process.* San Francisco: Jossey-Bass.

Koestler, A. (1978). *Janus: A summing up.* New York: Vintage Books.

Millar, F., & Rogers, L. E. (1987). Relational dimensions of interpersonal dynamics. In M. Roloff & G. Miller (Eds.), *Explorations in interpersonal processes: New directions in communication research* (pp. 117–139). Newbury Park, CA: Sage.

Rogers, L. E., & Escudero, V. (Eds.). (2004). *Relational communication: An interactional perspective to the study of process and form.* Mahwah, NJ: Erlbaum.

Rogers, L. E., & Farace, R. (1975). Analysis of relational communication in dyads: New measurement procedures. *Human Communication Research, 1,* 222–239.

Sigman, S. (1995). *The consequentiality of communication.* Hillsdale, NJ: Erlbaum.

Sigman, S. (1998). Relationship and communication: A social communication and strongly consequential view. In R. Conville & L. E. Rogers (Eds.), *The meaning of "relationship" in interpersonal communication* (pp. 47–67). Westport, CT: Praeger.

von Bertalanffy, L. (1968). *General systems theory: Foundations, development, applications.* New York: Braziller.

Watzlawick, P., Beavin, J., & Jackson, D. (1967). *Pragmatics of human communication.* New York: Norton.

Wiener, N. (1948). *Cybernetics.* Cambridge: MIT Press.

26

Relational Dialectics Theory

Crafting Meaning from Competing Discourses

Leslie A. Baxter and Dawn O. Braithwaite

Relational Dialectics Theory (RDT) is a theory of the meaning-making between relationship parties that emerges from the interplay of competing discourses. "Discourses" are systems of meaning that are uttered whenever we make intelligible utterances aloud with others (or in our heads when we hold internal conversations). In its broadest sense, a discourse is a cultural system of meaning that circulates among a group's members and which makes our talk sensical. For example, in the United States the discourse of individualism helps us to understand and value an utterance such as, "I need to find myself first before I commit to a serious relationship with another person." Similarly, the discourse of "romantic love" helps us understand an utterance such as, "It was love at first sight." Systems of meaning can be more localized, as well. For example, when partners refer to one another with a favorite idiom, such as "chickadee," they might be invoking a core meaning system about themselves as a biracial couple. Whenever we communicate, we are invoking—often indirectly and by implication—multiple systems of meaning. These discourses often compete, oppose, and struggle with one another, however. We often hear these discursive struggles when people talk. Consider this statement about dating by a college student: "Well, I'm kinda, like, seeing him, but we're not, ya know, serious." This utterance displays a struggle in meaning. It draws on a discourse of connection or closeness ("I'm seeing him"), yet it also draws on a discourse of autonomy or distance ("We're not serious"). RDT focuses on the struggles in meaning—the discursive tensions—that frequent interpersonal communication. However, the position of the theory is not that competing discourses are negative. Instead, they are the heart of the meaning-making enterprise. The central claim of RDT is that such discursive tensions are both inevitable and necessary.

Purpose and Meta-theoretical Assumptions

If the paradigmatic menu of choice is the "Big Three"—post-positivistic, interpretive, and critical—RDT fits best within the interpretive camp. Like many interpretive theories, the goal of RDT is to show how particular meanings are socially constructed and sustained through everyday communicative activities. It relies primarily on qualitative methods with a goal of rendering a rich, evocative understanding of the meaning-making process, privileging the words and perspectives of the participants themselves. Thus, it works with meanings as its core analytic unit, not variables as found in the post-positivistic project. These meanings are local, or situated, rather than universal. The goal of RDT is not generalizability, but rather understanding particular, situated communication. Unlike the post-positivistic orientation, which seeks causal and predictive explanation, RDT seeks intelligibility, or understanding. The benchmark of assessment is thus its ability to be heuristic—to facilitate understanding of the meaning-making process.

However, as Deetz (2001) recently noted, interpretive studies are evolving. Some interpretive researchers have begun to challenge interpretivism's focus on consensual, unified, and shared meanings, emphasizing instead the fragmented and contested nature of meaning-making. Furthermore, some interpretive researchers have moved from the subjective sense-making of individual participants to focus on language use and discourses uttered between people. Deetz opened up a fourth paradigmatic orientation to capture this move away from unitary conceptions of meaning to a view of meaning-making as a contentious and fragmented process and away from individual consciousness to discourse. He called this fourth orientation "dialogic," and RDT best fits within this emerging tradition. RDT is grounded in the dialogism of the Russian philosopher Mikhail Bakhtin, thus it is not surprising that RDT aligns with the core assumptions of Deetz's dialogic orientation. Dialogic studies bears a "family resemblance" to the interpretive tradition, but challenges its focus on meanings as shared and seamless and its focus on the subjective experiences located inside individuals. We'll elaborate on both of these points as our discussion of RDT unfolds.

Main Features of the Theory

We present RDT by articulating three of its central propositions. Many complexities of the theory cannot be addressed here, and we refer the reader elsewhere for more extensive treatments (Baxter, 2004; Baxter & Montgomery, 1996). Although we present these propositions in list form, they mutually inform one another and must be understood as a whole.

Proposition 1. Meanings emerge from the struggle of different, often opposing, discourses.

Following Bakhtin (1984), all meaning-making can be understood metaphorically and literally as a dialogue, that is, the simultaneous fusion and differentiation of different systems of meaning, or discourses. To engage in everyday dialogue, participants must fuse their perspectives to some extent while sustaining the uniqueness of their individual perspectives. Conversation is a unity constructed from the interplay of different perspectives. All meaning-making can be understood as a "dialogue," which is the interpenetration of different, often opposing, perspectives or discourses. Bakhtin (1981) described language use as "a contradiction-ridden, tension-filled unity" of "verbal-ideological" tendencies (p. 272). "Verbal-ideological tendencies" are discourses.

RDT uses the term "dialectical" rather than "dialogic," although for our purposes the terms are interchangeable (Baxter & Montgomery, 1996). However, it is important to note that not all uses of "dialectical" are synonymous with Bakhtin's core metaphor of dialogue. Bakhtin (1986) was, in fact, quite critical of the deployment of Hegelian/Marxist dialectics that characterized the Stalinist Russia of his earlier life. In particular, he found this brand of dialectics to be overly mechanistic in its thesis-antithesis-synthesis conception of change. The tension-filled dynamic envisioned by Bakhtin is not represented well by the positioning of two logically binary forces (the thesis and the antithesis) which then get resolved in a synthesis. He was critical of dialectics removed from "living words"—which make up communication. Bakhtin's sense of dialogism is much closer to the sense of dialectics articulated by Murphy (1971), who argued that dialectics represents a general worldview that is "destructive of neat systems and ordered structures, and compatible with the notion of a social universe that has neither fixity or solid boundaries" (p. 90).

To argue that meaning-making is a process of dialectical flux between different, often opposing, discourses is to argue against a view of meaning as stable, consensual, and unitary. However, it would be false to conclude that RDT leaves us with semantic chaos and the inability to ever produce any meanings! We produce meaning all of the time when we interact with one another through the interplay of different discourses.

For example, let's consider the following conversational excerpt between two friends, Jill and Kathy:

1   Kathy: So, what's up, best-friend-since-3rd-grade? Haven't seen ya in a few

2   weeks—exams, job, life hassles, ya know, the usual stuff!

3 Jill: Yeah, it's been ages, it seems. Not uh, much, I uh guess. I sorta met

4 this new guy, Rob

5 Kathy: So, are you an "item" yet? Tell me all about it!

6 Jill: Well, we hooked up after that party, you know, the one

7 Kathy: after the losing game?

8 Jill: Yeah, that one. Well, it was great, and then, uh, he didn't uh, get back

9 to me in a few days, and I thought it was over but then, he called!

10 I think he just might be "the one," but it scares me to hear myself say that out loud!

11 Kathy: So, wanna bring him to my birthday party next week and "go public"?

12 Jill: We're not ready to be a couple yet! He's sorta uptight about getting involved

13 so soon after he broke up with his old girlfriend.

14 And I totally understand, I mean, I'm still hurt

15 Kathy: Remember your ex, Dave?? You were you know, a mess for a

16 month! Actually, you're still lickin' some wounds from that one!

17 Jill: We're kinda, ya know, taking it slow, just between us, so we don't get

18 uh, ya know, hurt.

19 Kathy: Ahhh, come on! If he's "the one," it's time! I wanna meet him!

We can identify several competing discourses that are at play in the process of meaning-making between Jill and Kathy. A discourse of romantic love renders intelligible Jill's statement that, after a few short weeks, she thinks she might have found "the one." However, playing with and against this discourse is Jill's statement that both she and Rob are hesitant about getting involved so soon after breaking up with their respective ex-partners. A discourse of individualism can be heard here that legitimates the value of "taking it slow" in order to protect self-interests and not get hurt. We can hear other discourses in play, also. Kathy is giving voice to a discourse of community in inviting Jill to "go public" with her new boyfriend, a discourse that expects relationships to have public identities embedded in social networks of friends and family. However, Jill declines the invitation, invoking a discourse of privacy in which relationship business is legitimated as private between the two parties. We can also hear a discourse of friendship, as the two jointly negotiate their friendship status.

The central proposition of RDT is that all of communication is rife with the tension-filled struggle of competing discourses—the discursive oppositions of sociality. An analysis of communication framed by RDT seeks to understand this dialectical process by (a) identifying the various discourses that are directly or indirectly invoked in talk to render utterances understandable and legitimate, and (b) asking how those discourses interpenetrate one another in the production of meaning. In this first proposition, we have elaborated on the first analytic step. The second analytic step will be emphasized in the second proposition.

> Proposition 2. The interpenetration of discourses is both synchronic and diachronic.

In the context of the second proposition, "diachronic" simply means occurring over time, whereas "synchronic" refers to one moment in time. Meanings do emerge in interactional moments, and in this sense, they are, at least momentarily, fixed and stable. But meaning is also fluid, which means that it is ultimately unfinalizable and "up for grabs" in the next interactional moment. In subsequent interactions, parties might jointly construct meaning to reproduce the old meaning, or they could jointly produce a new meaning. In either case—reproduction or production—meaning-making is envisioned as ongoing communicative work that results from the interanimation of different, often competing, discourses. RDT encourages us to tack between synchronic (in the moment) and diachronic (over time) analytic perspectives.

Some constructed meanings function to elide, or skirt, the struggle of discourses. For example, parties can jointly construct meaning centered in one discourse only, thereby privileging that discourse and muting other competing discourses. If Jill and Kathy conclude their exchange by agreeing to the privacy of Jill and Rob's relationship, this meaning will center the discourse of privacy over community. If over time Jill and Kathy repeatedly find themselves deferring to the discourse of privacy—allowing one another the right to keep secrets, and so on—then privacy has become what Bakhtin (1981) referred to as authoritative. Authoritative discourses are taken-for-granted or default meanings, accepted as "true" or "reasonable" on their face. However, Bakhtin argued that it is exceedingly effortful for parties to sustain authoritative discourses. Communication holds potentiality for rupture, challenging taken-for-granted meanings; centrifugal discourses, while removed from the authoritative center, are never completely eradicated.

The struggle of competing discourses is also evaded when relationship parties jointly construct meanings that involve an inversion across time with respect to which discourses are centered and which discourses are marginalized. This diachronic ebb and flow moves back and forth, with centered and marginalized discourses changing places in the meaning-making process. Let's return to Jill and Kathy. Let's suppose that on this occasion they agree to grant privacy to Jill and Rob's relationship. However, the next time they meet, Kathy persuades Jill to bring Rob to a dinner and movie. At a later point, Jill and Rob retreat once again into privacy. Such ebb-and-flow inversions are common patterns of meaning-making by relationship partners (Baxter, 2004), but they elide the discursive struggles by constructing them in the form of either-or dilemmas.

Discursive struggles are also skirted when relationship parties construct ambiguous or equivocal meanings. One of the meanings "at stake" in this sample exchange is the identity of Jill and Kathy as best friends. A discourse of friendship makes sensical several utterances in the exchange. For example, Kathy opens the conversation in Line 1 by reminding Jill that they have been best friends since third grade, which she follows up with an excuse for why she has not behaved like a best friend lately. This excuse evidences a discourse of individualism, in which the events of Kathy's life took priority over taking time out to keep in touch with Jill. Yet the act of providing an excuse recognizes that an expectation of friendship was violated. Jill's reply in Line 3 functions to construct ambiguity surrounding the status of Kathy's identity as a best friend. Jill does not directly refute Kathy's failure to attend to her, nor does she directly affirm that Kathy has been her best friend since childhood. A discourse of privacy renders intelligible her evident hesitation to disclose about her new boyfriend, who only later we discover might be "the one." Jill equivocates in Line 3, saying, "Not much, I guess." However, the discourse of friendship would not have anticipated such hesitation and equivocation on Jill's part in sharing what is such important news in her life. Kathy's response in Line 5 challenges the ambiguity of Jill's utterance with respect to the "new guy," but interestingly she lets stand the ambiguity of Jill's statement with respect to their best friendship. The rest of the conversation can be read at one level as discursive work by Jill and Kathy to restore their best friendship, although this is done "between the lines" throughout. Notice that by the end of the conversation we do not have an explicit commitment from Jill about whether she will be attending her best friend's birthday party and whether she will defer to Kathy's desire to meet Rob—further evidence of ambiguity concerning Kathy's identity as a "best friend." The ambiguity that surrounds Kathy's identity as a "best friend" slips between the discourses of friendship, privacy, and individualism. All discourses can be heard as legitimated, depending on how one wishes to interpret the ambiguity. In this sense, ambiguity functions as a discursive lubricant that allows meaning to maneuver between discourses.

In contrast to the kinds of meaning constructions discussed to this point is communicative work characterized by a mixture of competing discourses. One of these discursive mixtures is what Bakhtin (1981, p. 358) called a "hybrid," which is a mixing of discrete discursive meaning systems. Think of hybrids as salad dressing made by mixing oil and vinegar. The discourses (oil and vinegar) are distinct, yet they combine to form a new meaning—salad dressing. Let's suppose that Jill and Kathy strike a compromise meaning at the end of their conversation: Jill agrees to bring Rob to Kathy's birthday party, but he is not to be introduced as Jill's boyfriend. This compromise meaning is a hybrid.

It combines the discourses of friendship (Jill complies with her friend's request, and Kathy honors her friend's desire not to be hurt) with the discourse of community (with Jill and Rob going to Kathy's party) and the discourse of privacy (with Rob's status as "the one" being kept secret).

Another kind of discursive mixture is what Bakhtin (1990, p. 67) referred to as an aesthetic moment—that is, meaning-making in which discourses are no longer framed as oppositional but instead merge in a way that profoundly alters each meaning system. These aesthetic meanings of consummation or wholeness are crafted along new discursive lines. Think of aesthetic moments as akin to what chemists call "reactions."[1] For example, two molecules of hydrogen combine with one molecule of oxygen to produce an entirely new entity—water. Let's suppose that Jill and Kathy continue to talk and verbalize that the key to their best friendship since third grade is that they have always given each other the room to grow in separate directions and that this always brings them even closer. Such a construction—one that transforms independence and closeness in a way that no longer positions them as oppositional but rather reinforces them as integral to one another—might be classified as an aesthetic moment in their relationship. It functions to consummate the meaning of their friendship in ways that implode heretofore opposing discourses.

We have not exhausted the domain of possible ways in which meaning-making emerges from the play of different discourses, but we trust we have given you a concrete feeling for what the interpenetration process looks like. Interpenetration, in turn, is the linchpin for the third proposition.

Proposition 3. The interpenetration of competing discourses constitutes social reality.

In the third proposition, RDT joins a growing number of theories committed to a constitutive view (see Craig, 1999, for a review). This view positions communication as constitutive of the social world, not merely representational of an objective world that precedes communication. As Bakhtin (writing as Voloshinov, 1973, p. 85) put it, "It is not experience that organizes expression, but the other way around—expression organizes experience." What is unique about RDT is its articulation of the mechanism by which such construction takes place: the tensionality of difference (Baxter, 2006).

The constitutive process includes a decentering of the sovereign self, a construct that has been with us since the Enlightenment and that undergirds most theories of interpersonal communication. According to these theories, the sovereign self's dispositions, attitudes and beliefs, social positions, and goals are thought to precede communication. Communication is deployed by the sovereign self to serve that self's goals, typically to represent internal states, feelings, beliefs, and thoughts. By contrast, according to RDT, consciousness and identity are formed through communication with an Other. In everyday life, we encounter different Others and serve as an Other on an ongoing basis.

Fluidity characterizes this process of Other-ing, because a given Other is never stable but always in the process of becoming someone else. Consciousness and identity, then, are fluid and dynamic relations between different perspectives. For RDT the question is not how individuals, conceived as sovereign selves, deploy communication to represent their internal states or to self-present to others. Rather, the question is how difference constructs consciousness and identity. Consciousness and identity are meanings forged from the interpenetration of differences, just as any other meanings are. They are the consequence of discursive tensions. We examined above how Kathy's identity as Jill's best friend was discursively constructed in the talk between Kathy and Jill. We could just as easily shift our gaze to Jill's identity and ask how she is constructed as someone who is (not) part of an "item."

By extension, relationships are also meaning-ed, and thus constructed from the interpenetration of discursive tensions, just as consciousness and identity are. In contrast to other theories in which relationships are positioned as containers in which communication occurs (the communication-in-relationships view), RDT inverts this logic and articulates a relationships-in-communication view (Baxter, 2004). Relationships are made through the ongoing discursive competitions of everyday interaction between the parties and between the parties and members of their social network. The conversation between Kathy and Jill above functioned to construct their relationship as friends, perhaps reproducing it, perhaps giving it a new meaning. At the same time, the exchange between Jill and Kathy functioned to construct the Jill-Rob relationship by giving it a social identity short of "item" status.

The constitutive proposition in RDT moves us away from questions about individual subjectivity and the strategic deployment of communication to accomplish desired goals. Instead, it moves us to a focus on discourse and the joint communicative activities of parties.

Conceptualization of Communication in the Theory

As should be evident from the third proposition of RDT, communication is given constitutive force. Rather than presupposing that the world exists "out there" prior to communication, a view that positions communication as a representational device, RDT joins other social constructionist theories in positioning communication as the constitutive mechanism through which we make the social world meaningful. Of course, as we discussed in the second proposition, meanings can be reproduced and produced. If meanings are reproduced long enough, we come to think of them as representations of phenomena that are "real." Reproduced meanings take on an authoritative force. But even entrenched, reproduced meanings hold the potential for emergent meanings, according to dialogism and RDT.

Uses of the Theory

Space limitations do not permit us more than a summary of the kinds of research questions and methods that have been framed by RDT (for more extensive reviews of research, see Baxter, 2004; Baxter & Montgomery, 1996). In general, most researchers to date have emphasized only the first proposition of RDT, identifying competing discourses.

Several researchers have asked, "What are the oppositions that animate X?" where "X" can be a relationship type, an interpersonal process, or a given social phenomenon. When this question is answered inductively, scholars usually analyze qualitatively textual data of some kind, often interview transcripts, in search of their underlying oppositions. Typical of this approach is a study of elderly residents of a retirement community conducted by Williams and Guendouzi (2000). These authors interviewed elderly residents with an eye toward identifying the discursive oppositions that organized their familial relationships and their relationships with peers. Discourses of autonomy and connection were pervasive in the data.

Researchers have functioned deductively and quantitatively in answering the generic question, "What is the salience of given oppositions for X?" where X is again a relationship type, an interpersonal process, or a given social phenomenon. These researchers start with given oppositions and then determine participant perceptions of their salience or intensity. For example, Pawlowski (1998) presented married partners with a set of six commonly identified oppositions identified in the research literature (Werner & Baxter, 1994) and asked them to indicate, on five-point scales, the degree of importance for each of three kinds of relationship turning points identified by the participants. Although quantitative studies such as this are useful in identifying the relative salience of abstract oppositional pairs, they lack rich, evocative insight into the situation-specific dynamics of discursive oppositions.

Researchers have also focused narrowly on a single pair of opposing discourses, examining this opposition in depth. For example Sahlstein (2004) focused narrowly on the basic opposition of togetherness and apartness that constitute long-distance romantic relationships.

Much less attention has been given to RDT's Propositions 2 and 3. Researchers have provided us with a rich list of discursive oppositions across various relationship types, processes, and phenomena, but they have paid insufficient attention to how these oppositions interpenetrate and the meanings that are constituted from this interplay. Baxter and Braithwaite (2002) provided us with an example of a study that focuses on the synchronic construction of meaning through the interanimation of discursive oppositions in their study of marriage renewal vows. Through interviews with long-term married couples, these researchers identified a dominant discourse of community and a more muted discourse of individualism. Together, the interplay of these competing discourses in the enactment of the renewal event constructed what marriage meant to these couples: it is a complex semantic cloth woven from strands of public accountability to others, social embeddedness with family and friends, the expectation of permanence, romantic love, individual choice, and individual growth.

To the extent that research examines the diachronic construction of meaning, it lacks a longitudinal focus. Instead, researchers have inferred diachronic processes by asking participants to provide recollections of how their relationship communication has changed over time. For example, Johnson, Wittenberg, M. Villagran, Mazur, and P. Villagran (2003) interviewed participants from a relational dialectics perspective to solicit their retrospective identification of turning points—points of increased or decreased closeness—in friendship types.

We end this section with a brief discussion of misuses of RDT. We caution readers against certain kinds of research efforts, because they are incompatible with RDT. First, so-called one-hand-clapping research does not inform us about discursive tensions. A one-hand-clapping study examines a single discourse and attempts to draw inferences about the validity of RDT. For example, determining which topics are avoided by relationship parties is a legitimate topic of interest, but we can infer nothing relevant to RDT unless we simultaneously examine how the discourse of discretion, which renders topic avoidance intelligible, interanimates with the discourse of candor, which would declare all topics appropriate for discussion. Second, discursive tensions are not psychological needs or motivations. RDT decenters the sovereign self in the shift to discourse as the focus of attention. When participants talk about their feelings and beliefs, they are discursively constructing the sovereign self, as well as invoking other discourses such as patriarchy, individualism, romantic love, and so on. Third, it is not fruitful to ask whether the presence or absence of discursive oppositions correlates with any variety of possible relationship outcomes, such as satisfaction. According to RDT, and dialogism more generally, discursive tensions are inherent in the meaning-making enterprise. The issue is not whether these tensions are good or bad, per se; rather, the issue is whether the relating parties constitute meaning from the interpenetration of opposing discourses in ways that are productive. Fourth, interpersonal conflicts are not the equivalent of discursive tensions. Interpersonal conflict is a genre of communication that emphasizes person-against-person. By contrast, RDT focuses on discourse-against-discourse. Sometimes a given person articulates one discourse and the other person aligns with an opposing discourse, in which case we have an instance of conflict that manifests an embodied discursive opposition. However, probably more often discourses do not have such a tidy one-to-one correspondence with embodied persons. Competing discourses often are articulated within the utterances of one person.

Strengths and Limitations of the Theory

Because RDT offers us a complex theory of meaning-making, a model that emphasizes fragmentation and struggle, it is not easy to understand or to master. To many, this is a limitation of the theory. However, this characteristic can be regarded as a strength, simultaneously. Because meaning-making is complex, it necessitates a theory that captures this complexity. An additional strength of RDT is that it gives us a theory centered directly in communication, rather than a theory rooted in psychological or sociological constructs. Furthermore, RDT is a theory about process, a feature most scholars of interpersonal communication regard as central. To us, and to many of our students, RDT succeeds in helping us understand the pushes and pulls implicated in communication in our relationships. However, we will let you, the reader, have the final judgment on the heurism of the theory. If you find it illuminating about communication in relationships, then you share our view that RDT fares well on the heurism criterion.

We often hear RDT criticized because it fails to predict anything about communication in relationships. We agree that the theory lacks prediction capacity, but we would note that this criterion is suited to the post-positivistic project, not the interpretive paradigm. We hear the criticism that the theory has no new news—that researchers keep identifying the same basic discursive tensions over and over again. We think that this criticism holds merit, with the caveat that sometimes apparent similarity belies nuanced differences that are situation specific. Nonetheless, we urge researchers to move beyond the first proposition to engage the issue of how meanings are constituted from the interpenetration of opposing discourses. In doing so, RDT research will be more responsive to the criticism of, "So what?" It means little for researchers to simply list discursive tensions unless they also take the next step of rendering intelligible how the struggle of competing discourses constitutes meaning.

Directions for Future Research and Applications

RDT researchers need to move beyond the listing project of Proposition 1 to address the interpenetration process emphasized in Propositions 2 and 3, because meanings are made when discourses are in play with and against one another. A second suggestion for future research is the need for longitudinal work that allows us to better understand meaning-making as a synchronic and diachronic process. Third, researchers need to study discourses, not the internal states of sovereign individuals. RDT does not view the uttered word as a window to a person's internal subjectivity; rather, RDT views uttered words to be understandable as traces embedded within larger meaning systems: discourses. Fourth, and last, in order to do justice to the integrity of the concept of discourse, researchers will need to embed utterances in a richer "chain of speech communion" (Bakhtin, 1986, p. 93) than is characteristic of RDT research to date. Shifting from isolated utterances, or even single conversations, to the more complete utterance "chain" will involve taking into analytic account three different kinds of data. The first kind of data is the discursive history of past utterances in the relationship. Such a discursive history helps contextualize talk in the present between parties, placing their past in conversation with their present. The second kind of data is the broader cultural discourse that relationship parties jointly draw on as resources in making intelligible utterances in the present. We have emphasized this analytic move in this chapter, thereby illustrating how the study of communication in relationships moves outside the boundary of the relational dyad. The third kind of data is the anticipated responses from others (including the relationship parties themselves) in the future. Anticipated responses include those of generalized others (e.g., society in general), providing parties with a moral anchor by which to assess the appropriateness of their utterances in the present. This moral anchor provides parties with discourses of the ideal.

Note

1. The authors thank Meryl Carlson for the chemical analogy.

References

Bakhtin, M. M. (1981). *The dialogic imagination: Four essays by M. M. Bakhtin* (M. Holquist, Ed.; C. Emerson & M. Holquist, Trans.). Austin: University of Texas Press.

Bakhtin, M. M. (1984). *Problems of Dostoevsky's poetics* (C. Emerson, Ed. and Trans.). Minneapolis: University of Minnesota Press.

Bakhtin, M. M. (1986). *Speech genres and other late essays* (C. Emerson & M. Holquist, Eds.; V. McGee, Trans.). Austin: University of Texas Press.

Bakhtin, M. M. (1990). *Art and answerability: Early philosophical essays by M. M. Bakhtin* (M. Holquist & V. Liapunov, Eds.; V. Liapunov, Trans.). Austin: University of Texas Press.

Baxter, L. A. (2004). Distinguished scholar article: Relationships as dialogues. *Personal Relationships, 11*, 1–22.

Baxter, L. A. (2006). Communication as dialogue. In G. J. Shepherd, J. St. John, & T. Striphas (Eds.), *Communication as . . . perspectives on theory* (pp. 101–109). Thousand Oaks, CA: Sage.

Baxter, L. A., & Braithwaite, D. O. (2002). Performing marriage: Marriage renewal rituals as cultural performance. *Southern Communication Journal, 67,* 94–109.

Baxter, L. A., & Montgomery, B. M. (1996). *Relating: Dialogues & dialectics.* New York: Guilford Press.

Craig, R. T. (1999). Communication theory as a field. *Communication Theory, 9,* 119–161.

Deetz, S. (2001). Conceptual foundations. In F. M. Jablin & L. L. Putnam (Eds.), *The new handbook of organizational communication* (pp. 3–46). Thousand Oaks, CA: Sage.

Johnson, A. J., Wittenberg, E., Villagran, M. M., Mazur, M., & Villagran, P. (2003). Relational progression as a dialectic: examining turning points in communication among friends. *Communication Monographs, 70,* 230–249.

Murphy, R. (1971). *The dialectics of social life.* New York: Basic Books.

Pawlowski, D. R. (1998). Dialectical tensions in marital partners' accounts of their relationships. *Communication Quarterly, 46,* 396–412.

Sahlstein, E. M. (2004). Relating at a distance. *Journal of Social and Personal Relationships, 21,* 689–710.

Voloshinov, V. N. (1973). *Marxism and the philosophy of language* (L. Matejka & I. R. Titunik, Trans.). Cambridge, MA: Harvard University Press.

Werner, C. M., & Baxter, L. A. (1994). Temporal qualities of relationships: Organismic, transactional, and dialectical views. In M. L. Knapp & G. R. Miller (Eds.), *Handbook of interpersonal communication* (pp. 323–379). Newbury Park, CA: Sage.

Williams, A., & Guendouzi, J. (2000). Adjusting to "the home": Dialectical dilemmas and personal relationships in a retirement community. *Journal of Communication, 50,* 65–82.

27

Stage Theories of Relationship Development

Charting the Course of Interpersonal Communication

Paul A. Mongeau and Mary Lynn Miller Henningsen

Shrek: [Yelling] Layers! Onions have layers. Ogres have layers. Onions have layers. Ogres have layers. You get it? We both have layers.

Donkey: Oh, you both have layers. You know, not everybody likes onions.

(Warner, Williams, Katzenberg, Adamson, & Jenson, 2001)

C lose personal relationships with friends, coworkers, and lovers adapt, evolve, and change over time. This chapter focuses on two Stage Theories that attempt to describe how people initiate, escalate, and dissolve relationships. More specifically, these theories explain how and why interpersonal communication changes as relationships move from strangers or acquaintances to close friends or romantic partners, and perhaps back again. In this chapter, we describe and then evaluate the functions of Stage Theories, the stages proposed in two theories, and the role of communication in these theories.

This chapter describes two Stage Theories: Social Penetration Theory and the Staircase Model. Before defining the theories, we want to explain why we call Social Penetration a theory but refer to the Staircase as a model. In most social scientific scholarship, theories provide both explanations of, and predictions about, a phenomenon. Social Penetration Theory both describes relationship development through stages and provides a number of predictions (framed in terms of resources, costs, benefits, and outcomes) about movement among stages. Conversely, the Staircase Model provides a description of relationship stages, and does not develop clear predictions concerning movement among stages. We will consistently refer to Social Penetration "Theory" and the Staircase "Model," but we will use the term "theory" when referring to both together (i.e., Social Penetration Theory and the Staircase Model).

Purpose and Meta-theoretical Assumptions

PURPOSE OF STAGE THEORIES

To fully explain Stage Theories, we need to start with a brief history lesson (see also Chapter 1, this volume). Until the early 1970s, there were virtually no undergraduate courses, textbooks, or even much thinking about interpersonal communication. The common view of interpersonal communication was situational, where interpersonal communication occurred whenever a small number of people communicated face to face with immediate feedback and with no mediating devices (e.g., telephones, e-mail, or text messaging) coming between them (Miller & Steinberg, 1975). During the 1970s, the situational view of interpersonal communication was replaced by a developmental view where the physical context was deemed less important than who the partners were to each other and how (and what) they communicated. In short order, scholars in social psychology (Altman & Taylor, 1973), sociology (Davis, 1973) and the new subdiscipline of interpersonal communication (e.g., Knapp, 1978; Miller & Steinberg, 1975) focused scholarly attention on how and why interpersonal communication in relationships changed and developed over time. Several scholars tried to identify the stages of relationship development and deterioration. Although other theories were developed about the same time (e.g., Berger & Calabrese, 1975), we will focus our chapter on two related efforts: the stages in Altman and Taylor's (1973) Social Penetration Theory and Knapp and Vangelisti's (2005; see also Knapp, 1978) Staircase Model.

PARADIGMATIC ASSUMPTIONS OF STAGE THEORIES

Stage Theories have post-positivistic roots, but they also have both dialectic and social constructionist elements. Stage Theories' post-positivistic roots stem from Social Penetration Theory (Altman & Taylor, 1973), which included a series of broad, a priori hypotheses about the causes and effects of interpersonal communication. Researchers could directly observe and measure social penetration and could compare these observations to the theory's predictions.

Although Stage Theories have clear objectivist roots, they share assumptions with both social constructionist and dialectical perspectives. Stage Theories describe relationships, their development, and their de-escalation as communicative processes where people construct, reconstruct, and deconstruct their relationships through verbal and nonverbal communication. Furthermore, Altman, Vinsel, & Brown (1981) cast social penetration and relationship development in dialectical terms, suggesting that relational development is not a one-way street toward greater openness, intimacy, and understanding. Instead, a number of contradictory forces simultaneously draw partners toward both greater openness and greater privacy (see also Chapter 26, this volume).

Main Features of the Theories

The three major features of Stage Theories of Relationship Development are (a) the stages themselves, (b) the rules concerning movement through stages, and (c) the ways that interpersonal communication differs across stages. We focus on the first two features in this section and discuss the role of communication in the next.

RELATIONSHIP STAGES

These theories (i.e., Stage Theories of Relationship Development; Altman & Taylor, 1973; Knapp & Vangelisti, 2005) share several important assumptions and characteristics. This is true, in large part, because Knapp and Vangelisti (2005) acknowledged the intellectual contribution of Social Penetration Theory in the development of their model. First, both Stage Theories (i.e., the Social Penetration Theory and the Staircase Model) presume that relationship development is characterized by changes in interpersonal communication. Specifically, as relationships develop, communication shifts from superficial and noninterpersonal to intimate and personal. Second, both theories focus on the development and on the deterioration of relationships. Altman and Taylor (1973) argued that the process of relationship de-escalation is the opposite of relationship development (i.e., like a video clip shown in reverse). In relationship de-escalation, partners work through the same relational stages, but they are going in the opposite direction. Third, both theories use a similar organizing metaphor (i.e., social penetration or social intercourse).

Although there are important similarities between the theories there appear to be two basic differences, as well (for detailed comparison, see K. Miller, 2005). First, Knapp and Vangelisti's (2005) model presents separate sets of stages for escalation and de-escalation. Second, Knapp and Vangelisti focus almost exclusively on communication, while Altman and Taylor (1973) balance both communicative and psychological processes (e.g., assessments of rewards and costs; impression formation).

STAGES OF SOCIAL PENETRATION

According to Social Penetration Theory (Altman & Taylor, 1973), relationships develop and de-escalate via changes in verbal, nonverbal, and environmentally oriented behaviors (e.g., access to special possessions or places). Changes in verbal communication focus on self-disclosure (i.e., the process of telling the other person things about the self). Altman and Taylor described the development of self-disclosure using an onion metaphor (which explains our opening quotation from the movie *Shrek*). Imagine that all the information about yourself is somewhere inside an onion. The onion has four layers: the surface, the periphery, and the intermediate and central layers. As information is disclosed, the layers of the onion are peeled back, signifying the development of the relationship.

Information on the "surface" includes the things that others can learn just by looking at you (e.g., sex, race, and approximate age). Just below the surface is the "peripheral" level. This level includes information that you would share in just about any social circumstance (e.g., your first name, college major, hometown). Peeling layers from the periphery leads to the "intermediate" layers. This layer contains information that you share occasionally, but that you do not exactly keep hidden. For example, Paul does not tell just anyone that his freshman year in college were the four happiest years of his life, and Min does not often share that she loved the History of Concrete episode of *Modern Marvels*. (OK, we just told everyone reading this book, but we are all good friends now, right?) Finally, peeling layers beyond the intermediate levels leads to the "central" levels where information is private and is disclosed cautiously (Altman & Taylor, 1973).

Altman and Taylor (1973) presented four stages of relationship development that are defined by the depth (i.e., how personal the information communicated is) and breadth (i.e., the sheer number of topics discussed) of self-disclosure (see Table 27.1). An initial interaction between strangers would be a typical example of Altman and Taylor's first stage, "orientation." These interactions typically involve little personal sharing. New coworkers, for example, might share a broad range of surface information such as where they went to school or their hometowns, but no information past the periphery.

The second stage, "exploratory affective exchange," includes relationships such as casual acquaintances or people known only from work or school, and involves mutual disclosure of a wider array of information. Disclosure continues and broadens in topic at the periphery, and, on certain topics may include information from the intermediate levels. Partners exhibit nonverbal cues (e.g., eye contact, facial expressions, touch, and body movements) that reflect a

Table 27.1   Social Penetration Theory Stages, Definitions, and Examples from the Movie *Shrek*

Stage	Definition	Example from Shrek
Orientation	Initial interactions between strangers that involve very little personal sharing	When Shrek and Fiona initially meet . . . Fiona: You're an ogre. Shrek: Oh, you're expecting Prince Charming? Fiona: Well, yes, actually. This is all wrong. You are not supposed to be an ogre.
Exploratory affective exchange	Mutual disclosure between the dyad on a wider range of topics (though the topics largely remain at the periphery and occasionally intermediate levels)	Shrek and Fiona are eating rotisserie style swamp rat . . . Shrek: Maybe you can come and visit me in the swamp sometime. I'll cook all kinds of stuff for you—swamp toad soup, fish eye tartar. You name it. Fiona: I'd like that.
Affective exchange	Communication between the members of the dyad: open at the periphery with increasing disclosure at the intermediate and central levels	Just after Fiona turns into an ogre . . . Shrek: Fiona,[He pulls Fiona closer] I love you. Fiona: Do you really? Shrek: Really, really. Fiona: [Sighs] I love you, too.
Stable exchange	Communication open at all levels (i.e., surface, peripheral, intermediate, and central)	Fiona is permanently transformed into an ogre and passes out on the floor. Shrek pulls her to her feet . . . Shrek: Fiona? Are you all right? Fiona: Well, yes . . . But I don't understand. I was supposed to be beautiful. Shrek: [Smiling] But you are beautiful.

SOURCE: Warner et al., 2001.

desire to get to know the partner and that correspond to the increases in the depth of verbal disclosures. At this stage, information at the central level remains closely guarded and not disclosed.

Altman and Taylor's (1973) third stage, "affective exchange," includes close friendships or romantic relationships "in which people know one another well and have had a fairly extensive history of escalation" (p. 139). In this stage, communication at the peripheral layers is open and broad. Important to this stage, though, is heightened activity at the intermediate and central levels. Partners have removed many barriers that inhibited communication on private issues. Unlike earlier stages, communication at the central level does occur, but it is guarded and is not performed as freely as communication at the peripheral and intermediate levels.

Partners in few relationships reach the final level of "stable exchange." At this level, partners are likely granted access to nearly all information on all topics and at all levels (i.e., surface, peripheral, intermediate, and central). Consequently, partners know each other extremely well. However, Altman and Taylor (1973) cautioned that social penetration is never total, and despite considerable verbal, nonverbal, and environmentally oriented exchanges, partners are still somewhat of a mystery to each other. Predictive and explanatory abilities are never perfect.

In Social Penetration Theory, Altman and Taylor (1973) refered to relationship deterioration and dissolution as a social depenetration process, and claimed that it was the mirror of the penetration process. In particular, relationships break up because partners withdraw intimate self-disclosure on an increasing number of topics over time.

KNAPP AND VANGELISTI'S STAGES OF DEVELOPMENT AND DETERIORATION

A communication scholar, Knapp (1978), developed his own stages of relationship development and deterioration, based, in part, on the stages from Social Penetration Theory. The metaphor Knapp (1978; Knapp & Vangelisti, 2005) chose was a staircase, where each relational stage represented a different step. Relational development was represented by movement up the steps along the left-hand side of the staircase, while dissolution was represented by movement down the steps along the right-hand side of the staircase. Between the two sets of stages is a stabilizing section where partners can remain if the state of the relationship is acceptable to both parties.

Knapp and Vangelisti (2005) proposed five stages of coming together. First, "initiating" involves opening channels of communication and initial contact between partners. Second, "experimenting" allows partners to get to know each other better by moving from superficial to more personal communication. Third, Knapp and Vangelisti asserted that partners complete the "intensifying" stage: acknowledge the unique and special nature of their relational connection. The fourth stage of relationship development is "integrating," when the two partners figuratively become a single entity. Communication becomes easy between partners and they share nearly everything with each other, even their most personal secrets. Through the integrating phase, Knapp and Vangelisti's stages are similar to Altman and Taylor's (1973). The final stage of relational development in Knapp and Vangelisti's model, "bonding," has no analogue in Altman and Taylor's theory. Bonding, such as a marriage ceremony, represents the formalization and public recognition of the couple and cements a legal, personal, and social bond between partners.

Knapp and Vangelisti (2005) also described five stages of relationship dissolution that mirror, for the most part, their stages of development. First, "differentiating" involves partners separating themselves from the couple and focusing on their uniqueness. The next stage of dissolution is "circumscribing," where partners engage in less frequent and less personal communication. In the third dissolution stage, "stagnating," partners communicate negative feelings nonverbally and tend to imagine interaction (e.g., "I'll say this and then she'll say that and then she'll slam the door and then I'll go drink with my buddies") rather than repeat past fights. In the fourth stage, "avoiding," the partners attempt to increase physical and psychological space to prepare themselves for life without their partner. The final stage of dissolution is "termination" or the actual ending of the relationship (i.e., couple or friendship). Termination can occur during an initial interaction, after a long relationship, or anywhere in between.

MOVEMENT ACROSS AND BETWEEN STAGES

Social Penetration Theory (Altman & Taylor, 1973) presumes that rewards and costs associated with interpersonal interactions drive relationship development. People seek relationships that provide maximum rewards with minimum costs, in both present interactions and interactions projected to the future. Altman and Taylor's definitions of rewards and costs are similar to those described in Social Exchange Theories (see Chapter 28, this volume). Essentially, relational development is predicted if rewards exceed costs (i.e., outcomes are positive), outcomes surpass general expectations for relationships (i.e., outcomes are greater than comparison level, or *CL*), and perceived outcomes from the next best alternative (perhaps even being alone) are less than current outcomes (i.e., outcomes are greater than comparison level for alternatives, or *CL*alt).

Knapp and Vangelisti (2005) also presented a number of guidelines for movement between stages. In particular, they argued, "Movement is generally systematic and sequential. Movement may be forward. Movement may be backward. Movement occurs within stages. Movement is always to a new place" (p. 47). In addition, they claim that partners should not skip stages because he or she might miss important information concerning the partner.

Both theories (Altman & Taylor; 1973; Knapp & Vangelisti, 2005) describe processes of development and dissolution that appear to be linear (i.e., a gradual progression toward increased or decreased intimacy). Closer inspection of both theories, however, suggests that movement through stages may not be linear. For example, Altman and Taylor claimed that relationship development "ebbs and flows, does not follow a linear course, and cycles and recycles through levels of exchange" (p. 135). The Staircase Model suggests that movement through the model can be unpredictable. Just because a couple advances to intensifying does not mean that integrating is the inevitable next stage. Instead, they could move back to experimenting, slide to circumscribing, or terminate altogether. Further discussion about the linear nature of these theories can be found in the section below on the strengths and limitations of Stage Theories.

Conceptualization of Communication in the Theories

"Communication is critical in developing and maintaining interpersonal relationships" (Taylor & Altman, 1987, p. 257). Communication is not only the mechanism through which relationships develop (and dissolve) but also a marker for the movement through stages. Both Stage Theories differentiate stages from one another through verbal and nonverbal communication. As relationships develop and dissolve, a number of important changes occur in the nature of interpersonal communication.

Within Social Penetration Theory (Altman & Taylor, 1973), relationships develop by increasing the breadth and depth of self-disclosures as well as corresponding changes in nonverbal and environmentally oriented communication. The reverse would be true of dissolving relationships. Within the Staircase Model (Knapp & Vangelisti, 2005) as relationships develop, communication changes along a number of dimensions. Specifically, as relationships develop, communication becomes more unique, that is, more specific to the two individuals involved (i.e., a stylized-unique dimension). Specific verbal and nonverbal behaviors come to have a private meaning available only to the two people involved. In addition, communication becomes more efficient (i.e., the difficult-efficient dimension). More information is communicated through fewer behaviors, in part because of the idiosyncratic meaning systems that are generated. Communication also becomes better synchronized (i.e., communication meshes better; i.e., the awkward-smooth dimension). Partners can finish each other's sentences and engage in animated discussions without interrupting. Finally, partners gain the ability to communicate the same meaning in a number of different ways (i.e., substitutability). For example, comforting a close partner can occur verbally, but the same meaning can be communicated in other ways as well (e.g., a calm tone of voice, a shoulder rub, or a hug).

Uses of the Theories

The use of Stage Theories is a bit of a contradiction. Even though they have helped generate a better understanding of interpersonal communication, there have been few direct tests of these theories (for reasons we will describe in the next section). Although rarely tested directly, Stage Theories have been credited with generating scholarly interest in a wide variety of communication topics. For example, Welch and Rubin (2002) argued that Knapp's (1978) early explication of relationship dimensions (i.e., narrow-broad, public-personal, stylized-unique, difficult-efficient, rigid-flexible, awkward-smooth, hesitant- spontaneous, overt judgment suspended–overt judgment given) contributed to other scholars' interest in the way relationships are defined (often implicitly) through communication (e.g., Burgoon & Hale, 1987). Researchers still study the dimensions underlying the relational meaning of communication (e.g., Dillard, Solomon, & Palmer, 1999; see also Chapter 8, this volume).

Katherine Miller (2005) similarly argued that research on self-disclosure in a variety of contexts owes an intellectual debt to Social Penetration Theory. Reviews of self-disclosure research (e.g., Dindia, 2000) remain supportive of many of the roles and functions of communication in relationship development as outlined within Social Penetration Theory. Recent research on self-disclosure in specific contexts such as same-sex friendships (e.g., Sanderson, Rahm, & Beigbeder, 2005), doctor-patient interactions (e.g., Agne, Thompson, & Cusella, 2000), and research on avoiding communication in families (e.g., Afifi, 2005) reaffirm the importance of the Stage Theories of Relationship Development.

Other research owes an intellectual debt to the Stage Theories we are examining in this chapter. Duck (1982) developed a model of relationship dissolution (without a corresponding set of states for relationship development) that focused as much on the surrounding social network as it does the couple involved. Moreover, Duck contended that the disengagement process lasts far beyond termination. Even our own work on date initiation and romantic relationship transitions—how relationships make the shift from platonic (or nonexistent) to romantic—stems in important ways from these Stage Theories (Mongeau, Serewicz, Henningsen, & Davis, 2006). For example, the nature of the transition differs strongly depending on the couple's previous developmental stage.

Despite the heuristic value and the role the Stage Theories have had in generating scholarship, the theories are not without problematic elements. In the next section we briefly discuss the strengths and limitations of Stage Theories.

Strengths and Limitations of the Theories

The breadth and range of Stage Theories represents both a strength and a limitation. Few communication theories can boast the scope or influence of Social

Penetration Theory. Due in part to its broad perspective, Social Penetration Theory and the other Stage Theories generated a great deal of interest in the study of close personal relationships. These Stage Theories provided scholars and students with an initial road map of how relationships might develop and dissolve and have allowed scholars to gain a much better understanding of these processes. Stages of relationships, whether from Social Penetration Theory or the Staircase Model, provided a clear description of coming together, escalating, de-escalating, and ending relationships.

In describing Social Penetration Theory, Miller (2005) stated, "the theory has been widely used as a model in teaching about interpersonal relationships and as an overarching framework for considering relational development" (p. 175). The Stage Theories offer a step-by-step view of relationships. Understanding the progression from stage to stage, the mechanisms for moving forward and backward, and the stabilization of relationships at certain levels of closeness are important, parsimonious devices for students of relationship research. Few theories in interpersonal communication can claim the scope of the Stage Theories.

The breadth and scope of Social Penetration Theory, however, makes it difficult to adequately test it as a whole (see also Miller, 2005). Few attempts have been made to follow relationships from initial interaction to termination. Indeed, the logistical and ethical implications of investigating any relationship for such an extended period make the process difficult at best. Even Welch and Rubin (2002), who offered an operational definition of Knapp's (1978) stages, used cross-section rather than longitudinal data in their study. This means that rather than follow relationships over time, they investigated a large number of relationships (that were at all points of development) at a single point in time.

As we previously noted, a second limitation of the Stage Theories is that there is confusion concerning the linear nature of the stages. Although both Altman and Taylor (1973) and Knapp and Vangelisti (2005) noted that relationships may not follow a linear progression, the vocabulary that we have to describe relationship development and deterioration—as well as the rules for moving between stages—implies a linear path. For example, at one point, Knapp and Vangelisti (2005) argued that the process of relational development may not be linear, but they later stated, "Many people experience a general sequencing effect because: (1) each stage contains important presuppositions for the following stage; (2) sequencing makes forecasting adjacent stages easier; and (3) skipping steps is a gamble on the uncertainties presented by the lack of information that could have been learned in the skipped step" (p. 48). This clearly implies that relationships either do follow, or should follow, a linear path for development. Along similar lines, even though Altman and colleagues (1981) provided a dialectical view of social penetration processes (which presume that neither openness nor privacy is preferred), their later work equated good communication with openness: "Communication and disclosure intimacy appear to be the sine qua non of developing satisfying interpersonal relationships" (Taylor & Altman, 1987, p. 257), suggesting a one-way, or linear, view of relationship development.

Baxter and Montgomery (1996) provided a stinging critique of the linear nature of Stage Theories. In part, they took aim at the assumption that relationships progress in a one-way manner toward greater intimacy, closeness, and certainty. According to the linear view, healthy relationships grow while sick relationships decline. Baxter and Montgomery (1996), instead, presented a dialectical view where "relationships change in fluid patterns of more or less openness, more or less intimacy, more or less certainty and so forth" (pp. 58–59). Moreover, they argued that relationships do not reach a balance or stabilization. Instead, relationships are constantly moving and changing as they are buffeted by opposing forces (e.g., the simultaneous need for certainty and the desire for spontaneity; see Chapter 26, this volume).

Another limitation of Stage Theories is that they are not described specifically enough. Both Altman and Taylor (1973) and Knapp and Vangelisti (2005) described the stages relatively briefly. In fairness, the stages are only a small part of the larger Social Penetration Theory. Moreover, Knapp and Vangelisti never really presented the Staircase Model as theoretical (thus, our reticence to call it the Staircase Theory in this chapter). Moreover, neither theory was meant to be taken as the only way that relationships develop. Altman and Taylor claimed that "to speak of a set number of stages of the social penetration process is artificial" (p. 135). Knapp and Vangelisti implied that any direction of movement is possible from any point of the model.

Movement through stages is unique and may or may not be linear. The amount of time a couple spends at a particular stage depends on the circumstance, the people, and their relationship. For example, while Shrek and Fiona develop a romantic relationship through a reasonably linear path, Shrek and Donkey develop a friendship that jumps among stages of development and dissolution as they bicker. Rather than a staircase, perhaps a better metaphor for relationship development might be a rollercoaster in near total darkness. There are twists and turns, steep climbs, and perilous falls that, for the most part, we cannot see coming.

Social Penetration Theory's final limitation is Altman and Taylor's (1973) use of economic concepts (such as rewards and costs) from Social Exchange Theories (see Chapter 28, this volume). People disagree strongly on the utility of rewards and costs in the context of close personal relationships. Most of our students (and communication scholars, for that matter) either really like or absolutely hate the idea of using rewards and costs to explain relationship development and dissolution. There tends to be little middle ground on this particular matter. Some people find the idea of using rewards and costs to assess the attractiveness of relationships to be both natural and useful. Research indicates that including rewards and costs increases the accuracy of our explanations of relationship development (e.g., Sunnafrank, 1990). Others argue that there is something special and unique about close relationships that makes the cold, calculating accounting of rewards and costs totally inappropriate. For example, Wood (1997) claimed that "relationships are not governed by and cannot be explained by economic principles or cost-benefit considerations" (p. 234). Knapp and Vangelisti (2005) and other scholars (e.g., Berger & Calabrese, 1975) got around this issue by focusing on the role of communication in relationship development and by ignoring reward-cost notions altogether.

In short, Stage Theories fall short in terms of theoretical clarity and specificity. In order to develop into a strong "theory" of relationship development, these Stage Theories need to be explicated much more completely. As a metaphor spurring our scholarly imaginations, however, these theories have been an overwhelming success.

Directions for Future Research and Applications

From our analysis of the strengths and weaknesses of Stage Theories, two clear directions for future research emerge. First, communication scholars should undertake longitudinal studies to investigate how and why communication differs as relationships escalate, de-escalate, and stabilize. Second, researchers should attempt to evaluate communication in the development and dissolution of different types of relationships. The stages are supposed to apply to all relationships; this notion, however, has not been widely researched. Certainly characteristics such as the voluntary (e.g., dating partners and friends) or involuntary (e.g., in-laws and coworkers) nature of the relationship, the nature of the culture partners come from (e.g., would Social Penetration Theory work as well in Japan as the United States?), or differences among individuals (e.g., age, relational experience, or sexual orientation) could influence communication and relational development processes.

References

Afifi, T. D. (2005). The chilling effect in families and the pressure to conceal secrets. *Communication Monographs, 72,* 192–216.

Agne, R. R., Thompson, T. L., & Cusella, L. P. (2000). Stigma in the line of face: Self-disclosure of patients' HIV status to health care providers. *Journal of Applied Communication Research, 28,* 235–261.

Altman, I., & Taylor, D. A. (1973). *Social penetration: The development of interpersonal relationships.* New York: Holt, Rinehart, & Winston.

Altman, I., Vinsel, A., & Brown, B. B. (1981). Dialectic conception in social psychology: An application to social penetration and privacy regulation. In L. Berkowitz (Ed.), *Advances in experimental social psychology* (Vol. 14, pp. 107–160). New York: Academic Press.

Baxter, L. A., & Montgomery, B. M. (1996). *Relating: Dialogues and dialectics.* New York: Guilford Press.

Berger, C. R., & Calabrese, R. J. (1975). Some explorations in initial interaction and beyond: Toward a development of theory of interpersonal communication. *Human Communication Research, 1,* 99–112.

Burgoon, J. K., & Hale, J. L. (1987). Validation and measurement of the fundamental themes of relational communication. *Communication Monographs, 54,* 19–41.

Davis, M. (1973). *Intimate relations.* New York: The Free Press.

Dillard, J. P., Solomon, D. H., & Palmer, M. T. (1999). Structuring the concept of relational communication. *Communication Monographs, 66,* 49–65.

Dindia, K. (2000). Sex differences in self-disclosure, reciprocity of self-disclosure, and self-disclosure and liking: Three meta-analyses reviewed. In S. Petronio (Ed.), *Balancing the secrets of private disclosures* (pp. 21–35). Mahwah, NJ: Erlbaum.

Duck, S. W. (1982). A topography of relationship disengagement and dissolution. In S. W. Duck (Ed.), *Personal relationships 4: Dissolving personal relationships* (pp. 1–30). New York: Academic Press.

Knapp, M. L. (1978). *Social intercourse: From greeting to goodbye.* Needham Heights, MA: Allyn & Bacon.

Knapp, M. L., & Vangelisti, A. (2005). *Interpersonal communication and human relationships* (5th ed.). Boston: Allyn & Bacon.

Miller, G. R., & Steinberg, M. (1975). *Between people: A new analysis of interpersonal communication.* Chicago: Science Research Associates.

Miller, K. (2005). *Communication theories: Perspectives, processes, and contexts* (2nd ed.). Boston: McGraw Hill.

Mongeau, P. A., Serewicz, M. C. M., Henningsen, M. L. M., & Davis, K. L. (2006). Sex differences in the transition to a heterosexual romantic relationship. In D. J. Canary & K. Dindia (Eds.), *Sex differences and similarities in communication: Critical investigations of sex and gender in interaction* (2nd ed., pp. 337–358). Mahwah, NJ: Erlbaum.

Sanderson, C., Rahm, K. B., & Beigbeder, S. A. (2005). The link between the pursuit of intimacy goals and satisfaction in close same-sex friendships: An examination of the underlying processes. *Journal of Social and Personal Relationships, 22,* 75–98.

Sunnafrank, M. (1990). Predicted outcome value and uncertainty reduction theories: A test of competing perspectives: *Human Communication Research, 17,* 76–103.

Taylor, D. A., & Altman, I. (1987). Communication in interpersonal relationships: Social penetration processes. In M. E. Roloff & G. R. Miller (Eds.), *Interpersonal processes: New directions in communication research* (pp. 257–277). Newbury Park, CA: Sage.

Warner, A., Williams, J. H., Katzenberg, J. (Producers), Adamson, A., & Jenson, V. (Directors). (2001). *Shrek* [Motion picture]. United States: DreamWorks SKG.

Welch, S. A., & Rubin, R. B. (2002). Development of relationship stage measures. *Communication Quarterly, 50,* 24–40.

Wood, J. T. (1997). *Communication theories in action: An introduction.* Belmont, CA: Wadsworth.

28*

Social Exchange Theories

Calculating the Rewards and Costs of Personal Relationships

Laura Stafford

"I just wasn't getting anything out of that relationship." "He wasn't worth the effort." "She was too high maintenance." We often hear people give reasons like these for ending a romantic involvement. Such reasons implicitly indicate decisions and actions based on perceptions of costs (what we are putting into a relationship) versus rewards (what we are getting out of a relationship). The idea that interpersonal interaction is guided by calculations of costs and rewards is central to theories of social exchange. Rather than attempt to cover all Social Exchange Theories or even all that have been or might be applied to interpersonal communication, this chapter presents the major premises and concepts common among these theories. In doing so, three variations of Social Exchange Theories—Resource Theory, Interdependence Theory, and Equity Theory—are highlighted.

Purpose and Meta-theoretical Assumptions

Exchange Theories can be traced to psychologists Thibaut and Kelley (1959) or sociologists Homans (1961) and Blau (1964), and have roots in economics (rewards and costs) or behaviorist psychology (rewards and punishments). The common thread among these theories is the analogous connection to economic exchange. Just as in a profit-motivated economic exchange, in social exchange, decisions are based on projections of the rewards and costs of a particular course of action. We decide to invest money in one stock as opposed to another because of our expectations of the dividends we will earn. Similarly, according to Social Exchange Theories we make decisions about and engage in behaviors we expect to be rewarding. In both arenas, we act in a manner we believe will be profitable. The idea of thinking about relationships in terms of the return on our investments may seem somewhat cold and calculating. Exchange Theory does not presume that we always seek to maximize our rewards and minimize our costs, nor that we are only interested in maximizing our own profits at the expense of others: reciprocity and fairness are also part of Exchange Theory.

Social Exchange Theories are post-positivist in orientation; they largely rest on propositions that can be tested. Like other social scientific approaches, the primary purpose of Social Exchange Theories is to predict and explain behavior. According to Social Exchange Theories, we can predict and explain behavior through an understanding of the factors that individuals take into account (rewards and costs) in making decisions about their actions. Humans are seen as rational creatures who, on some level, engage in a cost-benefit analysis: a weighing of the pros and cons of interpersonal interaction and relationships.

Main Features of the Theory

Social Exchange Theories share basic assumptions: Social behavior is a series of exchanges. Individuals attempt to maximize their rewards and minimize their costs. When individuals receive rewards from others, they feel a sense of obligation (Sprecher, 1998). Embedded within these assumptions are two main concepts: self-interests and interdependence. Self-interests drive individuals to act in accordance with perceptions and projections of rewards and costs associated with an exchange, or potential exchange, of resources. Interdependence refers to the extent to which one person's outcomes depend on another person's outcomes. Before delving into detail about these basic components, we must understand the "social" aspects of social exchange, as well as consider more specifically what constitutes rewards and costs.

THE SOCIAL IN SOCIAL EXCHANGE

An exchange is simply a transfer of something in return for something else (Roloff, 1981). This does not necessarily involve more than one individual. It can occur between an individual and the environment. However, "social" exchange requires a connection with another human. Social exchange is also somewhat different from economic exchange. Economic exchange typically involves legal obligations, whereas social exchange relies on trust or goodwill. In other words, social exchange is voluntary. Economic exchange demands an exact specification of the rewards and costs of both parties, whereas social exchange leaves the rewards and costs open. Economic exchange involves a set, and often short, time frame for the exchange to occur. When you go to out to dinner, the restaurant expects you to pay the check at the end of the meal. Of course the time period for exchange may be long term such as in the case of car payments or mortgages. Economic exchange frequently involves bargaining or negotiating and is similar from person to person. In social exchange the time frame is more likely to be undetermined and flexible. It seldom involves explicit bargaining and is more likely to be individualized. Consider the following conversation between friends:

I need a ride home.

What's in it for me?

If you give me a ride, I'll bake you two dozen homemade brownies.

Make it three dozen.

Okay, three dozen. Let's go.

Not so fast. We need to specify the terms. I want them this weekend and you bring them to my house.

I'm the one without a car. You pick them up and it will have to be next weekend. But I will make them double chocolate chip.

All right, double chocolate chips are worth the wait. Deal.

Okay. Let's go.

Hold on. We need to draw up a contract, both sign it, and have it notarized before you get in my car. How do I know you will bake the brownies if I don't have it in writing?

Likely this conversation feels quite odd, and a friend who negotiates how many brownies a ride is worth is probably not someone we'd want to keep as a close friend. It is certainly not the way close friends generally ask for and grant favors. The reason the interaction sounds peculiar is because it is more akin to economic exchange than social exchange, and exchanges between friends are supposed to be social, not economic.

Let us break down the negotiation for a ride to illustrate the manner in which it is "economic" as opposed to "social." A legal obligation is created (via a written contract). The type and amount of a resource to be exchanged is explicit (one ride for three dozen brownies), and direct negotiations concerning the amount and time frame take place (three dozen brownies, not two, for next weekend, not this weekend).

Though different, it is debatable as to how distinct social and economic exchanges really are. Friends **could** have a conversation like the one of above, though it would be atypical. And squabbling siblings may retort to a request with, "What's in it for me?" Romantic partners do sometimes directly negotiate: "I walked the dog last time. It's your turn now." Not all economic exchanges involve bargaining. In the United States, we seldom negotiate with the grocer how much we should pay for milk or bread, but we expect to "haggle" over the price of a car.

Also obligations, though seldom legally enforceable (except, e.g., in the case of child support), do exist among family members, friends, and romantic partners, and thus may not feel voluntary: "My brother let me crash on his couch for a week last summer. Now I have to let him spend the night at my place." Likewise feelings of obligation typically thought of as social exchange can emerge in economic exchange. For example, long-term business partners may develop unspoken exchange patterns based more on trust than legalities (Roloff, 1981).

SELF-INTERESTS AND INTERDEPENDENCE

As already noted, Social Exchange Theories are based on the concepts of self-interests and interdependence. Individuals are motivated to interact with others in ways that serve their self-interests. Though this might mean we seek to maximize our profits at the cost of others, this is not always the case. Often it is in our best interests to cooperate so that both parties' profits are maximized. In addition, considerations of fairness or justice come into play.

To understand "interdependence," it is useful to think about independence and dependence. Total independence occurs when one's outcomes are based solely on one's own efforts, and complete dependence occurs when one's outcomes are based solely on the efforts of another. Complete independence can be illustrated by considering an individual's actions in a physical environment. The enjoyment (reward) of thriving plants in your apartment is based on your own efforts to water and care for them. Complete dependence is exemplified by a parent-infant relationship: a baby is entirely dependent on a caregiver for rewards.

Interdependence means that each person's outcomes or rewards are influenced by the other's efforts. In a long-term relationship, for example, each person's satisfaction (a reward) is influenced by the efforts of the other person. If within a particular marriage the husband enjoys being home with the children while the wife pursues her career, and she enjoys pursuing her career while her husband stays home with the children, both are receiving their desired rewards with the aid of the actions of the other. If she did not earn enough income, he could not afford to stay home with the children; if he did not care for the children, she would not be able to pursue her career. Such interdependence (or degree of dependence) is subject to the availability of alternative sources to satisfactorily meet needs. If the wife has other equally suitable childcare options, her reward of pursuing her career is less dependent on her husband.

Obviously this example is oversimplified. Individuals have many different needs and desires; a partner might provide needs in one arena and not in another. In a long-term relationship the level of dependence or interdependence, overall, refers to the "extent to which an individual 'needs' a relationship and relies primarily on a given partner and relationship for the fulfillment of important needs" (Rusbult, Drigotas, & Verette, 1994, p. 117), needs an individual believes cannot be acceptably met elsewhere.

COSTS, REWARDS, AND RESOURCES

Social exchange is based in the give and take of resources. These resources constitute rewards when they provide pleasure and costs when they provoke pain, anxiety, embarrassment, or mental and physical effort. Resource Theory, an exchange theory developed by Foa and Foa (1976) identifies types of resources: money, goods, status, love, services, and information. These resources vary in how concrete they are and how individualized they are. Some resources are more tangible than others. Fudge brownies (a good) are tangible; popularity (status) is not. Resources also vary in how unique they are to a particular individual. Consider love: Love is abstract. It is difficult to quantify or even define. It is intangible. It is highly individualized. No matter how fuzzy, abstract, and unquantifiable love may be, it is given specifically and uniquely to another. Money, on the other hand, is quite concrete. It is also universal. We know what a dollar is and how much it is worth. One $10 bill is as good as another, and can be given to many different people in the same way, with no particular individual or unique qualities attached.

Some resources are more similar than others and we are more satisfied when similar resources are exchanged (Foa & Foa, 1976). Goods, like groceries, cars, or clothes, are more similar to money than they are to love. Therefore an exchange involving money for money (exchanging a $10 bill for two $5 bills) or money for goods (money for groceries) is more likely to be gratifying than an exchange of money for love.

Relationship type also influences the exchange of resources. Money for services is expected between a mechanic and a customer. The next time you need an oil change your offer of love is unlikely to been seen as an acceptable exchange. Among friends, on the other hand, exchanging money for services is not generally appropriate. If your friend covers for you at work, you are more likely to reciprocate with—and it is more likely for both of you be content with—not an exchange of money, but rather with an understanding that "I owe you one."

Conceptualization of Communication in the Theory[1]

Communication can serve social exchange in two ways: (a) Communication is the means through which bargaining about the exchange occurs. That is, communication is the tool of negotiation, as illustrated in the "conversation" offered earlier in this chapter. (b) At other times, however, communication **itself** is the resource to be exchanged, the reward or cost. A hurtful comment from a friend may be a cost of that friendship, and a compliment might be a reward.

Though Roloff (1981) conceived of exchange as a transfer, implying a loss by one party, he later contended, in regard to communication, that one might give away that resource, thus rewarding another, and keep the resource. Consider someone who has a juicy piece of gossip. That person can give this gossip to many other people, and that person might also receive rewards (more gossip from others). But the traders of the gossip do not lose the information. That is they have not traded it away as they would in exchanging money for services. Each still possesses her or his original item of gossip. Similarly, you might compliment several different individuals. Such a compliment may be a reward for the other, but to what extent it is traded, exchanged, or a cost to the giver is more questionable, yielding Social Exchange Theory more complicated. Though this is especially noticeable in communication, this holds true for many resources of social exchange. You can give love without giving love away.

Communication can also be misconstrued, further complicating the social exchange. Communication intended to be a reward for another (praise) could be interpreted as sarcastic and insincere, and the recipient could believe that a punishment or cost has been incurred instead. In fact, interpersonal conflict is often the result of different meanings or values placed on the resources exchanged. If you give your partner advice or offer help (in your mind a reward) your partner might think you are implying incompetence, and thus feel it is a punishment or cost, and not a reward.

Uses of the Theory

Two variations of Social Exchange Theory are particularly well known in the field of interpersonal communication and relationships: Interdependence Theory and Equity Theory.

INTERDEPENDENCE THEORY: ALTERNATIVES AND COMPARISON LEVELS

Interdependence Theory was developed by Thibaut and Kelly (1959; Kelley, 1979; Kelley & Thibaut, 1978) and has at its core the control of resources.

Individuals assess the rewards of their relationships through comparison levels (*CL*) and alternatives (comparison levels of alternatives, or *CLalt*). The *CL* can be thought of as what one believes one **should** be receiving and the *CLalt* as what one believes one could be receiving.

The *CL* is the standard an individual uses to judge how attractive or satisfactory a particular relationship is (Thibaut & Kelley, 1959). Individuals contemplate how well the outcome of a current situation meets the standards or expectations of what they believe they deserve. If your girlfriend forgets your birthday **again**, you might find yourself contemplating, "Why am I still with this loser? I deserve so much better!" If so, you are thinking about or comparing the rewards of your current situation to what you believe you **should** be receiving from a romantic partner, one who appreciates you enough to remember your birthday.

The *CLalt* is the lowest level of rewards deemed acceptable when considering possible alternative relationships (Thibaut & Kelley, 1959). Just because we think romantic partners should remember our birthday does not mean we actually believe that a relationship with someone who meets our expectations of what a relationship should be like is possible. We might continue a relationship because we believe that the relationship is better than any alternatives open to us. It is your *CLalt* you are considering when a relationship does meet your minimum standards. Even though you believe you **deserve** better, you do not believe you can **do** better.

In sum, Interdependence Theory makes the point that satisfaction—and thus decision making and action—is based on how much above or below one's comparison level the outcomes of a particular situation are, as well as how much above or below the projected outcomes the outcomes from alternatives are perceived to be. We consider to what extent our outcomes are controlled by a particular partner or relationship. We contemplate what we believe we **should** receive as well as what we believe we **could** receive, and we act accordingly. This does not mean that our projections are accurate. Research suggests that the more committed we are to a partner and the more we have invested in a relationship, the more likely we are to mentally downplay possible alternatives and perceive our current relationship as superior to others' relationships (Rusbult, Van Lange, Wildschut, Yovetich, & Verette, 2000). No matter how faulty our perceptions might be, Interdependence Theory poses that our dependence on a relationship is stronger, and therefore the chances of staying in that relationship are higher, when the rewards we receive in that relationship are greater than what we believe we might receive without that relationship (Rusbult et al., 1994).

EQUITY THEORY

Up to this point, it seems that Social Exchange Theories characterize individuals as profit mongers: we want the most profit we can achieve, regardless of the costs to others. Theories of social exchange do not assume that humans will seek to gain the most from others regardless of the costs to others. Equity Theory holds that, in addition to consideration of one's own profits, we also consider reciprocity and fairness.

Fairness can be thought of as equity in the distribution of costs and rewards. It can be considered in the short run: "I cooked dinner. You do the dishes." In intimate relationships, fairness is also considered in the long run: "I'll finish my degree first while you put me through college, then it will be your turn." Actually, in close long-term relationships, fair exchange seldom involves specification of the time frame or resources. Instead, a sense of equity or inequity accumulates over the course of a relationship that is not apparent in any one interaction. Though the time of reciprocity may be elongated and the nature of the resources exchanged implicit, equity theorists propose that inequity will catch up to us at some point, because we prefer relationships that are equitable.

Whereas Independence Theory emphasizes dependence on or control of resources, Equity Theory emphasizes fairness. A forerunner of today's Equity Theory, Adams's (1965) notion of "distributive justice" contends that people think and act so that rewards are distributed in accordance with their efforts. Three types of (in)equity might occur: (a) You might consider whether the ratio of your rewards to costs is equal to your partner's ratio. (b) You might consider the exchange relationship you and your partner have with a third individual. (c) You might compare your relationship to others in similar circumstances. Each of these is explained below.

First, you might perceive the ratio of your rewards to costs to be equal to your partner's. Consider a situation wherein neither relational partner is putting much into the romantic relationship, and neither is getting much out of it; the ratio of inputs to outcomes is the same. Both may desire a casual "no-strings-attached" relationship, requiring little effort on either part. In this instance equity exists and both are satisfied with the arrangement. Similarly, if both invest heavily, sinking many costs into the relationship, and both are greatly rewarded, again equity exists. Inequity occurs when one person's effort to outcome ratio is out of sync with the other person's. If one person contributes a great deal to the relationship and the other contributes little, then even though the first person may feel the relationship is rewarding, inequity occurs if the second person is reaping the same benefits without the same efforts.

In the second type of (in)equity we look at the exchange relationship we and another person have with a third individual. When we perceive our efforts to be on par with another person's efforts with the same exchange partner (a third party), we again perceive equity. If you and a classmate engage in a joint project, if you share the workload and the teacher gives you the same grade, the ratio of input (work on the project) to outcome (the grade) is equal. Conversely, if you do most of the work and your lab partner does little but you receive the same grade, you likely will see the distribution of rewards as unfair.

The third type of inequity discussed by Adams (1965) is determined by evaluating one's own situation in contrast to others in similar situations. Suppose I work hard at a relationship and my partner doesn't, yet all of my friends also work just as hard as I in their relationships and none of their partners contribute to their relationships either. If my ratio of inputs to outputs in my romantic involvement is the same as my perception of the ratio of inputs to outputs of others in the same circumstance, I may then perceive my arrangement to be fair.

If partners' relative contributions are unequal then the relationship is inequitable. This inequity results in emotional distress—and the greater the inequity the greater the distress. Inequity fosters anger or guilt (Sprecher, 2001). Given our emphasis on maximizing profits it seems logical that the one who is "underbenefited" often experiences anger: "Why am I the one to do all of the work in this relationship?" Alternatively, feelings of guilt may emerge if we are the "overbenefitted party" who perceives that we are getting more out of a relationship than we are giving. If people prefer fairness to profits, or believe in a norm of reciprocity, then feeling guilty about our profitable relationship makes sense.

Given that inequity causes distress, we attempt to restore equity through changing our outcomes or inputs. Adams (1965) proposed that we attempt to maintain equity by changing our actions or our perceptions. You might equalize the balance by not putting so much effort into your relationship, convincing your partner to put more into the relationship, or ending the relationship. Another course is to distort your perceptions of rewards and costs: "I'm really not working any harder than my roommate. I enjoy mowing the lawn; it's good exercise. I'm outside in the fresh air. It's not really work." If you change your perception of a cost into a reward, equity is restored. In short, Equity Theory poses that rules of fairness or justice outweigh our desire to get the most we can. Therefore, we prefer equitable relationships.

Strengths and Limitations of the Theory

Most criticisms have been aimed at the primary premises of exchange perspectives. Three are offered here. Some relationships transcend social exchange. People are not necessarily "self-serving." People are not as rational as Social Exchange Theories seems to portray them.

Critics contend that some relationships cannot be explained by Social Exchange Theories. Relationships based in "true love" simply are not subject to an exchange perspective; love in its pure form is selfless as opposed to self-serving (Fromm, 1956). Long-term intimate relationships, it has been argued, are, or become, communal relationships wherein each person's concern is primarily for the other's welfare (Mills & Clark, 1982, 2001).

Similarly, it has been said that even outside of "true love" people are not always interested in what serves them the best. Social exchange does not allow for altruism; some proponents of social exchange agree with this criticism. Blau (1964) considered altruism as "beyond the scope" of social exchange. Others (e.g., Homans, 1961), however, contended that altruism is a reward because the negative feelings that come with inequity, such as anger or guilt, are themselves costs: when we act in ways to eliminate these feelings, we are ultimately acting in our own self-interest, not out of concern for others.

Continuing with the second criticism—that people are not necessarily self-serving—it has been argued that individuals differ in the degree to which they feel they ought to repay or be repaid. Some individuals may have more of an "exchange orientation" than others (Murstein, 1971). Those high in exchange orientation more actively calculate or keep score, whereas those low in exchange orientation care little about reciprocity or equity. Also, some cultures seem to value and foster exchange orientations more than other cultures do (Van Yperen & Buunk, 1990).

A third critique of social exchange is that people simply are not rational: we aren't human calculators constantly computing income and expenses. Many supporters of social exchange tend to agree that people are not always rational. As Roloff (1981) explained, we might go for long periods without considering our rewards and costs. At some point, though, perhaps a critical incident transpires, and we take notice of (in)equity. Recall that social exchange ideas as applied to long-term close relationships do not involve immediate reciprocity; rewards and costs are distributed and accumulated gradually. It is unclear as to how long one waits for the scales to be balanced, or even before one realizes that they are not balanced, before computations begin. Yet equity theorists contend that at some point inequities will be recognized and dealt with.

Social Exchange Theories also have a number of strengths. Theories are often evaluated as to their parsimony, heuristic value, predictive value, and falsifiability. Parsimony refers to how simple or complex a theory is. If one explanation is complicated and another equally good explanation is simple, the more parsimonious (simpler) explanation (theory) is preferred. In spite of the numerous variations of Social Exchange Theories, the central premises are few and simple, making Social Exchange Theories as a group parsimonious.

Theories that prompt further investigation are considered heuristic. Social Exchange Theories have generated a significant amount of research, which demonstrates their heuristic value. Within the confines of interpersonal communication and close relationships alone, Social Exchange Theories have generated a great deal of research. The theories have been applied to self-disclosure (Altman & Taylor, 1973), relationship initiation and development (Cate, Lloyd, & Long, 1988), sexual activity (Sprecher, 1998), conflict (Roloff, 1981), and the maintenance of romantic, friend, and family relationships (Canary & Stafford,

2001; Rusbult, 1980; Vogl-Bauer, Kalbfleisch, & Beatty, 1999), to give only a few examples.

Overall, Exchange Theory also fares quite well in terms of predictive value. That is, it has been found to offer a fair explanation of how people behave. In summarizing research based in interdependence theory, Rusbult and colleagues (1994) reported that "abundant evidence suggests that when individuals are more dependent on their relationships—that is, when they are more committed, more satisfied, more heavily invested, and perceive that their alternatives are poor—their relationships are more likely to persist over time" (p. 132). The work of Hatfield (formerly Walster) with main focus on the comparison of one's ratio to one's partner's ratio wherein interdependence is presumed (Hatfield, Traupmann, Sprecher, Utne, & Hay, 1985; Walster, Berscheid, & Walster, 1973; Walster, Walster, & Berscheid, 1978) supports social exchange assumptions. Other research has supported the proposal that equity is associated with relational satisfaction (Canary & Stafford, 1992; Stafford & Canary, 2006; Van Yperen & Buunk, 1990).

Theories are also judged on their "falsifiability." Can the ideas be tested? Some abstract ideas are difficult to test. It is likely impossible to determine if altruism is enacted—not out of the desire to serve or help others, but because it makes us feel good about ourselves, leaving these theories open to criticism on this front.

Directions for Future Research and Applications

General support has been found for the central premises of social exchange, yet debate continues about the degree to which Social Exchange Theories can account for human behavior, if exchange principles are "universal," and—if not—under which conditions and in which relationships what individuals consider and act on social exchange. Research is exploring the idea that individuals vary in their exchange orientation or that equity theories are not universal but rather are a product of individualistic capitalistic societies. Also, many distinctions among variations of social exchange have not received as much research attention. Perhaps more importantly for communication scholars, a profitable direction for research would be greater consideration of communication as the resource of exchange itself, and not simply the means to broker exchanges.

Note

1. I would like to acknowledge Michael Roloff's contribution, through discussion, to the ideas offered in regard to the role of communication in social exchange.

References

Adams, J. (1965). Inequity in social exchange. In L. Berkowtiz (Ed.), *Advances in experimental social psychology: Vol. 2* (pp. 267–299). New York: Academic Press.

Altman, I., & Taylor, D. (1973). *Social penetration: The development of interpersonal relationships.* New York: Holt, Rinehart, & Winston.

Blau, P. (1964). *Exchange and power in social life.* New York: John Wiley.

Canary, D. J., & Stafford, L. (1992). Relational maintenance strategies and equity in marriage. *Communication Monographs, 59,* 243–267.

Canary, D. J., & Stafford, L. (2001). Equity in the preservation of personal relationships. In J. Harvey & A. Wenzel (Eds.), *Close romantic relationships: Preservation and enhancement* (pp. 133–151). Mahwah, NJ: Erlbaum.

Cate, R. M., Lloyd, S. A., & Long, E. (1988). The role of rewards and fairness in developing premarital relationships. *Journal of Marriage and the Family, 50,* 443–452.

Foa, E., & Foa, U. (1976). Resource theory of social exchange. In J. Thibaut, J. Spence, & Carson (Eds.), *Contemporary topics in social psychology* (pp. 99–131). Morristown, NJ: General Learning Press.

Fromm, E. (1956). *The art of loving.* New York: Harper & Row.

Hatfield, E., Traupmann, J., Sprecher, S., Utne, M., & Hay, M. (1985). Equity in close relationships. In W. Ickes (Ed.), *Compatible and incompatible relationships* (pp. 91–117). New York: Springer-Verlag.

Homans, G. (1961). *Social behavior: Its elementary forms.* New York: Harcourt Brace Jovanovich.

Kelley, H. H. (1979). *Personal relationships: Their structures and processes.* Hillsdale, NJ: Erlbaum.

Kelley, H. H., & Thibaut, J. W. (1978). *Interpersonal relations: A theory of interdependence.* New York: Wiley.

Mills, J., & Clark, M. S. (1982). Exchange and communal relationships. In L. Wheeler (Ed)., *Review of personality and social psychology* (Vol. 3, pp. 121–144). Beverly Hills, CA: Sage.

Mills, J., & Clark, M. S. (2001). Viewing close romantic relationships as communal relationships: Implications for maintenance and enhancement. In J. Harvey & A. Wenzel (Eds.), *Close romantic relationships: Maintenance and enhancement* (pp. 13–25). Hillsdale, NJ: Erlbaum.

Murstein, B. K. (1971). A theory of marital choice and its applicability to marriage adjustment. In B. I. Murstein (Ed.), *Theories of attraction and love* (pp. 100–151). New York: Springer.

Roloff, M. E. (1981). *Interpersonal communication: The social exchange approach.* Beverly Hills, CA: Sage.

Rusbult, C. E. (1980). Commitment and satisfaction in romantic associations: A test of the investment model. *Journal of Experimental Social Psychology, 16,* 172–186.

Rusbult, C. E., Drigotas, S. M., & Verette, J. (1994). The investment model: An interdependence analysis of commitment processes and relationship maintenance phenomena. In D. J. Canary & L. Stafford (Eds.), *Communication and relational maintenance* (pp. 115–140). New York: Academic Press.

Rusbult, C. E., Van Lange, P. A. M., Wildschut, T., Yovetich, N. A., & Verette, J. (2000). Perceived superiority in close relationships: Why it exists and persists. *Journal of Personality and Social Psychology, 79,* 521–545.

Sprecher, S. (1998). Social exchange theories and sexuality. *Journal of Sex Research, 35,* 32–43.

Sprecher, S. (2001). Comparison of emotional consequences of and changes in equity over time using global and domain-specific measures of equity. *Journal of Social and Personal Relationships, 18,* 477–501.

Stafford, L., & Canary, D. J. (2006). Equity and interdependence as predictors of relational maintenance strategies. *Journal of Family Communication, 6,* 227–254.

Thibaut, J. W., & Kelley, H. H. (1959). *The social psychology of groups.* New York: Wiley.

Van Yperen, N. W., & Buunk, B. P. (1990). A longitudinal study of equity and satisfaction in intimate relationships. *European Journal of Social Psychology, 20,* 287–309.

Vogl-Bauer, S., Kalbfleisch, P. J., & Beatty, M. J. (1999). Perceived equity, satisfaction, and relational maintenance strategies in parent-adolescent dyads. *Journal of Youth and Adolescence, 28,* 27–49.

Walster, E., Berscheid, E., & Walster, G. W. (1973). New directions in equity research. *Journal of Personality and Social Psychology, 25,* 151–176.

Walster, E., Walster, G., & Berscheid, E. (1978). *Equity: Theory and research.* Boston: Allyn & Bacon.

29

Social Information Processing Theory

Impressions and Relationship Development Online

Joseph B. Walther

S imilar to those who work in organizations that have offices around the world, or to student project groups in which partnerships are formed strictly via the Internet, or to people who meet online and never in person, there is often a great deal of concern about what those distant partners are like: whether they are reliable, hard working, enjoyable, and if they have a good sense of humor. We are liable to think, with only e-mail or text-based messaging to connect us, that finding the answer to these queries is impossible. And yet, a matter of weeks (or several late nights of chatting) later, people are grinning at each others' messages, developing rapport, and at times becoming friends, sometimes to their great surprise. From the perspective of the Social Information Processing Theory (SIPT) of computer-mediated communication (CMC) this transition is not surprising. The SIPT of CMC explains how people get to know one another online, without nonverbal cues, and how they develop and manage relationships in the computer-mediated environment (Walther, 1992).

Purpose and Meta-theoretical Assumptions

When people encounter each other for the first time in a face-to-face setting, there is abundant information, immediately available and soon forthcoming, about who each person is. People make many first impression judgments based on the physical appearance of others. They rely on obvious physical features such as body type, physical attractiveness, the slogan on the other person's tee shirt or the designer label on their eyeglass frames. Even more subtly, people make inferences about others' personalities based on the quality of their voices, the distance at which they approach or to which they retreat, and myriad other cues. An individual makes initial "hypotheses" about who others are based on physical cues, and then tests those first-impression hunches through conversations, in which one senses what they say and how they say it, their conversation management style, and their other paralinguistic cues such as vocal cues, posture, facial expression, and gestures (Snyder & Stukas, 1999). We know this is so. Even though we are inclined to shun first impressions based on physical data, we nevertheless make such impressions and are generally comfortable doing so.

When we encounter other people via CMC, on the Internet, we most frequently do not have the variety, abundance, simultaneity, and relative effortlessness of means by which to size up others and by which to signal the characteristics we want them to associate with our selves. This can be unsettling. We can feel unsure of how to act when we do not have a sense of who others are. Some theories have suggested that the lack of nonverbal cues that characterize various teleconferencing technologies causes us to refrain from making inferences about the characteristics of others (e.g., Short, Williams, & Christie, 1976). This prevents impression formation and leads to uncertain or even hostile interpersonal behavior (Siegel, Dubrovsky, Kiesler, & McGuire, 1986). Other research suggests that, in the absence of individuating information about other persons with whom we interact online, we respond to them based on what social groups we believe they belong to, such as sophomores versus seniors, Wolverines versus Spartans, or some other easy categorization that is obvious at the moment. When those frames of mind are activated, we relate to others either as members of an in-group, in which case we assume they are similar to us and we treat them favorably, or as members of an out-group, in which case we distance ourselves from them through dislikable evaluations and responses. The tendency to "see" others this way is raised when, as is the case in CMC, we cannot literally see them (see, for review, Reicher, Spears, & Postmes, 1995).

The SIPT of CMC differs from either of these positions. SIPT predicts that people may indeed get to know one another online, albeit more slowly and through different mechanisms than through face-to-face interaction. The theory offers several preliminary assumptions about human motivations, the comparability of verbal and nonverbal communication, and the qualities of mediated channels that affect the rate of exchange of information used to relate to others. Thus the theory is a post-positivist theory because it bears these characteristics: The SIPT lays out certain assumptions (regarding people's motivations to develop impressions and relations despite channel differences, the capacity to express social information through mediated channels, and the rate at which social information flows vis-à-vis CMC versus face-to-face communication). From the root assumptions and definitions, certain propositions are derived, from which a number of testable hypotheses may be deduced (such as the assertion that online and offline relationships become similarly well developed when communicators experience ample time). From propositions such as these, researchable hypotheses may be (and have been) derived, several of which have been tested empirically in various contexts and relationships in which CMC takes place. The assumptions, propositions, and several hypothesis tests will be elaborated in the discussion to follow.

Main Features of the Theory

SIPT explains how we develop impressions and social relationships with one another, over time, online, without recourse to nonverbal cues. There are two central arguments to the theory that allow it to operate. The first pertains to the alteration of impression-bearing, emotional, and relation-managing information (i.e., social information rather than task-related information) much of which is typically expressed nonverbally offline; and how it is translated into verbal and textual symbols online. The second recognizes that this translation produces message exchanges that are not as efficient or quick as face-to-face, multi-cue conversations, and that the medium of CMC is itself often slower than speech. Thus, the second central aspect of SIPT is its argument about the rate of information in various forms of CMC relative to face-to-face communication. The different rates of social information exchange and information accrual affect the time it takes for impression formation and subsequent relational development and management in CMC compared to face-to-face interaction. Thus, the theory posits that when sufficient time elapses so that ample communicative exchanges are made, personal and relational information accrues and CMC is no less effective than face-to-face interaction at developing impressions and managing interpersonal relations (Walther, 1992).

TRANSLATION OF CUES

One way in which SIPT differs from theories of CMC that preceded it has to do with the functions of impression-bearing and relational cues, and the degree to which nonverbal and verbal or textual cues may perform them. Preceding theories asserted that the absence of nonverbal cues from CMC does two things: (a) It causes users to lose interest in one another as real individuals; and (b) It blocks the ability to express descriptive, emotional, personal, or relational messages. In contrast, SIPT explicitly assumes that individuals are motivated to form impressions and develop relationships of some kind, no matter what medium they are using. Therefore, according to SIPT, when non-verbal cues are unavailable—as they are in text-only e-mail or online chat—the remaining communication systems are employed to do the work of those that are missing. In other words, that which is typically nonverbal elsewhere is verbal (and typed) in CMC. Language and writing are held to be virtually inter-changeable with nonverbal cues, and no less useful than nonverbal cues in the management of impressions and relationships.

This argument, although simple enough, stands in contrast to many individuals' intuitions about nonverbal cues, as well as those of academic theorists and researchers in the past. Many people feel that a person needs to see someone to tell who he or she really is; that it is not possible to get an accurate impression of others until they are seen in person, or until they react in person. Many theorists also equate nonverbal information as isomorphic with the functions that nonverbal information often performs. That is, there is no doubt that facial expressions express emotions, or that invading another person's personal space can convey dominance or threat. Expressing emotions and conveying dominance are both social "functions," and nonverbal cues are quite natural and generally effective symbols used to perform those functions. However, if we make a distinction between the functions and the symbols used to achieve those functions, a number of possibilities arise. It is possible that a variety of nonverbal cues or cue combinations can convey a particular function. It also becomes possible that language—its style and the verbal content of the articulated message—can engender the social functions. There is good research evidence supporting this argument; it is a cornerstone of what some theorists call a functional approach to communication analysis (see Burgoon, Buller, & Woodall, 1989). Nevertheless, it is not intuitive to most people to think about how a variety of communication behaviors, not just a subset of nonverbal behaviors, can signal a particular emotion or characteristic. (This is true even though people make functional inferences all the time from any number of cues, and everyone knows what a "love letter" is.) Nevertheless, the interchangeability of cues has been ignored in most of the early thinking about CMC, which focused primarily on the expected impersonal effects of a medium with no nonverbal behaviors (e.g., Siegel et al., 1986).

A recent study sought to demonstrate the exchangeability of verbal and nonverbal cues between CMC and face-to-face settings. In an experiment we conducted (Walther, Loh, & Granka, 2005), a number of unacquainted people had two-person conversations about a moral dilemma. Half the conversations took place face-to-face, with each pair of participants in one room. The other half of the conversations took place with the two people each in a different room, using a popular CMC chat program. Unbeknownst to one partner, we asked the other partner to adopt one of two social attitudes after the first minute of interaction. In half the dyads, we asked individuals to act as if they really liked their partner and wanted to make that person like them, too. In the other half of the dyads, we asked our confederate to behave as if he or she grew to dislike the partner strongly, and wanted the person never to contact them again. We did not tell these confederates "how" to display these attitudes, because a major part of the study was to see what behaviors they employed more or less spontaneously. After the conversations, the couples were separated. The naïve individuals who had not been prompted to behave one way or another rated their partners in terms of immediacy and attraction.

The analyses and results of this study provided clear indications of the SIPT hypotheses. First, there was no difference between CMC and face-to-face in terms of how immediate and affectionate the partners were; the only significant difference was whether the partner was asked to be nice or be mean. The results of the analyses of face-to-face audio and video recordings and CMC transcripts showed a number of specific cues that are associated with variations in liking. As we expected, the face-to-face participants conveyed liking and disliking primarily through variations in vocalics (e.g., vocal pleasantness and pauses during speech), followed by kinesics (e. g., body relaxation, smiling, and gaze). No language effects in the face-to-face conversations were associated with liking judgments. In CMC, on the other hand, a good variety of verbal cues were associated with liking or disliking. These included outright statements of affection (e.g., "I like you") as well as the ways that people expressed disagreement with one another. For example, ignoring a partner's idea and flatly offering an alternative in response was associated with decrements in liking. All in all, the amount of attitude conveyed through language in CMC was no less than the amount conveyed through voice, movement, and facial expression face-to-face.

TIME AND RATE

The second manner in which SIPT differs from most other theories of CMC is in its considerations of communication rate and how the rate of information exchange differs in CMC from face-to-face communication, thus expanding the time frame required for CMC to be effective in social situations. As mentioned above, SIPT recognizes that verbal and textual cues are those that convey social and affective information in CMC, and that these written cues are the only cues to convey that information within text-based online communication. In face-to-face communication, the concurrent exchange of verbal messages along with appearance, kinesics (body movement and facial expression), vocalics (quality and use of the voice), proxemics (increases, decreases, and uses of space), and haptics (touch) provide an abundance of information all at once. The various cues do not always duplicate one another in terms of meaning;

they complement, contradict, accentuate, or minimize verbal cues and other nonverbal expressions (Ekman & Friesen, 1969). These simultaneous expressive systems allow us to process, rapidly and intuitively (although imperfectly), a great deal of task and social information. When one code system alone must do the work of all potential code systems—in this case, language is performing all expressive systems—we expect that less information may traverse a single message utterance than if more numerous cues were involved. For this reason, according to SIPT, the rate of social (and task) information is slower in CMC relative to face-to-face communication. Less information travels per exchange, thus requiring more exchanges to reach the same levels of impression development and relationship status as occurs more quickly face-to-face. When we add to this general retardation of information the fact that some people do not type as fast as others, things are slower yet. When we further add the recognition that asynchronous CMC such as e-mail does not take place in real time, and that a single question-and-answer turn may take days to complete, we start to appreciate how the rate of information interacts with time communicating to explain why, as research has shown, CMC takes longer to facilitate impressions (Walther, 1993) and to develop more levels of relational communication (Walther & Burgoon, 1992).

The SIPT originally addressed some contradictions in the research findings about online groups and virtual communities. Many experiments using synchronous CMC and face-to-face groups that took place in the 1980s and 1990s depicted CMC as reducing social information and leading to hostility and negativity. These results formerly were attributed to the CMC medium, and its lack of nonverbal cues was characterized as a source of uncertainty and discomfort (Hiltz, Johnson, & Turoff, 1986).

While these experiments accumulated, other reports were gaining attention that portrayed CMC much differently. "Virtual communities" in which people exchanged information, advice, and chatter were being reported in the popular press (Rheingold, 1993). Friendships developing among purely network-connected individuals arose, in some cases intensely. Reports of playful uses of organizational CMC networks were documented (Ord, 1989). Steinfield (1986) found that existing online work groups were actually fun and sociable—until they got close to their deadlines, when they began to look more cold and impersonal, just as the short-term group experiments showed. These reports contrasted those of the group experiments quite strongly, and challenged the idea that the lack of nonverbal cues alone could be a defining and depersonalizing characteristic of CMC.

The SIPT offered a way to make sense of these otherwise conflicting findings. From SIPT's perspective, the short time limits provided to CMC groups in the early experiments did not provide enough time and message exchanges for users to develop impressions and relate to one another sociably online. SIPT's information-rate proposition—that CMC requires more time to exchange an equivalent amount of information than in a face-to-face interaction—suggests that CMC experimental groups may have needed more time to develop. Were CMC groups given ample time, they might show the kind of sociability seen in face-to-face groups, as well as virtual communities, ongoing organizational work groups, and eventually, friendships (Walther, 1992).

Conceptualization of Communication in the Theory

Within SIPT, communication symbols are functionally interchangeable, communication is a process, and relationships are developmental. Functional interchangeability of symbols means that SIPT assumes that there are many ways to express social characteristics, emotions, and interpersonal attitudes. When nonverbal cues are unavailable for such expressions, individuals can find other ways to render the same connotation through word content, style, frequency and length of messages, and other CMC-based behavior.

The SIPT is a process theory in the sense that it views interpersonal meanings as accumulating iteratively—that is, in association with a build-up of information over a series of communicative interactions in order to build a psychological model of one's online partners (see Miller & Steinberg, 1975). At first glance this view may seem at odds with the functional interchangeability view, above. After all, if a person can achieve the same thing using words as by using gestures, why does he or she need many exchanges to transfer meanings? The SIPT view is that some information channels (such as face-to-face interaction) transmit many types of symbols quickly, whereas other channels move fewer types of symbols slowly. The symbols that CMC carries move slowly and need more exchanges to accrue functional utility.

The SIPT also sees relationships as developmental. Work groups, friendships, and other relatively enduring relationships do not appear out of nowhere full-blown. Rather, communication fosters the evolution of these relationships over time. Thus, when communication goes slowly, relationships accrue slowly; new CMC relationships do not become as well developed as traditional relationships in an equal amount of time. Thus, the interchangability of cues and the speed or rate at which different cues collect over time across communication process episodes impact the rate of development of relationships. Like physical distance, relational distance is a function of rate by time.

Uses of the Theory

Although SIPT's basis in assumptions and derived propositions may suggest a certain abstraction and formality to the theory, these structural qualities have allowed the theory to be applied rather broadly to several contexts of CMC, including virtual groups, friendships, education, and dating. For instance, even though e-mail and bulletin boards were the dominant forms of CMC when the theory was first articulated in the early 1990s, it has been useful in understanding new, synchronous (real-time) CMC platforms such as chat rooms and instant messaging systems, and has helped to distinguish interpersonal effects of such new tools compared to older, asynchronous ("store-and-forward") channels such as e-mail and videoconferencing (Nowak, Watt, & Walther, 2005). Its abstract nature has allowed it to be derived and applied to CMC use in such settings as online work groups and virtual teams (Walther & Bunz, 2005; Wilson, Straus, & McEvily, 2006), online role-playing games, either text-based (Parks & Roberts, 1998) or graphical fight games (Peña & Hancock, 2006), electronic classrooms and distance education (Schweizer, Paechter, & Weidenmann, 2001), as well as chat rooms (Henderson & Gilding, 2004), newsgroups (Parks & Floyd, 1996), online dating services (Gibbs, Ellison, & Heino, 2006), online romance (Baker, 2005), and even online gender-swapping (Jaffe, Lee, Huang, & Oshagan, 1999; Roberts & Parks, 1999).

Indeed, SIPT has been used to illuminate how people develop friendships and romantic relationships online. Parks and Floyd (1996) interviewed and surveyed a number of Usenet News users, and found that most users had formed at least one friendship online, and that these relationships were about as well developed on many measures as the participants rated their off-line friendships. One major factor associated with the likelihood of forming a relationship online is the amount of time a user has been or is on the Internet. Likewise, a survey of individuals who were in exclusively online romantic relationships found that both the length of time the relationship had lasted, as well as the amount of time spent communicating with one's partner, were significantly associated with perceived attitude similarity, commitment, intimacy, and trust (Anderson & Emmers-Sommer, 2006). It is noteworthy that both rate/time and message dimensions—frequency of message exchanges, and the accumulation of sufficient messages over time—acknowledged by SIPT were both potent factors that affected relationship quality in this study. Time online and communication frequency were also related to relationship formation in a German online, text-based role-playing game (Utz, 2000). Even in an avatar-based online swordfight game (in which players control cartoon representations who chat and fight on the screen), time online was associated with greater levels of socioemotional comments (Peña & Hancock, 2006). These studies assessed time online as a player's history, i.e., the amount of time since she or he joined that game. This is not exactly the way SIPT conceptualized time; in SIPT, time is an interval in which a number of messages accrue, regardless of an individual's personal history with a medium. The work of Liu, Ginther, and Zelhart (2001), however, has shown that both the frequency as well as duration of messages—focusing on messaging rate, not history—affect impression development in CMC, in line with SIPT's predictions.

Another important aspect of online impressions and relations that SIPT has informed is self-disclosure. Disclosure increases intimacy in traditional relationships, too, and it is a verbal behavior that we all recognize as a means to and reflection of relationship development. It is not hard to see why it may be potent in CMC. Indeed, several studies suggest that disclosure is more likely and more intense in CMC than in face-to-face settings (e.g., Henderson & Gilding, 2004). There are several reasons why this might be the case, but the simplest is that, aside from self-disclosure, there are not many ways to convey intentional information about oneself online. A great amount of self-disclosure among strangers is somewhat off-putting offline, yet online there is a positive relationship between the amount of self-disclosure one gives and a partner's rating of the discloser's conversational effectiveness (Tidwell & Walther, 2002).

While these acquaintanceship development processes are part and parcel of dyadic social relationships, they also have been shown to pertain to project-oriented online groups. That is, the gradual impression development and relational growth also accrue in settings where work, rather than games or socializing for socializing's sake, is the focus. In these settings, student group members developed deeper impressions of one another over the course of three projects spanning six weeks of asynchronous interaction, even though it took parallel face-to-face groups a single meeting to develop as strong an impression of their partners (Walther, 1993). Their affection, trust, informality, and other relational dimensions also increased over time, sometimes approaching or exceeding that of face-to-face groups. One recent study offered rewards and punishments to online groups depending on their adherence to a rule requiring frequent interaction (Walther & Bunz, 2005). The researchers found that the incentives not only raised communication frequency, but also increased message explicitness, feedback, and affection. These results, in turn, increased group members' trust for one another and the quality of the work that they did.

Strengths and Limitations of the Theory

SIPT appears to be a popular theory of CMC for two contrasting reasons: (a) its intuitive application, on the one hand, and (b) its formal articulation of assumptions and propositions, on the other. Many individuals have encountered each other for the first time online, and although many new networking systems promote picture exchanges, many do not. It is still quite common, as it became through the 1990s, for people to have first contact with others in a text-based online hobby discussion, technology discussion, or other kinds of chat rooms, bulletin boards, games, and other venues. People grow to recognize one another and attribute characteristics to one another, liking develops, and ongoing relationships take shape. These developments were theoretically unaccounted for before SIPT's introduction, both for academic researchers as well as other people who become ensconced within the Internet.

When theories formally identify their underlying assumptions and propositions, it is easier for researchers to see precisely which aspect of a theory is being tested, extended, or challenged by any particular study or observations. Additionally, it is easier to assess where research results that do not support the theory seem to be challenging the theoretical framework. For instance, Roberts, Smith, and Pollock (1996) found a rapid progression from no familiarity to intimate relating among some users of an online synchronous chat facility. Roberts and colleagues suggested that this challenges the proposition in SIPT about CMC requiring a longer time in order to achieve a relatively high level of intimacy (although this finding does not challenge SIPT's social information conversion proposition regarding nonverbal cues into verbal cues). Such assertions challenge researchers to extend their thinking: Can the interaction goals or context modify the rate of relationship development in CMC? Or does synchronous online chat approach the rapidity of face-to-face communication and thus, although bereft of nonverbal cues, provide a similar amount of message exchanges in a limited amount of time than we would see over a much longer time in e-mail or bulletin boards? Whichever of these two possibilities turns out to be the case, it will have subtle implications for the understanding specifically of the rate/time aspect of SIPT.

Other research has challenged SIPT's assumption that people are generally motivated to develop impressions and relationships with one another. Prior to the recognition that this assumption was questionable, cases in which the online behavior predicted by SIPT did not accrue made it unclear whether the theory as a whole was false or if it pertained some times and not others. By testing systematic variations in people's motivation to impress or relate with others online; by testing factors that heighten or dampen this motivation; and by finding corresponding changes in online affinity, the boundaries of the theory will become narrower, but the theory will become more precise and useful. For instance, one study (Walther, 1994) drew on previous offline research on the effect of anticipated future interaction as a factor that propels greater uncertainty reduction and liking. In a CMC setting, strangers were brought together and either led to anticipate more future interaction with one another doing several online tasks, or led to anticipate interaction on a single online task. Indeed, the degree of anticipated future interaction affected the positivity of online relational development quickly and powerfully enough that relational levels among those with greater anticipated future interaction were no different from an offline comparison condition. As a result of these refinements, we no longer suggest that SIPT dynamics will happen in every CMC encounter. However, when longer-term online interaction is expected, SIPT is more likely to take effect, and we know a bit more precisely that anticipating ongoing inter-action is one of the motivating theoretical dynamics.

Directions for Future Research and Applications

Like any theory, SIPT is subject to continued modification, extension, and refinement. Unlike most theories of interpersonal communication, SIPT includes as a central construct aspects of communication technology, and the ways these technologies develop are in rapid flux. The Internet was not origi-nally developed with human communication as its central purpose. However, its contemporary use as a communication medium seems to eclipse any other function to most people. As new Internet communication tools develop, we are forced to ask how SIPT can account for the most modern applications, if it can do so at all. For instance, new networking tools such as Facebook and MySpace have emerged that allow users to provide pictures, biographies, and overt spec-ifications of who their friends are, among other features. These tools also pro-mote asynchronous text-based communication through e-mail links and connections to blogs, as well as to instant messenger connections. These and unforeseen developments will guide exploration of whether SIPT can account for the dynamics that such applications provide.

A sample of these questions is already under exploration: Does the presence of photographs in these applications make SIPT irrelevant, or is SIPT still rel-evant when visual cues are static, and interpersonal acquaintanceship comes yet later through interactive exchanges? How do visual and verbal (but not vocal) cues combine? Initial answers suggest that photos anchor interpersonal impressions in a way that interactive chat does not diminish (Walther, Slovacek, & Tidwell, 2001), making SIPT's domain of application limited to CMC that is devoid of photographs (but that may nevertheless employ icons or avatars; Nowak & Biocca, 2003).

New social networking applications allow some users to leave messages publicly for others on a "message wall" (i.e., to leave messages for someone that yet other people can see, even though the receiver did not sanction the mes-sages and may not even yet have seen them). Such third-hand cues about users may have some role to play in developing impressions, but are not under the person's control the way one's e-mail and chat messages are. They are not within SIPT's theoretical boundaries, but they do impinge on the interpersonal phenomena for which SIPT would otherwise account. Do third-hand messages override self-generated self-descriptions? It appears they do (Walther, Kim, Van Der Heide, Westerman, Ton, & Langwell, in press). Future research must explore the relative weights and values that Internet users apply to information about a person that they glean from search engines, databases, auction sites, and online newspapers—sources of information that people other than the target may have generated—compared to online discussion archives, dating profiles, and other sources of self-generated information that individuals create to represent themselves, but in past contexts and for specific audiences, that other users may nevertheless access online.

At the same time, there is a good deal of Internet communication that is strictly text based and that takes place among individuals who do not yet know each other elsewhere, much of which is in a context that hints at continued interaction. Under these circumstances, SIPT offers considerable potency, although a degree of porousness with which to intermingle with other theoretical ideas will be necessary to make it more broad and enduring as new characteristics of technology become part of the interpersonal process.

References

Anderson, T. L., & Emmers-Sommer, T. M. (2006). Predictors of relationship satisfaction in online romantic relationships. *Communication Studies, 57,* 153–172.

Baker, A. (2005) *Double click: Romance and commitment among online couples.* Creskill, NJ: Hampton Press.

Burgoon, J. K., Buller, D. B., & Woodall, W. G. (1989). *Nonverbal communication: The unspoken dialogue.* New York: Harper & Row.

Ekman, P., & Friesen, W. V. (1969). The repertoire of nonverbal behavior: Categories, origins, usage, and coding. *Semiotica, 1,* 49–98.

Gibbs, J. L., Ellison, N. B., & Heino, R. D. (2006). Self-presentation in online personals: The role of anticipated future interaction, self-disclosure, and perceived success in Internet dating. *Communication Research 33,* 1–26.

Henderson, S., & Gilding, M. (2004). "I've never clicked this much with anyone in my life": Trust and hyperpersonal communication in online friendships. *New Media & Society, 6,* 487–506.

Hiltz, S. R., Johnson, K., & Turoff, M. (1986). Experiments in group decision making: Communication process and outcome in face-to-face versus computerized conferences. *Human Communication Research, 13,* 225–252.

Jaffe, J. M., Lee, Y., Huang, L., & Oshagan, H. (1999). Gender identification, interdependence, and pseudonyms in CMC: Language patterns in an electronic conference. *Information Society, 15,* 221–234.

Liu, Y., Ginther, D., & Zelhart, P. (2001). How do frequency and duration of messaging affect impression development in computer-mediated communication? *Journal of Universal Computer Science, 7*(10), 893–913.

Miller, G. R., & Steinberg, M. (1975). *Between people: A new analysis of interpersonal communication.* Palo Alto, CA: Science Research Associates.

Nowak, K. L., & Biocca, F. (2003). The effect of the agency and anthropomorphism on users' sense of telepresence, copresence, and social presence in virtual environments. *Presence, 12,* 481–494.

Nowak, K. L., Watt, J., & Walther, J. B. (2005). The influence of synchrony and sensory modality on the person perception process in computer-mediated groups. *Journal of Computer-Mediated Communication, 10*(3). Retrieved June 1, 2006 from. http://jcmc.indiana.edu/v0110/issue3/nowak.html.

Ord, J. G. (1989). Who's joking? The information system at play. *Interacting with Computers, 1,* 118–128.

Parks, M. R., & Floyd, K. (1996). Making friends in cyberspace. *Journal of Communication, 46,* 80–97.

Parks, M. R., & Roberts, L. D. (1998). "Making MOOsic": The development of personal relationships on-line and a comparison to their off-line counterparts. *Journal of Social and Personal Relationships, 15,* 517–537.

Peña, J., & Hancock, J. T. (2006). An analysis of socioemotional and task communication in online multiplayer video games. *Communication Research, 33,* 92–109.

Reicher, S., Spears, R., & Postmes, T. (1995). A social identity model of deindividuation phenomena. *European Review of Social Psychology, 6,* 161–198.

Rheingold, H. (1993). *The virtual community: Homesteading on the electronic frontier.* Reading, MA: Addison-Wesley.

Roberts, L. D., & Parks, M. R. (1999). The social geography of gender-switching in virtual environments on the Internet. *Information, Communication, and Society, 2,* 521–540.

Roberts, L. D., Smith, L. M., & Pollock, C. (1996, September). *A model of social interaction via computer-mediated communication in real-time text-based virtual environments.* Paper presented at the annual conference of the Australian Psychological Society, Sydney, Australia.

Schweizer, K., Paechter, M., & Weidenmann, B. (2001). A field study on distance education and communication: Experiences of a virtual tutor. *Journal of Computer-Mediated Communication, 6*(2). Retrieved June 1, 2006, from http://jcmc.indiana.edu/v016/issue2/schweizer.html.

Short, J., Williams, E., & Christie, B. (1976). *The social psychology of telecommunications.* London: John Wiley.

Siegel, J., Dubrovsky, V., Kiesler, S., & McGuire, T. W. (1986). Group processes in computer-mediated communication. *Organizational Behavior and Human Decision Processes, 37,* 157–187.

Snyder, M., & Stukas, A. A. (1999). Interpersonal processes: The interplay of cognitive, motivational, and behavioral activities in social interaction. *Annual Review of Psychology, 50,* 273–303.

Steinfield, C. W. (1986). Computer-mediated communication in an organizational setting: Explaining task-related and socioemotional uses. In M. L. McLaughlin (Ed.), *Communication yearbook 9* (pp. 777–804). Newbury Park, CA: Sage.

Tidwell, L. C., & Walther, J. B. (2002). Computer-mediated communication effects on disclosure, impressions, and interpersonal evaluations: Getting to know one another a bit at a time. *Human Communication Research, 28,* 317–348.

Utz, S. (2000). Social information processing in MUDs: The development of friendships in virtual worlds. *Journal of Online Behavior, 1*(1). Retrieved June 25, 2006, from http://www.behavior.net/JOB/v1n1/utz.html.

Walther, J. B. (1992). Interpersonal effects in computer-mediated interaction: A relational perspective. *Communication Research, 19,* 52–90.

Walther, J. B. (1993). Impression development in computer-mediated interaction. *Western Journal of Communication, 57,* 381–398.

Walther, J. B. (1994). Anticipated ongoing interaction versus channel effects on relational communication in computer-mediated interaction. *Human Communication Research, 20,* 473–501.

Walther, J. B., & Bunz, U. (2005). The rules of virtual groups: Trust, liking, and performance in computer-mediated communication. *Journal of Communication, 55,* 828–846.

Walther, J. B., & Burgoon, J. K. (1992). Relational communication in computer-mediated interaction. *Human Communication Research, 19,* 50–88.

Walther, J. B., Kim, S., Van Der Heide, B., Westerman, D., Tong, S. T., & Langwell, L. (in press). The role of friends' appearance and behavior on evaluations of individuals on Facebook: Are we known by the company we keep? *Human Communication Research.*

Walther, J. B., Loh, T., & Granka, L. (2005). Let me count the ways: The interchange of verbal and nonverbal cues in computer-mediated and face-to-face affinity. *Journal of Language and Social Psychology, 24,* 36–65.

Walther, J. B., & Slovacek, C., & Tidwell, L. C. (2001). Is a picture worth a thousand words? Photographic images in long term and short term virtual teams. *Communication Research, 28,* 105–134.

Wilson, J. M., Straus, S. G., & McEvily, B. (2006). All in due time: The development of trust in computer-mediated and face-to-face teams. *Organizational Behavior and Human Decision Processes, 99,* 16–33.

Index

About the Editors

Leslie A. Baxter (PhD, University of Oregon) is F. Wendell Miller Distinguished Professor of Communication Studies at the University of Iowa. Her research interests are centered in communication and relating in personal and familial relationships. She has published more than 100 articles and chapters, and has written or coedited six books. She has been the recipient of numerous scholarly awards, including the National Communication Association's Bernard J. Brommel Family Communication Award, the Woolbert Award for outstanding scholarship, and the Knower and Miller Awards in interpersonal communication. She is a Past President of the Western States Communication Association.

Dawn O. Braithwaite (PhD, University of Minnesota) is a Willa Cather Professor of Communication Studies at University of Nebraska-Lincoln. She focuses her scholarship on understanding communication in personal and family relationships, via relational dialectics, rituals, and social support. She has published 70 articles and book chapters and four books. She received the National Communication Association's Bernard J. Brommel Family Communication Award. She is a Past President of the Western States Communication Association. She has been the Research Board Director of the National Communication Association and will be the association's President in 2010.

About the Contributors

Walid A. Afifi (PhD, University of Arizona) is an Associate Professor in the Communication Department at the University of California at Santa Barbara. His primary research program revolves around development and testing of the Theory of Motivated Information Management, a framework that examines uncertainty processes and information-seeking decisions. He and his chapter coauthor are currently involved in an extension of that work involving crisis management. He is an author of more than 35 articles and chapters, and has served on the editorial board of several flagship journals.

Charles R. Berger (PhD, Michigan State University) is a Professor and the Chair in the Department of Communication at the University of California, Davis. His research interests include the role that goals and knowledge structures play in the production and processing of verbal discourse and nonverbal behavior, and the ways in which threat-oriented messages are processed by rational and experiential information processing modalities. He is a Fellow and Past President of the International Communication Association.

David B. Buller (PhD, Michigan State University) is a Senior Scientist at Klein Buendel, Inc., a health communication firm in Golden, Colorado. His research encompasses the strategic processes in deceptive communication and the effectiveness of traditional and new communication technologies in preventing chronic disease. His research on deception has been supported by grants from the U.S. Army Research Institute and Research Office. He has published three books and more than 100 articles and chapters.

Judee K. Burgoon (EdD, West Virginia University) is a Professor of Communication and Site Director for the Center for Identification Technology Research, University of Arizona. Her deception-related research has centered on cues to deception in face-to-face and mediated contexts, training in deception detection, and development of tools for automated detection. This research has been supported by the Department of Defense and Department of Homeland Security. She has published seven books and more than 250 articles and chapters.

Brant R. Burleson (PhD, University of Illinois, Urbana-Champaign) is a Professor of Communication at Purdue University. His research examines communication skill acquisition and development, emotion in communication, effects of communication skills, and supportive forms of communication such as comforting. Author of more than 100 articles and chapters, he edited *Communication Yearbook* and recently coedited *The Handbook of Communication and Social Interaction Skills*. His research has been recognized by awards from several regional, national, and international scholarly societies.

William R. Cupach (PhD, University of Southern California) is a Professor of Communication at Illinois State University. His research pertains to problematic interactions in interpersonal relationships, including such contexts as embarrassing predicaments, relational transgressions, interpersonal conflict, and obsessive relational pursuit. He previously served as Associate Editor for the *Journal of Social and Personal Relationships* and is a Past President of the International Association for Relationship Research.

James Price Dillard (PhD, Michigan State University) is a Professor and Head of Communication Arts and Sciences at Pennsylvania State University. His teaching and research focus on the communication processes by which individuals attempt to change the opinions and behaviors of others. Dillard has received the John E. Hunter Award for Meta-Analysis and the National Communication Association Golden Anniversary Award for article of the year. He coedited *The Persuasion Handbook* and served as editor of *Human Communication Research*.

Wesley T. Durham (PhD, University of Nebraska-Lincoln) is an Assistant Professor of Communication Studies at the University of Southern Indiana. His research agenda focuses on how individuals disclose health-related topics and issues to other family members. His primary research interests include disclosure and privacy processes in the contexts of family planning and crystal methamphetamine addiction.

Kory Floyd (PhD, University of Arizona) is an Associate Professor of Human Communication and Director of the Communication Sciences laboratory at Arizona State University. His research focuses on the communication of affection in families and in other personal relationships, and on the physiological correlates of relational communication. He has received a number of awards for his research, including the G. R. Miller Early Career Achievement Award from the International Association for Relationship Research. He is currently Chair of the Family Communication Division of the National Communication Association, and is currently editor of *Journal of Family Communication*.

Howard Giles (PhD, DSc) is an Assistant Dean of Undergraduate Studies, Director of the Center on Police Practices and Community, and Professor of

Communication at the University of California, Santa Barbara. His research has won numerous awards, and has explored facets of applied interpersonal and intergroup communication research and theory. On editorial boards of dozens of journals across disciplines, he has been Founding Editor of two of his own, and is Past President of the International Communication Association.

Daena J. Goldsmith (PhD, University of Washington) is an Associate Professor of Communication at Lewis and Clark College. She studies social support in personal relationships, with a particular focus on how relational partners cope with chronic illness. Other interests include the influence of gender and culture on communication patterns. She is the author of *Communicating Social Support*, and numerous articles and chapters.

John O. Greene (PhD, University of Wisconsin, Madison) is a Professor of Communication at Purdue University. His interests include communication theory, interpersonal communication, nonverbal communication, and aging and communication. He is a recipient of the National Communication Association's Woolbert Award, and is a past Editor of *Human Communication Research*.

Laura K. Guerrero (PhD, University of Arizona) is a Professor in the Hugh Downs School of Human Communication at Arizona State University. Her research focuses on relational communication, with emphases in attachment, emotion, and nonverbal messages. She has published more than 70 articles and chapters, as well as several books, including *Nonverbal Communication in Close Relationships* and *Close Encounters: Communicating in Relationships*. She received the Early Career Achievement Award from the International Association for Relationship Research.

Mary Lynn Miller Henningsen (PhD, University of Wisconsin) is an Associate Professor in the Department of Communication at Northern Illinois University. She has published articles and book chapters on dating relationship initiation, flirting and sexual harassment, group influence, and group decision making. She cochaired the Local Arrangements Committee for the 2004 National Communication Association convention in Chicago, and is the current book review editor for the *Journal of Social and Personal Relationships*.

Colin Hesse (MA, Arizona State University) is a doctoral student in human communication at Arizona State University, where he also works in the communication sciences laboratory. His research focuses on the communication of affection and its associations with physical and mental health. He is currently coauthoring a book on biology and communication, and is serving as editorial assistant for *Journal of Family Communication*.

James M. Honeycutt (PhD, University of Illinois) is a Professor of Communication Studies at Louisiana State University, Baton Rouge. He studies communication and physiology in personal and family relationships, conflict resolution, and cognitive processes, including mental imagery and imagined interaction in a variety of contexts. He has published three books and more than 60 articles and chapters.

Jeff Judd (BA, Arizona State University) is a masters student in human communication at Arizona State University, where he also works in the communication sciences laboratory. His research focuses on the physiology of interpersonal communication. He has coauthored several journal articles and book chapters, and has served as editorial assistant for *Journal of Family Communication.*

Jody Koenig Kellas (PhD, University of Washington) is an Assistant Professor of Communication Studies at the University of Nebraska-Lincoln. She specializes in relational and family communication, including research on the processes, identity negotiation, and relational qualities associated with individual and joint storytelling in families, postdissolutional communication, face-work, and attributions. Her research has been published in *Communication Monographs, Human Communication Research, Journal of Family Communication, Journal of Social and Personal Relationships* and in several book chapters.

Leanne K. Knobloch (PhD, University of Wisconsin, Madison) is Assistant Professor in the Department of Speech Communication at the University of Illinois. Her research addresses how communication shapes and reflects people's understandings of close relationships, particularly with respect to relationship development, relational uncertainty, and interdependence.

Jenny Mandelbaum (PhD, University of Texas, Austin) is an Associate Professor in the Department of Communication at Rutgers University. She has published more than 20 journal articles and book chapters, and a book. Her research has focused on the organization of everyday interaction, with particular emphasis on storytelling and other communication practices through which relationships and identities are constructed and managed.

Valerie Manusov (PhD, University of Southern California) is a Professor of Communication at the University of Washington. Her primary focus is on nonverbal communication, with a particular interest in the attributions of meaning made for nonverbal cues. In 2001, she coedited, with John Harvey, a book focusing on attributions in close relationships, and she has written more than a dozen articles and chapters focusing on attributions in communication.

Masaki Matsunaga (MA, Seinan Gakuin University) is a Fulbright scholar and a doctoral candidate of the Department of Communication Arts and Sciences at Pennsylvania State University. His master's thesis investigated Japanese college students' face-work strategy use in romantic and sexual relationship initiation. He studies interpersonal and intercultural communication, as well as measurement and methodology issues in human communication research.

He also works with Dr. Walid Afifi in his research on ambient uncertainty and crisis communication.

Steven McCornack (PhD, University of Illinois) is an Associate Professor and Coordinator of the Undergraduate Program in the Department of Communication at Michigan State University. His scholarly interests include deception and deceptive message production, and betrayal in romantic relationships. He has published more than 20 articles in various scientific journals, and has received a number of honors for excellence in undergraduate teaching, including a Lilly Endowment Teaching Fellowship, the Amoco Foundation Excellence-in-Teaching Award, and the MSU Teacher/Scholar Award.

Rachel M. McLaren (MA, Pennsylvania State University) is a doctoral candidate in the department of Communication Arts and Sciences at Pennsylvania State University. Her research seeks to clarify the interplay of communication, cognition, and emotion in responses to significant experiences, such as hurtful interactions, within personal relationships.

Sandra Metts (PhD, University of Iowa) is a Professor in the School of Communication at Illinois State University. Her research interests include relationship disengagement, deception, sexual communication, emotional expression, face-work, and politeness. She is the former President of the Central States Communication Association has served as Editor of *Communication Reports,* and Associate Editor of *Personal Relationships* and *Journal of Social and Personal Relationships.*

Paul A. Mongeau (PhD, Michigan State University) is a Professor at the Hugh Downs School of Human Communication at Arizona State University, where he serves as Director of the Interdiscplinary PhD Program in Communication. His primary areas of scholarly interest focus on the earliest stages of dating relationships, including how relationships make the transition from platonic to romantic. He is currently editor of the *Journal of Social and Personal Relationships.*

Sandra Petronio (PhD, University of Michigan) is a Professor in the Department of Communication Studies at Indiana University–Purdue University, Indianapolis; Core Faculty in the Indiana University Center for Bioethics; and Adjunct Faculty in the Indiana Univeristy School of Nursing and the School of Informatics. She focuses on management of private disclosures. Her book, *Boundaries of Privacy,* won the International Association for Relationship Research Book Award and National Communication Association's Miller Book Award. She received the 2002 National Communication Association's Bernard J. Brommel Family Communication Award.

Gerry Philipsen (PhD, Northwestern University) is a Professor of Communication at the University of Washington. He studies culturally distinctive ways of communicating, communication in small task-oriented groups, and the modern history of the communication discipline. He is a recipient of numerous awards for distinction in teaching and for distinction in research. He has served as Department Chair and as Chair of the University of Washington faculty.

Jessica J. Rack (MA, University of Cincinnati) is a doctoral student in the Department of Communication at Purdue University. Her research interests include communication regarding grief, social support, child maltreatment, communication apprehension, racism in language, and marital communication. She has coauthored two book chapters and has presented several authored and coauthored papers at regional and national conferences.

L. Edna Rogers (PhD, Michigan State University) is a Professor of Communication at the University of Utah and a Past President of the International Communication Association. Her research interests include interpersonal and relational communication, with a central focus on the interactional study of marital and family relationships.

Denise Haunani Solomon (PhD, Northwestern University) is a Professor of Communication Arts and Sciences at Pennsylvania State University. She studies the role of communication in relationship transitions, such as forming social relationships with coworkers, establishing a committed dating relationship, and coping with breast cancer. Her work appears in journals devoted to both communication and personal relationships research. She serves on the editorial boards of five journals, and she is an Associate Editor of *Personal Relationships*.

Brian H. Spitzberg (PhD, University of Southern California) is a Professor of Communication at San Diego State University. His primary focus is on interpersonal communication competence and on the dark side of interpersonal communication, including the study of conflict, stalking, and intimate violence. In 2004, he coauthored with William Cupach a book on the dark side of relationship pursuit, and coedited, with Professor Cupach, a new book collection of scholarly essays on the dark side of interpersonal communication.

Laura Stafford (PhD, University of Texas, Austin) is a Professor of Communication at the University of Kentucky. Primary areas of research are relationship maintenance and long-distance relationships. She has published numerous research articles and chapters and two books. She has served as chair of the Interpersonal Communication Division of the National Communication Association and the International Communication Association. She is an Associate Editor of the *Journal of Social and Personal Relationships* and is Editor-Elect of *Journal of Applied Communication Research*.

Karen Tracy (PhD, University of Wisconsin) is a Professor of Communication at the University of Colorado, Boulder. She is a discourse analyst who studies communicatively interesting and problematic institutional practices. She is the author and editor of five books and more than 50 articles and chapters, and is a past Editor of the journal *Research on Language and Social Interaction.*

Joseph Walther (PhD, University of Arizona) is a Professor in the Departments of Telecommunication, Information Studies and Media, and Communication at Michigan State University. He studies interpersonal communication via computers, in personal relationships, work groups, and education. He has held appointments in psychology, information science, and education in the United States and in England. He was chair of the Organizational Communication and Information Systems division of the Academy of Management, and the Communication and Technology division of the International Communication Association.

Cindy H. White (PhD, University of Arizona) is an Associate Professor of Communication at the University of Colorado, Boulder. She conducts research on interpersonal communication that explores how patterns of interaction form the foundation for personal relationships. She has published work on deception, relational loss, social support, and health communication. Her current research considers how communicators understand conceptual models or principles of communication, and how they learn to enact communication practices in training situations, such as parenting education and conflict mediation programs. She is coeditor of *Together Alone: Personal Relationships in Public Spaces.*

Julia T. Wood (PhD, Pennsylvania State University) is the Lineberger Professor of Humanities and professor of Communication Studies at the University of North Carolina at Chapel Hill. She teaches and conducts research on personal relationships, intimate partner violence, feminist theory, and intersections of gender, communication, and culture. She also consults with attorneys on cases of sex and gender discrimination. During her career, she has published 23 books and has published more than 80 articles and chapters in books. She has received 13 awards for her research and 12 awards for her teaching.